The Reception of Jesus in the First Three Centuries

8

Editors
Chris Keith, Helen Bond and Jens Schröter

The Reception of Jewish Tradition in the Social Imagination of the Early Christians

Edited by
John M. G. Barclay and Kylie Crabbe

LONDON • NEW YORK • OXFORD • NEW DELHI • SYDNEY

T&T CLARK

Bloomsbury Publishing Plc

50 Bedford Square, London, WC1B 3DP, UK
1385 Broadway, New York, NY 10018, USA
29 Earlsfort Terrace, Dublin 2, Ireland

BLOOMSBURY, T&T CLARK and the T&T Clark logo are trademarks of
Bloomsbury Publishing Plc

First published in Great Britain 2022
This paperback edition published 2023

Copyright © John M. G. Barclay, Kylie Crabbe and contributors, 2022

John M. G. Barclay and Kylie Crabbe have asserted their right under the Copyright, Designs
and Patents Act, 1988, to be identified as Editors of this work.

Cover design: Charlotte James
Cover image: The Good Shepherd, fresco (3rd century) in the Catacomb of Priscilla,
Rome, Lazio, Italy (© INTERFOTO / Alamy Stock Photo)

All rights reserved. No part of this publication may be reproduced or transmitted
in any form or by any means, electronic or mechanical, including photocopying,
recording, or any information storage or retrieval system, without prior permission
in writing from the publishers.

Bloomsbury Publishing Plc does not have any control over, or responsibility for, any
third-party websites referred to or in this book. All internet addresses given in this
book were correct at the time of going to press. The author and publisher regret any
inconvenience caused if addresses have changed or sites have ceased to exist, but
can accept no responsibility for any such changes.

A catalogue record for this book is available from the British Library.

Library of Congress Cataloging-in-Publication Data
Names: Barclay, John M. G., editor. | Crabbe, Kylie, 1977– editor.
Title: The reception of Jewish tradition in the social imagination of the
early Christians / edited by John M.G. Barclay and Kylie Crabbe.
Description: London ; New York : T&T Clark, 2021. |
Series: The reception of Jesus in the first three centuries ; 8 |
Includes bibliographical references and index. |
Summary: "A reconsideration of the reception of Jewish traditions and texts
in early Christianity by leading international contributors"–Provided by publisher.
Identifiers: LCCN 2021009051 (print) | LCCN 2021009052 (ebook) |
ISBN 9780567695994 (hardback) | ISBN 9780567696007 (pdf) |
ISBN 9780567696021 (epub)
Subjects: LCSH: Church history–Primitive and early church, ca. 30–600. | Christianity
and other religions–Judaism. | Judaism–Relations–Christianity. | Identification (Religion)
Classification: LCC BR166 .R43 2021 (print) | LCC BR166 (ebook) | DDC 270.2–dc23
LC record available at https://lccn.loc.gov/2021009051
LC ebook record available at https://lccn.loc.gov/2021009052

ISBN: HB: 978-0-5676-9599-4
PB: 978-0-5677-0272-2
ePDF: 978-0-5676-9600-7
ePUB: 978-0-5676-9602-1

Series: The Reception of Jesus in the First Three Centuries

Typeset by Newgen KnowledgeWorks Pvt. Ltd., Chennai, India

To find out more about our authors and books visit www.bloomsbury.com
and sign up for our newsletters.

Contents

List of Contributors — vii
List of Abbreviations — viii

Introduction — 1
John M. G. Barclay and Kylie Crabbe

Part 1   The reception of Jewish texts

1   The early Christian reception of the legend of the Greek translation of the scriptures — 15
    Judith M. Lieu

2   The Law and Prophets as Origen's Gospel — 31
    Devin L. White

3   The reception of the Watchers tradition in Tertullian with regard to 1 Cor. 11.2–16 — 47
    Stephen C. Carlson

Part 2   The reception of Jewish themes, images and categories

4   'Not like the gentiles who do not know God' (1 Thess. 4.5): The function of Othering and anti-gentile stereotypes of sexual wrongdoing in early Jewish and Christian texts — 63
    Christine Gerber

5   Patterns of Christian reinterpretations of the Maccabean martyrdoms — 87
    Jan Willem van Henten

6   'The blind and the lame': An adapted category in early Christian communal self-understanding — 107
    Kylie Crabbe

7 The ethics of Eden: Luxury, banqueting and the New Jerusalem   129
   Candida R. Moss

8 Scribes, Pharisees, Sadducees and Trypho: Jewish leadership and Jesus
   traditions in Justin's construal of Christian and Jewish identity   145
   Benjamin A. Edsall

Part 3 The reception of Jewish practices

9 Denial of forgiveness and the Spirit: 'Anxiety of influence' and the
   Christian demotion of John's baptism   163
   Joel Marcus

10 Tradition and authority in scribal culture: A comparison between the
   Yaḥadic Dead Sea Scroll texts and the Gospel of Matthew   179
   Loren T. Stuckenbruck

11 Remember the poor: Early Christian reception of a Jewish communal
   responsibility   197
   John M. G. Barclay

Bibliography   213
Index of Ancient Sources   233
Index of Authors   257
Index of Subjects   262

Contributors

John M. G. Barclay is Lightfoot Professor of Divinity, Department of Theology and Religion, Durham University.

Stephen C. Carlson is a Senior Research Fellow, Institute for Religion and Critical Inquiry, Australian Catholic University.

Kylie Crabbe is a Senior Research Fellow, Institute for Religion and Critical Inquiry, Australian Catholic University.

Benjamin A. Edsall is a Senior Research Fellow, Institute for Religion and Critical Inquiry, Australian Catholic University.

Christine Gerber is Professor of New Testament Studies, Theological Faculty, Humboldt-University, Berlin.

Jan Willem van Henten is Professor of Religion, Department of History, European Studies and Religion, University of Amsterdam and Extra-Ordinary Professor, Department of Old and New Testament, Stellenbosch University.

Judith M. Lieu is Lady Margaret's Professor of Divinity Emerita, University of Cambridge.

Joel Marcus is Emeritus Professor of New Testament and Christian Origins, Duke Divinity School.

Candida R. Moss is Edward Cadbury Professor of Theology, University of Birmingham.

Loren T. Stuckenbruck is Chair of New Testament Studies (with emphasis on Ancient Judaism), Ludwig Maximilian University, Munich.

Devin L. White is Research Fellow in Biblical and Early Christian Studies, Institute for Religion and Critical Inquiry, Australian Catholic University.

Abbreviations

Abbreviations used in this volume are in keeping with Bloomsbury Publishing, *House Style Guidelines for Authors and Editors*, 1.2 (September 2016) (Biblical texts) and *The SBL Handbook of Style*, 2nd edn (Atlanta: Society of Biblical Literature, 2014).

Introduction

John M. G. Barclay and Kylie Crabbe

The essays collected in this volume stand at the interface between two related questions. First, how were Jewish traditions and texts received (taken up, adapted and altered) within communities that expressed loyalty to the person of Jesus and came to identify themselves, over time, as 'Christians'? Second, how did these early Christians think of themselves as a social phenomenon? The two questions are interlinked, because the reception of Jewish tradition took place within communities, not just in individual minds and lives, and because that process of reception inevitably kept raising the question of the identity and purpose of the communities involved. The ideas, practices and terminology with which Christians constructed their identities were in most cases heavily dependent on – indeed, directly derived from – the Jewish tradition that they inherited and reworked. But in that reception, they also subtly reimagined themselves as its heirs: they altered not just its accents but also its *reference*, and reconfigured ancient traditions as in some sense properly *their own*. Thus the social imagination of the early Christians – the way they configured their social identity – was essentially intertwined with their reception of Jewish tradition, and the varied forms and processes of this reception are an index of the ways in which the first Christians forged their new, but derivative, identity. This social phenomenon turns out to be a classic case of reception, and one with far-reaching consequence for the Western cultural tradition.

This volume forms the second published product of the project, 'Texts, Traditions, and Early Christian Identities' that is housed and funded by the Australian Catholic University (ACU).[1] It arises from a highly productive colloquium that took place at the ACU campus in Rome in late September 2019. All the essays gathered here were presented in that congenial and challenging environment and revised afterwards in light of the colloquium discussions. The colloquium encompassed the reception of Jewish texts, concepts and practices up to the early third century CE, and our conversation moved back and forth between individual case studies and the larger patterns they represent. In this introduction, we summarize some of the key general findings of our work and offer a precis of each of the essays, grouped in three sections.

---

[1] The first volume is Francis Watson and Sarah Parkhouse (eds), *Telling the Christian Story Differently: Counter-Narratives from Nag Hammadi and Beyond* (London: T&T Clark, 2020).

In his groundbreaking study of the moral traditions that form contemporary culture, *After Virtue*, Alasdair MacIntyre describes a 'living tradition' in terms that provide a frame for our analysis of reception:

> A living tradition ... is an historically extended, socially embodied argument, and an argument precisely in part about the goods which constitute that tradition.[2]

Adapting this statement slightly for our purposes, we may use it to encapsulate three dimensions of reception that are particularly apposite to the reception of Jewish tradition in the social imagination of the early Christians.

Reception as the historical extension of a living tradition

Whatever may be said about early Christian reception of Jewish tradition, it is important to be clear from the start that this was (and remains) a *living* tradition within Judaism, constantly adapted and developed, 'on the move' before, during and after the rise of Christianity. The early Christians did not receive a static, fixed or frozen tradition but one that was inherently mobile and malleable, constantly supplementing and changing its meaning in varied historical and social contexts. As several essays here illustrate, the reception of Jewish tradition within ancient Judaism was a continuous, active process, and it should come as no surprise that that creativity was continued within circles that drew their inspiration from the Jewish figure of Jesus, both those that considered themselves to be Jewish and those that did not. The focus here on *living* tradition exposes the fact that reception is not a passive phenomenon, in which inert 'bearers' of tradition serve merely as conduits. Nor is their role simply that of inheriting and transmitting, repeating and reproducing what they have received. On the contrary, their extension of a living tradition involves many forms of adaptation, choice and revision, *even when* they think they are doing no such thing. Of course, there is a spectrum here of degrees of intervention: some forms of reception are more 'conservative' than others. But what we cannot overlook is the *agency* involved in reception, its active, adaptive modes of appropriation. That is a necessary facet of historical extension, as the tradition is ever reframed and reapplied in new historical circumstances.

This is no singular or linear process. Traditions spawn multiple interpretations and social formations that branch off in various directions at the same time. Second Temple Judaism was, as we have learned in recent decades, a highly diverse phenomenon. At times one can identify decisive moments of change, like points-switches on a railway track – when a text is translated into a new language or takes root in radically changed historical or social environments. When Hebrew scriptures are translated into Greek, when texts about the agricultural conditions of Judea are applied to city dwellers in the Diaspora, when statements about ancient kingdoms are reapplied to the Roman

---

[2] Alasdair C. MacIntyre, *After Virtue: A Study in Moral Theory*, 3rd edn (London: Bloomsbury Academic, 2014), 257.

world, when texts written for and about Jews are read by non-Jews as if addressed to *them*: these are all significant moments of change that provide new social and cultural frames for the interpretation of Jewish tradition. But there are many minor and subtle forms of adaptation taking place all the time and in every historical environment in the reception of a living tradition, as the 'arguments' continued in a tradition receive new answers, or generate new questions.

Reception as a socially embodied argument

MacIntyre's reference to the social dimensions of a living tradition echoes analysis of interpretation in the twentieth century, which has emphasized the ways in which understanding is embedded in the social and historical conditions of the interpreter(s). Within the field of hermeneutics, both Gadamer and Jauss underlined the historicized nature of reception such that the well-known term *Wirkungsgeschichte* indicates not just 'the history of reception' (or 'history of effects') but also the ways in which history shapes how traditions are received.[3] A large part of that shaping is caused by the social context of interpretation – the community of interpreters and their assumptions, horizons, and interests. As interpreters, even *virtuosi* are shaped by their social contexts – whether (to take some examples discussed in this book) the Teacher of Righteousness, John the Baptist, Jesus, Paul or Origen. If we take such figures, or individual texts, out of their social context and analyse their ideas in disembodied form, we are apt to miss the import of what they are saying and to misread their creative significance. An essential aspect of the complexity and diversity of reception within the Jewish tradition is the difference in context between Diaspora and homeland, between city and countryside, and between pre- and post-70 conditions. Similarly, reception of Jewish tradition is deeply influenced by the social configuration of communities of interpretation – whether that be the temple environment of Jerusalem, the desert community of Qumran, the court, the synagogue or the school. As those traditions get taken up within early Christian circles, their reception is shaped by the ethnicity of interpreters, their social and educational status, their physical location and their linguistic culture. As a socially embodied *argument*, such reception is also shaped by its argumentative context, the communities to which it is opposed, the audiences to which it is addressed and the social threats to which it feels exposed. Our evidence rarely reveals as much about these social dimensions of reception as we would like, but we should seek to understand it, as far as possible, in such terms. In fact, acts and processes of reception are not only constructed by their social environment but serve themselves to construct it. As they reconfigure and reframe the traditions they receive, the agents of reception are themselves configuring and framing the communities they address, creating a social imagination for the world they wish to inhabit.

---

[3] See the careful discussion of this matter in Robert Evans, *Reception History, Tradition and Biblical Interpretation: Gadamer and Jauss in Current Practice* (London: Bloomsbury T&T Clark, 2014).

Reception as, in part, an argument about the people who constitute that tradition

To match the purposes of this volume, we have here adapted the last part of MacIntyre's formulation, shifting attention from 'the goods which constitute that tradition' to '*the people* who constitute that tradition'. Traditions have no demographic boundaries: even if they have a primary home and social context, they easily 'leak out' to other groups and interested parties, sometimes by intention, and sometimes not. The (guarded) openness of Jewish communities to the participation of non-Jews always bore the potential that Jewish traditions could be taken up by others, and the missionary impetus of Jewish Christ-believers, from the first generation, ensured that the complex weave of Jewish texts, concepts and practices was available for further creative adaptation and reapplication. The reception of these traditions in mixed Jew-Gentile communities, and then in communities made up entirely of non-Jews, was bound to create a profound and complex argument concerning the people to whom they belonged: to whom did these texts refer, who were they written for and who were their authoritative interpreters in the ongoing saga of their reception? How should these practices be continued (or not), and by whom?

We can watch such questions arise already in the letters of Paul, who cites the Jewish scriptures but claims, when writing to communities of (mostly) non-Jews, that 'these things were written down to instruct us' (1 Cor. 10.11) and that 'whatever was written in former days was written for our instruction, so that by steadfastness and by the encouragement of the scriptures we might have hope' (Rom. 15.4). Here the scriptures are received as a tradition if not *about* 'us' at least *for* 'us' – a bold claim that opens the door for a multifaceted argument about who *constitutes* that tradition in its historical continuation. Many of these texts, though written for and about Israel, depict their model figures in non-specific terms, as 'the righteous', 'the holy', 'the wise' or 'brothers'. That rendered them readily transferable to those who claimed no Jewish ethnicity, supplying to novel communities of Christ-believers narratives and tropes which populated their imagination in powerful ways. These communities were bound together by common allegiance to Jesus, whose status as Jewish Messiah was often evoked, and whose rootedness in Jewish tradition could be denied only by an extreme effort of historical amnesia. That fact made it hard to dislocate these traditions entirely from Judaism and ensured that the argument over their 'proper' reception was urgent and frequently heated. A complex duality emerged: at one level, the appropriation of Jewish traditions for non-Jewish communities, accompanied by claims to superior understanding or definitive fulfilment; at another, the 'Judaizing' of Gentile communities, who gained a history, an ancestry and an identity from the Jewish traditions they claimed as their own.

Nomenclature is important. What we label 'Jewish' scripture could be considered simply 'scripture' – without ethnic label or community assignment. The categories and classifications that have become familiar in scholarly discourse are, of course, our own construction, and when we label traditions 'Christian' or 'Jewish' we find ourselves sometimes echoing and sometimes overriding the categories deployed by the texts themselves. If the early 'Christians' claimed the Maccabees as their own martyr-heroes (see the essay here by Jan Willem van Henten), *we* may regard such reception as an act of appropriation, even supersession, of an evidently 'Jewish' phenomenon. But from a world view where the all-important category is the witness of the faithful to God, ethnicity may not be as salient in the reception of this tradition as we are apt to assume. The history of 'the faithful' may be traced all the way back to Abraham, and its continuation claimed in Daniel, the Maccabees and others in a seamlessly continuous tradition through to early Christian martyrs. If we label this phenomenon the continuation of a Jewish tradition or, alternatively, its 'deJudaizing', we place ourselves not in a neutral, objective position but in a particular location within a still-ongoing argument about the people who constitute that tradition.

The essays in this volume seek to illuminate such processes of reception, with particular focus on its role in forming the social imagination of the early Christians. They divide into three groups as studies in: the reception of Jewish texts; the reception of Jewish themes, images and categories; and the reception of Jewish practices. A brief overview will serve to bring out their interconnections.

Under the heading of *The Reception of Jewish Texts*, three essays explore the ways in which Jewish scriptural traditions are the subject of creative processes of reception in early Christianity. *Judith Lieu* explores 'The early Christian reception of the legend of the Greek translation of the scriptures'. She sets the scene by summarizing and questioning a common but erroneous scholarly narrative structured by a simple binary: that Christians appropriated the LXX translation, while Jews repudiated the LXX and either reverted to the Hebrew or sponsored their own revised translations. Not only is this account historically untrue, but it masks a far more complex process by which texts and their translations enter into competing claims for authority and competence. Lieu then focuses on three Christian retellings of the famous translation legend, two by Justin Martyr and one by Irenaeus. In his *Dialogue with Trypho*, Justin invokes the legend to mount a competitive claim to authority over against Trypho's Jewish teachers, and thereby displays the anxieties created by an unstable and multivocal text. By contrast, in his *First Apology*, the legend serves to guarantee the value of a text that has royal patronage and demands serious attention in the domain of high culture. Differently again, Irenaeus uses the tradition about the translation to defend the prophetic qualities of the Emmanuel text (Isa. 7.13–14) and to develop an overarching scheme of soteriology, played off against both Jews and 'heretical' Christians. There are multiple layers of reception encapsulated here: the reception of the Hebrew texts in Greek translation, the reception of the translation in the legend recounted by The Letter of Aristeas and the reception of that legend in multiple Christian forms for various rhetorical and social purposes. The stages analysed by Lieu show this living textual tradition embroiled in a multifaceted argument, where the stakes were high and different groups laid claim to that textual tradition as an integral part of their social identity.

Devin White explores Origen's reading of the difference between Jewish and Christian reception of shared texts in 'The Law and Prophets as Origen's Gospel'. Third-century Judaism and Christianity were both textual communities, and an important element in their rivalry was their competing claim to a shared text. White explores

Origen's explanation of this rivalry as a matter of more than social difference, but of a profound distinction in *ontological* status. Exploring first Origen's critical references to Jewish 'literalism' and then his programmatic comments on the nature of 'gospel' in the prologue to his *Commentary on John*, White spotlights Origen's emphasis on 'spiritual' understanding, which is possible only for those who have undergone the ontological transformation entailed in participation in the Logos. For Origen, although there are degrees of intensity with which texts reveal Christ, all scriptural texts, including the Law and the Prophets, are to some degree 'gospel' inasmuch as they point towards Christ, when properly understood. But that understanding is only accessible to those who, in Paul's words, have the 'mind of Christ' (1 Cor. 2.16), and Origen uses this and other Pauline motifs to advance a Christian version of the philosophical axiom that 'only like can know like'. Thus, for Origen, the sociological difference between Jews and Christians is secondary to their more basic ontological distinction, which is revealed in their differing hermeneutics. Thus, the Christian reception of the Jewish tradition is central to the ways in which Christians imagined themselves as 'spiritual' people, and Origen makes a bold claim that the texts are oriented to Christian readers, as the goal of their long-evolving tradition.

Finally in this part, *Stephen Carlson* examines an intriguing episode in the layered reception of texts in 'The reception of the Watchers tradition in Tertullian with regard to 1 Cor. 11.2–16'. As he points out, the source of the argument in this case is an obscurity in Paul's text that has significant implications for the social, and specifically the gendered, configuration of Christian churches in Carthage in the early third century. What did Paul mean when he said that 'a woman should have authority on her head *because of the angels*' (1 Cor. 11.10)? Who are these angels? And what 'women' are required by Paul here to cover their heads: all women (so Tertullian) or only married women (so a succession of bishops in Carthage)? The ambiguities are resolved by Tertullian by appeal to 1 Enoch, a Jewish text that participates in a long Jewish argument about the interpretation of Gen. 6.1–4, and whose authority as scripture was defended by Tertullian against other Christians of his day. Thus a Pauline text is received and interpreted by reference to an intertext, both of which are part of a living tradition used to shape the ways that Carthaginian Christians regulated their social roles, especially the anomalous role of mature unmarried *virgines*. As Carlson shows, Tertullian's text gives us a tantalizing glimpse of the argument conducted by the *virgines* themselves (or at least, the defenders of their unveiled appearance in church) and thus allows us to see how competing versions of the early Christian social imagination were argued out by reference to a long, complex and sometimes opaque tradition.

The second part of this volume concerns *The Reception of Jewish Themes, Images, and Categories*. The five essays here address a variety of examples related to the reception and recategorization of traditions about peoples, characters, themes and images related to communal life. *Christine Gerber* opens this part with an examination of the reception of stereotypes about gentiles, idolatry and sexual behaviour, and their application to a new context in early Christianity, in her essay '"Not like the gentiles who do not know God" (1 Thess. 4.5): The function of Othering and anti-gentile stereotypes of sexual wrongdoing in early Jewish and Christian texts'. Sparked by an observation about varied uses of τὰ ἔθνη in Eph. 3.1 and 4.17–20 – the first to describe the addressees positively and the latter referring to a negative group of 'others', with whom the recipients are presumed no longer to identify – Gerber's essay considers other examples in which writers align gentiles with both idolatry and sexual wrongdoing. Examining texts from Alexandrine Judaism (Pseudo-Aristeas, Joseph and Asenath, and Wisdom) and then 1 Thessalonians and Ephesians, she argues that these 'Gentile Bashing' stereotypes provide a shortcut for early Christian writers to associate groups with legitimacy or deviance, thus providing a boundary marker and strengthening in-group identity as superior to 'others'. Here lack of knowledge of God results in both sexual wrongdoing and idolatry, dovetailing with ideas that are already connected in Jewish texts. But Gerber observes that by highlighting sexual wrongdoing, early Christian writers such as the author of Ephesians create an 'inclusive ethos' with non-Jewish readers who would also seek to distance themselves from such wrongdoing; she finds the language sufficiently vague as to make sense in diverse cultural settings, from Jewish sources to Stoic ethics. Thus, Gerber's analysis of the function of anti-gentile rhetoric reveals an overlooked but important element of group identity formation among early Christians, as the 'Othering' applied to gentiles in Jewish texts is reworked in settings for Christian readers from non-Jewish backgrounds. Significantly, despite the new addressees' background, this rhetoric enables these readers to identify with the superior ethos described by the Christian, anti-gentile text – even if this were in fact not so different from the ethos espoused by other, 'gentile' groups with which they might previously have identified.

Jan Willem van Henten explores 'Patterns of Christian reinterpretation of the Maccabean martyrdoms'. In so doing, he sets out an example in which early Christian writers not only draw on but appropriate Jewish characters so that their Jewish identity is elided and they become Christian heroes. Van Henten explores the earliest Christian reinterpretations of the Maccabean martyrs (approx. 100–260 CE), considering any role played by the original context and Jewish identity of the martyrs in later interpretations, as well as the ways in which these later reinterpretations portray the Maccabean characters' motives for choosing martyrdom and their function as role models for Christians. He notes that, despite some passing references to elements related to Jewish identity, for example, their 'ancestral language', the Maccabees have been 'historized' (i.e. attributed to a Christian past) and 'scripturalized' (integrated into Christian scripture). With the striking omission of the Jewish commitments such as dietary practices that are central to the martyrs' motivations in 2 and 4 Maccabees, the reinterpretations focus on attributes such as faith, virtue and end-time vindication, which represent the martyrs as heroes within Christian salvation history and exemplars for the Christian readers who are addressed as the heirs of this tradition. Thus the early Christian reinterpretation of the Maccabean martyrs facilitates a sense of communal Christian identity which is grounded in a salvation history that reaches into the past, inspiring steadfast self-sacrifice in the face of conflict with worldly authorities and assurance of vindication.

Highlighting the diversity among both Jewish and early Christian sources, *Kylie Crabbe* considers the role of impairment and disability in social identity in '"The blind and the lame": An adapted category in early Christian communal self-understanding'. Crabbe begins by examining passages which refer to 'the blind' and 'the lame' in the

Hebrew Bible, as well as some significant points of difference in the Greek text of key passages (e.g. Jer. 31.8–9). She identifies among these texts various ways in which the treatments of characters with visual and mobility impairments interact with communal identity, and then considers how the categories identified help to make sense of the references to 'the blind' and 'the lame' in texts which build on Hebrew Bible traditions, both among texts found at Qumran and in the New Testament. Some passages reflect an 'inclusion/exclusion' dynamic that may manifest in three ways: the groups with impairments are explicitly excluded from the community's identity as a whole or from significant roles within it, or they are explicitly included within communal identity (often with allusion to the exclusionary passages they seek to counter), or these groups of characters may undertake a process of inclusion to exclusion through healing such that the community arrived at no longer includes those with impairments (as in the case of passages that align the healing of 'the blind and the lame' with eschatological transformation, e.g. Isa. 29.18; 35.5–6; Mt. 11.5; Lk. 7.22). Other passages, she suggests, reflect an 'identification' dynamic – by which 'the blind' and/or 'the lame' become metaphorical categories for the experience of the community as a whole (as in examples in which the remnant of Israel limps on the promised return from exile, e.g. Mich. 4.6–7; Zeph. 3.19–20). Building on the study of these pilgrimage texts, she considers the role of 'the blind' and 'the lame' in the temple in Mt. 21.14 and Luke's banquet parable in Lk. 14.21–4 as metaphors for communal self-understanding. Recognizing the risks such metaphors run of appropriating (or eclipsing) the lived experience of those with visual and mobility impairments, she notes that the choice of metaphor is striking and potentially revealing of a role for disability and weakness in early Christian communal identity.

Candida Moss explores how images of the afterlife in Jewish and Christian texts interact with claims about ethical practices in 'The ethics of Eden: Luxury, banqueting and the New Jerusalem'. Moss highlights an intriguing tension between early Christian expectations of post-mortem luxury and gluttony, on the one hand, and ethical commitments to asceticism, on the other. Focusing on two key areas in which this tension is particularly pronounced, she considers portraits of wealth and the heavenly city (at times inspired by images of Eden's paradise) and post-mortem feasting – whether in a temporary millennial kingdom or in an eternal kingdom. Moss's analysis highlights diversity on these themes in both Jewish and Christian literature. For instance, while she describes the heritage of luxury in the Septuagint as 'ambiguous' – noting the positive portrayal of the luxury of Eden, or in Ezekiel's promise to the Lord's sheep of rest and luxury, as compared to the prophets' indictment of luxury and decadence – she highlights Philo's concern about τρυφή in Eden. And in terms of feasting, she considers Second Temple texts that indicate a sense of community meals anticipating an eschatological banquet (such as in Qumran), alongside rituals of present and post-mortem banqueting in catacombs, and contrasts these latter with cases where early Christian fasting in this life is part of the preparation for post-mortem feasting. Indeed, for Tertullian, the consequences of dietary restraint even *facilitate* resurrection, through the simpler mechanics of raising an emaciated body. Contrastingly, Moss draws out strands of early Christian literature that come to criticize expectations of post-mortem decadence. In instances in which the appropriation and subversion of

Jewish sources serve broader polemical purposes, Jerome and Origen label traditions of post-mortem luxury and decadence as part of Jewish chiliasm, leveraging anti-Jewish sentiment and suspicion of wealth and luxury to foster their challenge to the status of the Book of Revelation. Such themes highlight an early Christian social framework that imagines its present communal life in abstinence and displays diverse attitudes towards eschatological decadence, reflecting differing self-understandings about the early Christian community's relationship to Jewish groups, their (diverse) eschatological traditions and practices arising from these commitments.

The final contribution to this part is Benjamin Edsall's 'Scribes, Pharisees, Sadducees and Trypho: Jewish leadership and Jesus traditions in Justin's construal of Christian and Jewish identity'. Here Edsall explores how Justin Martyr, in his *Dialogue with Trypho*, conflates, modifies and adapts (i.e. creatively receives) gospel traditions in their depiction of Jewish leaders and links them to contemporary controversies between Christians and Jews. Edsall's close analysis shows the special prominence given to Pharisees in Justin's reception of 'the Memoirs of the Apostles', and the ways in which Justin turns the gospel critiques into charges against Trypho's Jewish community, by associating the leaders excoriated by Jesus with 'teachers of your race' and 'Pharisee teachers', who influence the 'synagogue leaders'. As Edsall acknowledges, it is extremely difficult to know how far we may read this text as evidence for social reality in Justin's day. But what is important, in any case, is how Justin *constructs* his social situation and *imagines* his Christian community as the heirs of Jesus in continuing conflict with the Jewish heirs of Jesus's opponents one hundred years down the track, even if both sides also have internal battles with 'heretical' groups within their communities. Thus the dynamic process of reception continues through Justin's work, as literary figures in the gospels are interpreted with a view to second-century configurations of Christian and Jewish identity. In imagining his own disputes with Jews as a continuation of Jesus's controversies with Pharisees, Justin forges an image of the Christian community with far-reaching implications for 'the parting of the ways'.

The final part of this book concerns *The Reception of Jewish Practices*. Joel Marcus opens this part with an essay entitled 'Denial of forgiveness and the Spirit: "Anxiety of influence" and the Christian demotion of John's baptism'. Building on his recent monograph, Marcus here questions the gospel accounts of John the baptizer, and offers a case study in the creative, interested adaptation of tradition through successive stages of reception. Biblical material about the Spirit and forgiveness, often associated with water, was variously received in Second Temple Judaism, and was of particular significance to the Qumran sectarians, as evident in 1QS. On Marcus's account, John, once a member of that movement, adapted this tradition in a radical way to present himself as the eschatological figure who provides access to forgiveness and the Spirit through his special rite of baptism. Jesus, or at least the post-Easter followers of Jesus, subsequently downgraded the status of John, denying to his baptism the benefits of forgiveness and Spirit in order to associate those with Jesus himself. The developing competition between the John-movement and the Jesus-movement required the rewording of sayings attributed to John, while Josephus reinterpreted John's baptism for different reasons. This rolling history of adaptive reception is not simply an intellectual matter. It concerns practices crucial to the identity of competing religious movements, especially as the baptismal rite was central to the early Christians' understanding of themselves as a social entity. In that sense, reception of tradition was fundamental to the argument about who constituted the elect community and what efficacy could be attributed to their initiatory rite.

Loren Stuckenbruck considers scribal practice as a source of authority in his essay 'Tradition and authority in scribal culture: A Comparison between the *Yaḥadic* Dead Sea Scroll texts and the Gospel of Matthew'. Here Stuckenbruck explores the way in which Matthew's portrait of Jesus as an authoritative teacher supports or reflects the evangelist's own claims to authority, made implicitly and explicitly in how he sets out his gospel. In doing so, Stuckenbruck analyses the rhetorical use of the Teacher of Righteousness in numerous texts from among the Dead Sea Scrolls, including various Pesharim and the Damascus Document. These Qumran sources align multiple temporal moments by recounting the Teacher's authoritative interpretation of earlier scriptural traditions within the author's time some generations later. Stuckenbruck argues that, for both figures (the Teacher of Righteousness and the Matthean Jesus), the texts focus on an account of the past while applying the teaching to pressing considerations of the writers' own times. He suggests that the writers not only find connections between their own time and that of their teachers (for instance, blending the portrait of the teachers' opponents with the opponents of their own times), but that they leverage the authority of the teacher to support their own scribal authority. Thus Stuckenbruck advances two parallel cases in which earlier Jewish tradition is not only deployed but also adapted, added to and reframed, to authorize a contemporary phenomenon which claims merely to continue the past, with implications for how authority is transmitted within the early Christian community.

Finally, *John Barclay* analyses social practices of economic support in 'Remember the poor: Early Christian reception of a Jewish communal responsibility'. He emphasizes first the importance of socio-economic support as a matter of communal commitment (not just personal morality) and thus its significance as a 'symbolic clamp', holding together communities of differing social ranks in relations of reciprocal recognition and solidarity. Barclay discusses samples of the multiplex Jewish traditions on this matter, beginning from Deuteronomy 15 and following this tradition forward in such varied Jewish texts as The Damascus Document and Tobit. One of the features that makes this tradition malleable is its use of the label 'brother', chosen because kinship relations entail the strongest moral bonds of obligation. But 'brother'-language can be adopted readily by a variety of communities, such as those oriented to Christ, who reapplied these Jewish traditions of economic practice to support – indeed, to constitute – new networks of social commitment. Paul's communities, and Paul's attempts to link them via monetary collections to 'the poor among the saints' in Jerusalem, are good examples of this reapplied tradition, while The Shepherd of Hermas indicates how the same tradition was used to clamp together the assembly in Rome, tying the rich into the community by persuading them to contribute to the support of poorer fellow Christians. Thus Barclay demonstrates that the Christian reception of this fundamental, community-forming practice is both a continuation of the Jewish tradition and a creative adaptation, which serves to underpin in practical ways Christian self-definition and self-understanding as a community who 'remember the poor'.

We hope these summaries have whetted the reader's appetite for the feast of scholarship that follows, and that these essays will continue to enrich an important scholarly tradition (and argument) concerning what we mean by 'reception' and how to understand early Christian formation in its Jewish matrix. It remains to thank Australian Catholic University (and particularly its Deputy Vice-Chancellor for Research, Wayne McKenna) for generosity in funding both the wider project of which this is part and the colloquium of which this is the fruit. We are grateful to each of the authors for their insight and rigour in addressing these themes and to all who participated generously with the discussion in Rome. In particular, we would like to thank those who engaged in depth with the papers as respondents at the colloquium: Simon Gathercole, Christine Gerber, Judith Lieu, Candida Moss, Jens Schröter, Joseph Verheyden and Francis Watson. In the preparation of this volume we are grateful to Hilary Howes for her meticulous attention to detail and Richard Phua for compiling the main indexes (also funded by ACU), and to Bloomsbury Academic for their commitment to this volume from the very beginning.

Part 1

The reception of Jewish texts

1

The early Christian reception of the legend of the Greek translation of the scriptures

Judith M. Lieu

The world of Jewish thought from the Second Temple period and the emergence of what would become Christianity cannot be understood apart from the translation of the Hebrew scriptures into Greek. This statement might be explored purely in terms of the historical and cultural context, and particularly of the indispensable role of Greek for communication through the Empire. More important, however, is the symbolic freight that is carried in terms such as 'scriptures' and 'translation' – something that varies according to the perspective from which the statement is made – and the implicit claims that lie buried within them. Furthermore, whereas in the past such a claim would have been deemed as of primary interest to historians of the period, it is now inextricably bound up in the newly competing discourses of translation theory, of postcolonial analysis, of the understanding of the sacred and of the construction of religion and of identity.[1] If it ever was, translation is no longer limited to the esoteric interests of the philologist but both offers a window into and is itself an agent within the dynamics of social power relations. The aims of this essay are necessarily more focussed and modest, although it seeks to be alert to and perhaps to contribute to that new environment; its concern is not to answer the familiar questions of the origins and use of the Greek Bible but to explore the purposes to which such questions could be put, and were put, as individuals and communities positioned themselves in relation to received tradition and to the surrounding society. Although a thorough exploration would require the analysis of a range of writings, constraints of space mean that this essay will set the context and then focus on two writers of the second century, Justin Martyr and Irenaeus.[2]

Within older accounts of the so-called 'Parting of the Ways' the Greek translation of the scriptures played an important and fairly well-defined role which may be summarized as follows: Although the translation into Greek of the Hebrew scriptures

---

[1] See the special number of *Religion* 49.3 (2019), especially Hephzibah Israel, 'Translation and Religion: Crafting Regimes of Identity', 323–42.
[2] For a full account of the history of the tradition see Abraham Wasserstein and David J. Wasserstein, *The Legend of the Septuagint: From Classical Antiquity to Today* (Cambridge: Cambridge University Press, 2006), although they are more concerned to trace a linear development of uses of the legend without analysing in detail its function in each context.

(conventionally, the Septuagint) predated the time of Jesus, the early Christians very quickly adopted it in their efforts to demonstrate that Jesus was the Messiah promised by God through the prophets, and more generally that Jesus Christ and the church founded in his name were the true heirs of the scriptural narrative of salvation. This move is already evident to various degrees in the reliance on the Septuagint by the main witnesses in the New Testament even when authors' knowledge of the Hebrew or recourse to independent (or their own) translation remain matters of discussion. Recourse to the Greek translation was necessitated by the spread of the Gospel beyond the land of Israel-Palestine into a predominately if not exclusively Greek-speaking environment, and inevitably it helped to ensure the success and eventual dominance of the gentile mission. Alongside this standard, more or less neutral, account was the parallel assertion that the Jews then, or concurrently, distanced themselves from the Septuagint: Emanuel Tov's summary, reprinted as recently as 2015, expresses this in terms that might match the concerns of this volume very clearly:

> A statement referring to the Septuagint as both Jewish and Christian would be imprecise, since the LXX was never both Jewish and Christian at the same time. The translation started off as a Jewish enterprise, and was accepted by the early Christians when they were still a group within Judaism. From that time on, when the Jews had abandoned the LXX, Christianity held on to the LXX as Scripture.[3]

This conventional narrative is routinely continued with the further claim that the Jews turned instead to alternative translations into Greek (such as that of Aquila) that followed the Hebrew more closely, even where they did so to the point of incomprehensibility. Thus, James Dunn, who surprisingly even asserts, 'In contrast, the synagogues continued to read the scriptures in Hebrew', describes the translation by Aquila as 'intended as a replacement for the Christianized Septuagint' or what had become 'Christian scripture', and as 'part of the rabbis' campaign to rabbinize their Greek-speaking co-religionists.'[4] Marcel Simon brings together the Christian appropriation of the Septuagint and their appeal to it 'to confound the Jews', with the assumption that the Jews 'abandoned it' by the third century, substituting new translations such as that of Aquila, to which he also adds the prohibition in rabbinic sources against the teaching of Greek wisdom (m. Sotah 9.14; b. Sotah 49b).[5]

Such accounts have sometimes adopted a mildly self-critical note, using, as did Simon, the language of appropriation or 'take over', although few would now go so far as Adolf von Harnack, 'Such an injustice as that inflicted by the Gentile church on Judaism is almost unprecedented in the annals of history. The Gentile church stripped

---

[3] Emmanuel Tov, 'The Septuagint between Judaism and Christianity', in *Textual Criticism of the Hebrew Bible, Qumran, Septuagint: Collected Essays III*, VT.S 167 (Leiden: Brill, 2015), 449–69, 449.
[4] James D. G. Dunn, *The Partings of the Ways between Christianity and Judaism and their Significance for the Character of Christianity*, 2nd edn (London: SCM, 2006), 314. Cf. Marcel Simon, *Verus Israel: A Study of the Relations between Christians and Jews in the Roman Empire (AD 135–425)*, trans. H. McKeating (Oxford: Oxford University Press, 1986), 153, 'prompted by this lack of confidence in the Septuagint and by the need to refute the interpretations the Christians based upon it'.
[5] Simon, *Verus Israel*, 294–301.

it of everything: she took away its sacred book.'[6] It has been pointed out, justifiably, that such a narrative is itself an act of (ex-)appropriation, denying the use of the Greek scriptures to the continuing story of the Jewish people, and serving to reinforce models of the survival of the people only through the medium of Hebrew and rabbinic literature, too often largely incomprehensible to the scholars making such claims.[7] Such binary models have a long history, which itself should make them suspect, implicitly if not explicitly identifying the Jews with 'the letter' and 'literalism', Christians with 'the spirit'.[8] They adopt a starkly antithetical and 'zero-sum' model of the 'parting of the ways'; each stage on one side must correspond to a parallel (re-)action on the other, in a quasi-double-entry bookkeeping of gains and losses. Yet, even where monochrome or flat reimaginings of 'the parting' themselves have been abandoned, the binary template too often survives.

However, it is not just the underlying model that is suspect: a growing body of scholarship has demonstrated that the narrative itself is no longer viable. The Greek translations of the prophets found among the Dead Sea Scrolls, inter alia, have demonstrated that what are now more often called 'Old Greek' translations which adopted a method involving closer imitation of the Hebrew structure predated the emergence of Christianity, and so were not a response to it; the same is true of their more formal heirs in the second and third centuries ('the Three', namely Aquila, Symmachus and Theodotion). Although time does not allow a fuller discussion of the sources and the debate, there is little to support the model of Aquila as the mouthpiece of the rabbis, or possibly even as reflecting rabbinic policies and exegesis, and use of his translation likely extended beyond the sphere of their operations.[9] Perhaps more importantly, the sometimes circular arguments that have claimed that surviving scroll fragments with a LXX text must be Christian have been persuasively questioned by Robert Kraft.[10] More emphatically, there is substantial and increasingly well-documented evidence of the continued use of the LXX as well as of other forms of Greek translation by the Jews at least through the Byzantine period, if not, in some circles, later.[11]

---

[6] Adolf von Harnack, *The Expansion of Christianity in the First Three Centuries*, 2 vols, trans. James Moffatt (London: Williams & Norgate, 1904), 81.

[7] Cf. Tessa Rajak, *Translation and Survival: The Greek Bible of the Ancient Jewish Diaspora* (Oxford: Oxford University Press, 2009), 286–94; Rajak, 'Theological Polemic and Textual Revision in Justin Martyr's *Dialogue with Trypho the Jew*', in *Greek Scripture and the Rabbis*, ed. T. M. Law and Alison Salvesen (Leuven: Peeters, 2012), 127–40, 127–8.

[8] For this pattern see Simon, *Verus Israel*, 301: 'Judaism became more rigidly devoted to meditation exclusively on the law, and to the practice of its ancestral rituals.'

[9] See Alison Salvesen, 'Aquila, Symmachus and the Translation of Proof-Texts', in *Die Septuaginta: Texte, Wirkung, Rezeption*, ed. Wolfgang Kraus and Siegfried Kreuzer (in Verbindung mit Martin Meiser und Marcus Sigismund), WUNT 325 (Tübingen: Mohr Siebeck, 2014), 154–68.

[10] An overview of Kraft's questions and contributions can be found via http://ccat.sas.upenn.edu/rak//earlylxx/jewishpap.html (accessed 26 March 2020).

[11] Cameron Boyd-Taylor, 'Afterlives of the Septuagint: A Christian Witness to the Greek Bible in Byzantine Judaism', in *The Jewish-Greek Tradition in Antiquity and the Byzantine Empire*, ed. James Aitken and James Carleton Paget (Cambridge: Cambridge University Press, 2014), 135–51; Nicholas de Lange, 'Jewish Transmission of Greek Bible Versions', in *XIII Congress of the International Organization for Septuagint and Cognate Studies*, ed. Melvin K. H. Peters (Atlanta, GA: SBL Press, 2008), 109–17.

However, the particular concern of this essay is to set within this wider discussion the part played by the narrative or 'legend' of the origins of the LXX, as best known in, whether or not initiated by, the Letter of Aristeas. This story was not only retold within subsequent Jewish tradition but was taken up by Christians in a process that often has served as a subsection of the broader narrative of appropriation already described.[12] These successive retellings in Christian sources of the 'Septuagint Legend' have been regularly rehearsed elsewhere, with particular attention often being paid to the developing emphasis within them that divine intervention in the process ensured the complete unanimity of the translation produced, in contrast to the original narrative where that unanimity was the result of their careful collaboration (*Ep. Arist.* 306).[13] Nevertheless, such studies have struggled to detect a neat progressive process, particularly in the early period; more importantly, because their interest has been in attempting to do so, frequently they have ignored the rhetorical framing of the individual retellings.

It is not the concern of this essay to engage in the debates surrounding the origins of the translation into Greek of the Jewish scriptures, or those concerning to what degree, if any, the Aristeas story can be sifted for kernels of historical truth as to the personnel, the dating and the intentions or needs at work in the original undertaking. Generally, under the influence of recent translation studies, attention has moved from relating the Letter of Aristeas to the production of the translation towards understanding it in relation to the reception of the latter.[14] However, while this shift is important both for interpreting the Letter of Aristeas and for any discussion of the apologetic narrative defences of the Septuagint translation (however it actually arose), for the purposes of this discussion the version given by the Letter of Aristeas probably remains the starting point for any investigation of its Christian retellings.[15]

Nonetheless, two insights from translation studies will continue to provide the backcloth to this investigation: first, debates about translation are not simply about the possibility of, or the expectations regarding, linguistic equivalence but represent or embody questions of cultural equivalence or differentiation – in the words of Naomi Seidman, 'translating [its] semeiotic operations into cultural and philosophical converse'.[16] In terms of a model of translation as colonial appropriation, in the Letter of Aristeas the appropriation is as much by – rather than primarily of – the source language/text/culture. At the same time, the Jews also benefit from the exchange, not for the liturgical or educational reasons often discussed in scholarship but by acquiring high cultural value and status. Second, it is more generally true that, in the words of Lynne Long, 'a new translation can be a serious means of challenging the orthodox readings of a holy text … or the means of creating a new cultural identity through

---

[12] Cf. Rajak, *Translation and Survival*, 282–4.
[13] Wasserstein and Wasserstein, *Legend of the Septuagint*.
[14] See Benjamin G. Wright, 'The *Letter of Aristeas* and the Reception History of the Septuagint', *BIOSCS* 39 (2006), 47–68; Wright, 'The Letter of Aristeas and the Question of Septuagint Origins Redux', *Journal of Ancient Judaism* 2 (2011), 304–26.
[15] The question whether the account by Aristobulus is independent is not material to this essay.
[16] Naomi Seidman, *Faithful Renderings: Jewish-Christian Difference and the Politics of Translation* (Chicago: University of Chicago Press, 2006), 46–9.

separation from the established traditions'.[17] Undoubtedly the Letter of Aristeas can be read as negotiating this situation, while Christian rereadings, whether consciously or not, are implicated in it.

Glimpses of how the legend had a continuing life, serving different purposes, in Jewish writings can be traced through its use by Philo (*Vit. Mos.* 2.5-7 (25-44)) and by Josephus (*Ant.* 1.3 (9-13); 12.2.1-15 (11-118)).[18] In their account of the tradition, Abraham and David Wasserstein follow these by their description of the various rabbinic references, primarily from the Babylonian Talmud, before they then turn to the Christian ones. In part this is because of their conviction that the tradition in b. Meg. 8b-9b, according to which King Talmai separates the seventy-two translators into seventy-two houses although his efforts are ultimately thwarted by divine wisdom, must predate the separation of Judaism and Christianity and so is to be dated prior to the Bar Kochba revolt. This conclusion seems highly unlikely, and it is more probable that the baraita arose in Babylonian circles and was mediated, whether directly or indirectly, through fourth-century Christian sources.[19] Consequently, even if the precise transmission of the legend remains unclear, the functions assigned to it and the strategies adopted for this purpose by the early Christian sources can be explored in their own terms.

Justin Martyr

Justin Martyr has often been seen as exemplifying the supposed 'take over' of the Septuagint as described earlier; further, it is apparently with him that the legend first appears in Christian circles. As shall be seen, in the *Dialogue with Trypho* he refers to the tradition only by allusion, but he does assume some level of recognition of it, and even of shared respect for it, by his adversary, and by implication by his readers, whoever they might be – a matter where there is as yet no consensus. In the *First Apology*, on the other hand, he introduces a summary form of the legend as something unknown to his purported Roman (if not actual) audience. Since the *First Apology* was written prior to the *Dialogue*, but the events described by latter are set several years earlier,[20] it is not possible to trace any development in Justin's own knowledge of the tradition. What is of greater importance are the specific literary context and generic intention in each case; it would be a mistake to appeal to what he says in one text in order to interpret the other or to reconstruct a synthesis between them.

---

[17] Lynne Long, 'Introduction: Translating Holy Texts', in *Translation and Religion: Holy Untranslatable?*, ed. Lynne Long (Bristol: Multilingual Matters, 2005), 1-15, 6.

[18] Wasserstein and Wasserstein, *Legend of the Septuagint*, 27-50, discuss Aristobulus, Philo and Josephus. Whether there were other Hellenistic-Jewish retellings is unknown, so conclusions should not be drawn from their 'absence'.

[19] Wasserstein and Wasserstein, *Legend of the Septuagint*, 51-83, esp. 68-9; for the alternative position see Guiseppe Veltri, *Ein Tora für den König Talmai: Untersuchungen zum Übersetzungsverständnis in der jüdisch-hellenistischen und rabbinischen Literatur*, TSAJ 41 (Tübingen: Mohr Siebeck, 1994).

[20] *Dial.* 120.6 refers to the *Apology* (dated to c.150 CE, *1 Apol.* 46.1), while Justin's original encounter with Trypho is set soon after the Bar Kochba revolt (*Dial.* 1.3).

The *Dialogue*

The *Dialogue* will be treated first here because, as just noted, Justin alludes to the Septuagint tradition without directly citing it, and an analysis of the literary function of this technique should not be clouded by what he does in the *Apology*. Yet, like most readings of the *Dialogue*, the exercise necessarily faces the challenge of distinguishing between treating it as an unfolding exchange set in the 130s, even if as a fictionalized version of such, and as a literary composition perhaps from the 160s, conceived and planned as a whole – that is, of distinguishing between Justin as implied narrator-protagonist within the text and Justin as implied author. Presumably belonging to the latter stage are the extended scriptural quotations – necessarily dependent on literary composition – even when the exegetical interest of the 'protagonist-Justin' is limited to a few verses of phrases from them. The former, together with the textual variations in and with the specific passages he subsequently discusses, which are sometimes but not always noted by him, have provoked considerable debate regarding the ways in which either as protagonist or as author he accessed the scriptural text – for example, whether he was able to consult full manuscripts in some cases, perhaps available to him through synagogues, and/or whether he depended on earlier testimonia collections; a further debate concerns the relationship both between these and between them and the forms of the Septuagint as then or as subsequently in circulation.[21]

Formulated as a vigorous defence to a Jewish interlocutor of the Christian message and existence, the *Dialogue* is constructed, without specific justification, around the interpretation of scripture, assumed to be a text or set of texts which on one level both sides recognize as the ultimate point of appeal. Justin's quasi-biographical introduction of his journey through the various philosophical options had climaxed in an encounter with an old man who introduced him to the prophets, those who 'were much older than the philosophers', 'who only spoke what they heard and saw' and 'whose writings remain even until now' (*Dial*. 7.1–2).[22] Thus prophecy and their written form are established as the centre point, but while they are superior to the philosophers there is no cultural or linguistic divide between the two.

Surprisingly, the old man implies that the coming of the Christ is one of the factors that authenticates the status of the prophets, but he gives no reason why that Christ, whom these prophets made known, should be the object of belief. However, using this as his starting block, Justin's efforts move in the opposite, and more obvious, direction, namely demonstrating that the scriptures (primarily the prophets, including the Psalms) do point towards the beliefs and practices of the Christians. In keeping with the dialogue genre, the argument develops by means of objections posed by Justin's interlocutor or, frequently, anticipated by Justin himself – although the author-Justin is necessarily responsible for both. When he turns more explicitly to the status and person of Jesus Christ these objections take the form of alternative interpretations of the passages to which he appeals that (he claims)

---

[21] For a detailed analysis see Oskar Skarsaune, *The Proof from Prophecy: A Study in Justin Martyr's Proof-Text Tradition: Text-Type, Provenance, Theological Profile*, NT.S. 56 (Leiden: Brill, 1987).

[22] The theme of 'remaining' occurs also in the Jewish accounts of the translation; cf. also *1 Apol.* 31.5 below.

his interlocutors or their teachers 'are so presumptuous' as to offer; for example, they apply the words of the royal Psalms to Hezekiah or to Solomon rather than to the Christ (*Dial.* 33.1 (Ps. 110); 34 (Ps. 72.1); 36.2 (Ps. 24); cf. 64.5 (Pss. 99; 72); 83 (Ps. 110)); they misidentify 'homonyms', or terms with double reference, such as 'law' (34.1); and they theologize or grandstand over the – for him irrelevant – addition of an α to 'Ἀβραάμ' and of a ρ to Σάρρα, while they fail to investigate the reason, which for him is deeply symbolic, as to why Moses gave the name Ἰησοῦς to Αὐσῆς (113.1–2).[23] For him these are failures in interpretation (ἐξηγοῦμαι), and in properly understanding to whom the passages refer (εἰς [ὃν] εἰρῆσθαι), that is, they are failures in knowing 'how to read'.

Within this litany of exegetical competition an appeal to Isa. 7.14 appears surprisingly late; indeed, in terms of the line of argument it is prompted by a prior appeal to Isa. 53.8, 'who can recount his generation [γενεά]?' (*Dial.* 43.3).[24] Here Justin manages to blend the mystery of his 'becoming' (γένεσις), the inexpressible character (γένος) of his death and the way in which he was born (γεννηθείς) and came into the world; it was this latter that was prophesied in advance by Isaiah (7.10–16a), another of his long quotations (*Dial.* 43.5–6). At this point he immediately complains that they (or their teachers) not only once more apply the verse with which he is concerned to Hezekiah 'who was their king' but even claim that what 'is said in the prophecy' was not that a 'virgin' (παρθένος) but that a 'young woman' (νεᾶνις) would conceive (43.8).[25]

Although Justin promises Trypho that he will shortly prove the proper application of the prophecy to 'the Christ confessed by us', he only does so after a considerable diversion; again he begins by quoting the same extended passage from Isaiah 7 in order to demonstrate that 'being begotten from a virgin and his having been born through a virgin' was prophesied through Isaiah (*Dial.* 66).[26] At this point Trypho, for the first time but as predicted by Justin, does protest, 'The passage does not read, "Behold the virgin shall conceive" ... but "Behold the young woman shall conceive ..."', and continues, 'The whole prophecy is spoken with reference to Hezekiah' (*Dial.* 67.1).[27] Immediately taking the offensive, Trypho goes on to object that by introducing

---

[23] For the change of names of Abra(ha)m, Sara(h) and Joshua see Gen. 17.5, 15 and Num. 13.16; Justin's identification of the changes is dependent on the LXX, particularly in the case of the LXX's use of Ἰησοῦς for the Hebrew יְהוֹשֻׁעַ. That Joshua becomes the successor of Moses and leads the people into the land is fundamental for Justin.

[24] Isa. 52.10–54.6 had been quoted as early as *Dial.* 13.2–9 (where the final phrase of Isa. 53.8 is read as ἥκει εἰς θάνατον as opposed to the LXX ἤχθη εἰς θάνατον (= *Dial.* 43.3)); subsequently, in *Dial.* 32.2, there is another allusion to Isa. 53.8 (τὸ γένος αὐτοῦ ἀδιήγητον) together with other verses from Isaiah 53 in the context of Justin's defence of a 'two parousias' scheme.

[25] In his long quotation in this chapter and at *Dial.* 66.2–3 the text is ἡ παρθένος ἐν γαστρὶ λήψεται καὶ τέξεται υἱόν, but the text he accuses them of rejecting is ἡ παρθένος ἐν γαστρὶ ἕξει in favour of ἡ νεᾶνις ἐν γαστρὶ λήψεται καὶ τέξεται υἱόν. See further, n. 27.

[26] The text is the same as at *Dial.* 43.5–6 except that whereas that had καὶ καλέσεται τὸ ὄνομα αὐτοῦ Ἐμμανουήλ here the verb is either καλέσουσι (following the marginal correction) or καλέσει. This clause is not repeated in his subsequent discussions of the passage.

[27] On this occasion Trypho uses the formula ἐν γαστρὶ λήψεται in both cases; Justin returns again to 'their' application of the text to Hezekiah and their distortion of it in *Dial.* 71.3 (with λήψεται), and again in 84, where he reads ἐν γαστρὶ λήψεται but reports their distortion of the text as ἡ νεᾶνις ἐν γαστρὶ ἕξει. The variation between λήψεται and ἕξει, and in the person of the verb 'call' (n. 26), is also found in LXX manuscripts at Isa. 7.14. The appeal at *Dial.* 84 is prompted by his preceding citation

the language of virginal conception Justin is borrowing ideas from pagan mythology, which have no place in the interpretation of scripture (67.1-2). What is at stake here is not only whether Jesus fulfils Isaiah by virtue of, in Justin's eyes, his undoubted but unparalleled birth from a virgin but also whether such a birth would be an appropriate demonstration that he was the promised Christ.[28]

After a further characteristic diversion, albeit with the assumption that Isaiah's prophecy did speak of 'the virgin', Justin loops round to winning Trypho's agreement that the prophets often used obscure or symbolic words and actions that required interpretation (ἐξηγοῦμαι) by 'the prophets who came after them' (68.6). It is only at this point that he adds a significant new weapon in his defence: by denying a reference to 'our Christ' in favour of one to Hezekiah Trypho ('you' pl.) is, he asserts, mistakenly following 'your' teachers who are so presumptuous as to deny 'the validity of the interpretation (ἐξήγησις) made by your seventy elders who were in the presence of Ptolemy king of the Egyptians' (68.7).[29] Although this whole debate is sometimes labelled a text-critical debate, Justin presents more as at stake: he is unequivocal that it is evidence of the extent to which their self-interest will take them, 'For when things in the scriptures patently refute their foolish and self-serving opinion, they are so bold as to say that this is not how these things were written' (68.7). This goes to prove further that their repeated attempts to refer this and other passages to Hezekiah rather than to 'our Christ' is not just confusion or misunderstanding but deliberate deceit.

Having unexpectedly introduced the appeal to 'the seventy' as a trump card from up his sleeve, Justin replays it repeatedly as part of a sustained attack on them for falsifying (παραγράφειν) the scriptures and introducing alternative 'interpretations' (παρεξηγεῖσθαι) (71.2; 73.5; 84.3-4). So, for example, in addition to their misrepresentation of Isa. 7.14, he charges them with removing (ἀφαιρεῖν, περικόπτειν) 'many passages from the interpretations (ἐξήγησις) undertaken by the elders in the presence of Ptolemy who was king of the Egyptians', when these would clearly demonstrate the one crucified to be God and man, whose death was proclaimed – and when pushed by Trypho he proceeds to provide some examples of such supposed deletions from Ezra, Jeremiah and the Psalms (*Dial*. 71.2; 72-3).[30] He goes on to identify other disagreements between how they 'interpret' the text and how 'the seventy' did, although he pointedly refrains from disputing over what he calls 'terminology' (λέξις) – which presumably does not include the 'virgin'/'young woman' alternative – and on occasion he even declares himself for the sake of the

---

of Ps. 110.1-4, where v. 3 reads 'from the womb (ἐκ γαστρός) before the dawn I begat you' (*Dial.* 83.2, although 'from the womb' is omitted in the manuscript but may be supplied from the reference back in 83.4; the passage is also quoted at 32.6; 63.3; cf. 76.7).

[28] Trypho adds that they ought to recognize that Jesus was born as 'ἄνθρωπος ἐξ ἀνθρώπων' and prove that he was the Christ by his manner of life according to the law.

[29] λέγειν τὴν ἐξήγησιν ἥν ἐξηγήσαντο οἱ ἑβδομήκοντα ὑμῶν πρεσβύτεροι παρὰ Πτολεμαίῳ τῷ τῶν Αἰγυπτείων βασιλεῖ γενόμενοι (ctr. 71.1 γενομένῳ βασιλεῖ) μὴ εἶναι ἔν τισιν ἀληθῆ). This again follows an appeal to Isa. 53.8 (cf. above).

[30] In one case (Jer. 11.19) there is no textual evidence of the omission; in the others the supposed 'deletions' are probably Christian elaborations.

argument ready to adopt their reading (ἐξήγησις) rather than that of the seventy (120.4–5; 124.2–3; 131.1; 137.3).

Although many scholars have seen a reference in these debates to alternative translations, such as those of Aquila and Theodotion, which do read νεᾶνις at Isa. 7.14, there is nothing to suggest that Justin knows these or other extended written versions.[31] At the same time, however, the text which Justin asserts represents the work of the seventy is not in fact consistently that of the Septuagint, while that which he dismisses as held by his opponents frequently is.[32] It seems evident that the texts with which he was familiar and that he inherited and those that he consulted when composing the *Dialogue* diverged, sometimes at crucial points, and where this potentially undermined his argument, he used a motif common in contemporary disputes over authoritative texts, that of 'distortion', in order to defend his position.[33] From a narrative perspective, the textual dilemma appears as something that became progressively more apparent during the encounter: towards the very end (*Dial.* 137.3) he admits that his reading of Isa. 3.10 (LXX) has shifted during the course of the debate from 'let us bind the righteous one' at the beginning (17.15; but cf. 133.7) to the supposedly authentic ('as the seventy interpreted') 'let us do away with the righteous one' (119.17; 136.2).[34] Although he offers as a post-hoc justification for this shift that initially he was making concessions to how they wanted to read it (137.3), from a rhetorical, literary perspective this is a clumsy concession, and may reflect the complex genesis of the *Dialogue*. Yet it also confirms what has become apparent here, that textual forms were not separated neatly along 'religious' lines but were fluid and complex in ways that had not previously mattered.

In all this the 'legend' serves a significant rhetorical role. Oskar Skarsaune has suggested that some form of the legend prefixed Justin's supposed testimonia source and that this bolstered his conviction that the latter presented the authentic text over against that which he subsequently encountered, perhaps from his Jewish rivals; however, whereas the original purpose of the prefatory legend may have been in a missionary context, Justin used it for text-critical purposes.[35] However, Skarsaune's argument depends on harmonizing the narrative of the legend in the *First Apology* (see below) with the epigrammatic reference in the *Dialogue*, whereas the brevity of the description and its late emergence within the structure of the *Dialogue* do little to support him. Furthermore, as Tessa Rajak has argued, in practice in the *Dialogue* it is theological polemic that dominates with little evidence of serious textual analysis.[36] Instead, the legend serves more fundamental polemical purposes for Justin.

---

[31] For example, he ignores the present tenses in those translations, 'is pregnant and bears'; cf. Salvesen, 'Aquila, Symmachus'.
[32] Skarsaune, *Proof*, 42–5.
[33] This is all evidently happening at the level of the composition of the *Dialogue*: how it could work in a chance oral encounter is not at all clear.
[34] The Septuagint reading is 'bind'.
[35] Skarsaune, *Proof*, 45–6, 295.
[36] Rajak, 'Theological Polemic'.

In the second half of the *Dialogue*, following its first introduction in *Dial.* 71, the formulaic moniker, 'seventy elders in the presence of Ptolemy', possesses a sort of talismanic quality which provides an authority to his scriptural text, over against that which, at best, his interlocuters 'prefer', and, at worst, is the result of the mutilation their teachers have carried out. Although rhetorically Justin takes for granted both the authority implied in the moniker and that those elders were theirs ('your'), Trypho is given no opportunity to challenge any of the claims Justin makes about them. Yet, contrary to those who have suggested that Trypho appeals to the meaning of the Hebrew as opposed to Justin's secondary Greek translation, this is not how Justin represents the situation. Trypho speaks and thinks as exclusively in Greek, and in Greek modes of reading texts, as does Justin himself: for Trypho the correct reading is νεᾶνις without any reference to the existence still less the form of the Hebrew original, or to questions of appropriate equivalence such as occupied later debate.[37] For both it is not a matter of philology or of translational accuracy but of what 'was written', and the proper establishment of that.

Despite his occasional use of the terminology of textual analysis and debate,[38] Justin avoids the dominant vocabulary of 'translation' which is found in the Letter of Aristeas and in other sources (ἑρμηνεύειν); instead, for him all these debates, including those over 'what was said', are matters of interpretation (ἐξηγοῦμαι, ἐξήγησις). By avoiding the topos of translation Justin-as-author avoids acknowledging that the Jews might have any intrinsic insight into the scriptures, insofar as they were originally written in their own tongue, and hence he also steers clear of any debate about the quality and nature of translation itself. Instead, all these disputes belong under the umbrella of what is his preferred and undifferentiated vocabulary throughout both the *Dialogue* and the *First Apology* for all 'exegetical' activity explaining the true meaning of scripture.[39] Furthermore, as already noted, that interpretation is equated with the activity undertaken by the prophets themselves of explicating earlier, opaque, prophetic words and acts (68.6 above), while it is also grounded in the quasi-mythic authority of the 'seventy elders'.

To some extent what Justin is attempting here exemplifies the observation of Naomi Seidman, 'Jews are the target of Christian missionary hopes, but they are also the source of Christian genealogical anxieties – the reliance of Christianity on the texts, and indeed on the translations, of a rival religious group.'[40] Yet it is not only reliance on 'the other' that is at work here but reliance on texts themselves, which are inherently unstable and necessarily multivocal. What the *Dialogue* reflects is not a moment of translational or even exegetical divergence, as in classic accounts of 'the Christian appropriation of the Septuagint', but precisely such anxieties and the necessary negotiation of the authority of the interpreter.

---

[37] Ctr. Seidman, *Faithful Renderings*, 40, 'Trypho, claiming privileged access to Hebrew sources and Jewish readings'. On the later philological debate see Adam Kamesar, 'The Virgin of Isaiah 7:14: The Philological Argument from the Second to the Fifth Century', *JTS* 41 (1990), 51–75.

[38] See above pp. 22–23.

[39] ἐξηγοῦμαι, ἐξήγησις; cf. also Rajak, 'Theological Polemic', 135.

[40] Seidman, *Faithful Renderings*, 8.

The *First Apology*

The legend functions in an entirely different way within the *First Apology*, to the extent that despite shared elements it should be described as a different story. It is again central to Justin's apologetic argument that the whole Christian narrative from the birth of Jesus through to the mission to and the conversion of the gentiles had been prophesied in advance; in this case, however, it is the antiquity of such prophecy that matters – '5000, 3000, 2000, 1000 or 800 years' before the events happened (*1 Apol.* 31.8). Even so, he does not present this argument until after he had first denounced the beliefs and practices of the Graeco-Roman gods and those who followed them, even where these might seem to echo or to anticipate what Christians claimed about Jesus. For Justin it is prophecy that establishes that Jesus was not a practitioner of magical arts (such as Simon Magus, *1 Apol.* 26), while the comprehensive coverage anticipated in detail by prophecy pre-empts any challenge to any particular claim made about Jesus, or any alternative explanation of them.

The obvious objection to this would be, 'what authenticates prophecy?', especially since to a large extent Justin treats prophecy as a distinctively Jewish phenomenon, and as requiring appropriate interpretation. In part, the answer is that just as prophecy authenticates the interpretative account of the life and significance of Jesus, so also the manifest actuality of these events, inasmuch as they primarily lie in the past, authenticates prophetic truth. Yet, as if to anchor what could be dismissed as an imaginative closed circle, Justin drops in a few supposedly irrefutable guarantees already known or available to his audience: the census returns in the time of Quirinius (*1 Apol.* 34), the destruction of Jerusalem and prohibition of Jewish entry (47), the 'Acts of Pilate' (35, 48). However, the crucial authentication of prophecy (and his use of it) comes at the very beginning of the argument (31): here Justin opens by introducing the 'certain men among the Jews who became prophets of God and through whom the prophetic spirit proclaimed in advance things that were going to happen before they took place' (31.1). He immediately follows this up with an account of how these prophecies came to be translated into Greek and were preserved 'among the Egyptians to the present day as well as everywhere among all the Jews' (31.5). Added to this is his own place in this evidentiary succession, 'we found in the books of the prophets proclaimed beforehand, becoming present, begotten through a virgin ... Jesus our Christ' (31.7).

The narrative flow in this account allows for no break in the transmission of the prophecies or for any possibility of malign interference; the prophets, through whom the prophetic spirit had pre-announced, themselves collected the prophecies into books, precisely as spoken, in their own tongue, Hebrew, while the Judaean kings of their time took possession of these and protected them. The translation itself is presented as the result of a straightforward exchange between Ptolemy, king of the Egyptians, who was setting up a library and keen to include in it the writings of all humankind, and Herod who 'at that time' was himself king of the Jews. Herod initially sends the books of the prophecies, as requested, in Hebrew, whereupon Ptolemy further requested men to translate (μεταβάλλω) them into Greek because their contents were unintelligible to the Egyptians. Once this was done – the actual process is not recounted – these books, by implication both in Hebrew and the translation into Greek, remained among the Egyptians 'until now' (*1 Apol.* 31.1–5).

Unsurprisingly, scholars have debated the presence of Herod, although it is most probable that in the context of an Apology Justin simply wanted two plausible 'Kings', particularly in continuity with the earlier protective role of 'kings', without any interference from librarians or high priests as in earlier accounts. The single other appearance of Herod in the *Apology*, as part of the conspiracy against Christ (40.6), is not enough to establish an intentional irony that it was he who inadvertently enabled the translation into Greek of the prophecies which would disprove all his efforts. Likewise, Justin refers only in general terms to 'the men who translated (τοὺς μεταβαλοῦντας) them into the Greek tongue', without detailing their number or their status, in stark contrast to the *Dialogue*'s sole focus on this. Writing in a world well aware of the requirements for translating official documents, he ignores any disclaimers of collusion or hints of the miraculous, which might invite suspicion. More pointed is the unbroken transition from the Egyptian narrative to the availability of these prophecies universally among the Jews, and thence to the double-sided inability of the latter to make sense of the prophecies and their hostile aggression against Christians (31.5–6).

Within Justin's apologetic task this account brings the potentially arcane disputes between Jews and Christians over opaque and archaic texts into the world of royal diplomacy, cultural institutions, acknowledged centres of learning and writings which are of documented provenance, self-evidently of serious value, and available for dispassionate consultation. This was more or less where Josephus in his account had also located the translation (*Ant.* 12.2.1–15 (11–118)). However, at the same time, Justin makes this a matter exclusively about the prophetic character of these writings: unlike the Jewish tradition there is no reference to the law. This does not mean Justin had in mind only the books usually labelled 'prophetic', as is indicated by his claim that some went back five thousand years, presumably to Adam,[41] while he immediately proceeds to describe Moses as 'the first of the prophets' with a citation from Gen. 49.10–11 (*1 Apol.* 32.1).

This account also provides the basis for the assertion that he repeatedly makes thereafter that the Jews 'possess the books of the prophecies' but fail to understand them, presumably either in their own tongue or in translation (36.3; 49.5; 53.6; 63.11); they are not written in some unintelligible language but are available for reading and argument. At the same time the Jews thereby become unwilling witnesses to the truth of the Christian claim and to their own hard-heartedness – a *topos* that will go on to have a long life.[42] Essential to this strategy is the absence of any suggestion that there might be debates by anyone, including by the Jews, about the correct wording of the text, including that of Isa. 7.14 (33.1).[43] In a society familiar with translation any such admission would potentially legitimize conflicting ways of reading; the neutral term μεταβάλλω similarly pre-empts further debate. Hence the translation has been

---

[41] Theophilus of Antioch describes Gen. 2.23–4 as a prophecy by Adam (*Autol.* 2.28).

[42] This is made explicit in Ps.-Justin, *Cohortatio*, 13.

[43] ἡ παρθένος ἐν γαστρὶ ἕξει καὶ τέξεται υἱόν, καὶ ἐροῦσιν ἐπὶ τῷ ὀνόματι αὐτοῦ Μεθ' ἡμῶν ὁ θεός. Cf. n. 27; the second clause is not septuagintal but cf. Mt. 1.23.

established here as a publicly available document, boasting antiquity, guaranteed provenance and significant patronage, and requiring no religious authentication or authorization; what matters is the ability to read and to understand it appropriately. From this point on, without any further reference back to Ptolemy, the ability to do so will provide the crux of his argument in the *Apology*; the tone here is not one of anxiety or negotiation but of cultural confidence.

Irenaeus

Irenaeus offers a further demonstration both of the malleability and of the possibilities for reinvention inherent in the story. Although he shares what was to become an ever more focalized concern with Isa. 7.14, there is little to suggest that he inherited the legend through Justin – evidence perhaps of its wider currency. When he introduces it, the wider context is what is an axiomatic principle in his overall system, namely that those whom he labels 'heretics' challenge the tradition which the church holds from the apostles and dispute the appeal to scriptural proof which similarly goes back to those apostles (*Haer*. 3.1–5). Much of his constructive argument turns on the unity of the scriptural and apostolic testimony, in particular regarding the unity of God as Creator and Father, and regarding the fleshliness of Jesus's salvific incarnation, the two principles that he identifies as lying at the heart of heretical denial.

The Matthean birth narrative and the epithet 'Emmanuel', which initially occupy only a supporting role in his Christological debate (3.9), increasingly take centre stage as he turns to challenge those who claim that Jesus was 'a mere man, begotten by Joseph' (3.19.1). Within his theological scheme of salvation, the possibility of human participation in immortality demands that the Word of God had first 'become that which we also are'. That the son of God was born from Mary, but as of a virgin, guarantees both his human generation as son of man and that he is Emmanuel, 'God with us'; it finds its authentication in the scriptural testimony, or rather the sign (*signum*; σημεῖον) given of his own accord by God himself (*Haer*. 3.19.3; cf. Isa. 7.13–14). On this basis, Isa. 7.13–14, reduced to the catch phrases 'he who from the virgin is Emmanuel' or 'the sign of the virgin',[44] carries the burden of his developing argument.

However, this promptly provokes the acknowledgement that it is indeed contrary to the claims of those who 'now dare to interpret/translate (μεθερμηνεύειν) the scripture, "behold, a young woman shall conceive and bear a child"'.[45] Irenaeus ascribes this translation to Theodotion of Ephesus and to Aquila of Pontus, both of whom he describes as 'Jewish proselytes' (Ἰουδαῖοι προσήλυτοι), but whom he claims are followed by the Ebionites (one of his 'heretical' groups) when they say that Jesus

---

[44] *Haer*. 3.20.2 (Latin only), 'eum qui ex virgine Emmanuel'; 3.21.1 (cf. Eusebius, *Hist. eccl.* 5.8.10), τὸ τῆς παρθένου σημεῖον.

[45] *Haer*. 3.21.1, τῶν νῦν μεθερμηνεύειν τολμώντων τὴν γραφήν, ἰδοὺ ἡ νεᾶνις ἐν γαστρὶ ἕξει καὶ τέξεται υἱόν (Latin: *ecce adolescentula in ventre habebit et pariet filium*; ctr. 3.21.5 *ecce adolescentula in ventre concipiet*). There is nothing to suggest that Irenaeus has direct knowledge of the translations of Theodotion or Aquila.

was begotten from Joseph (*Haer.* 3.21.1; cf. Eusebius, *Hist. eccl.* 5.8.10).⁴⁶ However, he immediately continues that this is an act of sabotage against the divine plan and prophetic testimony is demonstrated by the fact that this prophecy had been made long before the Babylonian exile, that is, before the empire of the Medes and Persians, and that it had been translated into Greek by the Jews themselves (*ab ipsis Iudaeis*) long before the coming of Christ, sure evidence that there had been no collusion with those like Irenaeus.

With this, Irenaeus embarks on his account of that translation, which he firmly dates to the period of Macedonian rule, prior to the Roman conquest, emphasizing at beginning and end how long this predates the coming of Christ and the appearance of Christians (3.21.2). His narrative summarizes the key themes of Ptolemy and his intention that the library in Alexandria contain all human writings, his request for a Greek translation (μεταβεβλημέναι) of the scriptures⁴⁷ and the sending of 'seventy elders highly experienced in the scriptures and both languages'; a novelty, however, is that Ptolemy is identified as son of Lagus, not Philadelphus, and the request is made to 'the Jerusalemites'.⁴⁸ The clear implication is that since they were then subject to the Macedonians, the Jerusalemites have no choice but to submit to their ruler's demand;⁴⁹ indeed, reinforcing that note of compulsion, Ptolemy deliberately guards against any potential collusion or subversion of the truth by separating the translators and insisting that they operate independently but write the same translation.⁵⁰ However, the complete agreement 'in words and terms' of their individual translations becomes evident only when they are read in the presence of Ptolemy, and this immediately convinces all present of the divine character of the scriptures and of the intent behind their translation.

Irenaeus then goes further to locate this within God's continuing purposes: it is of a piece with the time when God had previously inspired (ἐμπνεύω) Ezra to collate the words of the prophets from the past⁵¹ and to restore the Law after their corruption during the Babylonian exile: since Irenaeus had stressed the original prophecy as predating the exile and return under the Persians this may also by implication pre-empt any suggestion of its corruption. Furthermore, the preservation of the scriptures 'for us' in Egypt echoes the preservation of Jacob's family and that of the family of

---

⁴⁶ Strikingly, Irenaeus makes no reference to his earlier brief account of the Ebionites (*Haer.* 1.26) which referred to their 'curious exposition of the prophets' and their 'Jewish way of life', and to their exclusive use of the Gospel of Matthew without any suggestion of disagreements as to the meaning of the opening chapters. Evidently, due caution should be exercised in relying on both of these references to the Ebionites as representing an actual group. Epiphanius, *Pan.* 30.13.6; 14.3, claims that the Ebionites have excised the first two chapters of Matthew, which for him is a Hebrew Gospel.
⁴⁷ Irenaeus uses the general term γραφαί, presumably including at least the law and prophets.
⁴⁸ Clement of Alexandria, *Strom.* 1.22.148, knows and keeps open both identifications of the Ptolemy.
⁴⁹ This is reinforced if the Latin text 'to do what he determined' is preferred to the Greek as preserved by Eusebius, *Hist. eccl.* 5.8.10–12, 'God doing what he determined', which may be influenced by Clement, *Strom.* 1.22.149.
⁵⁰ Irenaeus explains the separation as, 'and he did this with respect to all the books'; it is not clear whether this refers to the whole of the scriptures or implies it was his usual practice.
⁵¹ προγεγονότοι προφηταί; L. Michael White and G. Anthony Keddie (eds), *Jewish Fictional Letters from Hellenistic Egypt: The Epistle of Aristeas and Related Literature* (Atlanta, GA: SBL Press, 2018), 241; the translation, 'former prophets', is misleading.

'our Lord' also in Egypt, whither each had fled.⁵² Brought alongside these events the implication may be that the translation marks a distinct stage in God's economy of revelation.

Irenaeus draws further conclusions from the narrative and his framing of it. First, any alternative translations, which earlier he had described as 'recent' (νῦν), are shown to be 'deliberate and audacious' attempts to contradict 'our' appeal to the scriptures and the faith in the coming of God's son grounded on it. Second, both through the legend and through the Jewish proselyte identity of the recent translators, the Jews are presented not only as the active opponents of the axis of truth but also as its unwitting enablers, all within God's overall economy. Indeed, even before embarking on his narrative, he claims that had the Jews known the use that Christians would make of the scriptures they would almost certainly have burned them (3.21.1).

Finally, in his next step, Irenaeus blends this whole excursus into his overall conception of the unity of scripture, church and tradition. Not only have the scriptures been translated as described but the proclamation of the church is similarly free of corruption. The Apostles, who themselves are older than these recent upstarts, agree with the translation just as the translation agrees with the tradition of the apostles: Peter (i.e. Mark), John, Matthew and Paul (i.e. Luke) proclaimed the prophetic passages exactly as in the 'translation of the elders'. Thus, the same spirit was at work within the prophets, within the translation of the elders and within the proclamation of the Apostles – with which he returns to his starting point, now explicitly uniting Lk. 1.35; Mt. 1.23 with Isa. 7.10–17.⁵³

However, Irenaeus has not yet done; interpreting Mt. 1.23 through the lens of Lk. 1.42, he proceeds to demonstrate that the promise to David and his progeny ('from his belly', Ps. 132.11) is evidently not fulfilled through Joseph, inasmuch as according to Matthew the latter was descended from Joachim and Jeconiah, who were ejected from the throne of David. The failure of those 'who altered what Isaiah said' to make any changes to any of these other passages is itself, he asserts, evidence of their duplicity (*Haer.* 3.21.5–9).

What is at stake throughout this complex passage is the nuanced Christological argument on which Irenaeus's soteriology depends. It is contextualized within opposing positions which take to the extreme each side of the human-divine tension that for him has to be maintained. A single verse, or rather a single term, serves to embody the either/or of heretical or authentic confession, and that differential is then projected onto a rereading of the origins of the scriptures. The various attempts to translate the scriptures are divided into just two camps, those made by Jewish 'proselytes' and followed by heretics and that which, ironically, was the work of 'men who were the most skilled in the scriptures' but through which God's glory was demonstrated and which becomes the basis of Christian demonstration. Behind what starts and continues

---

⁵² Consciously or not, Irenaeus is reconfiguring the Sinai and Exodus allusions which are fundamental to the strategy of the Letter of Aristeas.
⁵³ 3.21.4, where only the Latin survives, reading Mt. 1.23 as *ecce virgo in utero concipiet*, and Isa. 7.14 as *ecce virgo in ventre accipiet*; for *ventris* see n. 27; there may be some intertextual influence from Lk. 1.42 (= κοιλία) together with the appeal in the next section to Ps. 132.11 (LXX 131), *fructu ventris*.

as a defence against alternative Christian views stalks an unmitigated displacement of the Jews, which renders it a more definitive act of appropriation. At the same time, this act belongs within the narrative of internal Christian differentiation as much as it does in that between Jew and Christian. Indeed, these two narratives feed into each other in ways that will resound through subsequent centuries.

Although space does not permit exploring subsequent retellings of the legend, what has become evident is that its Christian adoption does not mark a simple or univocal 'appropriation' of the Greek scriptures within the trajectory of Jewish and Christian differentiation and self-construction. Rather, it offers a window into a much more complex set of dynamics. Rereading and redescribing scripture are always part of a continuing process of textual navigation and of the interplay between textual competency and authority that is integral both to the Jewish and Christian scriptures themselves and to their textual communities, as well as to differentiation within and between them.

2

The Law and Prophets as Origen's Gospel

Devin L. White

The law becomes an 'old testament' only for those who want to understand it in a fleshly way ... But for us, who understand it spiritually and explain it spiritually and according to the gospel-meaning, it is always new.[1]

In recent years it has grown increasingly common to read ancient schools and religious groups as 'textual communities'.[2] Jane Heath, in a critical appraisal of the idea, suggests we understand a textual community as one 'whose life, thought, sense of identity and relations with outsiders are organised around an authoritative text'.[3] Applied to ancient Jewish and Christian relations, this notion of textual communities prompts several questions. For example, by what logic can ancient, gentile Christians define their own identities on the basis of authoritative writings received from and shared with their Jewish neighbours? Why did they conceive of themselves and those Jews as two textual communities and not one? While early Christian thinkers, beginning at least with the Apostle Paul, wrestled to clarify the place of the Law and Prophets in gentile Christian life and thought, few explained their appropriation of Jewish holy books with Origen of Alexandria's precision and candour.[4]

Some Christians before and after Origen both distinguished themselves from Jews and did so, at least in part, by opposing Law to Gospel, commandment to grace.

---

[1] Origen, *Hom. Num.* 9.2.4.
[2] Brian Stock, *The Implications of Literacy: Written Language and Models of Interpretation in the Eleventh and Twelfth Centuries* (Princeton, NJ: Princeton University Press, 1983), esp. 88–240. Regarding ancient Judaism, Jan Assmann uses the concept in his study of the Hebrew Bible's development in *Religion and Cultural Memory: Ten Studies*, trans. Rodney Livingstone (Stanford, CA: Stanford University Press, 2006), 63–80. For one influential application of the term to early Christianity, see, e.g. Judith M. Lieu, *Christian Identity in the Jewish and Graeco-Roman World* (Oxford: Oxford University Press, 2004), esp. 27–62.
[3] Jane Heath, '"Textual Communities": Brian Stock's Concept and Recent Scholarship on Antiquity', in *Scriptural Interpretation at the Interface between Education and Religion: In Memory of Hans Conzelmann*, ed. Florian Wilk (Leiden: Brill, 2019), 5–34.
[4] On Paul's understanding of Torah and his gospel, see esp. Dietrich-Alex Koch, *Die Schrift als Zeuge des Evangeliums: Untersuchungen zur Verwendung und zum Verständnis der Schrift bei Paulus*, BHT 69 (Tübingen: Mohr Siebeck, 1986); Francis Watson, *Paul and the Hermeneutics of Faith*, 2nd edn (London: T&T Clark, 2004).

Origen maintained the distinction between church and synagogue but collapsed the categories of Law and gospel.[5] All scripture, Origen insisted, including the books read by his Jewish neighbours, was gospel literature. In this essay I explain the theological reasoning undergirding Origen's nuanced position. My argument falls into two parts: first, an explanation of Origen's familiarity with and critique of 'literal' Jewish exegesis, including scholarly attempts to understand that critique; second, a summary reading of the prologue to Origen's *Commentary on John*, perhaps the Alexandrian's clearest discussion of the inherence of the gospel in the Law. This summary explains why Origen sets the boundary between Christians and Jews where he has.[6] For him, the ability to read the Law as gospel literature is a function of the reader's ontological (and not merely social) identity. The gospel is what spiritual Christians, transformed by their progressive union with the Logos, perceive when they read all biblical texts. This is the sort of spiritual reader presupposed by the epigraph above. To read the Law spiritually, the reader must first become spiritual. The secondary, social distinction between Christians and Jews, church and synagogue, results from this primary, ontological difference.

The literal sense between Jews and Christians

Origen is remarkable for having spent his entire life in two cities known for their vibrant Jewish communities: Alexandria, where he was born and raised, and, later, Caesarea, to which he relocated following a complicated, internecine row in the Alexandrian church.[7] His Jewish milieu left its mark on his thought. As is well known, credit for the preservation and early dissemination of Philo's works falls to Origen.[8] And even Origen's earliest writings reveal his familiarity with Jewish exegetical traditions preserved in rabbinic sources.[9] It is even probable that Origen's later works influenced the emerging rabbinic movement and vice versa.[10] This is the Origen who, near the

---

[5] In an attempt to reflect Origen's own nuanced distinction between the four canonical Gospels and the 'gospel sense' proper to all of Christian scripture, this essay refers to the four canonical witnesses to Jesus's life as 'Gospel' or 'Gospels' and to Origen's spiritual sense of scripture as 'gospel'.

[6] Readers unfamiliar with Origen's distinctive hermeneutic should consult especially Henri de Lubac, *History and Spirit: The Understanding of Scripture according to Origen*, trans. Anne Englund Nash (San Francisco, CA: Ignatius, 2007); Karen Jo Torjesen, *Hermeneutical Procedure and Theological Method in Origen's Exegesis*, PTS 28 (Berlin: de Gruyter, 1985); Elizabeth Ann Dively Lauro, *The Soul and Spirit of Scripture in Origen's Exegesis* (Leiden: Brill, 2005); Peter W. Martens, *Origen and Scripture: The Contours of the Exegetical Life*, OECS (Oxford: Oxford University Press, 2011).

[7] The makeup of the Jewish community Origen knew in late-second- and early-third-century Alexandria is disputed. Bietenhard suggests that Origen knew rabbis in Alexandria (Hans Bietenhard, *Caesarea, Origenes und die Juden* (Stuttgart: Kohlhammer, 1974), 19). De Lange suggests a synagogue community (Nicholas R. M. de Lange, *Origen and the Jews: Studies in Jewish–Christian Relations in Third Century Palestine* (Cambridge: Cambridge University Press, 1976), 24).

[8] David T. Runia, *Philo in Early Christian Literature: A Survey*, CRINT 3 (Minneapolis, MN: Fortress, 1993), 16–31.

[9] Maren R. Niehoff, 'Origen's *Commentary on Genesis* as a Key to *Genesis Rabbah*', in *Genesis Rabbah in Text and Context*, ed. Sarit Kattan Gribetz et al., TSAJ 166 (Tübingen: Mohr Siebeck, 2016), 129–53.

[10] De Lange, *Origen and the Jews*, 103. For rabbinic exegetical traditions in Origen, see Ruth Clements, '*Peri Pascha*: Passover and the Displacement of Jewish Interpretation within Origen's Exegesis'

end of his life, felt he knew his Jewish neighbours well enough to scoff at what was, in his estimation, Celsus's stilted Jewish interlocutor.[11] If any early Christian writer could confidently explain what his Jewish peers might or might not say, it was Origen.

Origen was also confident that, despite living in the same cities and reading the same sacred texts, he and his Jewish neighbours belonged to different religious groups. Yet, as Origen well knew, most of Christian scripture had come to him from the Jews. Because the two communities shared holy books, the efficacy of Origen's attempts to observe a border separating Jewish and Christian identity was, at very least, debatable. On one hand, Celsus attacked the authority of Christian scripture by 'oppos[ing] both Jews and Christians at once'.[12]

On the other hand, even some members of Origen's Caesarean church seem to have expressed a fascination with the Law's literal meaning that Origen found unsuited to Christian commitment. In reply, he warned that anyone who 'wishes to hear and understand these words literally … ought to gather with the Jews rather than with the Christians'. Instead, Origen continues, 'if he wishes to be a … disciple of Paul, let him hear Paul saying that "the Law is spiritual" [and] declaring that these words are "allegorical" when the law speaks of Abraham and his wife and sons' (Rom. 7.14; Gal. 4.24).[13] Origen also notes and opposes a general fascination with Jewish exegesis among the spiritually mature in his congregation, whom he refers to as 'priests'. Just as Levitical priests should not consume day-old sacrificial meat, neither should they take rabbinic exegesis as an authority: 'For if you bring that which you learned from the Jews yesterday into the Church today, that is to eat the meat of yesterday's sacrifice' (Lev. 7.15).[14]

Pastoral asides like these indicate that some Caesarean Christians around Origen not only read the books they shared with their Jewish neighbours but actively sought Jewish interpretations of those texts. Origen's sixth *Homily on Genesis* addresses exactly this situation and suggests a different approach for Christian interpretation of the Law:

> The Apostle Paul, 'Teacher of the Gentiles in faith and Truth' taught the Church which he gathered from the Gentiles how it ought to interpret the books of the Law (1 Tim. 2.7). These books were received from others and were formerly unknown to the Gentiles and were very strange. He feared that the Church,

---

(PhD diss., Harvard Divinity School, 1997). For Origen's influence on rabbinic exegesis, see Anna Tsvetkova-Glaser, *Pentateuchauslegung bei Origenes und den frühen Rabbinen* (Frankfurt am Main: Lang, 2010).

[11] Cf., e.g. Origen's objection in *Cels.* 2.28 that Celsus 'put into the mouth of the Jew what no Jew would have said'. Not all of Origen's modern readers have found Celsus's Jew so unbelievable. See, e.g. Maren R. Niehoff, 'A Jewish Critique of Christianity from Second-Century Alexandria: Revisiting the Jew Mentioned in *Contra Celsum*', *JECS* 21 (2013), 151–75.

[12] Cf. Origen's complaint that Celsus, when attacking the authority of Christian scriptures, 'opposes both Jews and Christians at once: the Jews who deny that Christ has come, but hope that he will do so; and the Christians who affirm that Jesus was the prophesied Christ' (*Cels.* 4.1).

[13] *Hom. Gen.* 6.1. Unless otherwise noted, all quotations of the *Homilies on Genesis* and the *Homilies on Exodus* are from *Origen: Homilies on Genesis and Exodus*, trans. Ronald E. Heine, FOTC 71 (Washington, DC: Catholic University of America Press, 1982). See further Franchesca Cocchini, *Il Paolo di Origene: Contributo alla storia della ricezione delle epistole paoline nel III secolo*, Verba Seniorum 11 (Rome: Edizioni Studium, 1992), 123–8.

[14] *Hom. Lev.* 5.8.3. Cf. *Hom. Jer.* 12.13.1–2.

receiving foreign instructions and not knowing the principle of the instructions, would be in a state of confusion about the foreign document. For that reason he gives some examples of interpretation that we also might note similar things in other passages, lest we believe that by imitation of the text and document of the Jews we be made disciples. He wishes, therefore, to distinguish disciples of Christ from disciples of the Synagogue by the way they understand the Law. The Jews, by misunderstanding it, rejected Christ. We, by understanding the Law spiritually, show that it was justly given for the instruction of the Church.[15]

This passage is remarkable not least for its presentation of Jewish biblical literature as exotic, alien and strange. By construing the Jewish 'text and document' as 'foreign', Origen underscores his assertion, common in his writings, that the synagogue and church are two distinct communities. Christians in his world may have received many of their scriptures from the Jews, Origen admits. But what distinguishes Christians and Jews is the manner in which they read those books.[16] Crucially, in Origen's estimation, Christian scripture itself guides its readers, through examples like the letters of Paul, to the interpretation of the whole.

In principle, Origen's explanation is clear enough. If scripture interprets scripture then let Paul's letters teach the church to read as he read.[17] But Origen's appeal to Pauline hermeneutical example does not mean that he or his audiences thought the division between themselves and their Jewish neighbours a simple one. His appeal to Paul as an exegetical standard is proof enough of this point. Origen's Paul, after all, never abandoned Judaism.[18] Even if he no longer consistently obeyed Torah's literal precepts, he could still circumcise Timothy when it suited his evangelistic purposes (cf. Acts 16.1–5; 1 Cor. 9.20).[19] Whether other first-century Jews, to say nothing of Origen's third-century Jewish peers, would have approved such flexibility is open to question.[20] But the point still stands that, for Origen, appealing to Paul as the model for gentile Christian exegesis is to appeal simultaneously to a Jewish exemplar, even if that exemplar was adapting his teaching to the special circumstances of his gentile audience. Nevertheless, the very ambiguity of Paul's Judaism may explain why Origen felt the need to clarify, time and again, what made him and his students Christians and

---

[15] *Hom. Gen.* 5.1. Cf. *Princ.* 4.2.1.
[16] For the purposes of this essay, I bracket Origen's discussion of Jewish-Christian groups like the Ebionites. Cf., e.g. *Princ.* 4.3.8; *Comm. Matt.* 11.12; *Hom. Gen.* 3.5; *Cels.* 2.1, 5.61–5. For Origen's critique of Ebionite biblical interpretation, see Martens, *Origen and Scripture*, 148–56.
[17] Cf. *Princ.* 4.2.4. On Paul as Origen's hermeneutical exemplar, see esp. de Lubac, *History and Spirit*, 77–86; Cocchini, *Il Paolo di Origene*, esp. 117–48; Martens, *Origen and Scripture*, 156–60.
[18] *Comm. Rom.* 10.39.2. See further Theresia Heither, *Translatio Religionis: Die Paulusdeutung des Origenes in seinem Kommentar zur Römerbrief* (Cologne: Bohlau, 1990), 290–9; Paula Fredriksen, 'Origen and Augustine on Paul and the Law', in *Law and Lawlessness in Early Judaism and Early Christianity*, ed. David Lincicum et al., WUNT 420 (Tübingen: Mohr Siebeck, 2019), 67–88.
[19] In *Cels.* 2.1, Origen writes that 'even Paul himself became a Jew to the Jews that he might gain Jews (1 Cor. 9.20). For this reason, as it is written in the Acts of the Apostles, he even brought an offering to the altar, that he might persuade the Jews that he was not an apostate from the law.' Cf. *Comm. Jo.* 1.41–2.
[20] See, e.g. David J. Rudolf, *A Jew to the Jews: Jewish Contours of Pauline Flexibility in 1 Corinthians 9:19–23*, 2nd edn (Eugene: Pickwick, 2016).

not Jews, why they ought to imitate Paul and not the rabbis. The choice facing Origen's audience was not Jewish or Christian exegesis but two divergent expressions of Jewish exegesis. Origen, after all, cites Rom. 2.29 and its identification of Christians as Jews 'in secret' when describing Christian readers of the Law.[21]

What, then, did Origen find problematic in non-Pauline, Jewish exegesis? Origen regularly warns his audience of the dangers of Jewish biblical interpretation, distilling his critique to a single, hermeneutically freighted term: 'literalism'. To Celsus, who had too closely correlated Jewish and Christian exegesis for Origen's liking, he replies,

> If we may give an exact answer to Celsus's words when he thinks that we hold the same opinions as the Jews about the stories he quotes, we will say that we both confess that the books were written by divine inspiration, but concerning the interpretation of the contents of the books we no longer speak alike. In fact, the reason why we do not live like the Jews is that we think the literal interpretation of the laws does not contain the meaning of the legislation.[22]

Much in this passage depends on Origen's use of the term 'literal' and its implied antithesis. In Origen's exegetical taxonomy, the contrast to 'literal' is not, in the simplest sense of the term, 'allegorical' but 'spiritual'. In other words, the fact that Christian spiritual interpretation takes the form of allegory does not imply that all allegory, like the kind practiced by Neoplatonists,[23] affords true access to the texts' spiritual referents.[24] Jews, that is, may not recognize the spiritual sense of the Law and Prophets, but not because they cannot read allegorically.[25]

Blindness to the spiritual sense nevertheless entails several consequences Origen finds alarming. Too strong an insistence on the literal sense, for example, leads some unnamed Jewish exegetes to excuse dissimulation on the grounds that they are only imitating Abraham's treatment of Sarah and Abimelech (Gen. 20.1–18).[26] In addition,

---

[21] Cf., e.g. *Princ.* 4.2.5; *Comm. Jo.* 1.1.
[22] *Cels.* 5.60. Translations of *Contra Celsum* are taken from *Origen: Contra Celsum*, trans. Henry Chadwick (Cambridge: Cambridge University Press, 1953).
[23] See, e.g. Robert Lamberton, *Homer the Theologian: Neoplatonist Allegorical Reading and the Growth of the Epic Tradition* (Berkeley: University of California Press, 1986). Note that not all viewed allegory as an appropriate interpretive method. For one example of grammatical opposition to allegory, see Francesca Schironi, *The Best of the Grammarians: Aristarchus of Samothrace on the Iliad* (Ann Arbor: University of Michigan Press, 2018), 138–42.
[24] Cf. *Hom. Gen.* 13.3, where Origen treats Isaac's re-digging of Abraham's wells as an example of Christian allegory over and against Hellenistic allegory, and *Hom. Lev.* 5.7.5, where he equates interpreting scripture with Hellenistic grammatical methods and adding leaven to the tabernacle's unleavened bread.
[25] Cf., e.g. *Hom. Gen.* 7.6; *Hom. Exod.* 12.1; *Hom. Lev.* 16.1–2; *Hom. Num.* 7.2.4; *Hom. Jes. Nav.* 6.1, 9.4; *Hom. Judic.* 2.5.
[26] *Hom. Gen.* 6.3:

> What edification will we receive when we read that Abraham, such a great patriarch, not only lied to king Abimelech, but also surrendered his wife's chastity to him? In what way does the wife of so great a patriarch edify us if she is supposed to have been exposed to defilements through marital indulgence? These things are what the Jews suppose, along with those who are friends of the letter, not of the spirit (2 Cor. 3.6).

Cf., e.g. Josephus, *Ant.* 1.207.

overly literal reading ensures logical contradictions. How, asks Origen, can bones be a source of impurity when a corpse dropped on Elisha's bones is resurrected (Lev. 5.2–3; 2 Kgs 13.21)?[27] These are the sorts of literal impossibilities that prove the existence of higher senses of meaning.[28] Cases like these also provide Origen with evidence that 'the meaning of the Scriptures was "taken away" from [the Jews]' (Mt. 21.43). No longer is the interpretation of the Law and the Prophets preserved with them, rather they are ones who read and do not apprehend spiritually.'[29]

This is strong language. But, even assuming that this quote from the *Homilies on Jeremiah* expresses Origen's enduring opinion on the matter (and not that his rhetoric has gotten the better of him), we must, as with any point of Origen's doctrine, consider the whole witness of his surviving corpus. Like all creative theologians, his thought modulated over time. And even when there is no reason to suppose that his ideas developed, he always adapted his instruction to suit the perceived abilities of his audience.[30] Origen's critique of Jewish literal interpretation should not be overstated. Without glossing over his frequently severe tone, we must also recognize that Origen elsewhere praises Jewish exegesis, even going so far as to present it as precedent for his own exegetical practice.

For example, early in the *Contra Celsum* he, the philosophically educated Alexandrian grammarian, claims that Jewish exegesis outclasses the hermeneutics practiced in pagan philosophical schools.[31] This sort of praise is entirely in keeping with Origen's view of Jews and their status relative to other people groups, since they alone of all peoples were not dominated by demonic influence.[32] Jewish exegesis similarly surpasses that practiced by heretical Christians. Against Apelles, the sometime disciple of Marcion, Origen appeals to Jewish exegetical tradition as a countervailing authority.[33] Origen also admires the Jewish practice of designating books which 'defile the hands'.[34] Though the surviving rabbinic evidence regarding this textual designation is notoriously cryptic, Origen reads it as an analogue to the production of a textual curriculum, in which some literature is held to be propaedeutic to other related texts.[35] For example, in Proclus's school, Plato's dialogues were taught in an order suited to a student's philosophical progress from novice to adept.[36] Origen suggests

---

[27] *Hom. Lev.* 3.3.1. For a lengthy list of such impossibilities, see *Princ.* 4.3.1–3.

[28] See, e.g. Lauro, *Soul and Spirit of Scripture*.

[29] *Hom. Jer.* 14.12.3. Translations of the *Homilies on Jeremiah* are taken from *Origen: Homilies on Jeremiah; Homily on 1 Kings 28*, trans. John Clark Smith, FOTC 97 (Washington, DC: Catholic University of America Press, 1998). Cf., e.g. *Hom. Exod.* 7.3; *Hom. Judic.* 8.4; *Hom. Jes. Nav.* 26.3.

[30] See Ronald E. Heine, *Origen: Scholarship in Service of the Church* (New York: Oxford University Press, 2010), vii–viii, 83–4; Anders-Christian Jacobsen, *Christ the Teacher of Salvation: A Study on Origen's Christology and Soteriology*, Adamantiana 6 (Münster: Aschendorff, 2015), 13–17.

[31] *Cels.* 1.43.

[32] *Cels.* 5.31.

[33] *Hom. Gen.* 2.2. On Apelles, cf. Eusebius, *Hist. eccl.* 5.13.

[34] Cf., e.g. m. Yad 3.5; t. Yad. 2.14.

[35] Martin Goodman, 'Sacred Scripture and "Defiling the Hands"', *JTS* 41 (1990), 99–107; Timothy H. Lim, 'The Defilement of the Hands as a Principle Determining the Holiness of Scriptures', *JTS* 61 (2010), 501–15.

[36] See, e.g. Dirk Baltzly, 'Plato's Authority and the Formation of Textual Communities', *CQ* 64 (2014), 793–807.

that, while Christians may have jettisoned 'defilement' as a technical term, the Jews have nonetheless taught them to scaffold Old Testament literature into a graduated curriculum. By categorizing the Song of Songs as a book that defiles the hands, Jews teach Christian exegetes the best order in which to read and teach Solomon's writings.[37] Again, following philosophical precedent, they should begin with Proverbs (ethics), continue through Ecclesiastes (physics) and conclude with the Song of Songs (enoptics).[38]

Even more radically, despite his consistent complaint that Jews are blind to all but scripture's letter, Origen admits that there have been some Jews who understood its spiritual sense. But, because of their great purity relative to their neighbours, God removed these persons from the midst of the community. In his discussion of the Jews entrusted with God's oracles (Rom. 3.2),[39] Origen writes,

> But if one of them was a wise and intelligent hearer and a wonderful counselor, it is said that the Lord removes them from Jerusalem because he was offended by the impieties of the people. For Isaiah says the following, 'Behold, the Lord, the Lord of hosts, shall remove them from Jerusalem and from Judea', and a little later, 'the prophet and the diviner and elder and the captain of fifty and the wonderful counselor and the wise builder and prudent hearer'. To such persons, then, it must be assumed that the divine oracles were first entrusted. We have to admit then that they possessed a great advantage in every way. There were moreover others like them, as the Apostle has mentioned is written in the books of Kingdoms, 'I have reserved for myself seven thousand men who have not bowed their knees to Baal'. Furthermore, Christ's apostles themselves and Paul, the chosen vessel, because he came from the Jews and from the circumcision, he too possessed a great advantage in every way over the Gentiles whom he was teaching. For the oracles of God had been entrusted to him.[40]

---

[37] *Comm. Cant.* Pr.1.

> I advise and counsel everyone who is not yet rid of the vexations of flesh and blood … to refrain completely from reading this little book. … For they say that with the Hebrews also care is taken to allow no one even to hold this book in his hands, who has not reached a full and ripe age. And there is another practice that we have received from them – namely, that the Scriptures should be delivered to boys by teachers and wise men … while at the same time the beginning of Genesis … the first chapters of Ezekiel … the end of the same … and this book of the Song of Songs … should be reserved for study till the last.

All translations of the *Commentary on the Song of Songs* are taken from *Origen: The Song of Songs, Commentary and Homilies*, trans. R. P. Lawson, ACW 26 (New York: Newman, 1956).

[38] *Comm. Cant.* Pr.3. See, e.g. Mark J. Edwards, 'Origen on Christ, Tropology, and Exegesis', in *Metaphor, Allegory, and the Classical Tradition: Ancient Thought and Modern Revisions*, ed. G. R. Boys-Stones (Oxford: Oxford University Press, 2003), esp. 245–6.

[39] *Comm. Rom.* 2.14.6.

[40] *Comm. Rom.* 2.14.7. All translations of the *Commentary on Romans* are taken from *Origen: Commentary on the Epistle to the Romans, Books 1 to 5*, trans. Thomas P. Scheck, FOTC 103 (Washington, DC: Catholic University of American Press, 2001); *Origen: Commentary on the Epistle to the Romans, Books 6 to 10*, trans. Thomas P. Scheck, FOTC 104 (Washington, DC: Catholic University of American Press, 2002). Such outlying examples of spiritual insight fascinate Origen. See, e.g. his discussion of Balaam in *Hom. Num.* 17.3.2.

There is reason to suppose, then, that Origen was always on the lookout for Jewish exegesis which did not fit his standard critique of Jewish literalism. His point is that 'to those who read and do not understand, and who read and do not believe, the letter alone is entrusted, concerning which the Apostle says, "The letter kills" (2 Cor. 3.6)'.[41] And while Origen grants that the Jews have an advantage as recipients of God's oracles, 'when it comes to faith', he argues, 'the Gentiles have a great advantage in every way'.[42] Perhaps this belief in a Jewish advantage regarding scripture, combined with a concession that some Jews have in fact read scripture's spiritual sense, explains why Origen frequently echoes Philo and other Jewish exegetical traditions (though usually without attribution).[43] We can only speculate about the identity and influence of Origen's unnamed Hebrew Master.[44]

What is literalism? Interpreting Origen's critique

Clearly, we must account for the full range of data when explaining Origen's view of Jewish exegesis. In this regard, recent scholarly reaction to Origen's critique appears scattershot. While all recognize Origen's persistent attempts to distance himself and his communities from Jewish 'literalism', interpretations of this tendency run a surprisingly wide gamut. Some read Origen as a bitter anti-Semite while others aim to rehabilitate Origen's hermeneutic as a paradigm for a non-supersessionist Christian reading of the Old Testament.

In my judgement, the former line of reasoning overlooks the theological contours of Origen's hermeneutic. Susanna Drake, for example, sees Origen's application of the Pauline categories 'flesh' and 'spirit' as the keys to Origen's distinction between Jew and Christian, and, hence, between Jewish and Christian biblical interpretation (cf. 1 Cor. 2.14–3.1).[45] She is not the first to recognize the centrality of this dyad for Origen's thought. Karen Torjesen's landmark dissertation ably demonstrated that Origen uses 'flesh' and 'spirit' not as fixed anthropological categories, as in some Jewish or Christian Gnostic exegesis of Genesis 1–2, but as heuristic terms demarcating stages of Christian progress.[46] Drake, by contrast, overlooks Origen's doctrine of the soul's ascent, suggesting instead that a preoccupation with Jewish sexuality undergirds Origen's evaluation of Jewish exegesis.[47] While she has correctly

---

[41] *Comm. Rom.* 2.14.8.
[42] *Comm. Rom.* 2.14.9.
[43] See, e.g. the list of Origen's citation of Philonic precedent in Runia, *Philo in Early Christian Literature*, 160–2. See too Jennifer Otto, *Philo of Alexandria and the Construction of Jewishness in Early Christian Writings*, OECS (Oxford: Oxford University Press, 2018), 91–135.
[44] Cf., e.g. *Comm. Jo.*1.215; *Princ.* 1.3.4, 4.3.14; Heine, *Origen*, 29–30, 56–7; Pierre Nautin, *Origène: Sa vie et son oeuvre* (Paris: Beauchesne, 1977), 346–7; Ruth Clements, 'Origen's Hexapla and Christian-Jewish Encounter in the Second and Third Centuries', in *Religious Rivalries and the Struggle for Success in Caesarea Maritima*, ed. Terence L. Donaldson (Waterloo: Wilfrid Laurier Press, 2000), 308.
[45] Susanna Drake, *Slandering the Jew: Sexuality and Difference in Early Christian Texts* (Philadelphia: University of Pennsylvania Press, 2013), 40.
[46] Torjesen, *Hermeneutical Procedure*, 35–43.
[47] 'In his rhetorical production of Jewish literalism and his argument for Christian interpretive superiority, Origen formulated a certain "discourse of sexuality" that characterized Jews as more fleshly and sexually depraved than their Christian counterparts' (Drake, *Slandering the Jew*, 40).

identified Origen's objection to Jewish exegesis, its satisfaction with scripture's letter, she has not contextualized this objection in light of Origen's system, which heavily emphasizes the soul's return to God. More attention to the theological superstructure of Origen's hermeneutic, a superstructure in which textual meaning and progressive participation in the Logos are fused, would better account for Origen's critiques of Jewish literalism.

Peter Martens provides a helpful counterpoint to Drake. For Martens, 'Origen does not think literalism plagues Jewish exegesis as a whole, but only the interpretation of particular ceremonial customs in the law'.[48] This explains how 'Origen created ample space for the selective retrieval and integration of Jewish exegesis into his own interpretive activity'.[49] Martens is correct, to a point. But, puzzlingly, given the soteriological tilt of his broader thesis, Martens might have mentioned that, for Origen, participation in the Logos is required for recognition of the Logos. Instead, Martens emphasizes the different exegetical strategies and interests proper to synagogue and church, suggesting that 'the Christian and Jewish communities of [Origen's] day could be demarcated simply in terms of their respective exegetical strategies regarding their shared Scriptures'.[50] To be sure, different methods for reading will produce different results, sometimes with difficult consequences for the parties involved. Thus, in Origen's corpus exegetical strategies construct readerly identities. As Martens notes, 'At stake, then, in this debate about Jewish exegesis was not simply a denial of *present* Christian identity, but also *past*, since the literal interpretation of the law and prophets was deeply implicated in the historical figure of Jesus himself: in the rejection of his ministry, including his exegetical tutelage, and, ultimately, in his crucifixion.'[51] On this point, Martens is certainly correct. But as we will see, Origen's exegetical distinction between Jew and Christian assumes that exegetical procedure not only forms or confirms identity but also reveals it. That is, Origen saw the application of distinct exegetical strategies as evidence of an ontological difference in the individual members of the communities.[52] In all Origen's surviving writings, perhaps his clearest discussion of the gospel meaning of the Law and Prophets – offered in tandem with a discussion of the reader's Christian identity – lies in the prologue to the *Commentary on John*.

---

[48] Martens, *Origen and Scripture*, 143.
[49] Ibid., 147.
[50] Ibid., 137.
[51] Ibid., 146. Emphasis Martens's.
[52] Martens may correctly identify the nature and consequences of Origen's critique of Jewish literalism – it both distinguishes Origen's exegesis from the exegesis of the synagogue down the street and allows Origen to reference that same exegesis in his own interpretations of the literal sense – but Martens's discussion leaves unaddressed a potentially troubling feature of Origen's critique of Jewish exegesis: is Origen's Christian allegory, with its attendant critique of Jewish exegesis, inherently supersessionist? This is the charge Daniel Boyarin levels against Origen and which David Dawson refutes. See Daniel Boyarin, *A Radical Jew: Paul and the Politics of Identity* (Berkeley: University of California Press, 1994); John David Dawson, *Christian Figural Reading and the Fashioning of Identity* (Berkeley: University of California Press, 2001).

The 'Gospel' and its readers (*Comm. Jo.* 1.1–89)

Origen introduces the *Commentary on John* by differentiating the Gospel of John's Christian readers from their Jewish neighbours.[53] Where Israel was divided into tribes, 'all the people of Christ', Origen suggests, 'according to "the hidden man of the heart" who bear the name "Jew inwardly" and who have been circumcised "in spirit" possess the characteristics of the tribes in a more mystical manner' (1 Pet. 3.4; Rom. 2.29).[54] These gentile Christians, saved from among the nations, are the 144,000 John depicts, with 12,000 from each tribe (Rev. 7.2–8).[55] If Christians exhibit the characteristics of Israel's tribes, Origen reasons, then some must occupy the place of the Levites. Whereas most Christians capitulate to the demands posed by 'the activities of life and offer a few acts to God', Levites are 'those who devote themselves to the divine Word and truly exist by the service of God alone'.[56] These Levites, 'although all their possessions consist of tithes and firstfruits, offer tithes to God through the high priest and, I think, firstfruits too'.[57] The Levitical offering of firstfruits implies for Origen-specific, exegetical ends:

> Since we are eager for those things which are better, all our activity and our entire life being dedicated to God, and we wish to have all our activity as the firstfruits of many firstfruits … what more excellent activity ought there be, after our physical separation from one another, than the careful examination of the gospel? For, indeed, one might dare say that the gospel is the firstfruits of all the Scriptures. What other firstfruits of our activities ought there to have been, then, since we have come home to Alexandria, than that devoted to the firstfruits of the Scriptures?[58]

Before examining Origen's definition of 'gospel' proper, we should note one feature of the argument as he has thus far developed it. Though it is common to read the prologue of the *Commentary on John* with an eye to what, exactly, constitutes Origen's gospel, note that Origen offers this definition only in concert with a soteriological

---

[53] On the structure and argument of the introduction to the *Commentary on John*, see esp. Agnès Aliau-Milhaud, who argues that Origen has arranged the prologue to correlate his doctrines of ascending senses of textual meaning with ascending stages of the exegete's Christian maturity ('La composition du prologue du Commentaire sur Jean d'Origène', *Adamantius* 22 (2016), 6–24). See too Aliau-Milhaud, 'Progrès du texte, progrès de l'individu dans le Commentaire de Jean d'Origène: les techniques d'exégèse appliquées au thème du progrès', in *Origeniana Nona: Origen and the Religious Practice of His Time*, ed. György Heidl and Róbert Somos, BETL 228 (Leuven: Peeters, 2009), 13–23.

[54] *Comm. Jo.* 1.1. Translations of the *Commentary on John* are taken from *Origen: Commentary on the Gospel According to John Books 1 to 10*, trans. Ronald E. Heine, FOTC 80 (Washington, DC: Catholic University of American Press, 1989), and *Origen: Commentary on the Gospel According to John Books 13 to 32*, trans. Ronald E. Heine, FOTC 89 (Washington, DC: Catholic University of American Press, 1993).

[55] *Comm. Jo.* 1.2–8.

[56] *Comm. Jo.* 1.10. For Origen's use of Levitical imagery to describe spiritually adept Christians, see Theo Schäfer, *Das Priesterbild im Leben und Werk des Origenes* (Frankfurt am Main: Lang, 1977), 45–63; John A. McGuckin, 'Origen's Doctrine of the Priesthood, I & II', *Clergy Review* 70 (1985), 277–86, 318–25; Theo Hermans, *Origène: Théologie des sacrificielle du sacerdoce des Chrétiennes*, TH 102 (Paris: Beauchesne, 1996), esp. 206–23.

[57] *Comm. Jo.* 1.9.

[58] *Comm. Jo.* 1.12–13.

discussion – the governing question is what, exactly, qualifies a reader to interpret the gospel, hence Origen's interest in dedicated, priestly exegetes.[59] These Levitical readers, it is clear, are (1) not Jewish and (2) excel other Christians by their devotion to scripture.[60] Origen even paints the intended recipient of the *Commentary*, his patron Ambrose, as a priestly aspirant, one 'eager to be spiritual'. 'Spiritual', here, is a biblical echo entailing the whole of Paul's distinction between sarkic, psychic and pneumatic Christians (1 Cor. 2.14–3.1).[61]

What parts of scripture, then, qualify as gospel? First, the law of Moses is said to be 'not Gospel', the firstling, but not the firstfruits of scripture.[62] 'It does not make known "him who is to come", but proclaims him in advance.'[63] Second, on the other hand, the entire New Testament is gospel, 'not only because it declares alike with the beginning of the Gospel, "Behold the Lamb of God who takes away the sin of the world" (Jn 1.29), but also because it contains various ascriptions of praise and teachings of him on account of whom the gospel is gospel'.[64] To the natural objection that epistles are, prima facie, not like the four Gospels, Origen replies that the same appellation can apply to distinctive objects in qualified senses; Christ says 'call no man teacher', yet Paul lists 'teacher' among one of the offices of the church (Mt. 23.8; Eph. 4.11). The Epistles, then, are not Gospels in the sense of the four, but they remain, nonetheless, gospel.[65]

This point allows Origen to order all biblical instantiations of gospel according to the intensity or clarity with which they reveal Christ. Hence, even among the four Gospels, the Gospel of John holds a special place, the firstfruits of the firstfruits, as it were, 'for none of those manifested his divinity as fully as John when he presented him saying, "I am the light of the world"; "I am the way, and the truth, and the life"; "I am the resurrection"; "I am the door"; "I am the good shepherd"' and so on (Jn 8.12; 10.7, 11; 11.25; 14.6).[66]

The designation of the Gospel of John as the Gospel of Gospels, firstfruits of firstfruits, prompts Origen to return to his first point about the reader qualified to handle such firstfruits, 'whose meaning no one can understand who has not leaned on Jesus' breast nor received Mary from Jesus to be his mother also'. In fact,

> He who would be another John must also become such as John, to be shown to be Jesus, so to speak. For if Mary had no son except Jesus, in accordance with those who hold a sound opinion of her, and Jesus says to his mother, 'Behold your son'

---

[59] See, e.g. the helpful discussion in Paul Saieg, 'Reading the Phenomenology of Origen's Gospel: Toward a Philology of Givenness', *MT* 31 (2015), 235–56.
[60] See Hans G. Thümmel, *Origenes' Johanneskommentar Buch I-V*, STAC 63 (Tübingen: Mohr Siebeck, 2011), 199–200.
[61] *Comm. Jo.*1.9.
[62] *Comm. Jo.*1.14.
[63] *Comm. Jo.*1.17.
[64] Ibid. This is not the only instance where Origen qualifies the entire New Testament as gospel. Cf., the third homily on Psalm 36, section 6, where he distinguishes τὰς γραφὰς τὰς παλαιὰς καὶ … τὰς εὐαγγελικάς (*Die neuen Psalmenhomilien: Eine kritische Edition des Codex Monacensis Graecus 314*, ed. Lorenzo Perrone, GCS N.F. 19/Origenes Werke 13 (Berlin: de Gruyter, 2016), 147).
[65] *Comm. Jo.* 1.19–20. On the importance of the four Gospels for Origen, see too Francis Watson, *Gospel Writing: A Canonical Perspective* (Grand Rapids, MI: Eerdmans, 2013), 398.
[66] *Comm. Jo.* 1.21–2.

(Jn 19.26), and not, 'Behold, this man also is your son,' he has said equally, 'Behold, this is Jesus whom you bore.' For indeed everyone who has been perfected 'no longer lives, but Christ lives in him' (Gal. 2.20), and since 'Christ lives' in him, it is said of him to Mary, 'Behold your son,' the Christ.[67]

In other words, the true, priestly interpreter of the gospel is shown to be none other than the one whom the Gospels proclaim, whose presence now enlivens his disciples. Because this point stands as the logical bedrock of Origen's argument in *Comm. Jo.* 1.1–89, it is worth noting that Origen makes the same point in *Peri Archon*, albeit via a different Pauline text. Playing on the semantic range of νοῦς to describe both the meaning of a word and the human mind, Origen argues that the precise sense (ὁ ἀκριβὴς νοῦς) of the gospel is the mind of Christ (νοῦς ... Χριστοῦ).[68] Origen reiterates exactly this theme a few lines later in the *Commentary on John*: 'He who will understand these matters accurately must say truthfully, "But we have the mind of Christ, that we may know the graces that have been given us by God" (1 Cor. 2.16).'[69] Writing later in the *Commentary on Romans*, Origen distinguishes Jewish and heretical devotion to the literal sense from the Christian possession of what he there terms 'the sense of Christ'.[70]

With the gospel's Christian, priestly reader so described, Origen offers a more abstract definition of 'gospel'. Gospel, he suggests, 'is a discourse containing a report of things which, with good reason, make the hearer glad whenever he accepts what is reported, because they are beneficial'.[71] On one hand, this description naturally suits the four Gospels.[72] But so capacious a definition introduces a new problem for Origen, since Christians believe the Law and Prophets also make their hearers glad.[73] Before Christ's advent, the presence of the gospel in the Law and Prophets was not clear but, 'since the Savior has come, and has caused the gospel to be embodied in the gospel, he has made all things gospel, as it were'.[74] Origen understands the correlation between the advent and the recognition of the gospel's presence in all scripture in Pauline terms. When Christ came, he 'removed the veil on the Law and prophets' (2 Cor. 3.14–18) and 'showed the divine nature of them all when he presented clearly to those wanting to become disciples of his wisdom what things were true in the law of Moses, which the ancients cultivated in a copy and shadow (Heb. 8.5), and what the truth was in the events in the stories, which "happened to them in a figure, and were written" on account of us "on whom the ends of the world have come"' (1 Cor. 10.11).[75]

The interpretation of this gospel, then, comprises the proper worship offered by those 'in whom Christ has dwelt'.[76] Origen nevertheless admits that this gospel, present

---

[67] *Comm. Jo.* 1.23. Cf. *Pasch.* 6.
[68] *Princ.* 4.2.3. See Bernhard Neuschäfer, *Origenes als Philologe*, 2 vols (Basel: Reinhardt, 1987), 1.120.
[69] *Comm. Jo.* 1.24. Cf. 10.172–3.
[70] *Comm. Rom.* 2.14.14.
[71] *Comm. Jo.* 1.27.
[72] *Comm. Jo.* 1.28–31.
[73] *Comm. Jo.* 1.32. Cf. 1.85, which offers, as additional evidence that the prophets are gospel, Phillip's preaching of the gospel from Isa. 53.7 to the Ethiopian eunuch (Acts 8.30–5).
[74] *Comm. Jo.* 1.33.
[75] *Comm. Jo.* 1.34.
[76] *Comm. Jo.* 1.35.

in the Law and Prophets but recognized only after Christ's advent, 'although it is stored up in all the Scriptures' is 'called "gospel" in a special sense', that is, to distinguish it from the four.[77] But what sets this gospel apart is the distinction between 'the gospel which is perceptible by the senses' and 'the intelligible and spiritual gospel', that is, the gospel which only the mind of Christ can see.[78] It will be Origen's task in the ensuing commentary, he suggests, to translate the spiritual gospel into a perceptible gospel, one suited to the edification of his audience.[79]

I have condensed Origen's initial discussion of the gospel and its readers in the prologue to the *Commentary on John* in order to make three fundamental observations. First, it should now be clear that, in Origen's schema, all scripture is gospel, even if in a qualified sense.[80] This includes biblical books which, as Origen knew, the church had received from the Jews. The Word described in the Johannine prologue is the same word who spoke through the prophets,

> For who is 'the word which came from the Lord' to Jeremiah or to Isaiah or to Ezekiel or anyone except the one in the beginning with God? I do not know any word of the Lord other than the one concerning whom the Evangelist said, 'The Word was in the beginning, and the Word was with God and the Word was God.'[81]

Or, as Origen vividly puts it in the *Commentary on the Song of Songs*,

> When Christ was coming, therefore, He stood awhile behind the wall of the house of the Old Testament. He was standing behind the wall, in that He was not yet showing Himself to the people. But when the time is come, and He begins to appear to the Church who sits inside the house, that is, within the letter of the Law, and to show Himself to her through the windows of the Law and the prophets, that is, through the things that had been foretold concerning Him, then He calls to her to come forth and come outside to Him.[82]

The Logos who coyly peeks through the lattices of the Law and Prophets may be the one Christ, but, on its face, Origen's definition of gospel in the *Commentary on*

---

[77] *Comm. Jo.* 1.36.
[78] *Comm. Jo.* 1.44.
[79] *Comm. Jo.* 1.47–74.
[80] The theme of scriptures reappears throughout Origen's works. Cf., e.g. Origen's citation of Jn 6.63 in *Hom. Lev.* 4.1.1:

> Hear our Lord and Savior when he speaks to his disciples, 'The words which I spoke to you are spirit and life.' If, therefore, we learned from the voice of the Savior himself that the words which he spoke to the Apostles 'are spirit and life', we ought by no means to doubt that we must believe that those which he spoke through Moses likewise are 'spirit and life'.

Cf. *Comm. ser. Matt.* 27. On Origen's doctrine of Logos as the unity of scripture, see, e.g., Rolf Gögler, *Zur Theologie des biblischen Wortes bei Origenes* (Düsseldorf: Patmos-Verlag, 1963), 262–4; Torjesen, *Hermeneutical Procedure*, 108–12.

[81] *Hom. Jer.* 9.1. Cf. *Philoc.* 15.19: ἀεὶ γὰρ ἐν ταῖς γραφαῖς ὁ λόγος σὰρξ ἐγένετο, ἵνα κατασκηνώσῃ ἐν ἡμῖν (SC 302: 438); *Pasch.* 26.

[82] *Hom. Cant.* 3.3.

John implies something like a sliding scale of gospel, with every book other than the four read as gospel in a limited sense, and Gospel of John set out even among the four as the firstfruits of the firstfruits. In the *Commentary on Romans*, Origen notes that Moses's and Elijah's presence with Christ at the transfiguration teaches that 'the law and prophets are shown to harmonize with the Gospels and to shine forth with the same glory when viewed and interpreted spiritually'.[83] While the glory is the same, the degree of radiance varies from book to book. An important counterpoint is warranted here. Namely, just as Origen can qualify all scripture as 'gospel' in the *Commentary on John*, so, in *Peri Archon*, a text written only a few years prior, he suggests that all scripture is equally 'law'.[84]

My second observation, proceeding from the first, is that Origen's conception of the spiritual gospel as the presence of the Logos in the Old Testament implies a reader competent to identify the Logos in those texts. Christ, revealing himself through the text, is scripture's spiritual sense, and only a reader possessed of the mind of Christ recognizes that sense. In this regard, Origen has applied a basic tenet of much ancient epistemology. Only like can know like. For true knowledge, knower and known must share some conjunction, and, in the case of human knowledge of the divine, ultimately, union.[85] While some Jews, from Moses to Paul, may have enjoyed the Logos's enlightening presence, Origen clearly thinks them outliers compared with the Logos's presence in Christians.

Third and finally, this ultimate union of knower and known forms the basis of Origen's distinction between Christian and Jewish biblical interpretation, and, by extension, 'Christianness' and 'Jewishness': Soteriology, characterized by distinctively Pauline language, explains that Christ dwells in individual Christians, enabling their perception of the spiritual gospel. Unless one turns to Christ, the veil of the letter remains in place. Because Christ does not dwell in unbaptized Jews, they do not see the glory of the gospel shining from behind the veil. Even the most detailed knowledge of the veil does not imply any acquaintance with the radiant face beneath (2 Cor. 3.14–18). Neither, however, does the face beneath the veil negate the veil itself.

Shared books, two textual communities

To translate Origen into contemporary, academic parlance, the Alexandrian's distinction between Christians and Jews, church and synagogue, assumes that sociology is secondary to and dependent upon theological ontology. What a group like the church is determines where its boundary lines fall. But when two or more groups define their identities with reference to the same texts, boundaries can prove difficult

---

[83] *Comm. Rom.* 1.10.3.
[84] E.g. *Princ.* 4.3.3 and its discussion in Cocchini, *Il Paolo di Origene*, 124–5. Cf. *Pasch.* 38, discussing τὴν ὁμοιότ[η]τα τοῦ νόμου τὴν πρὸς τὸ εὐ[α]γγέλιον (Octave Guéraud and Pierre Nautin (eds), *Origène: Sur la Pâque: Traité inédit publié d'après un papyrus de Toura* (Paris: Beauschesne, 1979), 228).
[85] See esp. Robert M. Berchman, *From Philo to Origen: Middle Platonism in Transition*, BJS 69 (Chico, CA: Scholars, 1984), 190–200.

to trace. Hence, Origen's appeal to the individual and communal practice of biblical interpretation. Ontological differences are clearly manifest in the results of shared practices.

To the confusion of observers like Celsus, an outsider to Christians and Jews alike, late antique Christians and Jews appeared in some respects identical because they shared the same holy books. But this apparent congruence masked what an insider like Origen took to be a crucial difference. That is, that Christians and Jews derived irreconcilably different meanings from the same text. The former saw Christ, the Logos, everywhere. The latter did not. Each community of readers produced interpretations proper to their ontological identities. Ethnic Israel remained Israel, but conversion to Christianity rendered a potential reader of the Law a 'Jew in secret', and such a reader found the gospel in each biblical composition (Rom. 2.29).[86] In this way, Origen explains how the same textual corpora, Israel's Law and Prophets, came to shape and reinforce the identities of two adjacent but discrete textual communities.

---

[86] *Comm. Jo.* 1.1.

3

The reception of the Watchers tradition in Tertullian with regard to 1 Cor. 11.2–16

Stephen C. Carlson

One of the ways that early Christians used to define themselves as a community was through texts. They wrote epistles and treatises to shape the practice of the communities they formed, whether it was Paul for the churches he planted or Tertullian for the communities he increasingly found himself alienated from. As with any text, the community-forming documents they produced were read and understood in light of the other texts and traditions they received. A particularly contested area of social formation lies at the intersection of gender, sex, marriage and dress.[1] How are Christian men and women to behave in their new communities, and how much of their behaviour is to differ from or align with the practices of the larger communities they find themselves in? In particular, are they to marry, and if they reject marriage in favour of celibacy, what does that say about their social status and how they dress? To answer these questions, Christians turned to the textual resources they had at hand, including Paul's directives in 1 Corinthians, as well as the Jewish scriptures they inherited. Through this process, it is evident that intertextuality affects interpretation, and this case study investigates a specific example of this: Tertullian's reading of Paul in 1 Cor. 11.2–16 in light of his reception of the pre-Christian, Jewish 'Watchers' tradition in 1 Enoch. In particular, this study explores how Tertullian's reception of texts with distinct social imaginations for a community of God's people facilitated still another social imagination of his own, for his Christian community in the early third century.

Community formation in Paul, 1 Cor. 11.2–16

The reception of 1 Corinthians is an excellent vehicle for exploring community formation by early Christians, because it is the most community-formative letter among Paul's epistles. Written in response to questions and concerns raised by

---

[1] See, e.g. Peter Brown, *The Body and Society: Men, Women, and Sexual Renunciation in Early Christianity* (London: Faber and Faber, 1988); Jennifer Wright Knust, *Unprotected Texts: The Bible's Surprising Contradictions about Sex and Desire* (New York: HarperOne, 2011).

Paul's informants, 1 Corinthians conveys the apostle's advice to the Corinthian community on a wide range of issues. For example, Paul dispensed guidance about how to treat a community member who was cohabitating with his father's wife (1 Corinthians 5). Paul also discouraged the Corinthian Christians from appealing to the Roman legal system without first settling the matter among themselves first (1 Corinthians 6). Interaction with the pagan world also comes up in 1 Corinthians 8–10 with Paul's direction concerning food sacrificed to idols. Chapters 12–14 involve Paul's instruction concerning the use of the gifts of the spirit: they should be for the edification of the church as well as unbelievers who may be attending their assemblies.

Most importantly for this study, 1 Corinthians also presents Paul's social imagination concerning sex and marriage, and the heart of his advice is found in 1 Cor. 7.8–9:

> Now I say to the unmarried and the widows, it is good for them if they remain as I am; if they do not exercise self-control, let them marry, for it is better to marry than to burn.[2]

Paul goes on to put this recommendation into eschatological perspective. In view of what he sees as the 'impending crisis', he gives his opinion that 'virgins' (i.e. never-married women) ought to remain unmarried.[3] This advice is consonant with Paul's general commendation of keeping the immediate status quo for Christians – whether over the state of their foreskin or the state of their liberty (vv. 17–24) – in order to focus upon the 'affairs of the Lord' (1 Cor. 7.32–5). For Paul, 'the pattern of this world is passing away' (v. 31 παράγει γὰρ τὸ σχῆμα τοῦ κόσμου τούτου), and he would rather have Christians devote their energies to saving souls than changing the human institutions that will not in any case survive God's wrath (cf. Rom. 1.18).

Paul's 'fraught argument' in 1 Cor. 11.2–16 about how men and women ought to dress their heads should be read in the same light.[4] Upon first impression, the passage is difficult to follow because its crucial terms are not defined, its logic lacks focus and, most importantly, its social context has become obscure to us.[5] A good illustration of the problems posed by the passage is the mention of angels in v. 10, 'For this reason, the woman ought to have (an?) authority upon her head because of the angels

---

[2] 1 Cor. 7.8–9 Λέγω δὲ τοῖς ἀγάμοις καὶ ταῖς χήραις, καλὸν αὐτοῖς ἐὰν μείνωσιν ὡς κἀγώ· εἰ δὲ οὐκ ἐγκρατεύονται, γαμησάτωσαν, κρεῖττον γάρ ἐστιν γαμῆσαι ἢ πυροῦσθαι.

[3] 1 Cor. 7.25-6 Περὶ δὲ τῶν παρθένων ... νομίζω οὖν τοῦτο καλὸν ὑπάρχειν διὰ τὴν ἐνεστῶσαν ἀνάγκην, ὅτι καλὸν ἀνθρώπῳ τὸ οὕτως εἶναι.

[4] On the difficulty of Paul's logic in this passage, see especially Benjamin A. Edsall, 'Greco-Roman Costume and Paul's Fraught Argument in 1 Corinthians 11.2–16', *JGRChJ* 9 (2013), 132–46. For a recent history of research for this passage, see Torsten Jantsch, 'Einführung in die Probleme von 1Kor 11,2–16 und die Geschichte seiner Auslegung', in *Frauen, Männer, Engel: Perspektiven zu 1Kor 11,2–16*, BTS 152, ed. Torsten Jantsch (Neukirchen-Vluyn: Neukirchener Theologie, 2015), 1–60; and for a detailed bibliography see Jacob Brouwer, 'Gott, Christus, Engel, Männer und Frauen: Chronologisch-thematische Bibliographie zu 1Kor 11,2–16', in *Frauen*, ed. Jantsch, 187–235.

[5] So, e.g. Brown, *Body and Society*, 52: 'A disquisition on hair and on the natural hierarchy that made men superior to women, so contorted and so heavy with unspoken anxieties, that modern scholars remain at a loss how to unravel it.'

(διὰ τοὺς ἀγγέλους).' The definite article should signal familiarity to the readers, but this is the first time angels were explicitly mentioned in the passage. Paul thus presumes some knowledge of angels by his recipients, and since angels are not part of Graeco-Roman mythology, most if not all they knew about angels would have to have come from his teaching.[6] Unfortunately, it is very difficult to nail down the content of Paul's prior teaching about angels.[7] Scholars have scoured his scriptures and suggested various scenarios for these angels, including lusty angels,[8] good angels maintaining the created order or assisting worship,[9] human messengers (whether Paul's opponents or empowered women in his ministry)[10] or congregants thought comparable to angels.[11] All of these proposals, unfortunately, are forced to assume a scenario for the angels that is hardly maintained in the text. Given Paul's assumption about the local knowledge of the Corinthian congregation,[12] it is likely that Tertullian and his interlocutors were no better off in understanding Paul's puzzling reference than we are today, making this verse ripe for intertextual illumination.

But it is not just v. 10 that is obscure. Scholars are divided about what the issue in Corinth even was. The traditional and still majority reading of the passage is that it involved head coverings, namely the veil as worn by various Graeco-Roman women, but, as we will see later, it was contested in Tertullian's own community whether such veiling ought to apply to all women in general or to married women in specific.[13] Other scholars hold that the issue involved the hairstyles of both men and women.[14] Nevertheless, whatever was going on in Corinth about how men and women wore their hair Paul was reluctant to change, as the final sentence makes clear: 'But if anyone

---

[6] Benjamin A. Edsall, *Paul's Witness to Formative Christian Instruction*, WUNT 2/365 (Tübingen: Mohr Siebeck, 2014), 117–18, 148–50, esp. 149.

[7] One wonders whether – as Edsall, *Paul's Witness*, 149, puts it – 'Paul simply overshot his communicative mark here'.

[8] E.g. Tertullian, *Or.* 22.5-6, *Virg.* 7.2; L. J. Lietaert Peerbolte, 'Man, Woman, and the Angels in 1 Cor 11:2–16', in *The Creation of Man and Woman: Interpretations of the Biblical Narratives in Jewish and Christian Traditions*, ed. Gerard P. Luttikhuizen, TBN 3 (Leiden: Brill, 2000), 76–92; Knust, *Unprotected Texts*, 161.

[9] E.g. Origen, *Hom. Luc.* 23.8; Mark Finney, 'Honour, Head-Coverings and Headship: 1 Corinthians 11.2–16 in Its Social Context', *JSNT* 22 (2010), 31–58; Jason David BeDuhn, '"Because of the Angels": Unveiling Paul's Anthropology in 1 Corinthians 11', *JBL* 118 (1999), 295–320; and Judith M. Gundry-Volf, 'Gender and Creation in 1 Corinthians 11:2–16: A Study in Paul's Theological Method', in *Evangelium-Schriftauslegung-Kirche: Festschrift für Peter Stuhlmacher zum 65. Geburtstag*, ed. Jostein Ådna et al. (Göttingen: Vandenhoeck & Ruprecht, 1997), 151–71 (angels as mediators of prophecy).

[10] Alan G. Padgett, *As Christ Submits to the Church: A Biblical Understanding of Leadership and Mutual Submission* (Grand Rapids, MI: Baker Academic, 2011), 113–15; Gordon D. Fee, *The First Epistle to the Corinthians*, NICNT (Grand Rapids, MI: Eerdmans, 1987), 522.

[11] Clement, *Hyp.* frag. 1.

[12] So Edsall, *Paul's Witness*, 149: 'However, Paul does not clarify his meaning. Rather, he assumes that the Corinthians will not be lost by such compressed arguments which suggests that he expects them to know something about angels and their cosmic and communal role.'

[13] In particular, Tertullian, *Virg.* 4, claims Paul's proscription applies for all women, regardless of marital status, while his Carthaginian opponents held that it applied to married women.

[14] E.g. Jerome Murphy-O'Connor, 'Sex and Logic in 1 Corinthians 11:2–16', *CBQ* 42 (1980), 482–500; Philip B. Payne, *Man and Woman, One in Christ: An Exegetical and Theological Study of Paul's Letters* (Grand Rapids, MI: Zondervan, 2009), 109–215. They propose that the issue is related to the promotion of heteronormativity and its concomitant homophobia.

is disposed to be contentious, we do not have such a custom nor do the churches of God.'[15]

Paul's short-term conservatism on such temporal matters was to have radical long-run consequences. Paul's commendation of celibacy in 1 Corinthians 7 encouraged Christians in the early centuries to renounce marriage and devote themselves to God.[16] The result of this is that many Christian communities would have a class of celibate Christian women called *virgines*, with a special status of their own, and one of these communities was the early-third-century Carthage. At the same time, however, it is unclear to what extent this development was considered by or even foreseeable to Paul when he made his remarks about how men and women should dress and groom their heads in Christian assemblies. There is certainly a sense of subsidiarity in Paul's comment for them to judge for themselves (1 Cor. 11.13 Ἐν ὑμῖν αὐτοῖς κρίνατε), though Paul's status quo bias probably militates against innovation in the gendered customs of dress. Ironically, however, it is Paul's status quo preference on marriage in chapter 7 that created the new social realities of Tertullian's day and rendered his chapter 11 advice so contextually bound as to become opaque to later interpreters. Tertullian's reinterpretation and extension of Paul's advice demonstrate the impact of his reception of Jewish texts and traditions.

Community formation in Tertullian in light of his reception of the Book of Enoch

Community formation is a constant theme in Tertullian's large body of work.[17] For example, he wrote tracts on how Christians should behave at public and pagan events (*De spectaculis, De idolatria*), and how they are supposed to handle persecution (*Ad martyras, De fuga in persecutione*). Much can be written about Tertullian's attempts to shape his community, but this study will focus on his reception of the Book of Enoch as he knew it, in conjunction with his interpretation of what women should be wearing in his tracts on prayer (*De oratione*), on the apparel of women (*De cultu feminarum*), on the soldier's crown (*De corona militis*) and on the veiling of virgins (*De virginibus velandis*).[18]

Written early during his 'Catholic' period, Tertullian's tract on prayer, *De oratione*, provides an intertextual reading of Paul's cryptic comment in 1 Cor. 11.10. The first part of the tract is an exposition of the several clauses of the Lord's Prayer, and the second half considers the proper circumstances for prayer. In chapter 20, Tertullian turns to the topic of women's dress and, appealing to 1 Pet. 3.3 and 1 Tim. 2.9, he urges that women dress modestly. Then, Tertullian brings up a matter of current dispute: whether

---

[15] 1 Cor. 11.16: Εἰ δέ τις δοκεῖ φιλόνεικος εἶναι, ἡμεῖς τοιαύτην συνήθειαν οὐκ ἔχομεν οὐδὲ αἱ ἐκκλησίαι τοῦ θεοῦ.
[16] For other factors, see Brown, *Body and Society*, 60–1.
[17] See generally Kristi Upson-Saia, *Early Christian Dress: Gender, Virtue, and Authority*, Routledge Studies in Ancient History 3 (New York: Routledge, 2011), 61–2.
[18] The only apparel-focused work not considered here is his tract on the philosopher's mantle (*De pallio*).

or not *virgines* ought to be veiled.[19] The reason for this dispute is that Tertullian wants them to be veiled, but both the current bishop and his predecessor apparently held to a local custom that *virgines* should not be forced to veil.[20]

Tertullian's response is exegetical. He argues that 1 Cor. 11.2–16 calls for all women to be veiled in prayer, not just married women as his opponents argue (*Or.* 21.2). The basic exegetical issue is the scope of the Greek term γυναῖκες that Paul uses in the passage, which can mean either women generally or married women specifically. Tertullian favours the former option and makes a number of arguments for it. The argument most relevant for this study is that he goes through the Pauline passage and contends that various statements in there about 'women' apply to both married and unmarried women. It is in the course of this argument that Tertullian reaches 1 Cor. 11.10, and he connects Paul's enigmatic reference to 'the angels' to the *Watchers* myth: 'Indeed, it is because of the angels that he says they ought to be veiled, because the angels defected from God because of the daughters of humans.'[21]

Two elements of Tertullian's analysis demonstrate that his main intertext is 1 En. 6.1–4 rather than its Gen. 6.1–4 hypotext, though their interpretation is necessarily intertwined because the Enochian passage is itself an interpretation of the Genesis passage. First, Tertullian identifies those who took wives for themselves as 'angels' as in 1 Enoch instead of 'sons of God' as in the Hebrew and Old Greek texts of Genesis 6.[22] Second, the angels are further characterized as estranged from God (so 1 En. 6.3–6). In other words, Tertullian read Paul's 'because of the angels' in 1 Cor. 11.10 in light of 1 Enoch 6 to conclude that the angels must have been the lusty, fallen angels of the Watchers. To be sure, many ancient exegetes made the same identification of the 'sons of God' as angels without directly appealing to 1 Enoch,[23] and this is a reflection of the ongoing, indirect influence of 1 Enoch on the interpretation of Genesis.[24] In Tertullian's case, however, we need not be satisfied with merely indirect influence, because as we will discuss further, Tertullian knows of the text and mounts a defence of its scriptural status.

Tertullian supplies two reasons for this intertextual reading. First, both virgins and married women are a source of sexual temptation, so if married women could tempt the

---

[19] *Or.* 21.1 (ed. Diercks): *Sed quid promiscue observetur per ecclesias quasi incertum, id retractandum est, velarine debeant virgines an non.*

[20] *Or.* 22.10 (ed. Diercks): '*Sed non putet institutionem unusquisque antecessoris commovendam.*' *Multi alienae consuetudini prudentiam suam et constantiam eius addicunt. Ne compellantur velari, certe voluntarias prohiberi non oportet.* With the final clause, the most that Tertullian seems to be able to hope for from the Carthaginian leadership is that modest *virgines* should not be pressured to give up the veil.

[21] *Or.* 22.5 (ed. Diercks): *Nempe propter angelos ait velari oportere, quod angeli propter filias hominum desciverunt a Deo.*

[22] Compare Gen. 6.1–2 (NRSV): 'When people began to multiply on the face of the ground, and daughters where born to them, the sons of God saw that they were fair; and they took wives for themselves of all that they chose' and 1 En. 6.1–2 (trans. Nickelsburg): 'When the sons of men had multiplied, in those days, beautiful and comely daughters were born to them. And the watchers, the sons of heaven, saw them and desired them. And they said to one another, "Come, let us choose for ourselves wives from the daughters of men, and let us beget children for ourselves."'

[23] E.g. Philo, *Gig.* passim; Justin martyr, *2 Apol.* 5.3; Irenaeus, *Haer.* 1.10.1, 4.16.2, and *Epid.* 18.

[24] See generally Annette Yoshiko Reed, *Fallen Angels and the History of Judaism and Christianity: The Reception of Enochic Literature* (Cambridge: Cambridge University Press, 2005).

angels, then so could unmarried women – indeed they would be even more tempting.[25] Second, the fact that the angels took them as wives shows that they were either not yet or no longer married: 'Also because it says, "and they took wives for themselves", it does so because they took wives of those who were free of course; but concerning those not free it would have been stated otherwise.'[26] In both cases, Tertullian's argument is that the scriptural phrase 'daughters of humans' is inclusive of both married and unmarried women, including both virgins and widows. The context of 1 Enoch is not restricted to prayer, so the internal logic of Tertullian's chosen intertext suggests that he would be open to having *virgines* be veiled outside of the context of prayer and even outside of the congregation. Tertullian does not go this far at this point in his career, but in appealing to the example of the veiled Rebecca meeting her betrothed in Gen. 24.65 he does argue that betrothed virgins should be veiled.[27]

Tertullian's reference to 1 Enoch as 'scripture' is no impediment to seeing it as his main intertext, because he strongly defends its scriptural status in a tract on the apparel of women, *De cultu feminarum*. Opening with an infamous apostrophe to Eve, calling her 'the Devil's gateway',[28] Tertullian contends that contemporary women ought to dress themselves modestly and without ornamentation. Much of the text concerns various ways in which women could enhance their appearance, all of which Tertullian rejects as improper for Christian women. Although this tract does not concern *virgines* specifically, it does demonstrate his reception of the *Watchers* myth of 1 Enoch on the matter of what women should wear:

> For those, too, who invented these things are condemned to the penalty of death, namely, those angels who rushed from heaven upon the daughters of men so that this ignominy is also attached to woman. For when these fallen angels had revealed certain well-hidden material substances, and numerous other arts that were only faintly revealed, to an age much more ignorant than ours – for surely they are the ones who disclosed the secrets of metallurgy, discovered the natural properties of herbs, made known the power of charms, and aroused the desire to pry into everything, including the interpretation of the stars – they granted to women as their special and, as it were, personal property these means of feminine vanity: the radiance of precious stones with which necklaces are decorated in different colors, the bracelets of gold which they wrap around their arms, the colored preparations which are used to dye wool, and that black powder which they use to enhance the beauty of their eyes.[29]

---

[25] *Or.* 22.5 (ed. Diercks): *Quis ergo contendat solas mulieres, id est nuptas iam et virginitati defunctas, concupiscentiae, nisi si non licet et virgines specie praestare et amatores invenire?*

[26] *Or.* 22.5 (ed. Diercks): *Etiam quod ait 'et acceperunt sibi in uxores', eo facit, quod accipiuntur in uxores quae vacant scilicet; de non vacantibus autem aliter enuntiasset.*

[27] *Or.* 22.5 (ed. Diercks): *De illis tamen quae sponsis dicantur constanter super meum modulum pronuntiare contestarique possum velandas ex ea die esse qua ad primum viri corpus osculo et dextera expaverint; omnia enim in his praenupserunt, et aetas per maturitatem et caro per aetatem et spiritus per conscientiam et pudor per osculi experimentum et spes per expectationem et mens per uoluntatem. Satisque nobis exemplo Rebecca est quae sponso demonstrato tantum notitia<e> eius nubendo velata est.*

[28] *Cult. fem.* 1.1.2 (ed. Turcan): *Tu es diaboli ianua.*

[29] *Cult. fem.* 1.2.1 (trans. Arbesmann, Daly and Quain, FC 40).

In other words, Tertullian blames the use of cosmetics, jewellery and other beauty aids upon the teachings of the fallen angels who took the daughters of humans as wives. These details are found in 1 En. 8.1–2.[30] For this argument to work, the reader has to accept 1 Enoch as authoritative, and Tertullian realizes that its scriptural status is not accepted by everyone: 'I know that the scripture of Enoch, which gives this order to angels, is not received by some because it is not admitted into the Jewish library.'[31] Tertullian, nonetheless, goes on to defend its status, arguing that Noah or the Spirit had preserved it from the Flood, that Jude testified to it and that the real reason Jews rejected it is that it prophesied about Christ (*Cult. fem.* 1.3.2–3). Regardless of how effective his defence of 1 Enoch as scripture was, it is clear that it is useful for attacking pagan practices he disapproves of.[32]

De corona militis is Tertullian's tract about what men should wear on their heads, but even here he makes comments about women. Writing upon the occasion of a Christian soldier's refusal to wear a laurel crown in acknowledgement of a monetary gift to the military ranks on the death of the Emperor Septimius Severus (d. 211), Tertullian argues that, in the silence of scripture, the custom of refusing such pagan honours should stand even at the cost of imprisonment, torture or execution.[33] In the course of his argument, Tertullian notes that there is a custom among Jews that unmarried women were veiled, citing Rebecca's example in Gen. 24.64–5.[34] Alluding to 1 Cor. 11.3, Tertullian argues that Christian men ought not wear anything on their heads, to symbolize their Christian liberty over the idolatry of the state, and that Christian women likewise should not wear such pagan headgear since their veil already symbolizes their submission (*Cor.* 14.1).[35] In this context, Tertullian again connects Paul's comment about the angels in 1 Cor. 11.10 to the *Watchers* myth and further speculates that the women seduced the fallen angels by wearing crowns, which, in his opinion, abrogates

---

[30] 1 En. 8.1–2 (trans. Nickelsburg)

> Asael taught men to make swords of iron and weapons and shields and breastplates and every instrument of war. He showed them metals of the earth and how they should work gold to fashion it suitably, and concerning silver, to fashion it for bracelets and ornaments for women. And he showed them concerning antimony and eye plaint and all manner of precious stones and dyes. And the sons of men made them for themselves and for their daughters, and they transgressed and led the holy ones astray. And there was much godlessness on the earth, and they made their ways desolate.

[31] *Cult. fem.* 1.3.1 (ed. Turcan): *Scio scripturam Enoch, quae hunc ordinem angelis dedit, non recipi a quibusdam quia nec in armarium Iudaicum admittitur.*

[32] Reed, *Fallen Angels*, 175: 'For others, such as Tertullian, the relevance of angelic descent for the polemic against pagan culture seems to have served as welcome confirmation of the value of the "book(s) of Enoch" as sources of Christian truth.'

[33] E.g. *Cor.* 2.4; 3.1; 4.1; 12.3; 14.1.

[34] *Cor.* 4.2 (ed. Fontaine): *Apud Iudaeos tam sollemne est feminis eorum velamen capitis ut inde noscantur. Quaero legem, apostolum differo. Si Rebecca conspecto procul sponso velamen invasit, privatus pudorlegem facere non potuit, aut, causae suae fecerit, tegantur virgines solae, et hoc nuptum venientes, nec antequam cognoverint sponsos.*

[35] *Cor.* 14.1 (ed. Fontaine): *Tanto abest ut capiti suo munus inferat idololatriae, immo iam dixerim Christo, siquidem caput viri Christus est: tam liberum quam et Christus, ne velamento quidem obnoxium, nedum obligamento. Porro et quod obnoxium est velamento, caput feminae, hoc ipso iam occupatum non vacat etiam obligamento. Habet humilitatis suae sarcinam.*

a woman's modesty and enhances her beauty into a seductive allure.[36] Although Tertullian does not specifically address unmarried women in this passage,[37] the logic of his appeal to the *Watchers* myth nonetheless does not discriminate on marital status. Indeed, it pertains most appositely to marriageable women.

By the time Tertullian enters his Montanist phase, his position becomes even more rigorist.[38] In his tract on the veiling of virgins, *De virginibus velandis*, Tertullian aims to demonstrate that all *virgines* ought to be veiled 'from the time when they made the transition of their age', regardless of their marital status.[39] This position is stricter than that espoused earlier in *De oratione*, in that Tertullian no longer limits his proscription to the context of prayer as with 1 Cor. 11.2-16 or to betrothed virgins as with Gen. 24.64-5. Rather, Tertullian calls for all *virgines* to be veiled, and a major contributing factor is his beloved intertext of the fallen angels in the Book of the Watchers of 1 Enoch.

The importance of the *Watchers* myth for the extension of Tertullian's injunction of the veiling of virgins beyond the contexts of prayer and betrothal is evident in how Tertullian rehearses and augments his exegetical arguments made earlier in *De oratione*. Even though Tertullian's thesis in *De virginibus velandis* is no longer limited to the communal prayer where 1 Cor. 11.2-6 is fully on point, it is still necessary to address that passage because, if Paul can be read as permitting *virgines* to not be veiled in church, then this allowance ought to apply more generally in public, where it was socially acceptable in Carthage for unmarried women to be seen without the veil. When Tertullian gets around to addressing the exegesis of 1 Cor. 11.2-16 in *Virg.* 7, he expands upon his earlier arguments from *Or.* 22. Important for our purposes, Tertullian does so by including additional details from the *Watchers* myth:

> Therefore, a face which is so dangerous and which has cast scandals from here to heaven, ought to be shaded in order that, standing in the presence of God before whom it is accused of being responsible for the angels being banished, it may blush before the other angels also, and may restrain that former evil freedom of its own head, [a freedom] which now ought not be placed before the eyes of men. But even if those angels had grasped after females who were already unclean, so much more

---

[36] *Cor.* 14.1 (ed. Fontaine): *Si nudo capite videri non debet propter angelos, multo magis coronato. Fortasse tunc illos coronato scandalizaverit. Quid enim est in capite feminae corona quam formae lena, quam summae lasciviae nota, extrema negatio verecundiae, conflatio illecebrae?*

[37] Perhaps the phrase 'submission to the veil' (*obnoxium velamento*) might suggest married women, but for Tertullian even the unmarried women ought to be veiled (*Virg.* 1.1). Geoffrey D. Dunn, 'Rhetoric and Tertullian's de Virginibus Velandis', *VC* 59 (2005), 1-30, 27, argues that Tertullian did not raise the issue of virgins veiling because in *De corona militis* Tertullian is upholding custom, while in *De virginibus velandis* Tertullian is attacking custom.

[38] It is tempting to connect Tertullian's more rigorist position on veiling in this phase with Montanism, but Tertullian nowhere makes the connection explicit. See Dunn, 'Rhetoric', 21 n. 92: 'The rigorism of Montanism would tend to suggest that they would be more likely to uphold a traditional practice like veiling virgins than more moderate Christians, unless one wished to argue that Tertullian was addressing some wayward Montanist virgins.' Perhaps, Tertullian's rigorism about the veil is a kind of compensation for the more permissive practice of female prophesying in Montanist congregations.

[39] *Virg.* 1.1 (ed. Bulhart): *Proprium iam negotium passus meae opinionis Latine quoque ostendam virgines nostras velari oportere, ex quo transitum aetatis suae fecerint; hoc exigere veritatem, cui nemo praescribere potest, non spatium temporum, non patrocinia personarum, non privilegium regionum.*

the virgins ought to be veiled 'on account of the angels', as the sin of the angels would have been greater on account of [them being] virgins.[40]

For Tertullian, then, the *virgines* are now even responsible at the final judgement for the sins of the fallen *Watchers*, who were forced to gaze upon their uncovered heads and be banished by God for their subsequent sins. As a result, Tertullian insists on the responsibility of *virgines* to cover their heads, not just in congregational contexts as in 1 Cor. 11.2–16 but also, more generally, in public and from the time of their maturity.[41]

Community formation among Carthaginian *Virgines* and later Christians

Tertullian was not the only person in Carthage to express an opinion about the veiling of virgins. His opponents also had views of their own, but our consideration of the views of the Carthaginian *virgines* is hampered by the fact that the bulk of Tertullian's tract on the veiling of virgins is a conversation 'between men'.[42] By and large, these women were talked about, not reasoned with. This is especially evident at *Virg.* 16.4, where Tertullian 'turns' to appeal to the Carthaginian women after talking about them in the third person: 'It still remains', he says, 'that we turn to them so that they would more freely admire those things', followed by a direct address to them to cover their heads, because 'every age of men is endangered' by them.[43] The rational part of his discourse, then, was not directed to them but to the leader of the community, the bishop, in order to convince him to 'prefer benefit to custom'.[44] That is, Tertullian wanted the bishop to force Christian women to adopt Tertullian's innovations in what they ought to wear, based on his particular social imagination for the Christian community.[45] Nevertheless,

---

[40] *Virg.* 7.3–4 (trans. Dunn).
[41] For further exploration of the role of veiling and the gaze of males in connection with these passages, see Mary Rose D'Angelo, 'Veils, Virgins, and the Tongues of Men and Angels: Women's Heads in Early Christianity', in *Off with Her Head! The Denial of Women's Identity in Myth, Religion, and Culture*, ed. Howard Eilberg-Schwartz and Wendy Doniger (Berkeley: University of California Press, 1995), 131–64. Also of interest are Lynn Cohick, 'Virginity Unveiled: Tertullian's *Veiling of Virgins* and the Historical Women in the First Three Centuries A.D.', *AUSS* 45 (2007), 19–34; and Karl Shuve, '"Put On the Dress of a Wife, So That You Might Preserve Your Virginity": Virgins as Brides of Christ in the Writings of Tertullian', in *The Symbolism of Marriage in Early Christianity and the Latin Middle Ages: Images, Impact, Cognition*, ed. Line Cecile Engh (Amsterdam: Amsterdam University Press, 2019), 131–54.
[42] On the rhetorical function of women in writings by men for men, see generally Eve Kosofsky Sedgwick, *Between Men: English Literature and Male Homosocial Desire* (New York: Columbia University Press, 1985); Kate Cooper, *The Virgin and the Bride: Idealized Womanhood in Late Antiquity* (Cambridge, MA: Harvard University Press, 1996); and Shelly Matthews, 'Thinking of Thecla: Issues in Feminist Historiography', *JFSR* 17 (2001), 39–55.
[43] *Virg.* 16.4 (ed. Bulhart): *Superest etiam, ut ad ipsas convertamur, quo libentius ista suscipiant. Oro te, sive mater sive soror sive filia virgo, secundum annorum nomina dixerim, vela caput, si mater, propter filios, si soror, propter fratres, si filia, propter patres: omnes in te aetates periclitantur.*
[44] Cf. *Virg.* 17.9 (ed. Bulhart): *utilitatem consuetudini praeponentibus.*
[45] See, e.g. *Virg.* 1.4, calling for 'the novelty of improvement' (*novitatem correctionis*). A striking indication of this novelty is that Tertullian tells the *virgines* to 'lie to some extent' by wearing the

since women were part of the community and participated in community-forming practices, we must be attentive for echoes of their voices, however muffled, in these texts.[46]

In terms of practice, it is fairly clear that most of the *virgines* presented themselves according to the standards of the local Carthaginian community and that the local church did not impose any special requirements. This state of affairs is evident at the beginning of *De virginibus velandis*, where Tertullian begins his argument against this practice by attacking the notion of 'custom' when it is incompatible with the 'truth' as he sees it: 'But our lord Christ calls himself *truth* not *custom*.'[47] Tertullian refers to the practices of *virgines* not veiling as an 'old custom',[48] and he calls for the 'novelty of improvement'.[49] Tertullian knows he is swimming against the tide.

Tertullian conveys not only what the practice of the *virgines* was but also some of their arguments. Perhaps the most extensive place where Tertullian shares their exegesis with us occurs in *Virg*. 4.1:

> 4.1 However, in so far as it is the custom to argue against the truth from the Scriptures, immediately it is put to us that no mention of virgins has been made by the apostle [Paul in the place] where he makes a ruling about the veil, but that only women were named, since, [it is argued,] if he had wanted virgins to be covered as well, he would also have written something about the virgins when the women were mentioned. In this way, it is said, in that [other] passage where he handles the issue of marriage, he declares what ought to be observed concerning virgins as well. And thus [it is said by my opponents that] those [virgins] are not included in the law about the veiling of the head [in the former passage] as they have not been named in this law but, on the contrary, from this [law comes the practice for virgins] to be unveiled. They who are not named are not commanded by it.[50]

Accordingly, the Carthaginian *virgines* and their supporters do not see 1 Cor. 11.2-16 as being about them at all. Rather, they hold that it concerns how married women should handle their veils in church. Recognizing that the key term women (γυναῖκες) is ambiguous between women generally and married women specifically, they note

---

veil (*Virg*. 16.5 *mentire aliquid ex his*), though not about their actual marital status (*Virg*. 16.6 *Quamquam non mentiris nuptam; nupsisti enim Christo*).

[46] On the need to listen for the silenced and muffled voices of women in such texts, see generally Catharine A. MacKinnon, *Are Women Human? And Other International Dialogues* (Cambridge, MA: Belknap, 2006). This is a difficult task. Due to the nature of the discourse 'between men', all the usual problems with mirror-reading present themselves here: see John M. G. Barclay, 'Mirror-Reading a Polemical Letter: Galatians as a Test Case', *JSNT* 31 (1987), 73-97, esp. 74:

> In the first place, Paul is not directly addressing the opponents in Galatians, but he is talking to the Galatians about the opponents. This means that it is not just a question of trying to piece together what is being said at the other end of the telephone, but of listening in to one side of a dialogue (between Paul and the Galatians) about a third party (the opponents).

[47] *Virg*. 1.2 (ed. Bulhart): *Sed dominus noster Christus veritatem se, non consuetudinem cognominavit*.
[48] *Virg*. 1.3 (ed. Bulhart): *vetus consuetudo*.
[49] *Virg*. 1.4 (ed. Bulhart): *novitatem correctionis*.
[50] *Virg*. 4.1 (trans. Dunn); see also *Or*. 22.1.

that their interpretation is consistent with Pauline usage in his chapter on marriage (1 Corinthians 7), where he distinguishes between virgins (παρθένοι) and married women (γυναῖκες).

Tertullian does take this argument seriously and devotes much space in *De oratione* and *De virginibus velandis* to refuting it. In particular, Tertullian rejects the exegetical distinction between married and unmarried women on the ground that it creates a 'monstrous' third kind of woman with a 'head of her own'.[51] In other words, while the married woman may be thought to have her husband as her head, and the premarital virgin to have her father as her head, the Carthaginian *virgines* do not have any man as their head, but only themselves. This is the 'monstrous' implication of their removal from the marriage market, as Kristi Upson-Saia put it: 'Because the virgins had renounced sexual activity, they no longer belonged to the category woman and should be thought of only as virgins (i.e., a third gender).'[52] Thus, the *virgines*' removal of their bodies from the marriage market, justified by their appeal to Paul's commendation of celibacy in 1 Corinthians 7, served to create an independent locus of authority within the Christian community, where adult women who have renounced marriage no longer have to answer to a domestic man in charge.

Renunciation of sexual activity is also key to Carly Daniel-Hughes's analysis that the theology of the body among the *virgines* is directly linked to their veiling practices.[53] Specifically, she argues that 'while Tertullian sees veiling as an indicator of a virgin's shame, women, who claimed the title "virgin", understood their unveiling as a sign that their sexual continence unmoored that link.'[54] Thus, the Carthaginian *virgines*, who were 'sharp-witted hermeneutes',[55] were able to carefully construe Paul's formative teachings on sex, gender and marriage in 1 Corinthians and apply them to the practicalities of social behaviour and dress within Christian communities.[56]

We do not know, however, exactly what the *virgines* thought of the enigmatic angels in 1 Cor. 11.10, because Tertullian did not convey it. Perhaps they did not think much of it, since they thought the passage concerned married women and therefore whatever the reason that married women should cover their heads would not apply to them. Nevertheless, it is worth exploring how they could have understood the reference to

---

[51] *Virg.* 7.2 (ed. Bulhart): *Si* caput mulieris vir est, *utique et virginis, de qua fit mulier illa quae nupsit, nisi si virgo tertium genus est monstruosum aliquod sui capitis*. ('If the head of the woman is the man, then also [it is the head] of the virgin, from whom is made the woman who veiled herself in marriage, unless the virgin is a third kind, something monstrous with a head of her own.') On this passage see generally Heather Barkman, 'Virgins, Monsters, Martyrs, and Prophets: Tertullian's Species of Women', *Ottawa Journal of Religion* 4 (2012), 41–57.

[52] Upson-Saia, *Early Christian Dress*, 63.

[53] Carly Daniel-Hughes, '"Wear the Armor of Your Shame!": Debating Veiling and the Salvation of the Flesh in Tertullian of Carthage', *SR* 39 (2010), 179–201; Carly Daniel-Hughes, *The Salvation of the Flesh in Tertullian of Carthage: Dressing for the Resurrection* (New York: Palgrave Macmillan, 2011).

[54] Daniel-Hughes, *Salvation of the Flesh*, 94.

[55] Ibid., 95.

[56] This new kind of Christian woman (viz. celibate adult females) is a long-term consequence of taking Paul's promotion of celibacy to heart, however unintended in the short term. It is Tertullian's use of Jewish texts and traditions, especially Genesis and 1 Enoch, which preceded and did not recognize Paul's eschatologically realized thinking about sexuality, that allowed him to 'domesticate' Paul's potentially radical teachings.

angels by examining other exegeses of this verse that have survived, in order to get a sense of the interpretative possibilities for this verse and to see that Tertullian's was not the only viable one in his day and age.

The oldest extant interpretation of 1 Cor. 11.10 is a Valentinian reading preserved by Irenaeus and Clement, where the woman in the verse represents Wisdom who veiled herself out of modesty when Jesus comes with his attendants, the angels.[57] The practical implications for the Carthaginian *virgines* of this allegorical reading are not immediately clear, however. Are they to veil themselves at the return of Christ?

Contemporaneous to Tertullian, Clement of Alexandria argues in a fragment from his lost *Hypotyposeis* that the angels cannot be heavenly beings because they can see right through the veil; rather, Clement holds that Paul's 'angels' refers to the righteous and virtuous men in the congregation who may be attracted by the beauty of the women.[58] On Clement's reading, Tertullian's function of the veil as a protective against the angels is not operative, but the veil still serves to protect the 'righteous and virtuous men' in the congregation from temptation.[59] Though Clement and Tertullian disagree on the particular exegesis of the term 'angels', their bottom line is the same: they both want to regulate what women should wear in church for much the same reason and in much the same way. It is not clear that the Carthaginian *virgines* would accept this interpretation because they lived in a society where uncovered unmarried women did not in general scandalize the men of the community. What is clear, however, is that the *Watchers* myth is not an intertext for Clement on this point.

A generation later than Tertullian, Origen offers an interpretation of 1 Cor. 11.10 in one of his homilies on Luke, where the angels are heavenly beings that have been assigned to each church. Origen explains, 'Angels are present in the church – at least in that church that deserved them and belongs to Christ. This is the reason why women are commanded to have "a veil on their heads" when they pray, "because of the angels."'[60] One major difference between Origen and Tertullian is their intertext. For Origen, the relevant intertext is Revelation 2, not 1 Enoch, and the angels are virtuous, not lustful.[61] As a result, Origen's reading has elements in common with both Clement and Tertullian. Like Tertullian, Origen's angels are heavenly beings, but like Clement, Origen's angels are righteous beings. Origen does not consider the distinction between married and unmarried women, and so it remains unclear how his reasoning would apply to unmarried women whose culture and custom deem it appropriate to go out in public with their heads uncovered. One may presume

---

[57] Irenaeus, *Haer.* 1.8.3; Clement, *Exc.* 44.2.
[58] Clement, *Hyp.* fr. 1 (ed. Stählin): «Διὰ τοὺς ἀγγέλους.» ἀγγέλους φησὶ τοὺς δικαίους καὶ ἐναρέτους. κατακαλυπτέσθω οὖν, ἵνα μὴ εἰς πορνείαν αὐτοὺς σκανδαλίσῃ· οἱ γὰρ ὄντως καὶ ἐν οὐρανοῖς ἄγγελοι καὶ κατακεκαλυμμένην αὐτὴν βλέπουσιν.
[59] Clement's logic implies that either the unvirtuous men in the congregations would not be similarly tempted or, more likely, that their temptation does not matter somehow.
[60] Origen, *Hom. Luc.* 23 (trans. FC).
[61] Origen also considers 1 Cor. 11.10 in *Princ.* 1.6.2, where he tautologically states that there is a rank of authorities 'that may exercise authority over those who need to have authority over their head' (trans. Behr), and allegorically in his commentary on the Song of Songs (35.13), interpreting the woman of 1 Cor. 11.10 as the church.

that the Carthaginian *virgines* could argue that since the righteous men in their communities do not have a problem with uncovered *virgines*, neither should the righteous angels.

Part of the reason for the difference in intertexts between Tertullian and Origin is, as Annette Yoshiko Reed has explained, that the Book of the Watchers of 1 Enoch fell out of favour among elite Christian interpreters over the course of the third century.[62] Nevertheless, Tertullian's basic reading of 1 Cor. 11.10 of the veil as apotropaic against lustful angels has survived in later interpreters, though without any explicit appeal or interaction with 1 Enoch. One example is Basil of Caesarea, who writes in his treatise on virginity as follows:

> So if there is nothing concealed which will not be revealed, on account of all the aforesaid words the one who is virgin and single will provide for her own sinlessness, feeling regard for, not the faces of the remaining men only, but even more, I say, those of the angels seeing everywhere. *For this reason,* he says, *the woman must keep control over her head on account of the angels.* For it is not necessary, even if the virgin is sitting by herself at home alone, because no one of the people is present, to be naked without discrimination. For very much, I say, the nature of the female is tempting for every male nature by itself to be attracted. And on this account not only is it necessary for her, always being suspicious, to be on guard against the abuses of the daemons, invisibly lying wait for us, but also she must, on account of those angels venerable for all, I say, keep control.[63]

In other words, for Basil, a virgin ought to be covered even in private because of the presence of both angels and demons. Like the Cheshire cat, Tertullian's prized intertext for his interpretation of 1 Cor. 11.10 has largely disappeared, but like the smile his basic position has not: even virgins must keep covered. The Carthaginian *virgines* and their supporters would not have agreed.

Conclusion

It is a truism that reception of one text affects our reading of other texts. After all, how can a text be said to be received if it does not have any effect on the receiver? Nevertheless, the particular ways in which reception affects reading are contingent

---

[62] Reed, *Fallen Angels*, 194–205.
[63] My translation of PG 30.737: Εἰ οὖν οὐδέν ἐστι κεκρυμμένον ὃ οὐκ ἀποκαλυφθήσεται, διὰ πάντας τοὺς προειρημένους λόγους ἡ παρθένος καὶ μόνη οὖσα, τῆς ἀναμαρτησίας ἑαυτῆς προνοήσεται, οὐ τὰς τῶν λοιπῶν ἀνθρώπων ὄψεις μόνον, ἀλλὰ πολλῷ πλέον, φημί, τὰς ἑαυτῆς καὶ τῶν ἁπανταχοῦ ὁρώντων ἀγγέλων ἐντρεπομένη. *Διὰ τοῦτο γὰρ, φησὶν, ὀφείλει ἡ γυνὴ ἐξουσίαν ἔχειν ἐπὶ τῆς κεφαλῆς διὰ τοὺς ἀγγέλους.* Οὐ γὰρ δεῖ, κἂν ἐν οἴκῳ μόνη καθέζηται καθ' ἑαυτὴν ἡ παρθένος, διότι μηδεὶς πάρεστι τῶν ἀνθρώπων, ἀδιαφόρως γυμνοῦσθαι. Πολὺ γὰρ, φημὶ, ἐπαγωγὸς ἡ φύσις τοῦ θήλεος, πᾶσαν ἄρρενα φύσιν καθ' ἑαυτῆς ἐπισπάσασθαι. Καὶ οὐ διὰ τοῦτο μόνον φυλάττεσθαι δεῖ τὰς τῶν δαιμόνων ἐπηρείας, ἀοράτως ἐφεδρευούσας ἡμῖν, ἀεὶ ὑποπτεύουσαν, ἀλλὰ καὶ διὰ τοὺς πᾶσιν, φησὶν, αἰδεσίμους ἀγγέλους ἐξουσίαν ἔχειν ὀφείλει.

upon specific readers in specific contexts. In this study, we looked at Tertullian's reading of 1 Cor. 11.10 in light of 1 Enoch, and we have seen that his reception of the latter text is so strong that it affected his application of the New Testament scripture beyond Paul's social imagination, extending even to the habits of unmarried women outside of the church context.

Part 2

The reception of Jewish themes, images and categories

4

'Not like the gentiles who do not know God' (1 Thess. 4.5): The function of Othering and anti-gentile stereotypes of sexual wrongdoing in early Jewish and Christian texts

Christine Gerber[1]

Bashing of gentiles – no problem?

A puzzle in dealing with the parenesis of the Letter to the Ephesians brought me to this question. This puzzling passage in Eph. 4.17–20 provides the motivation for pursuing proper moral conduct by means of a sharp denigration of the gentiles, to whom the addressees had formerly belonged. Their lack of knowledge of God, so the verses claim, leads to moral corruption:[2]

¹⁷ Τοῦτο οὖν λέγω καὶ μαρτύρομαι ἐν κυρίῳ,
μηκέτι ὑμᾶς περιπατεῖν, καθὼς καὶ τὰ ἔθνη περιπατεῖ ἐν ματαιότητι τοῦ νοὸς αὐτῶν,
¹⁸ ἐσκοτωμένοι τῇ διανοίᾳ ὄντες, ἀπηλλοτριωμένοι τῆς ζωῆς τοῦ θεοῦ διὰ τὴν ἄγνοιαν τὴν οὖσαν ἐν αὐτοῖς, διὰ τὴν πώρωσιν τῆς καρδίας αὐτῶν,
¹⁹ οἵτινες ἀπηλγηκότες ἑαυτοὺς παρέδωκαν τῇ ἀσελγείᾳ εἰς ἐργασίαν ἀκαθαρσίας πάσης ἐν πλεονεξίᾳ.
²⁰ Ὑμεῖς δὲ οὐχ οὕτως ἐμάθετε τὸν Χριστόν.

---

[1] I would like to thank May-Britt Melzer and Friederike Haller, as well as Lea Schmitt and Benedikt Skorzenski (Hamburg and Berlin), for their research assistance. I am highly grateful to Dr Dennis Slabaugh (Hamburg) for providing the English translation of this paper.

[2] Impurity and greed are rejected in Eph. 4.17–20; this rejection is affirmed and reinforced in Eph. 5.3–7: Πορνεία, ἀκαθαρσία πᾶσα ἢ πλεονεξία are not only forbidden among the holy, but they should, in fact, not even be addressed amongst them, and those who practice those vices are damned and must be avoided by the holy.

What astonished me about Eph. 4.17–20 was first of all the inconsistency in the use of ἔθνη: while in Eph. 3.1 the fictitious author 'Paul'[3] addresses the recipients of the letter as ἔθνη and thereby identifies them as non-Jews (cf. 2.11–13) and as such in a positive manner as a target group for the message of salvation (3.6, 8), here in 4.17 ἔθνη refers to the others, that is, as μηκέτι implies, to those to whom the addressees no longer belong. Thus it designates the negatively connoted non-believers.[4]

What puzzled me even more was that I found no critical analysis of this deprecating portrayal of the ἔθνη by means of stereotypes. Exegesis, of course, provides important hints for understanding these statements. It is pointed out that both early Jewish and Pauline[5] traditions are processed here. And it is acknowledged that the characterizations as such in general do not apply.[6] The consensus seems to be that the important message in these verses is the so-criticized ethos itself and the assurance of one's own identity through demarcation, and not the vilification of the 'gentiles'.

But, even if this assertion were true, can this explain and justify these denigrating statements? If the true subject was just the ethos, then it would have been sufficient to stigmatize the practices themselves and to explain in detail what is precluded. In addition, the description of the gentiles in Eph. 4.18–19 is obviously exaggerated. Paul in his Letter to the Romans – albeit in the sphere of different rhetorical interests – already attested to the ability of non-Jews to do what the Law requires (Rom. 2.14–15). Can one then exculpate texts like this by reference to their pragmatism, or are they, as rhetorical practice, to be treated as a problem?

While exegesis today – and rightly so! – is sensitive in regard to anti-Jewish remarks and names these as such in order to prevent their perpetuation, it tolerates such polemical statements as in Eph. 4.17–20, which one can designate only as 'anti-Gentilism'. This can be explained easily with two facts, namely that no one today identifies with the gentiles in the negative sense of the text and also that within mainstream Christianity no one applies this description to non-Christian contemporaries. However, in view of the highly virulent debate about the ethics of speech and the production of knowledge

---

[3] Ephesians is considered to be a pseudo-Pauline letter, that is, it also uses Pauline texts; see in detail Michael Gese, *Das Vermächtnis des Apostels: Die Rezeption der paulinischen Theologie im Epheserbrief*, WUNT II 99 (Tübingen: Mohr Siebeck, 1997).

[4] In the *Corpus Paulinum*, ἔθνος serves as an antithesis to Ἰουδαῖος (Rom. 2.24; 3.29; 9.24; 11.11–12; 1 Cor. 1.23; Gal. 2.11–15 and Eph. 3.6) and to Ἰσραήλ (Rom. 9.30–1; 11.25), in the reception of the linguistic usage of the LXX that is received especially in reference to Abraham (Rom. 4.14–15; Gal. 3.8, 14 as an interpretation of Gen. 12.3). Accordingly, the term designates non-Jews, to whom Paul believes himself to be sent (Rom. 1.5, 13; 11.13; 15.16, 18; Gal. 1.16–17; 2.2, 8–9; Eph. 3.1, 8; Col. 1.27, as well as – the only usage at all in the pastoral letters – 1 Tim. 2.7; 3.16; 2 Tim. 4.17); cf. the corresponding address in Rom. 11.13; Eph. 3.1. Only in 1 Cor. 12.2 and Eph. 2.11 (ὑμεῖς τὰ ἔθνη ἐν σαρκί), as well as Eph. 4.17, does it designate the addressees in reference to their pre-Christian period. The designation of those who do not believe in Christ as ἄπιστοι and the like (1 Cor. 6.6; 7.12–15; 2 Cor. 4.4; 6.14–15) can include Jewish persons. However, those designated as ἔθνη in 1 Cor. 5.1, Eph. 4.17 and 1 Thess. 4.5 are specifically non-Jews.

[5] Cf. Tet-Lim N. Yee, *Jews, Gentiles and Ethnic Reconciliation: Paul's Jewish Identity and Ephesians*, SNTSMS 130 (Cambridge: Cambridge University Press, 2005), 40–1. Close to this especially are, on the one hand, Wisdom of Solomon 13–14, and on the other Rom. 1.21–4 (see Gese, *Vermächtnis*, 58–60); see below.

[6] Cf. Ernest Best, *A Critical and Exegetical Commentary on Ephesians*, ICC 39.1 (Edinburgh: Clark, 1998), 424–5.

through hegemonic discourse (in the words of Foucault[7]), and in view of the efficacy of derogatory speech, these forms of speech, too, should be analysed more precisely in regard to their pragmatism and effect.

The question about the content and the function of such statements is part of the complex issue of how we today reconstruct the emergence of Christianity and its relationship to early Judaism (or better, 'Judaisms'), and with which models and analytical or descriptive categories (such as identity and ethnicity and religion) we do this.[8] In characterizing the state of discussion, I dare to formulate only a twofold relativizing tendency: old certainties about the ancient categories (ἔθνος, *genus*, *religio*), the character of Judaism as 'ethnicity' and early Christians' awareness of difference from Judaism have disintegrated. What has emerged is a heightened consciousness of the impact of the categories drawn upon for analysis and description, and the danger of perspectival or anachronistic distortion.

Taking up these considerations, the present paper aims to contribute to the theme of the conference, the reception of Jewish tradition in the social imagination of the early Christians, by offering a case study about the reception of 'gentile-bashing' as the practice of 'Othering'. This occurs from the vantage point of a view of the rhetoric of 'Othering' sharpened by postcolonial theory, which shows that discursive forms and social practices combine indissolubly. The article focuses by way of example on the stereotypical conjunction of the charge of idolatry and sexual wrongdoing (πορνεία, etc.)[9] which has already become visible in Eph. 4.17-20; 5.3-5. For this reason, the article asks why precisely the field of sexual practice is so relevant. Following this, the article provides exemplary texts from Alexandrine Judaism (Pseudo-Aristeas, Joseph and Asenath, Wisdom), and then turns to 1 Thessalonians and Ephesians as exemplary texts which share this stereotypical reproach against the gentiles. The review of the reception includes continuities and changes.

'Othering' as a concept in analysis

Sociological, ethnological and postcolonial theories lend exegesis a depth of focus for the interpretation of the texts and historical processes that have led to the emergence of distinct groups.[10] Analyses that work with the concept of 'identity' have been established for some time. Even if identity is conceived differently according to theoretical background,[11] it is clear that the production of identity is a discourse that clarifies

---

[7] Michel Foucault, *The Archaeology of Knowledge* (New York: Pantheon Books, 1969, repr. 1972), 135-40, 49.
[8] Apart from the many contributions to the 'Parting of the Ways Debate', see e.g. Judith Lieu, *Christian Identity in the Jewish and Graeco-Roman World* (Oxford: Oxford University Press, 2011), as well as the volume of collected texts by David G. Horrell and Katherine M. Hockey (eds), *Ethnicity, Race, Religion: Identities and Ideologies in Early Jewish and Christian Texts, and in Modern Biblical Interpretation* (London: Bloomsbury Publishing PLC, 2018).
[9] This translation of πορνεία is taken from William R. G. Loader, *Making Sense of Sex: Attitudes towards Sexuality in Early Jewish and Christian Literature* (Grand Rapids, MI: Eerdmans, 2013), in view of the dispute over whether 'fornication' really describes the content.
[10] On the problem of the sources and on essentialist approaches, see Lieu, *Christian*, 1-26.
[11] Cf. Christian Strecker, 'Identität im frühen Christentum? Der Identitätsdiskurs und die neutestamentliche Forschung', in *Religionsgemeinschaft und Identität: Prozesse jüdischer und*

self-understanding by using alterity or exclusion, a process that needs the Other in order to assure its own exclusivity.[12] In the reconstruction of the emergence of Christianity, these approaches help against essentialist theses about the 'suchness' of the groups and against little-differentiated explanations on the basis of mirror reading, which interpret the texts solely as a reaction to existing problems. They sharpen the perception of the interdependence of theology and social practice.[13] 'Boundary markers' are understood as a reaction to the fluidity of identities, including the category of the ethnos.[14]

The constructive factor is easily overlooked: differences are not simply given as such but rather receive their discriminating function through the discourse. The postcolonial discourse has especially emphasized that the opposing group, the 'Other', is first of all epistemically 'produced'.[15] Notwithstanding the differences between colonial times and the situation in Antiquity, the postcolonial framework is suitable for revealing the discursive exercise of power in the production of knowledge about the Others and, thereby, of the Others as such. This becomes clear in the example of two epoch-making theoreticians:[16] G. Spivak, indebted to deconstructionism, coined the concept of 'Othering'.[17] Analysing the action of the British colonizers at the beginning of the colonial period in India, she shows how language and symbolic practices ensure a 'power making the subordinate aware of who holds the power, and hence about the powerful producing the other as subordinate'.[18] E. Said, incorporating Foucault's analysis of the discourse of power practices, exposed 'Orientalism' as a discursive practice from a non-reflective and absolutely staid standpoint (the 'Occident'), producing the Other of one's self (the 'Orient') and, to be sure, above all through the use of stereotypes, reduction, distancing and pathologizing. 'Othering can thus be described as a twofold process: the "Others" are constructed through certain practices

---

christlicher Identitätsbildung im Rahmen der Antike, ed. Markus Öhler, BibS(N) 142 (Neukirchen-Vluyn: Neukirchener Theologie, 2013), on the history of the term and the various conceptions.

[12] Cf. esp. Lieu, *Christian*.
[13] Cf. esp. Michael Wolter, 'Identität und Ethos bei Paulus', in *Theologie und Ethos im frühen Christentum. Studien zu Jesus, Paulus und Lukas*, WUNT 236 (Tübingen: Mohr Siebeck, 2009), 121–69.
[14] Following Fredrik Barth, *Ethnic Groups and Boundaries: The Social Organization of Culture Difference*, reissued (Long Grove, IL: Waveland Press, 1969, repr. 1998), whose approach, from a present-day perspective, is nevertheless essentialist. Cf. Lieu, *Christian*, 108–26, on the marking of allegedly immutable boundaries in early Christian texts, and Teresa Morgan, 'Society, Identity and Ethnicity in the Hellenic World', in *Ethnicity, Race, Religion: Identities and Ideologies in Early Jewish and Christian Texts, and in Modern Biblical Interpretation*, ed. David G. Horrell and Katherine M. Hockey (London: Bloomsbury Publishing PLC, 2018), 23–45, in reference to the Hellenic world: there are no fixed criteria for ethnic identity. 'Ethnicity (like identity in general) is always a construct … not necessarily bipolar or adversarial' (27).
[15] Lieu, *Christian*, 269–97, under the keyword 'The Other', emphasizes that the other as a threat must be fenced in, and this specifically means, in early Christianity, adopting the disparagement of the gentiles in Judaism.
[16] On the development of the discourse, see Oscar Thomas-Olalde and Astride Velho, 'Othering and Its Effects – Exploring the Concept', in *Writing Postcolonial Histories of Intercultural Education*, ed. Heike Niedrig and Christian Ydesen, Interkulturelle Pädagogik und postkoloniale Theorie 2 (Frankfurt am Main: Peter Lang D, 2011), 28–34; María do Mar Castro Varela and Nikita Dhawan, *Postkoloniale Theorie: Eine kritische Einführung*, BibS(N) 12 (Bielefeld: Transcript, 2005).
[17] In her essay 'The Rani of Sirmur', cf. Gayatri C. Spivak, 'The Rani of Sirmur: An Essay in Reading the Archives', *HistTh* 24 (1985), 247–72.
[18] Sune Q. Jensen, 'Othering, Identity Formation and Agency', *Qualitative Studies* 2.2 (2011), 65.

of knowledge production which legitimize domination; at the same time, however, this [political, economic and cultural] hegemonic intention makes the resulting epistemological practices appear "plausible" and "useful." '[19]

These few lines will not at all do justice to the contribution of postcolonial studies, but they point to their heuristic valence. And in a process of continual reflection, it remains to investigate whether new essentialisms or dichotomies are produced and others are victimized. One may bear in mind Cataldo's caveat: 'Reading the biblical texts through a post-colonial lens exposes presuppositions ... that are themselves relics or artefacts of an imperialist-minded culture with a heavy hand in shaping the traditional paradigms of modern biblical scholarship.'[20]

In awareness of the limitations resulting from the source situation and from historical distance, at this point three aspects are important:

The discursive production of the others as Others

Texts are not simply descriptive and do not simply portray factual differences. Rather, they produce 'the Other' through speech acts qua discourse as such, that is, as different than one's own self. The others outside the early Jewish and early Christian communities were never a coherent group – neither ethnically, nor religiously, nor in regard to social status or gender. This appears to be a mere platitude, but exegesis still tends to thoughtlessly repeat this conformizing, disparaging manner of speaking.

The rhetoric of Othering

Typical linguistic devices serve in the production of the Others. Accordingly, the use of such devices can expose discursive power. In my observation, the following are especially efficacious:[21]

- Alienating: speech *about* others as 'they' from a 'we' position, but not speech *with* them
- under the premise of a binary opposition (*tertium non datur*) that is conceptualized
- through labeling
- through emphasis on differences
- through generalizations
- and exaggerations.
- The Others are often pathologized as irrational or abnormal.[22]

---

[19] Thomas-Olalde and Velho, 'Othering', 30.
[20] Jeremiah W. Cataldo, 'The Other: Sociological Perspectives in a Post-Colonial Age', in *Imagining the Other and Constructing Israelite Identity in the Early Second Temple Period*, ed. Ehud Ben Zvi, LHBOTS 591 (London: Bloomsbury, 2014), 1–9.
[21] The criteria are based upon my observations, suggested in part by Stephen H. Riggins, 'The Rhetoric of Othering', in *The Language of Politics of Exclusion: Other in Discourse*, ed. S. H. Riggins (Thousand Oaks, CA: Sage, 1997).
[22] Here the use of metaphors is especially effective (see on Eph. 4.17–19); cf. Luise Ahmed, *Bilder von den Anderen*, JAC Ergänzungsband Kleine Reihe 14 (Münster: Aschendorff Verlag, 2016).

- Since ascriptions are neither justified nor substantiated they suggest that actual facts are being presented.
- The use of the present tense generalizes the Others temporally in a kind of 'freezing'.[23]
- While differences are enhanced, possible commonalities are concealed.

The imbalance in power

In the early Jewish-Hellenistic and early Christian texts the external political circumstances are different from those illuminated by the postcolonial 'classics' Spivak and Said. They speak about the Others from a situation of external inferiority: the Jewish diaspora, for example in Alexandria, and the Christ-believers around 50 CE in Thessalonica or around 90 CE in Asia Minor represent a minority. Their acts of interpreting Others did not reach into the social life of those Others. Their portrayals are likely to be also at least a reflex prompted by their own experience of being declared to be 'the Others'.[24] This does not speak against the approach of analysing the texts as the practice of Othering, but rather demands that the production of power relationships in our texts be thought of as more complex.

What is the problem with πορνεία – Why is sexual wrongdoing so important?

The texts of our case study all deal with the connection between false worship of God and sexual practice. The fact that concepts about legitimate sexuality or sexual wrongdoing have a place in the centre of ethical and religious or cultural self-distinction is anything but surprising and valid to the present day. From this, one can deduce just how strongly the judgement of sexuality has been 'naturalized' and ontologized in discourse. It is then all the more important at least to ask why this is so.

This article can touch upon this question only briefly. The meaning of πορνεία and what can be assessed as sexual wrongdoing assumes, of course, the notion of legitimate forms and objects of sexuality. There is, however, not only an extensive, divergent discourse about sexuality in Jewish, Greek, Roman and Christian sources themselves, but this discourse also reveals differences within these cultures that in any case should not be presented as coherent. There is also a discourse about this discourse, which arrives at various assessments about the ideals, practices, divergences and the exertion of influence concerning sexuality.[25] Therefore, as regards the question about

---

[23] Cf. Johannes Fabian, *Time and the Other: How Anthropology Makes Its Object*, repr. (New York: Columbia University Press, 2014), who discusses the use of the present tense in ethnography (80–7): To say 'the x are y' 'freezes' them at a point in time and may even assume their inability to change (81).

[24] The question is, of course, dealt with in gender and political discourses: how do the 'othered' persons react to the othering; what is the impact on their selves? Cf. Stuart Hall, 'New Ethnicities', in *'Race', Culture and Difference*, ed. James Donald (London: Sage, 1992), 252–9.

[25] See, only for the Jewish and Christian discourse within its own time, Holger Tiedemann, *Die Erfahrung des Fleisches: Paulus und die Last der Lust* (Stuttgart: Radius, 1998); Jennifer Wright

the relevance of the concept of πορνεία and 'sexual wrongdoing', only a few general observations and references to texts must be sufficient:

1. The concepts are coined in vague terms. This is true, first of all, for the Greek term πορνεία, which becomes relevant in Jewish and Christian texts, but which has a broad sense of meaning: as legitimately accepted prostitution, but above all as illegitimate forms of sexuality, namely incest, adultery, extramarital sexual intercourse, homosexual intercourse and so on. Other terms used in the context, such as the Latin equivalents *stuprum* and *pudicium*, are no more clear in the extent of their meaning.[26] Since the language is indistinct, the things and concepts designated by it necessarily remain vague.[27] It is equally unclear whether what is not forbidden is actually allowed. Underlining the fact that there is a strict limit and that compliance with this limit is crucial, while at the same time keeping the extent of these limits vague, could oftentimes be a strategy.
2. Sexuality is cross-culturally connected with concepts of legitimacy and deviance.[28] It is, thus, especially suited as a boundary marker. For, regardless of the question of concrete limits, the idea that there is a necessary limitation of relationships and that this limitation must be implemented in practice is generally accepted. This is different, for example, in regard to the concept of 'idolatry' or food taboos, since the inherent denigration of those is not generally shared by other cultures.
3. The significance of the discourse about legitimate sexuality also lies in the fact that sexuality is never a theoretical question: 'Sex is not an optional extra. It is part of what and who we are.'[29] Sexuality concerns the relation to one's self and the most intimate relationships: the body, power relationships in families, and marriage rules. But it is also part of the discursive production of social hierarchies and gender orders, and even in violent form a part of the conduct of war. Community is founded upon sexual relationships; in the discourse about sexuality, the limits of permitted relationships are negotiated.

Knust, *Abandoned to Lust: Sexual Slander and Ancient Christianity*, Gender, Theory, and Religion (New York: Columbia University Press, 2006); Kathy L. Gaca, *The Making of Fornication: Eros, Ethics and Political Reform in Greek Philosophy and Early Christianity*, HCS 39 (Berkeley: University of California Press, 2003); as well as the extensive studies by William R.G. Loader, see nn. 9, 33.

[26] See Renate Kirchhoff, *Die Sünde gegen den eigenen Leib: Studien zu pornē und porneia in 1 Kor 6,12–20 und dem sozio-kulturellen Kontext der paulinischen Adressaten*, SUNT 18 (Göttingen: Vandenhoeck & Ruprecht, 1994), 18–37, on the semantics of πορνεία and the varying use in pagan and Jewish, or Jewish-Christian, texts; on the likewise changing significance of the Latin equivalents, see Jane F. Gardner, *Frauen im antiken Rom: Familie, Alltag, Recht* (München: C.H. Beck, 1995), 118–36.

[27] Gaca, *Making*: 'To seek from their texts what fornication means and why it is wrong is like following Josef K in his quest for a straight answer from the courts' (19). The literature – primary and secondary – is legion here, too, and cannot be assessed here.

[28] On the use of the accusation of fornication in ancient invective as well as in anti-heretical discourses in emerging Christianity, see Knust, *Abandoned*. The charge of fornication also has its part in the denigration in colonial discourses: colonies are considered to be breeding sites for sexual deviance, perceived with a mixture of abhorrence and interest, and at the same time for the ethical domestication of the others (see Castro Varela and Dhawan, *Postkoloniale Theorie*, 115–16; cf., in addition, Ann Laura Stoler, *Carnal Knowledge and Imperial Power: Race and the Intimate in Colonial Rule*, repr. (Berkeley: University of California Press, 2010)).

[29] Loader, *Making*, 1.

For the persons who have their bodies at their own command the option of following or transgressing rules concerning sexuality forms the space for giving expression to the personal ethos. However, the fact that this is not at all an option for everyone, but rather only for free men, is ignored too easily in exegesis.[30]

4. In the Jewish-Christian tradition, sexuality and the discourse thereon has been religiously charged 'since Adam and Eve', because commands and prohibitions are directly connected with God's creation, and they concern the holiness of the entire people (cf. only Leviticus 18 and 1 Corinthians 5). Leviticus 18 assumes that the people of God differ in sexual practice from the surrounding nations and this assumption is a fixed component of the determination of identity in early Judaism. For example, Josephus within his epitome of the Law, *Apion* 2.190–220, represents sexual and marital ideas as specifically Jewish – a claim that according to our knowledge of the sources can be valid only to a small degree. In *Apion* 2.199–201 he limits legitimate sexuality to heterosexual sexual intercourse, only to married couples, and only for the sake of procreation. The dissociation from homosexual practices is mentioned repeatedly as a specific characteristic of Judaism.[31] But it should not be overlooked that there were Greek and Roman parallels to all of the sexual ideals mentioned above.[32]

5. The firm connection between πορνεία and idolatry expresses a fear that illegitimate sexuality is not only a problem in and of itself but that it is inherently linked with another danger, namely that it 'spills over' into something else that is even worse. The internal connection can be unfolded in both directions: sexual wrongdoings lead to idolatry (see T. Reub. 4.6–7) and the other way around (e.g. T. Dan 5.5).[33] The metaphor of idol worship as whoring fixes this connection.[34]

6. The ideal of endogamy justifies and reflects this connection.[35] This is made clear in the Torah in Exod. 34.14–16 and Deut. 7.1–5, and is illustrated via the

---

[30] Gaca, *Making*, 5–6, correctly criticizes Foucault for a purely individualistic, male-oriented view of the moral subject.

[31] Lev. 18.22; 20.13; Wis. 14.26 (see below); Ep. Arist. 152 (see below); Sib. Or. 3.185–6, 594–600; see on the broad treatment of the theme, Loader, *Making*, 131–40. Cf. Matthias Konradt, *Gericht und Gemeinde: Eine Studie zur Bedeutung und Funktion von Gerichtsaussagen im Rahmen der paulinischen Ekklesiologie und Ethik im 1 Thess und 1 Kor*, BZNW 117 (Berlin: de Gruyter, 2003), 106, with footnote 484 for further texts.

[32] Presumably, one can also find examples outside of the Jewish-Christian tradition for every position or invective (e.g. Plutarch, Musonius, but also gossip in the lives of the emperors by Suetonius); exemplary is Tiedemann, *Erfahrung*, 252–66.

[33] Cf. on the Testament of the Twelve Patriarchs, William R. G. Loader, *Philo, Josephus, and the Testaments on Sexuality: Attitudes towards Sexuality in the Writings of Philo and Josephus and in the Testaments of the Twelve Patriarchs*, Attitudes towards Sexuality in Judaism and Christianity in the Hellenistic Greco-Roman Era (Grand Rapids, MI: Eerdmans, 2011), 368–435, and, along with the texts treated below, esp. Sib Or. 3.573–600, see William R. G. Loader, *The Pseudepigrapha on Sexuality: Attitudes towards Sexuality in Apocalypses, Testaments, Legends, Wisdom, and Related Literature*, Attitudes towards Sexuality in Judaism and Christianity in the Hellenistic Greco-Roman Era (Grand Rapids, MI: Eerdmans, 2011), 59–60.

[34] See especially Jer. 2.20 LXX and Hos. 4.12 LXX; cf. Lev. 17.7; 20.5–6; Num. 14.33; 15.39; 25.1; Deut. 31.16; Judg. 2.17; 8.27, 33; 1 Chron. 5.25; 2 Chron. 21.11, 13; Ps. 73.27; 106.39; Jer. 3.1–10; Ezek. 16.20–43.

[35] On this question, see Aliyah El Mansy, *Exogame Ehen: Die traditionsgeschichtlichen Kontexte von 1 Kor 7,12-16*, BWANT 206 (Stuttgart: W. Kohlhammer, 2015), who shows that there were various

marriages of the Israelite heroes with foreign women.[36] The polemics against the mésalliances of Solomon (1 Kgs 11.1–13) or Ahab (1 Kgs 16.31–3) are paradigmatic. According to Ezra 9–10, the scribe Ezra, after returning from exile, demands the separation of marriages already existing with foreign women. The virulence of the theme of mixed marriages in diaspora Judaism[37] is shown in the treatments of the biblical narratives that qualify or overwrite the marriages with non-Jewish women,[38] or add their conversion to Judaism later.[39] And it finds its expression in the narratives like those in the Book of Tobit (see especially Tob. 4.13) and the romance of Joseph and Asenath (see below).

This short, certainly simplifying survey shows that the relationship between belief in God, monolatry or monotheism, and sexuality is inscribed deeply in the – if this essentializing terminology is allowed – 'self-understanding' of ancient Judaism, and that this is expressed (ideally) in specific practices and relationships and boundaries. The concept of religiously justified endogamy is an effective boundary marker that takes clear limits to membership for granted and thereby at the same time essentializes them. The high esteem in which endogamy was held is of special interest for the question about the reception of the *topoi* in early Christianity. It is crucial that the ideal of endogamy was not upheld in the first Christian congregations: one could assume that the number of mixed marriages was not too small in the first Christian congregations (see below).

The *Topos* of theological and sexual difference between Jews and gentiles in early Jewish writings as rhetoric of Othering

The boundaries of legitimate sexuality often play a role in the early Jewish texts that implicitly or explicitly assume the encounter with non-Jewish people.[40] In connection with the critique of idolatry, they serve the process of Othering: the deprecatory demarcation over against others who become at the same time tangible and distanced as Others. Three examples from the Alexandrine diaspora show how this, with all the stereotypes, can serve different goals.

---

positions in Jewish texts, but that the adoption of the belief in God, as in Ruth, was always the condition of a mixed marriage.
[36] Here, specific nations are named, e.g. Judah and a Canaanite woman, Gen. 38.2; Moses and the Midianite woman, Exod. 2.21.
[37] Cf. John M. G. Barclay, *Jews in the Mediterranean Diaspora: From Alexander to Trajan (323 BCE– 117 CE)*, repr., HCS 33 (Berkeley: University of California Press, 2010), 107–8, 410–12: One was concerned not least of all with the continuance of the tradition through the children. The virulence of endogamy for Philo (see Loader, *Philo*, 195–9) and Josephus (ibid., 345–7) shows that it was a current theme also in the first century after Christ.
[38] See the abundance of examples in Loader, *Making*, 81–8.
[39] Cf. ibid., 88–91.
[40] Cf., on the texts of diaspora Judaism as varied reference to the environment, Barclay, *Jews*.

The Letter of Aristeas

The Letter of Aristeas (second half of the second century BCE),[41] written as a fictional report of the non-Jew Aristeas from Alexandria to his brother Philocrates, transmits a summary of the laws by the High Priest Eleazar (Ep. Arist. 130–71) within the framework of the report about the translation of the Torah in Alexandria. The text clearly aims at presenting the Jews as a philosophically superior, peaceful people recognized as such by the distinguished Greeks of Alexandria, above all by the King Ptolemy Philadelphos.[42] Here, we consider only the assessment of the other religions and their sexual morality and, therewith, in a certain partiality, Jewish self-distinction.

In Ep. Arist. 134–8 Eleazar depicts Moses as keeping his people from believing in a multiplicity of gods, as all other peoples do, and from worshipping images of stone or wood, that is, something made by human hands, or even animals, like the Egyptians who are mentioned by name. This kind of worship is vain and empty (ματαίως Ep. Arist. 134, κενὸν καὶ μάταιον, Ep. Arist. 135). Against this, Moses has erected regulations of the Law like a fence – together with Ep. Arist. 142 the most important linguistic reference in the sources for this popular boundary metaphor! – and, to be sure, this fence serves not only to prevent such vain worship but also to prevent mingling and contamination with the peoples who practice this worship, thereby ensuring that the Jewish people will be 'worshipping the one and almighty God above the whole creation'. As it says in Ep. Arist. 139:

συνθεωρήσας οὖν ἕκαστα σοφὸς ὢν ὁ νομοθέτης, ὑπὸ θεοῦ κατεσκευασμένος εἰς ἐπίγνωσιν τῶν ἁπάντων, περιέφραξεν ἡμᾶς ἀδιακόποις χάραξι καὶ σιδηροῖς τείχεσιν, ὅπως μηθενὶ τῶν ἄλλων ἐθνῶν ἐπιμισγώμεθα κατὰ μηδέν, ἁγνοὶ καθεστῶτες κατὰ σῶμα καὶ κατὰ ψυχήν, ἀπολελυμένοι ματαίων δοξῶν, τὸν μόνον θεὸν καὶ δυνατὸν σεβόμενοι παρ' ὅλην τὴν πᾶσαν κτίσιν.

This fence leads to a separation in various senses ('what we eat, or drink, or touch, or hear, or see', Ep. Arist. 142), and it certainly includes the avoidance of sexual relations with those who believe in the gods.[43] Eleazar emphasizes the necessity of this distinction in Ep. Arist. 151 (παρὰ πάντας ἀνθρώπους διεστάλμεθα), and he explicates *in sexualibus* specifically as a defiling mingling.[44] Even though he does not ascribe this transgression to all others, but only to 'most other men', the point is made abundantly clear, that is, 'we have been kept separate from these' (Ep. Arist. 152):

οἱ γὰρ πλείονες τῶν λοιπῶν ἀνθρώπων ἑαυτοὺς μολύνουσιν ἐπιμισγόμενοι, συντελοῦντες μεγάλην ἀδικίαν, καὶ χῶραι καὶ πόλεις ὅλαι σεμνύνονται ἐπὶ τούτοις. οὐ μόνον γὰρ προάγουσι τοὺς ἄρσενας,[45] ἀλλὰ καὶ τεκούσας ἔτι δὲ θυγατέρας μολύνουσαν. ἡμεῖς δὲ ἀπὸ τούτων διεστάλμεθα.

---

[41] Cf. George W. E. Nickelsburg and Michael E. Stone, *Early Judaism: Texts and Documents on Faith and Piety*, rev. edn (Minneapolis, MN: Fortress Press, 2009), 75–80.
[42] Cf. Barclay, *Jews*, 138–50, on the intention of the entire text.
[43] With Loader, *Pseudepigrapha*, 432.
[44] Cf. ibid., 433.
[45] It is an open question whether προάγουσι τοὺς ἄρσενας refers to same-sex relations or specifically male prostitutes (cf. ibid., 506: 'procuring males').

Although there is no direct connection between the worship of idols by 'most other men' and their promiscuous practices, this connection is insinuated by the use of the term 'mingling' (ἐπιμίσγω Ep. Arist. 139; 152).

In the cited passage Eleazar applies the rhetoric of Othering when he speaks about 'them' from a 'we' position, but not with them (although the narrative setting would have allowed for this). Different forms of idol worship are mentioned and criticized. There are, to be sure, differences in degree, but the basic problem is the worship of the creature (Ep. Arist. 136-9). Also, even if learned Greeks could join in this critique of the idol cult,[46] worshipping the one God is claimed as specifically Jewish. Thus originates the binary opposition of 'we' and οἱ λοιποὶ παρ' ἡμᾶς ἄνθρωποι (Ep. Arist. 152, cf. 151). Their conduct is branded as foolish, empty and without understanding. The description 'freezes' them via present tense and uses stereotypes, serving the process of pathologization. While differences are emphasized, commonalities – which definitely may have existed[47] – are not explicitly sought.

If we interpret Eleazar's speech as Othering, then not only does it draw a boundary, but it constructs the others as Others, thereby powerfully classifying them as 'subordinate'. On the one hand, this lies contrary to the situation of the Jews of Alexandria, who are presented as a minority and, in part, as an enslaved group (Ep. Arist. 11-15). On the other hand, the powerfully produced difference between the Jews and their 'subordinate' other counterparts is confirmed by the fictitious situation. It is the mouths of the non-Jew Aristeas and the Ptolemaic King Ptolemy Philadelphos who utter the high esteem for the Jewish idea of God, the laws and the Temple, as well as the High Priest Eleazar.[48] One could even learn from the example of the fictitious author 'Aristeas', who argues for the release of the Jewish prisoners, because he, exactly opposite to Eleazar's strategy of Othering, points out a commonality, namely that all worship the same one God and creator under different names (cf. Ep. Arist. 16).

These observations draw attention to an important aspect: Othering as a power of interpretation assumes a universe, a world in which this power of interpretation can claim validity. In the narrative world of the Letter of Aristeas, this power of interpretation lies with the Alexandrine Greeks. They, so it is told, look with interest and admiration upon the Jewish writings and laws and also Jerusalem. Within this fictitious world of acknowledgement, Jewish Othering can become effective as a power of interpretation and can make the others into a homogeneous subordinate Other vis-à-vis the Jews themselves. Remarkably, according to the fiction of the text, those who thus become subordinate Others themselves accept their culture as subordinate (cf. Ep. Arist. 235; 321-2). This skewed situation, however, remains implicit and is smoothed over by statements which praise the Greek παιδεία of the Jews (cf. Ep. Arist. 121-2) and emphasize mutual respect.[49] What remains are clear boundaries: 'The strategy ... is to

---

[46] Cf. ibid., 430.
[47] Cf. ibid., 434-5, on intersections with Greek ethics; remarks about 'moderation and self-control' that update Stoic ideas are to be added here (see ibid., 437-8).
[48] This fiction is peculiar in revealing 'how certain Jews wished themselves to be perceived by non-Jews and on what basis they wished their relationships to be conducted'; see Barclay, *Jews*, 139.
[49] Cf., ibid., 141-2, on the expressions of mutual respect, which, however, primarily the Greeks, or rather the Alexandrians, pay to the Jews, and on εὐσέβεια towards God as a commonly shared value.

illustrate Gentile recognition of Jewish religion, but that does not mean that Jews also recognize the validity of Gentile worship.'[50]

Joseph and Asenath

According to biblical tradition, Joseph in Egypt is the Other per se. From Gen. 41.45, one could even conclude that he has assimilated to the dominant culture, since he has been given an Egyptian name and has married Asenath, a priest's daughter. It is interesting to see how the novelistic narrative of Joseph and Asenath,[51] probably originating in the centuries around the turn of the era, succeeds in reversing the relationships by making Asenath the 'Other' and by 'naturalizing' specific Jewish aspects. For while the Letter of Aristeas only marginally implies the ideal of inner-Jewish endogamy, here in Joseph and Asenath it is invoked.[52] Endogamy (and dietary laws) – the occasion for the stereotypical charge of misanthropy against the Jews[53] – is made narratively plausible by way of identifying and filling a gap in the biblical text: Joseph married Asenath only after she had converted to believing in the living God. And even though this takes place in the world of the Egyptian priest Pentephres, Joseph has the power to play his role as the 'Other' in such a way that it is not he but rather the others who are subordinate. This becomes clear in the development of Asenath: she reviles Joseph because he is 'foreign' (ἀνὴρ ἀλλογενής), a refugee, someone who has been sold, and a shepherd's son from Canaan, an adulterer and an effeminate interpreter of dreams (Jos. Asen. 4.9–10) – but only until she sees him. Joseph distances himself from Asenath without being a subordinate 'Other': he sits, a highly symbolic gesture, on a throne and eats alone, since to eat with the Egyptians would be an abomination to him (Jos. Asen. 7.1[54]), and he leaves the court just in time to keep the Sabbath (Jos. Asen. 9.5). His power rests on his unearthly beauty (Jos. Asen. 6.4), which not only makes him the ideal son-in-law but also leads to the haughty daughter Asenath (Jos. Asen. 2.1) falling in love with him and recognizing her misguided life.

The entire novel juxtaposes the living God and the mute and dead idols (Jos. Asen. 8.5; 11.7–8; 12.5) that surround Asenath (Jos. Asen. 2.3; 3.6). The worship of idols

---

[50] Ibid., 143.
[51] Joseph and Asenath is quoted here according to the 'long text' in the reconstruction by U. B. Fink; see Eckart Reinmuth (ed.), *Joseph und Aseneth*, SAPERE 15 (Tübingen: Mohr Siebeck, 2009), 56–129. On introductory questions, especially the difficult dating, see Manuel Vogel, 'Einführung', in Reinmuth, *Joseph und Aseneth*, 3–31; I refer here only to the first part of the narrative, Jos. Asen. 1–21.
[52] The propagation of endogamy or conversion of the 'strange' marriage partner appears as an essential concern of the text; cf. Vogel, 'Einführung', 27–8; Eckart Reinmuth, 'Joseph und Aseneth: Beobachtungen zur erzählerischen Gestaltung', in Reinmuth, *Joseph und Aseneth*, 152–3; Karl-Wilhelm Niebuhr, 'Ethik und Tora: Zum Toraverständnis in *Joseph und Aseneth*', in Reinmuth, *Joseph und Aseneth*, 196–7, 200–1.
[53] Cf. John M. G. Barclay, 'Hostility to Jews as Cultural Construct: Egyptian, Hellenistic and Early Christian Paradigms', in *Josephus und das Neue Testament: Wechselseitige Wahrnehmungen. II. Internationales Symposium zum Corpus Judaeo-Hellenisticum. 25.-28. Mai 2006, Greifswald*, ed. Christfried Böttrich and Jens Herzer, WUNT I 209 (Tübingen: Mohr Siebeck, 2012); see Tacitus, *Hist.* 5.5, Josephus, *Apion* 2.148 and others.
[54] See the subtle overwriting of the statement from Gen. 43.32, that it is an abomination for the Egyptians (likewise βδέλυγμα) to eat with the Hebrews (with Barclay, *Jews*, 208).

is pathologized via the gods' association with darkness, death and so on, their being combated by God, and their depiction as 'foreign' (ἀλλότριος; cf. Jos. Asen. 11.7). Joseph is mindful of his father Jacob's warnings of companionship with foreign women (γυναῖκες ἀλλότριαι Jos. Asen. 7.5). The gesture of preventing Asenath's kiss in Jos. Asen. 8.5–7 powerfully expresses his rejection. When Asenath desires to approach Joseph, he keeps her at arm's length and declares, in a fine example of 'mansplaining', that such closeness is permitted only among the God-fearing within the family; cf. Jos. Asen. 8.5–6:

> οὐκ ἔστι προσῆκον ἀνδρὶ θεοσεβεῖ, ὃς εὐλογεῖ τῷ στόματι αὐτοῦ τὸν θεὸν τὸν ζῶντα καὶ ἐσθίει ἄρτον εὐλογημένον ζωῆς καὶ πίνει ποτήριον εὐλογημένον ἀθανασίας καὶ χρίεται χρίσματι εὐλογημένῳ ἀφθαρσίας, φιλῆσαι γυναῖκα ἀλλοτρίαν, ἥτις εὐλογεῖ τῷ στόματι αὐτῆς εἴδωλα νεκρὰ καὶ κωφὰ καὶ ἐσθίει ἐκ τῆς τραπέζης αὐτῶν ἄρτον ἀγχόνης καὶ πίνει ἐκ τῆς σπονδῆς αὐτῶν ποτήριον ἐνέδρας καὶ χρίεται χρίσματι ἀπωλείας.

Not only marriage and sexual relationship but even a kiss, like the ones that are exchanged between family members, is unseemly. The impossibility of even a kiss is made dependent upon the mouth of the woman, because it is by her mouth that her misguided relationship to God manifests itself through praying, eating and drinking – it is thus written into her body.[55] This massive act of Othering specifically targets the Egyptian culture, which Asenath represents.[56]

However, this act of Othering starts a process in which Asenath arrives at a rejection of the cult of idols through the encounter with Joseph and is transformed by a long rite of passage including self-dissociation, debasement and repentance (chs 10–17). She does not remain the 'Other' but, rather, by confessing the one living God, becomes the 'daughter of the Highest' (Jos. Asen. 15.7). The fact that her family acknowledges Joseph together with his God from the very beginning (Jos. Asen. 3.3–4; 4.7; 5.7) and that, at the end, the pair is married by Pharaoh (Jos. Asen. 21.2–9) tarnishes the narrative logic.[57] However, this acknowledgement creates a narrative space where the Jewish man can be the 'Other', the alien, in the view of Asenath, while still representing his culture as superior and desirable. Joseph and Asenath thus resorts to a sexist concept in order to strengthen the Othering: the *topos* of the dangerous 'foreign woman'. The good news from Joseph and Asenath is that a happy end with the right man is possible.

Wisdom of Solomon 13–15

The last example of gentile-bashing comes from the book of Wisdom from Alexandria that was handed down under Solomon's name. This text is probably somewhat older

---

[55] Cf. Reinmuth, 'Joseph', 149–57, on exclusions.
[56] Cf. Jürgen K. Zangenberg, '*Joseph und Aseneths* Ägypten: Oder: Von der Domestikation einer "gefährlichen" Kultur', in Reinmuth, *Joseph und Aseneth*, 183–5.
[57] Asenath's own statement, that her family hates her for the destruction of the gods (11.7), fits with what would be expected within the narrative logic, but nowhere in the story does the family actually make this statement.

than the letters of Paul[58] and deserves mention since it provides one of the strongest critiques of idolatry.[59] The language and arguments show Greek education. Though the Jewish origin is not explicit, it is visible via allusions, for example to King Solomon as the author.[60] The critique of worshipping idols manifests itself in a concentrically structured excursus in Wis. 13.1–15.19:[61] In contrast to a rather tolerant judgement of the veneration of the stars in Wis. 13.1–9, Wis. 15.14–19 strictly rejects the worship of animals, in the context of the overarching theme of animal plagues directed against the Egyptians (Wis. 11.15; 12.27; 16.1). Within this framework, Wis. 13.10–15.13 offers a detailed critique, indeed even, in part, an ironic treatment, of the worship of idols: the criticism of the manufacture of idols from wood (Wis. 13.10–19) and by potters (Wis. 15.7–13) contrasts with addresses directed to God, who preserves ships at sea (Wis. 14.1–10, in response to the keyword 'wood') and who accompanies 'us' with His forbearance (Wis. 15.1–6). In the centre of the concentric structure, Wis. 14.11–31 presents an analysis of the origin of idols – the veneration of images that represent someone who is absent – and of the consequences of idol worship (vv. 15–21). However, the core of the problem is the profanation of the unutterable name of God (Wis. 14.21b).[62] Moral failure ensues out of this lack of knowledge of God. This connection is especially important and, like a maxim, it frames the section in Wis. 14.12 (ἀρχὴ γὰρ πορνείας ἐπίνοια εἰδώλων) and 14.27 (ἡ γὰρ τῶν ἀνωνύμων εἰδώλων θρησκεία παντὸς ἀρχὴ κακοῦ).

The essence of evil (πορνεία, κακός) comes to light in a carefully composed catalogue of twenty-two vices.[63] The list contains all possible social transgressions that are also condemned outside of Judaism. However, in v. 25, the Decalogue is echoed as well.

²³ ἢ γὰρ τεκνοφόνους τελετὰς ἢ κρύφια μυστήρια ἢ ἐμμανεῖς ἐξάλλων θεσμῶν κώμους ἄγοντες

²⁴ οὔτε βίους οὔτε γάμους καθαροὺς ἔτι φυλάσσουσιν ἕτερος δ' ἕτερον ἢ λοχῶν ἀναιρεῖ ἢ νοθεύων ὀδυνᾷ

²⁵ πάντα δ' ἐπιμὶξ ἔχει αἷμα καὶ φόνος κλοπὴ καὶ δόλος φθορά ἀπιστία τάραχος ἐπιορκία

---

[58] On the dating at the turn of the era, see Karl-Wilhelm Niebuhr, 'Einführung in die Schrift', in Niebuhr, *Sapientia Salomonis (Weisheit Salomos)*, 30–3.
[59] 'One of the most sustained attacks on Gentile religiosity which we have from the pen of a Diaspora Jew', Barclay, *Jews*, 186, and Wisdom 13–15.
[60] Cf. Niebuhr, 'Einführung', 15–17.
[61] The structure and interpretation essentially follows Luca Mazzinghi, *Weisheit*, IECOT 21 (Stuttgart: W. Kohlhammer, 2018). On the reception of philosophical traditions, cf. Karl-Wilhelm Niebuhr, 'Die *Sapientia Salomonis* im Kontext hellenistisch-römischer Philosophie', in Niebuhr, *Sapientia Salomonis (Weisheit Salomos)*, 246–56.
[62] Cf. Mazzinghi, *Weisheit*, 375; profanation means that the title κύριος, which corresponds to the Tetragramm, was used in a profane sense for many divinities in the Greek world; the author omits its use in this excursus.
[63] The list corresponds to the number of letters in the inverted Hebrew alphabet, starting with τ (τεκνοφόνους τελετάς), ending with α (ἀσέλγεια); with ibid., 376–7.

²⁶ θόρυβος ἀγαθῶν χάριτος ἀμνηστία ψυχῶν μιασμός⁶⁴ γενέσεως ἐναλλαγή⁶⁵ γάμων ἀταξία⁶⁶ μοιχεία καὶ ἀσέλγεια.

This central passage, Wis. 14.11-31, also uses the rhetoric of Othering in that it speaks about 'them' and not with them. The catalogue (Wis. 14.23-9) uses the present tense ('freezing'). It relies on generalizations, assertions and a pathologizing, indeed, criminalizing, list of vices. The differences between the various forms of idol worship, Greek, Roman or Egyptian, while definitely addressed in the context, are minimized. The result is a binary opposition between the gentiles and the Jews.

However, in comparison with the other texts, there are conspicuous differences: first of all, there is no 'labelling'; practices, rather than human beings, are disparaged (cf. Wis. 14.12, 27). And while this is not the case in this central passage, the remainder of the excursus contains arguments regarding why the lack of knowledge of God leads to the production and veneration of idols.⁶⁷ Finally, the list of vices is understandable irrespective of cultural background. And in relationship to the number of vices, the proportion of the criminalized sexual offenses is small, but they carry special emphasis as they bring the list to a close.⁶⁸ The sexual offenses are not specified explicitly and do not echo the LXX.⁶⁹ Wis. 14.23-4 places the implied sexual offenses much more in the context of orgiastic cults.⁷⁰

While Othering undoubtedly disparages the Others, the critique focuses on idolatry itself and contrasts it to the veneration of the true God. The text, interpreted as a discourse of Othering, relies on the knowledge of these divergent practices and worshippers in order to manufacture the Others as subordinate. Knowledge justifies the dominance that is ascribed to God Himself here. It is remarkable that interpersonal relationships with the Others are not even mentioned.⁷¹ The discourse has created a distance and asymmetry between Jewish people and all the others, to the extent that relationships, such as intermarriage, no longer merit discussion.

---

⁶⁴ The expression is found already in Plato; cf. ibid., 378.
⁶⁵ This presumably means same-sex relations (with Loader, *Pseudepigrapha*, 421).
⁶⁶ This 'could refer to incestuous marriage' (ibid., 421), but it is not precise.
⁶⁷ This somewhat 'more relaxed' attitude is reflected in the debate around whether a cultural antagonism or even cultural aggression would be recognizable in Wisdom (so Barclay, *Jews*, 181-92; with him Trent A. Rogers, *God and the Idols: Representations of God in 1 Corinthians 8-10*, WUNT II 427 (Tübingen: Mohr Siebeck, 2016), 60-2) or whether Wisdom, despite its polemical thrust in the above passages, displays a high level of convergence with Greek culture, meaning that the Jews and Greeks in Alexandria shared a degree of contempt towards the Egyptian religiosity (so John J. Collins, *Jewish Wisdom in the Hellenistic Age* (Edinburgh: T&T Clark, 1997), 212-13; John J. Collins, *Between Athens and Jerusalem: Jewish Identity in the Hellenistic Diaspora*, 2nd edn, The Biblical Resource Series (Grand Rapids, MI: Eerdmans, 2000), 195-202).
⁶⁸ So Loader, *Pseudepigrapha*, 421.
⁶⁹ Cf. ibid., 398-426, on the understanding of sexuality. In the first part of the text, the sexual morality of Wisdom is unfolded, but not in reference to the idol worship.
⁷⁰ Cf. Mazzinghi, *Weisheit, ad loc.*
⁷¹ Rogers, *God*, 95.

Dissociation from the gentiles in the Pauline letters

It is only a small step from Wisdom 13–15 to the New Testament, since, after all, the text or its theology influenced Paul himself (see below). The figure of Othering against non-believers[72] is also used within the New Testament. However, since the 'nations' were included into the mission, the boundary shifted (cf. Eph. 2.14–15 with Ep. Arist. 139; 142!). Out of this shift arises the need for clarifications about life together in the congregations, above all in mixed congregations. Clarifications with relevance for daily life concern the question of commensuality (Gal. 2.11–16; cf. Acts 15.20, 29), the question of eating flesh offered to idols (1 Corinthians 8), the participation in cults (1 Corinthians 10), but also in the question of legitimate and illegitimate sexuality (see esp. 1 Corinthians 5–7). In contrast to early Judaism, however, some letters reckon with mixed marriages (cf. 1 Cor. 5.1; 7.12–16; Heb. 13.4; 1 Pet. 3.1–3; but see also 1 Cor. 7.39).[73]

'Not like the gentiles', 1 Thess. 4.3–8

1 Thessalonians is of particular interest, since, as an authentic letter, it is addressed to non-Jewish people who are not fictitious. They are described as 'turned to God from idols, to serve a living and true God' (1 Thess. 1.9).[74] However, nowhere are they designated as ἔθνη or something analogous, but rather as ἀδελφοί (1 Thess. 1.4; 2.1), as the elect (1 Thess. 1.4) and so on.

On the one hand, dissociations that one can conceive of as Othering mark the social situation of the addressees, who experience hardships (θλῖψις κτλ, 1 Thess. 1.6; 3.4, 7) as a consequence of their recent conversion. These hardships presumably include social marginalization, which can be understood as being othered. On the other hand, the rhetorical means of Othering are also used in the sharp invective directed against Judeans in 1 Thess. 2.14–16:[75] speech about others in the third person (in contrast to 'we', vv. 15 and 16, and 'you', vv. 13 and 14), as well as the construction of binary oppositions that is even doubled by means of the mimesis formula: the congregations of God in Judaea and 'we' versus the 'the Judeans' and 'you' and 'your compatriots'. Since the charges remain without any justification they appear to be above all doubt. By means of general accusations, οἱ Ἰουδαῖοι are stylized as Others. It is remarkable that in this juxtaposition the gentiles (τὰ ἔθνη) stand 'between the lines': they are not part of

---

[72] Cf. Col. 3.5–11 (without mention of the ἔθνη); 1 Pet. 4.1–6; cf. Rev. 2.14, 20–23.
[73] On the acceptance of mixed marriages by Paul, see El Mansy, *Ehen*, 245–68. A widow who marries should 'do so only in the Lord' (1 Cor. 7.39), but in an existing mixed marriage the believer should not initiate a separation (1 Cor. 7.12–17). 2 Cor. 6.14 could contain a negative assessment of mixed marriages, but hardly require their separation (see William R. G. Loader, *The New Testament on Sexuality*, Attitudes towards Sexuality in Judaism and Christianity in the Hellenistic Greco-Roman Era (Grand Rapids, MI: Eerdmans, 2012), 222–6, *ad loc*).
[74] On the conditions of formation presumed in the following, cf. Stefan Schreiber, *Der erste Brief an die Thessalonicher*, ÖTK 13,1 (Gütersloh: Gütersloher Verlagshaus, 2014), 41–59.
[75] On the analysis, the origins of the charges stemming from internal Jewish self-criticism and the anti-Judaism of Antiquity and the problems with the passage, cf. ibid., 148–71.

the 'we' or 'you' but rather the object of attention of 'us' – they are among the ones on whom salvation is to be bestowed through proclamation, exactly that which the Others seek to prevent (1 Thess. 2.16a). This changes in 1 Thess. 4.5.

'To please God' (θεῷ ἀρέσκειν, 1 Thess. 2.15b) becomes the positive standard of ethical action in the parenesis that was taught before and is inculcated again in the second part of the letter (1 Thess. 4.1). 1 Thess. 4.3–8 stands at the centre of our interest; this passage begins with a programmatic presentation of the 'will of God',[76] it sharpens sexual-ethical standards and it works with the dissociation from τὰ ἔθνη τὰ μὴ εἰδότα τὸν θεόν: they are currently the 'Others'. In contrast to Eph. 4.17–24 (cf. 1 Cor. 6.11; Col. 3.7), 1 Thess. 4.3–8 does not focus on the fact that at an earlier time in their lives the addressees had conducted themselves in the same manner.[77] There is no danger of the addressees measuring such allegations against reality and contradicting them as misrepresentations.

Apotreptic admonitions (vv. 3b; 5a; 6a) frame a protreptic one (v. 4) and conclude with a threat of judgement (v. 6), which is in turn justified with the reference to the calling to holiness and to God's claim on the life of the believers (vv. 7–8).

³ Τοῦτο γάρ ἐστιν θέλημα τοῦ θεοῦ, ὁ ἁγιασμὸς ὑμῶν, ἀπέχεσθαι ὑμᾶς ἀπὸ τῆς πορνείας,
⁴ εἰδέναι ἕκαστον ὑμῶν τὸ ἑαυτοῦ σκεῦος κτᾶσθαι ἐν ἁγιασμῷ καὶ τιμῇ,
⁵ μὴ ἐν πάθει ἐπιθυμίας καθάπερ καὶ τὰ ἔθνη τὰ μὴ εἰδότα τὸν θεόν,
⁶ τὸ μὴ ὑπερβαίνειν καὶ πλεονεκτεῖν ἐν τῷ πράγματι τὸν ἀδελφὸν αὐτοῦ, διότι ἔκδικος κύριος περὶ πάντων τούτων, καθὼς καὶ προείπαμεν ὑμῖν καὶ διεμαρτυράμεθα.
⁷ οὐ γὰρ ἐκάλεσεν ἡμᾶς ὁ θεὸς ἐπὶ ἀκαθαρσίᾳ ἀλλ' ἐν ἁγιασμῷ.
⁸ τοιγαροῦν ὁ ἀθετῶν οὐκ ἄνθρωπον ἀθετεῖ ἀλλὰ τὸν θεὸν τὸν [καὶ] διδόντα τὸ πνεῦμα αὐτοῦ τὸ ἅγιον εἰς ὑμᾶς.

While in 1 Thess. 2.16 the ἔθνη were specified as the target of the proclamation, here they have become negative counterparts.[78] It is crucial to see that the participial expression τὰ μὴ εἰδότα τὸν θεόν (1 Thess. 4.5) is not merely qualifying but also partitive: not all of the ἔθνη are the designated counterparts, but rather only those who have not, as the addressees have done, 'turned to God' (1 Thess. 1.9). The same formulation is found

---

[76] On the structure and arrangement, as well as on the exegetical details, cf. ibid., 204–25; Abraham J. Malherbe, *The Letters to the Thessalonians: A New Translation with Introduction and Commentary*, AB 32B (New Haven, CT: Yale University Press, 2004), 226–36; Konradt, *Gericht*, 100–15, especially also as a mine of information on the early Jewish traditions that may have found expression in 1 Thessalonians 4.
[77] Contra Konradt, *Gericht*, 110–11. This occurs only in the pseudepigraphical letters Eph. 4.17–20; Col. 3.1–7 (see below), which address the gentiles only in a fictional sense. In 1 Cor. 6.11, it generally means all possible previously enumerated vices.
[78] It can also turn out differently: The letter also demands decent treatment of οἱ ἔξω (1 Thess. 4.12) and doing what is good καὶ εἰς πάντας (1 Thess. 5.15).

in Jer. 10.25 LXX (cf. Ps. 78.6 LXX). These intertexts serve to activate the idea of other peoples as a threat to God's people who, for this reason, deserve God's judgement. Additionally, they call to mind the topical connection between lack of knowledge of God, misguided sexuality and the threat of judgement that is also found in Wisdom 14 (see above) and Romans 1 (see below).[79]

The keyword ἁγιασμός (vv. 3–4 and, as inclusion, v. 7; cf. τὸ πνεῦμα τὸ ἅγιον, v. 8) is a central interpretation of the will of God. It means that the holiness conferred by God (see 1 Thess. 3.13; 5.23) must be transferred into ethical conduct. Here, ἁγιασμός stands contrary to ἀκαθαρσία (v. 7) and to πορνεία (v. 3).[80] In the Old Testament tradition, the holiness of Israel is connected with Israel's separation from the nations.[81]

In accordance with the tradition that all evil begins with πορνεία,[82] the admonition begins with the exhortation to keep apart from πορνεία. This lends weight to sexual transgressions; however, it remains unclear what πορνεία actually is and where it begins. In view of the Jewish tradition, it most likely designates every form of sexual intercourse outside of marriage or binding partnerships.[83] The metaphor τὸ ἑαυτοῦ σκεῦος κτᾶσθαι ἐν ἁγιασμῷ καὶ τιμῇ (1 Thess. 4.4) is another notorious *crux interpretum*:[84] the vessel could be either one's own body (or more specifically the *membrum virile*) or the woman whom one is to marry, or the already existing wife or, gender neutral, the marriage partner (cf. 1 Cor. 7.2–6).[85] The emphasis upon each person's own possessions speaks in favour of the latter.

In these debates there is a tendency to overlook the possibility that this vagueness in expression in 1 Thess. 4.3–6 might be intended precisely because it is so open for different applications. This openness corresponds to the openness of the formulation ἐν πάθει ἐπιθυμίας in v. 5 that stands in direct opposition to ἐν ἁγιασμῷ καὶ τιμῇ in v. 4 and equally begs the question of which concrete conduct is described.[86] It does convey, however, a 'cross-culturally' understandable, negative judgement: ἐπιθυμία is equally denigrated in early Jewish texts – beginning with the prohibition in the Decalogue to lust after the wife of the neighbour (Exod. 20.17; Deut. 5.21)[87] – and in Stoic ethics.[88] Hence, the rejection of πάθος and ἐπιθυμία in sexual practices describes generally

---

[79] See also Jonah's sermon in Nineveh, according to Ps.-Philo, *De Jona* 27, 105–6.
[80] On the connection of conferred holiness with an ethical equivalent, cf. Schreiber, *Thessalonicher*, 212–13. On the antithesis of holiness and impurity, cf. Rom. 6.19; 1 Cor. 7.14; Eph. 5.3, as well as, e.g. Lev. 10.10; 2 Sam. 11.4 (in each case LXX).
[81] Cf. especially Lev. 20.24, 26; with Konradt, *Gericht*, 100.
[82] Cf. T. Sim. 5.3–4; cf. Konradt, *Gericht*, 101.
[83] This is the implication of 1 Cor. 7.2 and of the rejection of prostitution in 1 Cor. 6.12–20, and corresponds to Paul's Jewish socialization; cf. Konradt, *Gericht*, 102, with citations.
[84] On the extensive discussion about the significance of the controversial verses, cf. recently Matthias Konradt, 'Die Gefäßmetapher in 1 Thess 4,4: Ein neuer Versuch zur Deutung von 1 Thess 4,4f.', *BZ* 62.2 (2018), 245–69.
[85] Another possibility is that v. 6a marks out sexual boundaries. Cf., e.g. Loader, *Sexuality*, 159.
[86] Cf. Loader, *Sexuality*, 156: It could mean that sexuality is reserved solely for procreation, or it could describe an 'inappropriate sexual response'.
[87] On ἐπιθυμία as a fundamental sin, see Konradt, *Gericht*, 104, e.g. Apoc. Mos. 19.3; Philo, *Dec.* 173; Philo, *Spec. Leg.* 4.84; Rom. 7.7; on the connection of πάθη and ἐπιθυμία, e.g. 4 Macc. 1.3; cf. 2.6.
[88] Cf. Malherbe, *Thessalonians*, 229–30; there are also parallels to the demand for honourable treatment in marriage (Aristoteles, *Eth.nic.*; Xenophon; Plutarch; Musonius).

accepted views (cf. 1 Thess. 4.12), thus it could be an 'inclusive ethos'.[89] By ascribing these negatively connoted sexual practices to the non-believing gentiles, 1 Thess. 4.5 claims exclusivity.

These statements cannot be accurate, though, neither in regard to ideals nor in regard to concrete practices, at least not in this generality.[90] The more recent exegesis rightly emphasizes that the generalizing statements serve as demarcation in order to strengthen one's own group identity.[91] The vagueness in the statements about misguided sexual conduct on the part of the gentiles indicates that they aim at dissociation.[92] If the purpose of the statements had been to develop a specific sexual ethos, a clear content would have been possible and far more advantageous.[93]

Instead, the statements in 1 Thess. 4.3–8 show typical means of the Othering discourse: they speak about the others,[94] not with them, and they construct a binary opposition by focusing solely upon the differences. This passage does not distinguish between various ethnic groups although these definitely existed in Thessaloniki. The generalization is based on two stereotypes that are augmented by tradition (not knowing God, the passion of the desires). All negative aspects (πορνεία, πάθη ἐπιθυμίας, ἀκαθαρσία) are projected into the 'Others', who are thus pathologized. The present tense 'freezes' the Others within this pejorative posture. The lack of evidence suggests that these insinuations are facts.

The observations made in the texts from early Judaism discussed above lead to further considerations regarding 1 Thessalonians:

1. Just like in the Jewish texts from Alexandria, the power imbalance that becomes effective in Othering does not correspond to the true situation of the congregational members who have experienced suppression because of their conversion. This rhetoric can be interpreted here, too, as a discursive reversal of circumstances: the allegedly powerful are, in reality, the inferior Others. The sphere in which this superiority is valid is the transcendent world of God's sovereignty, in which the 'saints' participate (cf. v. 8).
2. The exhortations request the addressees to be different, to be 'the Other' in their conduct of sexuality. The text harks back to Jewish traditions that connect

---

[89] On the concept, cf. Wolter, 'Identität', 127–9, 144–5.
[90] Cf. Loader, *Sexuality*, 160: Paul uses generalizations as 'shaming rhetoric' while fully aware that there are similar ideals to his in the Pagan society and moral philosophy. Boris Paschke, 'Ambiguity in Paul's References to Greco-Roman Sexual Ethics', *ETL* 83.1 (2007), 169–92, points out that Paul in 1 Cor. 5.1 conversely claims that the nations would not tolerate the current case of πορνεία in the congregation. Both are rhetorical exaggerations.
[91] Cf. O. Larry Yarbrough, *Not Like the Gentiles: Marriage Rules in the Letters of Paul*, SBLDS 80 (Atlanta, GA: Scholar Press, 1985), 87: 'Paul employs traditional polemic concerning marriage ... in the service of general paraenesis'; Schreiber, *Thessalonicher*, 215, 219.
[92] Contra Konradt, *Gericht*, who assumes that Paul's sexual ethics, on the basis of Jewish self-understanding, are distinct. He refers to the fact that prostitution was tolerated in the environment, but not in the Christian community. Paul, according to Konradt, inculcates this sexual ethos as an essential sign of Christian existence (ibid., 103, 105–8, 115).
[93] See, similarly, Yarbrough, *Gentiles*, 81–2; Malherbe, *Thessalonians*, 237, 239.
[94] Here they are designated as ἔθνη, who do not know God, but in the context also as οἱ ἔξω 1 Thess. 4.12; οἱ λοιποὶ οἱ μὴ ἔχοντες ἐλπίδα 1 Thess. 4.13; see 1 Thess. 5.6.

sexual wrongdoing with idol worship, but without explicitly marking them as such. While belief in God actually is exclusive, the ideals of sexual practice could achieve a general consensus and, thus, an inclusive ethos. Thus, the text claims that what is in reality open for general social consensus is an exclusive ethos. The exhortations then create an area of daily life in which the converts can obey a supposedly exclusive ethos and thus express their feeling of superiority.
3. In view of the importance of the problem of mixed marriages in the Jewish texts, it is conceivable, though not previously discussed in exegesis, that here, too, the connection of sexual conduct and Othering could be addressing especially the question of the mixed marriage. After all, some congregational members could have lived in mixed marriages. The metaphorical request τὸ ἑαυτοῦ σκεῦος κτᾶσθαι ἐν ἁγιασμῷ καὶ τιμῇ (1 Thess. 4.4) then implies the demand to maintain the marriage, to acknowledge the non-believing partner as God's creation,[95] to act honourably in this relationship and to dissociate oneself from sexual practices that are associated with the non-believing gentiles. The request summons the believer to live by the identity-establishing boundary not through the repulsion of the person but rather through the practice of a superior ethos.

Anti-gentile polemics in a pseudepigraphic letter: Eph. 4.17–24; 5.3–5 as reception of Rom. 1.18–32

We come full circle and return to the text that prompted my reflections. By now it has become clear how much Eph. 4.17–19 uses *topoi* that originate in anti-gentile polemics. The connection between the ignorance of God and misguided sexuality calls to mind Wisdom 14 especially; however, the reception of this text, or rather this *topos*, is conveyed via Rom. 1.21–4, as the word-for-word contacts show.[96]

For this reason, let us take a short look at Rom. 1.18–32. Paul plays with the anti-gentile stereotypes that connect idolatry and sexual wrongdoing just as Wisdom 13–14 does; perhaps he even adopted them from this passage.[97] However, Paul claims a connection between the lack of understanding of God and the exchange of Creator and mortal creatures on the one hand and sexual perversion on the other hand that is much tighter than the one in Wisdom (Rom 1.24–7). For Jewish readers, it would have been natural to read Rom. 1.18–32 as a criticism of the gentiles, that is, as an act of Othering the gentiles. However, Rom. 2.1–2 at the very least requires an inclusive rereading of Rom. 1.18–32. The passage alludes to the narrative of Paradise as a description of the *conditio humana* in general (cf. ἀπὸ κτίσεως κόσμου, Rom. 1.20) and to the worship

---

[95] Cf. Konradt, 'Gefäßmetapher', 250, 253, on the possibility that the vessel metaphor is associated with aspects of creatureliness.
[96] Cf. Gese, *Vermächtnis*, 58–60. The recurrence of ματαιόω, σκοτίζω, ἀκαθαρσία as well as the motif of the heart (καρδία) lacking understanding from Rom. 1.21, 24 in Eph. 4.17–19 is especially indicative.
[97] On the theological proximities, see fundamentally Folker Blischke, 'Die *Sapientia Salomonis* und Paulus', in Niebuhr, *Sapientia Salomonis (Weisheit Salomos)*; on Rom. 1.18–32, Jonathan A. Linebaugh, 'Announcing the Human: Rethinking the Relationship between Wisdom of Solomon 13–15 and Romans 1.18–2.11', *NTS* 57.2 (2011), 214–37. It is remarkable that Rom. 2.4–5 can be read as a counter-text to Wis. 15.1–4 just as well.

of the Golden Calf by the Israelites (cf. Rom. 1.23 with Ps. 105.20 LXX).[98] The point of the text is that these accusations apply equally to *all* human beings who shut their hearts to the truth of God (Rom. 1.18), whether they are Jewish or non-Jewish. In this regard, 'unnatural sexuality', while mentioned only briefly in Wis. 14.26 as γενέσεως ἐναλλαγή, is for Paul the result of and the punishment for exchanging the Creator and the creature (Rom 1.24–7).[99] For Paul, criticizing sexual practices is not the goal of the account, but rather an instrument for defaming the Others. Their defamation, however, is in itself a means, namely, for the argumentative development of the 'Pauline Gospel' of the salvation of all believers, whether Jewish or gentile (Rom. 1.16). All of these, without distinction, are in need of salvation (cf. Rom. 3.22).[100] Rom. 1.18–32 thus falls only halfway into the category of gentile-bashing. It is remarkable that Paul can use these stereotypical polemics against gentiles in order to discursively eliminate the difference between Jews and gentiles, that is, 'to the inclusion of Israel within the scope of Israel's own polemical tradition'.[101]

Ephesians 4, though a close reception of Romans 1, leads the anti-gentile stereotypes back to their original polemical place and (re)shifts the focus: once again, the polemics are directed against τὰ ἔθνη. Their helpless situation was already described retrospectively in Eph. 2.11–12: they are the Others from the perspective of those who are called 'the circumcision', and they are alien to the promises of God (Eph. 2.12). Eph. 4.17–19 agrees with Wisdom 14, Romans 1 and 1 Thessalonians 4 that the problem arises out of the lack of knowledge of God. None of them display any interest whatsoever in being explicit about the details of sexual transgressions (just as one, indeed, should not even talk about them, see Eph. 5.3). The terms ἀσέλγεια and ἐργασία ἀκαθαρσίας leave space for imagination. The expressions πορνεία, πόρνος in Eph. 5.3–5, even though somewhat more to the point, remain general.

We do find, also in Eph. 4.17–19, the characteristics of the rhetoric of Othering: the gentiles are spoken about as 'them' from the standpoint of 'I' (Eph. 4.17) and (plural) 'you' by means of labelling (τὰ ἔθνη, Eph. 4.17). They are charged with sweeping accusations: lack of knowledge of God, moral corruption, the two being insolubly connected. The gentiles are pathologized in the truest sense of the term: they have a heart incapable of functioning and no sensitivity for pain; and all of this is fixed in the timeless present tense – the situation is self-imposed, but unavoidable.

In Eph. 4.17–24, however, the act of Othering not only distances the contemporary gentiles, but it also creates a gap between the past and present of each of the addressed former 'gentile' persons, with the clear implication that the past is to be laid aside like an old self (Eph. 4.22–4).

The admonition in Eph. 5.3–14 continues the line from Eph. 4.17–19 in that it relies equally on Othering; the verses construct a binary opposition and underscore it with a light-darkness metaphor (in Eph. 5.8–14). The Others are labelled as οἱ υἱοὶ τῆς

---

[98] Cf. ibid., 229–33, who includes the allusions to Genesis in Rom. 5.12–21; 7.7–13.
[99] Cf. Michael Wolter, *Der Brief an Römer: Röm 1–8*, EKKNT VI/1 (Neukirchen-Vluyn: Neukirchener Theologie, 2014), 145–6.
[100] Cf. on the pragmatics of Rom. 1.18–32 in the context of the Letter to the Romans, ibid., 160–2.
[101] Linebaugh, 'Announcing', 216.

ἀπειθείας, every bad characteristic is ascribed to them and judgement is proclaimed upon them (Eph. 5.5–6, cf. already 2.2–3). Since now they are characterized by their wrongdoing, it is not necessary to think only of non-believing gentiles; the Others could also be immoral people who belong to the congregation.[102] What does become evident is the demand not to have communion with such people (Eph. 5.7, 11).

What is all of this good for? The intention of Ephesians is notoriously controversial due to its lack of any situational allusion and concrete polemic.[103] The letter as a whole summons its readers to unity in belief (Eph. 4.1–16), in the local congregation (Eph. 4.25–32) and in the household (Eph. 5.22–6.9) without excluding others disparagingly, and especially without drawing up borders against the Jews. Having the question of mixed marriages connected with the topic in mind, one could presume the double demand not to have communion with them (Eph. 5.7, 11) to imply that the addressees are not to enter into marriages with unbelievers. The domestic code, in any case, overwrites 1 Cor. 7.12–17, for it knows marriage only between Christians (5.22–33).[104]

If we assess Eph. 4.17–19 as a discourse of Othering, then the power produced through knowledge about the others becomes visible: the assertions make the gentiles and the past of the fictitious addressees into a coherent, distanced and inferior 'Other'. In the series of deprecatory statements about gentiles that we have analysed here, this text is distinguished by the fact that τὰ ἔθνη now, as in the Jewish texts, is a negative label without any specification, like the one 1 Thess. 4.5 provides, and lays emphasis on the lack of knowledge of God. The moral disaster that ensues from this lack of knowledge of God is portrayed as all-encompassing, but remains vague. A particular sharpness lies in the supposed remoteness from God: the metaphors of physical pathology show that 'self-healing' is impossible. The retrospective glance on the conversion of the fictitious addressees implies, however, that there was a moment of 'healing' from this 'abnormal' lack of knowledge of God – it happened through the Gospel, the message of Christ (Eph. 4.20–1).

Evaluation of the case studies

Within the overarching question of the reception of the Jewish tradition in Christianity in the process of formation, the results of the fundamental reflections upon gentile-bashing and of the analysed texts will be assessed in five theses.

1. The process of reception: the *topos* of false veneration of God and of sexual wrongdoing associated with it has its basis in the Old Testament and is

---

[102] The fact that εἰδωλολατρία is equated with πλεονεξία in Eph. 5.5 speaks for this.
[103] Cf. Christine Gerber, 'Paulus als Ökumeniker: Die Interpretation der paulinischen Theologie durch den Epheserbrief', in *Reception of Paul in Early Christianity: The Person of Paul and His Writings through the Eyes of His Early Interpreters*, ed. Jens Schröter, BZNW 234 (Berlin: de Gruyter, 2018), 317–54.
[104] Cf. Christine Gerber, 'Die alte Braut und Christi Leib: Zum ekklesiologischen Entwurf des Epheserbriefs', NTS 59.2 (2013), 192–221.

widely used in early Jewish literature as a general means of demarcation over against other peoples. Early Christian parenesis takes up the Jewish *topos* of gentile-bashing. Just how familiar the tandem of idolatry and πορνεία was becomes evident in its 'playful' use in Rom. 1.18–32. The critique could be regarded as self-evident, as can be seen in the fact that the charges in the Christian texts did not need to be justified with the authority of scripture or tradition.

2. Othering as social practice: the texts that were investigated noticeably used rhetoric of Othering. The social function of this gentile-bashing for each community can be read in them: by emphasizing the differences with stereotypes and timeless attributions the Other as such was produced, derogated and thereby subordinated. Even when the power relationships in the real world are reversed, and precisely then, these texts claim superiority over the 'Others' within the Jewish and Christian discourse universe of the One God. Beyond this, the demarcation in the Jewish texts finds its direct social expression in the fundamental impossibility of mixed marriages.

3. The specific effect of gentile-bashing: while the practice of Othering (and the charge of sexual perversion) is omnipresent, the connection of the charges that are investigated here has a specific meaning. It states that distancing from idolatry leads to the 'unique feature' of Jewish and Christian worship, the superiority of which is only valid within the Jewish or Christian discourse universe. But the disparaging portrayal of the 'Others' harks back to a generally shared value, namely the necessary avoidance of illegitimate sexuality. Here, an 'inclusive ethos' is tangible, apart from differences in the notion of legitimate sexuality.

4. Changes in the Christian reception: Christian parenesis faced a challenge when using gentile-bashing, since a part of the believers themselves had formerly been 'gentile'. The ἔθνη were no longer simply the others; therefore, the boundary had to be renegotiated. The change in the meaning of ἔθνη in the Pauline letters[105] portrays this shift.

The challenge was especially great in the first generation of Christ-believers, since the stereotypical charge of sexual wrongdoing had to undergo a reality check. This explains why 1 Thess. 4.3–6 does not refer at all to the past of the addressees. Ephesians, a fictitious letter, takes more liberties in this regard, as seen in 4.17–19 and 5.3–5. In addition, both texts, in comparison with the Jewish tradition, remain vague in reference to sexual transgressions. The point of 1 Thess. 4.3–6 could rather lie in the reaction to mixed marriages: in this recommendation, 'first-generation Christians' who happened to live in a mixed marriage find a possibility for maintaining their marriage, even if their partner did not convert, but also an option for drawing a boundary over against allegedly pagan life, namely via a specific sexual ethos.

---

[105] Cf. footnote 4.

5. In conclusion: if these analyses and reflections have made gentile-bashing comprehensible as a *topos* of Othering, then they also warn against taking the reifying statements about the 'Others' at face value, and against believing the claim of a clear differentiation. The texts do not depict clear distinctions, but rather, in their stereotypical Othering, above all confirm the necessity of first fixing the others as Others in discourse – exactly because they were not so different at all.

5

Patterns of Christian reinterpretations of the Maccabean martyrdoms

Jan Willem van Henten

Introduction

In the early sixteenth century, the priest Helias Mertz (d. 1527) gave an enormous boost to the cult of the Maccabean martyrs in Cologne. Mertz was the rector and confessor of the monastery of the nuns of St. Benedict in Cologne.[1] Legend has it that the bones of the Maccabean martyrs were preserved in Cologne, after Archbishop Reinald von Dassel had transported them in 1164 from Milan to his own city, together with the remains of the Three Magi.[2] They were preserved under the high altar of the chapel of the Monastery of the Sisters of St. Benedict, where Mertz was in charge since 1491.[3] Mertz commissioned several books devoted to the Maccabean martyrs, one of which appeared in 1517 and was edited by Erasmus, the other being a festive manuscript of 1525 on parchment, in which the contents of 1517 were copied. He also commissioned a lavishly decorated gilded shrine as a new container for the Maccabean bones from the goldsmith Peter Hanemann, the exterior of which presents a complex set of reliefs that combine the martyrdom of the mother and her sons with the passion of Christ

---

[1] W. Schmid, *Stifter und Auftraggeber im spätmittelalterlichen Köln*, Veröffentlichungen des Kölnischen Stadtmuseums 11 (Cologne: Kölnisches Stadtmuseum, 1994), 122–4, 199–203; H. Molitor, 'Helias Marcaeus', in *Contemporaries of Erasmus: A Biographical Register of the Renaissance and the Reformation*, vol. 2, ed. P. G. Bietenholz and T. B. Deutscher (Toronto: University of Toronto Press, 1986), 381–2; D. J. Collins, 'The Renaissance of the Maccabees: Old Testament Jews, German Humanists, and the Cult of the Saints in Early Modern Cologne', in *Dying for the Faith, Killing for the Faith*, ed. G. Signori (Leiden: Brill, 2012), 209–45; J. W. van Henten and H. Walvoort, 'The Re-Interpretation of the Maccabean Mother and Her Sons by Frater Magdalius Iacobus Gaudensis in the Framework of the Cult of the Maccabees in Cologne', *LIAS* 46 (2019), 1–28.

[2] A. von Euw, 'Die Makkabäerbrüder. Spätjüdische Märtyrer der christlichen Märtyrerverehrung', in *Monumenta Judaica: 2000 Jahre Geschichte und Kultur der Juden am Rhein. Handbuch*, vol. 1, ed. K. Schilling (Cologne: Kölnisches Stadtmuseum, 1963), 782–6, 783; W. Peters, 'Der Anspruch des Kölner Makkabäer-Klosters auf einen Platz in der Ursula-legende', *Annalen des Historischen Vereins für den Niederrhein insbesondere das alte Erzbistum Köln* 211 (2008), 5–31; D. Joslyn-Siemiatkoski, *Christian Memories of the Maccabean Martyrs* (New York: Palgrave MacMillan, 2009), 139–51.

[3] I. Bodsch, 'Sacrarium Agrippinae', in *Ornamenta Ecclesiae. Kunst und Künstler der Romanik in Köln*, vol. 2, ed. A. Legner (Köln: Schnütgen-Museum, 1985), 157.

and the suffering of Mary.[4] Mertz consistently downplayed the Jewish identity of the Maccabean martyrs and Daniel Joslyn-Siemiatkoski concludes that he colonized the martyrs ideologically for his own purposes by reinscribing a new Christian identity into them.[5] In this contribution I will revisit most of the earliest Christian reinterpretations of the Maccabean martyrs. The aims for the reinterpretation of the martyrs in these early Christian writings may not be as explicit as in Helias Mertz's use of them in the early sixteenth century, but it may be worthwhile to study the reinterpretations in their wider context and see which purposes they may serve.

Our group of martyrs came to be known as 'the Maccabees', a name that is also connected with the Jewish freedom fighters who rebelled against the Seleucid King Antiochus IV Epiphanes (175-164 BCE), that is, the priest Mattathias and his five sons.[6] The group of Jewish martyrs who were tortured to death during the persecution organized by King Antiochus IV according to 2 and 4 Maccabees is often referred to as 'the Maccabean martyrs' or simply 'the Maccabees'. The Passion of Montanus and Lucius compares the mother of the martyr Flavianus with the mother of the seven sons and calls her a 'Maccabean mother' (*Machabaeica mater*, 16.4), that is, a mother in the tradition of the Maccabees (see also Pas. Mar. 13, below). From the fourth century onwards 'the Maccabees' becomes an established name for these martyrs within the East as well as the West. Gregory of Nazianzus (fourth century CE) calls the martyrs 'the Maccabees' right at the beginning of his discourse in honour of them.[7] Augustine refers several times to the mother as 'the mother of the Maccabees' (*mater Machabaeorum*)[8] and once mentions 'the example of Eleazar the Maccabee'.[9]

I focus in the remaining part of this contribution on the earliest explicit Christian reinterpretations of the Maccabean martyrs, covering roughly the period of 100-260 CE: the brief paraphrases and allusions through keywords in Heb. 11.35-6,[10] the brief allusions in the Passion of Montanus and Lucius 16 and the Passion of Marian and James 13, traditionally dated in the spring of 259 CE,[11] the paraphrases and quotations

---

[4] R. Hirner, 'Die Makkabäerschrein in St. Andreas zu Köln' (PhD diss., Rheinische Friedrich-Wilhelms-Universität Bonn, 1970); U. Rautenberg, *Überlieferung und Druck: Heiligenlegenden aus frühen Kölner Offizinen*, Frühe Neuzeit, vol. 30 (Tübingen: Max Niemeyer Verlag, 1996), 231-8; Collins, 'The Renaissance', 228-39.
[5] Joslyn-Siemiatkoski, *Christian Memories*, 143, 151.
[6] E.g. Eusebius, *Dem. ev.* 8.2.93.
[7] *Discourse* 15; *PG* 35.912.1; also 912.9; *Funerary oration* 74.
[8] E.g. *Serm.* 300 *PL* 38.1379-80 and *Serm.* 301 *PL* 38.1380.
[9] *Exemplo Eleazari Macchabaei*, see Augustine, *Brev. coll.* 3; cf. also the titles of John Chrysostom's homilies on the Maccabean martyrs: *PG* 50.617, 623, 625; his *Mart.* 50.647; *Eleaz. puer. PG* 63.525; Basilius, *Epist.* 6.2; John Malalas, *Chron.* 206-7; *Martyrologium Romanum* under August 1.
[10] Details in J. W. van Henten, 'The Reception of Daniel 3 and 6 and the Maccabean Martyrdoms in Hebrews 11:33-38', in *Myths, Martyrs, and Modernity: Studies in the History of Religions in Honour of Jan N. Bremmer*, ed. J. Dijkstra et al. (Leiden: Brill, 2010), 359-77. For the subsequent period of Christian reinterpretations of the Maccabean martyrs, see J. W. Knust, '"Who Were the Maccabees?": The Maccabean Martyrs and Performances on Christian Difference', in *Martyrdom: Canonisation, Contestation and Afterlives*, ed. I. Saloul and J. W. van Henten (Amsterdam: Amsterdam University Press, 2020), 79-103.
[11] The date of the martyrdoms according to tradition is spring 259 CE. H. A. Musurillo, *The Acts of the Christian Martyrs* (Oxford: Clarendon Press, 1972), xxxv-xxxvi; É. Rebillard, *Greek and Latin Narratives about the Ancient Martyrs*, Oxford Early Christian Texts (Oxford: Oxford University Press, 2017), 175-6. The Passion of Marian and James refers to the Decian persecution and the

in the *Commentary on Daniel* (2.20; 2.35) by Hippolytus of Rome (d. 235 CE), the paraphrases and quotations in Origen's *Exhortation to Martyrdom* (235 CE)[12] and finally the paraphrases and quotations in Cyprian's *Ad Fortunatum* (257 CE) and *Testimonies against the Jews* 3.16–17 (between 246 and 250 CE).[13] Writings in which allusions to the Maccabean martyrs are far from certain, like the letters of Ignatius, the Martyrdom of Polycarp, the Martyrdom of Lyons and Vienne and the Latin Martyrdom of Felicitas and her seven sons, will be left out of my discussion.[14] It is too speculative to build conclusions on the basis of passages of which it is far from certain that they are dependent on the Jewish source texts. I will undertake my discussion in three rounds, by focusing on the following questions: (1) What role do the original context and the Jewish identity of the martyrs play? (2) How are the motives of the martyrs for choosing martyrdom presented in the reinterpretations? (3) How do the martyrs function as role models for Christians and support or even legitimate Christian views, practices and identities?

Jewish context and Jewish identities in the reinterpretations

The first observation that should be made here is that there is little evidence of the Jewish context of the Maccabean martyrdoms and the Jewish identity of the martyrs as exemplary figures. By way of contrast it may be helpful to point to Augustine, who devoted three homilies to the Maccabean martyrs.[15] In his first homily (*Sermo* 300),

---

martyrdom of Cyprian (dated September 258; Passion of Marian 5.2; 6.10; similarly Passion of Montanus 11.2; 21.3).

[12] Discussions in D. DeSilva, 'An Example of How to Die Nobly for Religion: The Influence of 4 Maccabees on Origen's Exhortatio ad Martyrium', *JECL* 17 (2009), 337–55; J. W. van Henten, 'The Christianization of the Maccabean Martyrs: The Case of Origen', in *Martyrdom and Persecution in Late Ancient Christianity: Festschrift Boudewijn Dehandschutter*, ed. J. Leemans, BETL 241 (Leuven: Peeters, 2010), 333–52.

[13] M. M. Sage, *Cyprian*, Patristic Monograph Series 1 (Philadelphia, PA: Philadelphia Patristic Foundation, 1975), 377–83.

[14] The modes of reinterpretation concern explicit quotations, implicit quotations (with a minimum of at least three almost identical words from the source text, obvious differences between the vocabulary and the style of the quoted text and the passage with the quotation, or correspondences between both contexts as indicators), allusions (indicated by some sort of textual signal) and paraphrase, for criteria to distinguish these modes; see van Henten, 'Reception of Daniel 3 and 6', 360–2. Different views: O. Perler, 'Das vierte Makkabäerbuch, Ignatius von Antiochien und die ältesten Martyrerberichte', *Rivista di archeologia cristiana* 25 (1949), 47–72; W. H. C. Frend, *Martyrdom and Persecution in the Early Church: A Study of a Conflict from the Maccabees to Donatus* (Oxford: Blackwell, 1965), 18–19; M.-L. Guillaumin, 'Une jeune fille qui s'appelait Blandine', in *Epektasis: Mélanges patristiques offerts au Cardinal J. Daniélou*, ed. J. Fontaine and C. Kannengiesser (Paris: Beauchesne, 1972), 93–8; V. Saxer, *Morts. Martyrs. Reliques. En Afrique chrétienne aux premiers siècles. Les témoignages de Tertullien, Cyprien, et Augustin à la lumière de l'archéologie africaine* (Paris: Beauchesne, 1980), 260. Cf. J. W. van Henten, 'Zum Einfluß jüdischer Martyrien auf die Literatur des frühen Christentums (2: Die Apostolischen Väter)', in *Aufstieg und Niedergang der römischen Welt II.27/1*, ed. W. Haase and H. Temporini (Berlin: de Gruyter, 1993), 700–23.

[15] *Serm.* 300 and 301; *PL* 38.1376–85; Mayence 50; C. Brown-Tkacz, 'The Seven Maccabees, Three Hebrews and a Newly Discovered Sermon of St. Augustine (Mayence 50)', *REA* 41 (1995), 59–78.

Augustine refers to a hypothetical Jew who argues that the Christians cannot venerate the Maccabean martyrs because they were Jewish. Augustine rejects this objection by stating that the deeds of the martyrs imply that they were Christians in spite of the fact that their martyrdom preceded the incarnation of Christ: they died not only for the law but also for Christ, who was still a mystery at that time, but as a matter of fact Moses did write already about Christ. For Augustine, therefore, there is no principle difference between the Maccabees and the martyrs who imitated Christ, whether Christ was hidden under the law or revealed in the Gospel. Both categories of martyrs belong to the people of Christ as descendants of Abraham, and both were strengthened and crowned by him. Augustine's awareness of the Jewish identity of the Maccabean martyrs and his reinterpretation of that identity are fairly unique within the early Christian reception of the Maccabean martyrs.

The Jewish context and Jewish identity of the Maccabean martyrs remain implicit in most of the passages reviewed for our analysis. The implicit references to the Maccabees in the Letter to the Hebrews (11.34c: 'they were tortured in/on drums)'; 11.34d: 'refusing to accept release'; 11.35a: 'Women received their dead by resurrection'; 11.35e: 'in order to obtain a better resurrection'; 11.36ab: 'still others suffered flogging and mocking')[16] are part of a larger cluster that also includes Daniel and his three companions. The references in Heb. 11.33–8 are anonymous and consequently put in the plural and they are part of a continuous chain of witnesses of πίστις that culminates in Jesus Christ as the one who founded and perfected faith (12.2, below). The ethnic and cultural-religious identities of all these heroes are completely ignored in Hebrews. The information given in the list of examples in Heb. 11.33–8 is just enough for the informed reader to establish a connection with the story alluded to and leaves the context of the sufferings of the protagonists by and large open. The lists of exemplary figures presuppose an ongoing history culminating in the figure of Christ that functions as encouragement of the intended readers (below), and the Israelite and Jewish figures referred to are part of that history and therefore disintegrated from their original context.

The Passion of Montanus and Lucius and the Passion of Marian and James include brief references to the Maccabean mother. The deacon Flavianus is the most prominent martyr in the Passion of Montanus and Lucius and Flavianus's mother visits him in prison during his final days. She is called an exceptional mother (*incomparabilis mater*, 16.3) and a 'Maccabean mother' (*Machabaeica mater*, Pas. Mont. 16.4; cf. Pas. Mar. 13.1), who is to be counted among the ancient examples (*inter uetera exempla numerandam*). Her piety is highlighted as well (16.4). The praise for this mother links up with the brief section with praise for the mother in 2 Macc. 7.20–3, who was 'especially admirable'.[17] The passage constructs an analogy between both mothers and focuses on their ideal attitude of being prepared to sacrifice a child for a higher cause. The author highlights that the number of sons – the Maccabean mother had seven – did not play a role because the love of the Lord was the only thing that mattered, which

---

[16] Details: van Henten, 'Reception of Daniel 3 and 6'.
[17] Cf. 2 Macc. 7.20: 'The mother was especially admirable and worthy of honourable memory'; Rebillard, *Greek and Latin Narratives*, 285 with footnote 83.

creates an explicit analogy with the Maccabean mother 'since *she too* had surrendered to the Lord all of her love in a single pledge' (transl. Rebillard; my emphasis).[18] It should be noted that the Lord in this martyrdom is Jesus Christ (e.g. 7.5-6; 10.2, 5; 15.4). The Maccabean mother is presented here as a glorious model and forerunner of the mothers of Christian martyrs. There is no marker of a previous Jewish period or a Jewish context. The mother of Flavianus is also associated with the patriarchs and called 'a daughter of Abraham', but the author constructs a continuity between her and the previous models (*vetera exempla*), including Abraham and the Maccabean mother. This continuity and the analogy between the Maccabean mother and the mother of Flavianus extend that far that the author can state that both mothers had surrendered their love in a single pledge to Jesus Christ (Pas. Mont. 16.5).

Hippolytus of Rome's *Commentary on Daniel*, written in Rome, implies a persecution by Septimius Severus (202-203 CE), during which many Christians would have died as martyrs (*Comm. Dan.* 1.15-17; 1.20-1; 2.14-38).[19] His commentary on Daniel's fourth vision, which concerns Nabuchodonosor's statue (Daniel 3; *Comm. Dan.* 2.14-38) includes paraphrases of the martyrdom of the mother and her seven sons and several quotations of 2 Maccabees 7. Hippolytus's perspective on the interconnection of the Maccabees and contemporary Christian martyrs is clearly different from the Passion of Montanus and Lucius and the Passion of Marian and James.

Hippolytus presents the seven brothers as martyrs of the past, next to Daniel's companions. He is clearly familiar with Second Maccabees, so we can easily see what he includes and what he leaves out from this book.[20] In one of the two passages about the Maccabees (2.35) he mentions King Antiochus and the terrible sufferings ordered by the king:

> For we find also the seven martyrs (τοὺς ἑπτὰ μάρτυρας) who, under Antiochus (ἐπὶ Ἀντιόχου), endured terrible punishments (δεινὰς κολάσεις ὑπομείναντας) and were taken from the world. And so what of it? Was God not able to smite king Antiochus and to rescue the seven brothers? He was able, but he did not will to do this so that this example may become ours. (2.35.8; transl. Schmidt)

Hippolytus does not offer any specifics about the sufferings and the reason for the Maccabean martyrdoms. He does indicate that God had a purpose with the Maccabean martyrs: they could function as a model (ὑπογραμμός) for Hippolytus and his fellow

---

[18] Pas. Mont. 16.5: *nihil enim interest de numero filiorum, cum perinde et haec in unico pignore totos affectus suos domino manciparit.*

[19] G. Bardy and M. Lefèvre, *Hippolyte. Commentaire sur Daniel*, Sources Chrétiennes (Paris: Éditions du Cerf, 1947), 8-10, 15-16, 28-39. Several Christian writings imply such a persecution, e.g. Eusebius, *Hist. eccl.* 6.1; 6.2.2-4; Passion of Perpetua and Felicitas; Tertullian, *Scap.* 3.1; 5. Historia Augusta 17.1 only briefly refers to a ban to entry into the Christian community. Frend, *Martyrdom and Persecution*, 320-3, argues that there was a persecution and comments that it was directed against converts (320 with n. 138). Cf. P. Guyot and R. Klein, *Das frühe Christentum bis zum Ende der Verfolgungen: eine Dokumentation*, vol. 1, Texte zur Forschung 60 (Darmstadt: Wissenschaftliche Buchgesellschaft, 1994), 354-6, who are sceptical.

[20] In *Comm. Dan.* 4.3 Hippolytus refers to 1 Maccabees as a book.

Christians. Hippolytus neither mentions the old scribe Eleazar nor the Maccabean mother in 2.35.

A preceding passage is more specific and offers a cluster of allusions to and quotations of 2 Macc. 7.1–6, starting with 'Be educated, O man, about the things which happen under Antiochus' (2.20.2). Hippolytus reports that the seven brothers were arrested and struck with scourges and whips (μάστιξιν καὶ νευραῖς ἐτύπτοντο; 2.20.3), but he does not mention the reason for their arrest and their refusal to violate the Jewish food laws by eating a piece of pork (2 Macc. 6.18, 21; 7.2). But the spokesperson of the martyrs refers to the ancestral laws as the prime motivation for disobeying the king in Hippolytus's words (2.20.3) and all seven brothers encourage each other in their ancestral language (2.20.4). This passage offers a paraphrase of 2 Macc. 7.1–6 with very dense corresponding vocabulary and two longer quotations from 2 Maccabees: one from 2 Macc. 7.2 in *Comm. Dan.* 2.20.3 and one from 2 Macc. 7.6 in 2.20.4. There are several minor adaptations of the text of 2 Maccabees 7, but these are not very relevant for the issue of the Jewish context of the martyrdom. Hippolytus acknowledges that the martyrs are members of the Jewish people, which has its own laws and its own ancestral language, but he interprets the martyrs at the same time from a Christian perspective by creating a kind of continuous truth by stating that God's Spirit encourages the martyrs to contempt death and anticipate their posthumous reward, which is true for the Maccabees but also for later Christian martyrs (2.21.1). This leads to the main point that for Hippolytus every believer has to be faithful to the word of God and take up his or her cross (2.21.3), which is underpinned with quotations of Mt. 10.38; 16.24 and Lk. 14.33. This implies that Hippolytus interprets all martyrdoms, recent Christian ones as well as 2 Maccabees 7 and the stories in Daniel 3 and 6 through a Christian lens.

Martyrdom is a hot topic in the writings of the Carthaginian Bishop Cyprian, who died as a martyr himself on September 14, 258 CE.[21] There are two sections in his work wherein the Maccabean martyrs figure prominently. Cyprian's *Ad Fortunatum*, which is probably his latest work and written in 257 CE,[22] reads as an exhortation to martyrdom and the Maccabees are the most important examples in two lists of older martyrs in chapter 11. The *Testimonies against the Jews* is an earlier work, probably written between 246 and 250 CE, which also quotes the Maccabean martyrdoms.[23] *Ad Fortunatum* 11 focuses on the persecutions of the Christians that will take place at the end of times before Jesus Christ will return to earth. There are no details about the persecutions, which are described by a cluster of quotations of statements of Jesus Christ that anticipate the sufferings of his followers. The underlying message is that good and righteous Christians always benefit from afflictions and hardship. Cyprian indicates that there is nothing new in these sufferings, which he demonstrates with several lists that highlight heroes from the past, first a list from the Old Testament that mentions the names of the heroes (including Abel and Zechariah the priest; see 2 Chron. 24.20–2). He adds a short-hand paraphrase of their fate.[24] A second and

---

[21] *Acta proconsularia of St. Cyprian* 3–4 (CSEL 3.3, xii–xiii).
[22] Sage, *Cyprian*, 377–83.
[23] Ibid., 382–3.
[24] E. L. Hummel, *The Concept of Martyrdom according to St. Cyprian*, Studies in Christian Antiquity 9 (Washington, DC: Catholic University of America, 1946), 37.

more elaborate list of models interprets the previous and subsequent examples as martyrdoms and models of faith and virtue. This list creates a continuity from the era of the first humans up to the persecutions at the end of time. This section refers to a book about the Maccabees and somewhat later Cyprian writes about the Maccabean martyrs:

> And what do we read in the Maccabean Books (*Quid vero in Machabeis*), about seven brothers, equal in birth and virtues (*septem fratres et natalium pariter et virtutum sorte consimiles*), and filling up the number seven, by the sacrament of a perfect completion? Seven brothers, united in martyrdom (*in martyrio cohaerentes*), as the first seven days in the divine disposition.

Later on, it becomes apparent that Cyprian was familiar with Second Maccabees, because he paraphrases first 2 Maccabees 7 and then 2 Macc. 6.18-31. He mentions Antiochus's attempt to force the Maccabees to eat a piece of pork and alludes here to 2 Macc. 6.18-21; 7.2. Cyprian clearly indicates that eating pork was forbidden by the law for Eleazar: 'to eat what was supplied from among sacrifices and unlawful food'. He highlights in this context the offer to Eleazar by the king's representatives to pretend only to eat a piece of pork. This is no doubt a hint to his readers that they should not fall for the option to avoid martyrdom, but he does not make explicit in what way this could be done. Elsewhere he blames fellow Christians for obtaining a *libellum* that stated that they would have made the sacrifice demanded from the Roman government.[25]

In his rendering of the Maccabean martyrdoms Cyprian intersperses the references to 2 Maccabees with his own comments and he creates a new interpretative framework in this way. One example concerns the tortures of the first son, who acted as a spokesperson for the entire group. Cyprian alludes to the scalping of this martyr as described in 2 Macc. 7.4 and subsequently explains the meaning of this: 'He [Antiochus] pulled off the skin of his head with the hair, with obvious hatred, which had a meaning. For since Christ is the head of the man, and God the head of Christ, he who lacerated a head of a martyr, persecuted God and Christ in his head.' The head of the martyr triggers an association with 1 Cor. 11.3 (Christ is the head of every man and God the head of Christ) and the co-reading of both passages implies that Antiochus acts as enemy of God and Jesus Christ, which may also build on Antiochus's characterization as a θεομάχος in 2 Macc. 7.19. The third martyr imitates the form of Christ's passion by stretching forth his hands for punishment. The passages about the benefits and rewards of martyrdom in *Test.* 3.16-17 hardly add something about the original context of the Maccabean martyrdoms and the Jewish identity of the martyrs and the references to 2 Maccabees are given without their context.

Origen's *Exhortation to Martyrdom*, written in Caesarea Maritima (Palestine) in 235 CE during the persecution of Maximinus Thrax (235-238 CE),[26] is a hortatory

---

[25] Cyprian, *Laps.* 35; *Epistle* 21.1-3; 55.13-14; M. A. Tilley, 'North Africa', in *The Cambridge History of Christianity*, vol. 1, ed. M. M. Mitchell and F. Young (Cambridge: Cambridge University Press, 2006), 381-96, esp. 389.

[26] Eusebius, *Hist. eccl.* 6.28.

speech (*logos protreptikos*) about martyrdom.[27] Origen energetically exhorts his fellow Christians Ambrose and Prototectus to submit themselves to martyrdom, which is the highest form of Christian life in his view.[28] The section on the Maccabean martyrs (*Mart.* 22-7) in Origen's fairly loosely composed *Exhortation* functions as a cluster of previous models.[29] Ambrose and Prototectus should opt for martyrdom (6-21), their denial of Christianity during a trial would be idolatry (*Mart.* 6).

Strikingly, Origen focuses extensively in the middle of his speech (22-27) on the Maccabean martyrs, who are presented as model figures to his implied audience, next to Abraham and Daniel's companions, who are discussed only briefly (5; 33). Like Hippolytus Origen was clearly familiar with a collection of Maccabean books, because he notes that the story of the seven brothers was recorded in these books (23). He quotes 2 Maccabees and was probably also familiar with 4 Maccabees, but there is no explicit reference to this book.[30] Importantly, the Maccabean book from which he quotes is considered to be part of scripture (ἡ γραφή, *Mart.* 23).[31] This can be deduced from *Exhortation* 27, where Origen refers to his rendering of the martyrdoms as summaries from scripture (ἐπιτεμόμενος ἀπὸ τῆς γραφῆς).[32] His introduction of the martyrdoms, focusing on the seven brothers, mentions that their death was described in the '(Books of the) Maccabees' (Καὶ οἱ ἑπτὰ δὲ ἐν τοῖς Μακκαβαϊκοῖς ἀναγραφέντες ἀδελφοί, 23). A quotation from Ecclesiastes (simplified) frames the section, pointing to the martyrs' posthumous vindication: 'I [Solomon] praised all those who have died more than the living, as many are alive until now' (Eccl. 4.2).[33] Through the connecting motifs of 'praise' and 'death' Origen moves over to the martyrdom of Eleazar and he highlights its voluntary aspect: 'Which dead person could more justifiably be praised than he who preferred death for proper religion's sake (ὑπὲρ εὐσεβείας) of his own choice (αὐτοπροαιρέτως)?' He continues with a paraphrase and a partial quotation from 2 Macc. 6.19, the verse that indicates Eleazar's preference to be executed rather than violating the Jewish dietary laws, echoing αὐθαιρέτως 'of his own accord' (2

---

[27] The Codex Parisinus has Εἰς μαρτύριον προτρεπτικός as title of Origen's writing about martyrdom. J. J. O'Meara, *Origen, Prayer, Exhortation to Martyrdom: Translated and Annotated*, Ancient Christian Writers 19 (Westminster: Newman Press, 1954), 10; P. Hartmann, 'Origène et la théologie du martyre d'après le PROTREPTIKOS de 235', *ETL* 34 (1958), 773-824, 780-1. See also P. Bright, 'Origenian Understanding of Martyrdom and Its Biblical Framework', in *Origen of Alexandria: His Work and His Legacy*, ed. C. Kannengiesser and W. Petersen (Notre Dame, IN: University of Notre Dame Press, 1988), 180-99.

[28] Ambrose was a wealthy married man from Alexandria and a deacon, also a close friend and supporter of Origen (Eusebius, *Hist. eccl.* 6.23.2). Prototectus was a priest from Caesarea Maritima. Hartmann, 'Origène', 774-5.

[29] Discussions of the composition: P. Koetschau, *Origenes Werke 1, Die Schrift vom Martyrium. Buch 1-4 gegen Celsus*, GCS (Leipzig: J. C. Hinrich, 1899), xii-xiv; O'Meara, *Exhortation*, 12; J. E. L. Oulton and H. Chadwick, *Alexandrian Christianity*, The Library of Christian Classics (Philadelphia, PA: Westminster Press, 1954), 389; Hartmann, 'Origène', 782-3.

[30] Discussion: in DeSilva, 'Example of How to Die Nobly'; van Henten, 'Christianization'.

[31] For lists of books of scripture, see Origen's *Commentary on the Psalter*, *Commentary on Matthew* 1, *Commentary on John* 5 and *Homilies on Joshua* 7.1.

[32] R. A. Greer, *An Exhortation to Martyrdom, Prayer, First principles. Book IV, Prologue to the Commentary on the Song of Songs, Homily XXVII on Numbers. Translation and Introduction* (London: SPCK, 1979), 56; DeSilva, 'Example of How to Die Nobly', 353.

[33] Translations from Origen's *Exhortation* are from Oulton and Chadwick (see n. 29).

Macc. 6.19) with the related word αὐτοπροαιρέτως.³⁴ The elaborate paraphrase of the king's attempt to persuade the youngest son from 2 Maccabees 7 also emphasizes the determination of the martyrs with a double reference to their resolution (προαίρεσις, *Mart*. 26).³⁵ Origen quotes the section where Eleazar receives the opportunity to pretend to eat a piece of pork (2 Macc. 6.23–8) almost in its entirety, with small adaptations of the text. He highlights Eleazar's statement with his motivation for not accepting the king's representatives' offer with the addition of εἶπεν ὅτι. This long quotation is followed by an introduction to Eleazar's second statement in 6.30, which is also fully quoted. The voluntary aspect of Eleazar's death, Eleazar could have avoided his martyrdom by pretending to eat pork, is clearly important for Origen.³⁶ The case of Eleazar already shows that Origen's reinterpretation of the Maccabean martyrdoms in *Exhortation* 22–27 focuses on the martyrs' statements. He quotes most of them, some with adaptations.³⁷ The martyrs' motivations are reformulated, partly along the lines of 4 Maccabees, because the martyrs sacrifice their life for the proper worship of God (εὐσέβεια, e.g. *Mart*. 22, 23, 27)³⁸ and steadfastness (ὑπομονή, *Mart*. 23, 26).³⁹ In the next section we will see that both motives are reinterpreted from a Christian perspective.

Origen is not interested in the personal information about the martyrs and the reason for their arrest. Differently from Cyprian he omits the information about the sacrificial meal in which the martyrs are forced to participate, and the offer to Eleazar to pretend at least to eat a piece of pork (cf. 2 Macc. 6.20-2). He also leaves out most of the details of the torture and execution of the martyrs except the torture of the first son. The only item of the martyrs' Jewish culture and identity mentioned several times is the law.⁴⁰ Importantly, in none of these passages does Origen discuss the meaning of the law. He is not interested in the Jewish connotation of the law and seems to have a different kind of law in mind (below).

A striking reinterpretation of the Maccabean martyrdoms concerns the scalping of the first brother, which is also highlighted by Cyprian. Origen associates it with

---

[34] D. Bertrand, 'Typologie des références à la Bible dans le Discours sur la prière', in *Origeniana Sexta: Origène et la Bible/Origen and the Bible*, ed. G. Dorrival and A. le Boulluec, BETL 118 (Leuven: Peeters, 1995), 229–41, 232–3, who distinguishes four formal ways of Origen's rendering of scripture: (1) explicit quotation, (2) implicit quotation (not introduced), (3) allusion and (4) references through biblical names. He also notes that Origen not only quotes from scripture in order to comment upon the quoted passage but also uses quotations to illustrate his commentary or simply quotes out of his love for quoting scripture. Further discussion: B. Neuschäfer, *Origenes als Philologe*, 2 vols, Schweizerische Beiträge zur Altertumswissenschaft 18.1–2 (Basel: Friedrich Reinhardt, 1987); F. Young, *Biblical Exegesis and the Formation of Christian Culture* (Cambridge: Cambridge University Press, 1997).

[35] Note also the addition of ἑκουσίως 'voluntarily' to the quotation from 2 Macc. 7.18 (*Mart*. 25).

[36] Cf. Heb. 11.35.

[37] 2 Macc. 6.24–8; 6.30; 7.2, 9, 12 (with adaptations), 14 (with adaptations), 18 (with adaptations), 30 (with adaptations).

[38] See also *Mart*. 5; 25; 29; 42; 47.

[39] See also *Mart*. 2; 15; 23; 26; 34; 37; 39; 41–44; 49; 4 Macc. 9.6; 16.1; 17.7, 10, 23.

[40] *Mart*. 22, quotation of 2 Macc. 6.28; *Mart*. 23, quotation of 2 Macc. 7.2, referring to the ancestral laws; *Mart*. 24, quotation of 2 Macc. 7.9, referring to God's laws; *Mart*. 25, quotation of 2 Macc. 7.11, referring to God's laws; *Mart*. 26, adapted quotation of 2 Macc. 7.30, referring to the law given by God.

circumcision, a Jewish identity marker not mentioned in 2 Maccabees 7: 'And he [i.e. the first son] endured the scalping in the Scythian way (τὸν περισκυθισμόν) like others endure the circumcision for the sake of divine law (τὴν διὰ τὸν θεῖον νόμον περιτομήν), assuming that he would fulfil in this way the word of God's covenant' (*Mart.* 23). Scalping was a Scythian punishment for defeated enemies, and the Scythians were famous for their cruelty.[41] Origen's association of the Scythian scalping (περισκυθίζω; also 2 Macc. 7.4) with circumcision (περιτομή) is probably triggered by the assumption of some similarity of practice, the all-round taking away of human skin, note the περί– in both words, but his adaptation may be understood along theological lines. It has been suggested that Origen hints here at martyrdom as a second circumcision as a new entry to the people of the covenant, equivalent to martyrdom as a second baptism in the Christian context.[42] Origen creates an analogy between circumcision and dying a martyr's death here ('he endured ... like others endure'), but he does not refer to circumcision as a Jewish identity marker and the actual circumcision of a male baby on its eighth day (Lev. 12.3; Lk. 1.59). Origen probably interprets circumcision allegorically here, as he does elsewhere, for example in his much discussed *Homily on the Circumcision of Abraham*.[43] He may have been inspired by Paul's reference to the circumcision of the heart (Rom. 2.28-9) as indication of the proper attitude towards God leading to martyrdom, or by interpreting Jesus's circumcision in Luke (Lk. 2.21) as anticipation of the crucifixion along the line of the *imitatio Christi*.[44] The 'divine law' in *Exhortation* 23 should probably also be interpreted from a Christian perspective, referring to the Word of God and Jesus Christ, who was with God and is God (Origen, *Cels.* 8.6).[45]

In short, the ethnic and cultural-religious identities of the Maccabean martyrs have by and large become irrelevant in the Christian reinterpretations analysed here. Cyprian and Origen refer to the Jewish law and Hippolytus and Cyprian to the ancestral language of the Maccabees, but these references are unimportant or being reinterpreted from a Christian perspective. Origen's association of the scalping of the first Maccabean brother with circumcision in *Exhortation* 23 is a case in point. He ignores circumcision as a Jewish identity marker and reinterprets it allegorically from a Christian perspective, turning the Maccabees in this way into a model for

---

[41] Herodotus 4.46, 62, 64-5. See also 2 Macc. 4.47.
[42] H. Chadwick in Oulton and Chadwick, *Alexandrian Christianity*, 408 n. 13; M.-B. Von Stritzki (trans.), *Aufforderung zum Martyrium*, Origenes: Werke mit Deutscher Übersetzung (Berlin-Freiburg: de Gruyter-Herder, 2010), 63.
[43] *Hom. Gen.* 3.4-5; M. R. Niehoff, 'Circumcision as a Marker of Identity: Philo, Origen and the Rabbis on Gen. 17:1-14', *JSQ* 10 (2003), 89-123; M. Himmelfarb, 'The Ordeals of Abraham: Circumcision and the "Aqedah" in Origen, the "Mekhilta", and "Genesis Rabbah"', *Henoch* 30 (2008), 289-310; M. Kister, 'Allegorical Interpretations of Biblical Narratives in Rabbinic Literature, Philo and Origen: Some Case Studies', in *New Approaches to the Study of Biblical Interpretation in Judaism of the Second Temple Period and Early Christianity. Proceedings of the Eleventh International Symposium of the Orion Center for the Study of the Dead Sea Scrolls and Associated Literature, Jointly Sponsored by the Hebrew University Center for the Study of Christianity, 9-11 January, 2007*, ed. G. A. Anderson, R. A. Clements and D. Satran (Leiden: Brill, 2013), 133-83. See also Origen, *Comm. Matt.* 11.12; *Comm. Rom.* 10-11; 19.
[44] This was suggested to me by Shaye J. D. Cohen.
[45] See also Origen, *Cels.* 7.34.

Christian martyrs. Nowhere in the passages discussed is there any hint of a polemics with Jewish opponents or fellow Christians who were sympathetic to Jewish religious practices. The Christianization of the Maccabees seems to have been self-evident from the earliest stage of their Christian reception onward. This process may be an example of what Andrew Jacobs describes as the 'historization' of the Jew, a process that renders Jews merely 'historical' by transferring them or their heritage to an embodied, living Christian past. This discursive strategy demands a kind of death according to Jacobs: Jews are imagined as 'dead' once they have supplied Christians what they need for their own theological and practical projects.[46] I would add that this pattern of reinterpretation goes hand in hand with a trajectory that ends up in the 'scripturalization' of the Maccabees, as becomes explicit in Origen and Cyprian. The Maccabean martyrdoms are not only part of Christian history but they are included in Christian Holy scripture or at least closely associated with that, which automatically implies that their stories are read through a Christian lens. Elsewhere Origen refers to 'the Maccabean books', but he mentions those only once in connection with a list of twenty-two books of the Old Testament and their equivalents in the Hebrew Bible, indicating that the Maccabean books do not belong to the Old Testament.[47] At the same time he refers in the *Exhortation* to the martyrdom of the seven brothers as part of scripture (ἡ γραφή, *Mart.* 23; 27, above).[48]

The motives for choosing martyrdom

The motives of the Maccabean martyrs in Heb. 11.35–6 remain implicit apart from a double reference to their resurrection. Neither the Jewish law nor God is mentioned in these verses and the martyrdoms are reinterpreted in several ways. Heb. 11.35de alludes to Eleazar, but the plural phrase 'still others' presupposes that there were more witnesses who suffered the torture of the *tympanon*, because they rejected the opportunity to avoid torture and execution offered to them. The sufferings are presented as the overture to the 'better resurrection', which means that the focus is upon the vindication of the martyrs. The phrase κρείττων ἀνάστασις ('better resurrection') is specific to Hebrews (cf. Heb. 11.40) and is formulated in contrast to the resurrection mentioned at the beginning of the verse, which refers to resuscitations as a continuation of one's earthly life (Heb. 11.35ab).[49] The better resurrection must

---

[46] A. Jacobs, *The Remains of the Jews: The Holy Land and Christian Empire in Late Antiquity* (Stanford, CA: Stanford University Press, 2004), 111–12.
[47] Origen, *Sel. Ps.* 12.1084. Other references to the Maccabean books: *Cels.* 8.46; *Comm. Jo.* 1.17; 13.58; *Or.* 11.1; *Hom. Jer.* 7.1; *Philoc.* 27; *Fr. Ps.* 43.1; *Fr. Exod.* 12.268.
[48] There is ambiguity in Origen about the status of some of the other Deuterocanonical Books as well; see E. L. Gallagher and J. Meade, *The Biblical Canon Lists from Early Christianity: Texts and Analysis* (Oxford: Oxford University Press, 2017), 83–98; L. McDonald, *The Formation of the Bible, Vol. 1, the Old Testament: Its Authority and Canonicity* (London: Bloomsbury/T&T Clark, 2017), 319–20. For the gradual process of the canonization of 2 and 4 Maccabees and the early manuscript witnesses to these books, see also Knust, '"Who Were the Maccabees?"'.
[49] C. Rose, *Die Wolke der Zeugen: Eine exegetisch-traditionsgeschichtliche Untersuchung zu Hebräer 10,32–12,3*, WUNT 2. Series 60 (Tübingen: Mohr-Siebeck, 1994), 314; D. A. Hagner, *Hebrews*, NIBC 14 (Peabody, MA: Hendrickson, 1990), 206–7.

refer to the eschatological resurrection. The Maccabean witnesses support the author's parenetic argument about faith within the context of the larger section of 10.19–12.15, despite the contrast between the previous witnesses and the community of Christ: they did not receive God's ultimate promise given with Christ, but they will be rewarded with the believers in Christ when salvation comes (11.39–40).[50]

The allusions to the Maccabees in Heb. 11.33–8 are obviously part of an elaborate cluster of references to named heroes from the past as well as to anonymous figures (11.2–31, 32, 33–38).[51] The key concept that underlies the lists of heroes in Hebrews 11 is πίστις ('faith' or 'trust'), defined in the first verse as 'Now faith is the realization (NRSV: assurance) of things hoped for, the conviction of things not seen'. Πίστις probably has an eschatological connotation (cf. the 'things hoped for') and the figures in the list function as models who anticipate this future.[52] Πίστις functions at the same time as a principle or power for the heroes listed, who act by it.[53] The subsequent series of lists of heroes exemplify this concept of πίστις, focusing on persons who apply this faith, as the repetition of formulae with πίστις as introduction of the examples implies. The passages referred to in the allusions imply that several figures of the lists sacrificed their lives in the framework of πίστις, including the Maccabean martyrs, even if πίστις or a Hebrew equivalent is absent in the source text as a key phrase that highlights the deeds or attitude of the heroes involved.[54] This is also true for 2 Macc. 6.18–7.42, but it should be noted that πίστις or related vocabulary does occur a few times as alternative motive for εὐσέβεια ('piety', 'proper attitude to God') in 4 Maccabees.[55]

The two Latin Passions that highlight the exemplary behaviour of the martyrs' mothers by comparing them with the mother of the seven Maccabean brothers are quite different from Hebrews 11, but the little information they provide about the motives of the Maccabean martyrs points in the same direction. The focus is, of course, on the Christian mothers of the martyrs. The Passion of Montanus, for example, highlights the faith (*fides*) and piety (*religiose pia*) of the mother of Flavianus (16.3–4, above).[56]

The short passage in Hippolytus's *Comm. Dan.* 2.35 that alludes to the torture of the seven Maccabean brothers does not mention a motive for preferring martyrdom to living on in shame, but the longer passage in 2.20 that quotes parts of 2 Macc. 7.1–6 and is part of the commentary on Dan. 3.16–18 with the refusal to commit idolatry as *leitmotiv* mentions the martyrs' faithfulness to the ancestral laws as main motive (20.3). A second motive is referred to with the quotation of 2 Macc. 7.6 in 20.4: 'God our Lord

---

[50] Rose, *Wolke der Zeugen*, 323–31; P. M. Eisenbaum, *The Jewish Heroes of Christian History: Hebrews 11 in Literary Context*, SBLDS 156 (Atlanta, GA: Scholars Press, 1997), 145–6, 160, 167, 181–2.
[51] Rose, *Wolke der Zeugen*, 92–146.
[52] H. W. Attridge, *The Epistle to the Hebrews: A Commentary on the Epistle to the Hebrews*, Hermeneia (Philadelphia, PA: Fortress, 1989), 308; R. Brawley, 'Discourse Structure and the Unseen in Hebrews 2:8 and 11:1: A Neglected Aspect of the Context', *CBQ* 55 (1993), 81–98. See also D. Hamm, 'Faith in the Epistle to the Hebrews: The Jesus Factor', *CBQ* 52 (1990), 270–91.
[53] Eisenbaum, *Jewish Heroes*, 145–6.
[54] Eisenbaum, *Jewish Heroes*, 140, 146–7, 158.
[55] 4 Macc. 7.21; 17.2. J. W. van Henten, 'The Tradition-Historical Background of Rom. 3.25: A Search for Pagan and Jewish Parallels', in *From Jesus to John: Essays on Jesus and New Testament Christology in Honour of Marinus de Jonge*, ed. M. C. de Boer, JSNTSup 84 (Sheffield: JSOT Press, 1993), 101–28, 125–6.
[56] Cf. Pas. Mar. 13.1–3.

is watching and truly will have mercy with us, as Moses previously made clear in public, saying "And he will have mercy with his servants" [Deut. 32.36].' The martyrs state that they will be comforted by God, which in the context of Hippolytus's commentary plausibly refers to the martyrs' vindication by God. Hippolytus's minor adaptations of the quotation of 2 Macc. 7.6 and the passage's immediate context imply that the focus of the passage is most probably not on the Jewish people, and the solidarity with the people expressed by the martyrs, but on the martyrs only. The quotation is followed up by Hippolytus's more general statement that God's Spirit encourages the martyrs to contempt death and anticipate their posthumous reward (2.21), which would match the previous passage about the Maccabees well if that would end with a hint at the martyrs' vindication.

Cyprian's reinterpretation of the Maccabean martyrs in *Ad Fortunatum* 11 presents them as models of martyrdom (*martyrium*) and models of faith and virtue (*fidei et virtutis exempla*) as part of a continuous chain of heroes that starts with Abel. As in Hebrews 11 and the Passion of Montanus and Lucius 'faith' (πίστις, *fides*) is a key theme, which is at the same time a central motivation for the martyrs. The Maccabean martyrdoms are great manifestations of faith (*documenta fidei*) in Cyprian.[57] The conclusion of Cyprian's discussion focuses upon Eleazar and highlights once again that he rejected the option to deceive his fellows. It also points to *fides* as an important motive:

> His sincere faith and perfect and fully pure virtue (*Sincera ... fides et virtus integra ac satis pura*), had absolutely no thought for King Antiochus, only for God the Judge. He knew that it could not help him to reach salvation, if he took it lightly and deceived a human person [i.e., Antiochus], since God, who is the Judge of our conscience, and is only to be feared, can never be sported with, nor deceived.

Cyprian alludes here to 2 Macc. 6.26, where Eleazar points out that God would be aware of the deception and would punish him. Next to *fides* and *virtus* is 'salvation' a motive for Eleazar's decision in this passage, but it is not elaborated.

Cyprian expresses the martyrs' anticipation of being resurrected by God earlier on in this section, as several statements of the brothers indicate:

> But he [the second brother] being confident in his martyrdom, and promising himself the reward of resurrection because of God's vindication, exclaimed and said, 'You indeed, in your fury, rob us from this present life; but the King of the world shall raise us, who have died for his laws, unto the resurrection of life forever'. (quotation of 2 Macc. 7.9)

> ... [he, i.e., the fourth brother] said, 'It is preferable to those who are being put to death by humans to expect from God to be raised again by him; for you there shall be no resurrection to life'. (quotation of 2 Macc. 7.14)

---

[57] See also the fifth brother, who trampled by strength of faith (*fidei vigore*) upon the bloodshedding of the king, and the mother's truth of faith (*in fidei veritate*).

'[the mother] I may receive you again together with your brothers by this mercy [i.e., God's mercy]'. (quotation of 2 Macc. 7.29)

The resurrection of the martyrs is also highlighted with the help of quotations from 2 Maccabees 7 in *Testimonies against the Jews* 3.16–17. Cyprian leaves it open whether the vindication of the martyrs takes place immediately, as implied in 2 Maccabees, or at the end of times.[58] Additional motives concern the *imitatio Christi* and the undoing of sins by the martyrs. The third brother intended to imitate the passion of Jesus Christ by his way of stretching forth his hands for punishment. The sixth martyr acknowledges with a quotation of 2 Macc. 7.18 that he and his brothers were suffering because of their sins, which implies that their martyrdom was beneficiary for themselves. Cyprian does not elaborate these motives here. This is also true for the three additional motives connected with the mother: the law,[59] the fear of God[60] and her motherly love for her sons: '[the mother] … as became one, whose thoughts were toward the law and toward God, as became one, whose love for her children was severe rather than indulgent'.

Origen adapts the statements of the Maccabean martyrs. He expands, for example, the words of the youngest brother to the executioners in 7.30 that he and his brothers obey the law given by God (*Mart.* 26). He makes it explicit that in case of conflicting interests God's law is to be preferred to the law of the authorities, a view that is already implied by the stories of Daniel 3 and 6, as Origen himself points out in *Exhortation* 33.[61] A similar point is added to the direct speech of the youngest martyr (2 Macc. 7.30–8): 'We must not accept a command that is contrary to the divine words' (*Mart.* 26). Origen consistently reinterprets the Maccabean martyrdoms as deaths for the proper worship of God (εὐσέβεια), as the author of 4 Maccabees does (above). *Exhortation* 27, for example, focuses on the mother who had to witness the execution of her seven sons. Origen highlights her extraordinary capability of making the love for her children subordinate to the love for God, which may build on the praise for the mother in 4 Maccabees and matches a line of interpretation in early Christian homilies on the Maccabean martyrs: 'It enables us to see how proper worship and love for God (εὐσέβεια καὶ τὸν πρὸς θεὸν φίλτρον) are far more powerful than any other bond of affection against the most severe sufferings and the harshest tortures' (*Mart.* 27).[62] Origen emphasizes the public dimension of martyrdom and comments that the

---

[58] For the vindication in 2 Maccabees, see J. W. van Henten, *The Maccabean Martyrs as Saviours of the Jewish People: A Study of 2 and 4 Maccabees*, JSJSup 57 (Leiden: Brill, 1997), 172–82.

[59] Cf. Eleazar further on in the passage with an allusion to 2 Macc. 6.24–5: faithfulness to the law of God.

[60] Similarly, Eleazar ('I fear You'), who also wants to avoid the eternal penalties of an offended God (allusion to 2 Macc. 7.25–6). Also Cyprian, *Test.* 3.16–17.

[61] Van Henten, *Maccabean Martyrs*, 10–14.

[62] 4 Macc. 14.13–15.32. See also the image of fire in connection with motherly love (*Mart.* 27; 4 Macc. 16.3–4) and the feelings of the mother in her 'inmost parts' (*Mart.* 27; 4 Macc. 14.13; 15.23, 29), Hartmann, 'Origène', 796; DeSilva, 'Example of How to Die Nobly', 348–9. John Chrysostom further elaborates the motif of maternal love and fire and presents the mother's martyrdom as a triumph of spiritual fire over actual fire (*Homily 2 on the Maccabees*, PG 50 625.32–46, J. W. van Henten, 'The *Passio Perpetuae* and Jewish Martyrdom: The Motif of Motherly Love', in *Perpetua's Passions: Multidisciplinary Approaches to the Passio Perpetuae et Felicitatis*, ed. J. Bremmer and M. Formisano (Oxford: Oxford University Press, 2012), 118–33. About the mother in homilies, see

willingness to confess the only real God in public is the realization of the proper attitude to God (εὐσέβεια) in Christ (*Mart.* 42). This attitude is therefore enacted in contact with or through the mediation of Jesus Christ (διὰ τὴν εἰς θεὸν ἐν Χριστῷ εὐσέβειαν).[63] Other passages about martyrdom for the sake of proper worship should probably be interpreted from this perspective, like the reference to Eleazar's martyrdom as a death for εὐσέβεια (*Mart.* 22).[64] Origen's paraphrase of the martyrdom of the third brother (*Mart.* 25) introduces a motive that does not occur in Second Maccabees:

> *And the third* [the third brother] *did not care at all about the tortures* (2 Macc. 7.12) and trampled upon them out of his love for God (διὰ τὴν πρὸς τὸν θεὸν ἀγαπήν). *When he was asked for his tongue, he exposed it quickly and held out his hands with good courage* (2 Macc. 7.10), saying: '*I forgo these for* God's *laws and hope to receive them back from* God in the state in which he may give them to the athletes for proper worship (οἱ τῆς εὐσεβείας ἀθληταί) focused upon him'. (2 Macc. 7.11; the text of 2 Maccabees is given in italics)

This cluster of quotations shows in comparison to 2 Macc. 7.10-12 several adaptations and expansions. Origen makes the indirect reference to God as Heaven in 2 Maccabees explicit, but he is more vague about the recreation of the martyr's body as formulated in 2 Maccabees 7. He also introduces the motive of the love for God.[65] This is an important addition, since this motif is already mentioned in Origen's introduction of his writing.[66] In *Exhortation* 2-3 Origen connects the motif of the love for God with the themes of community with God and not being dependent on the body: 'I think that they love God with all their soul who withdraw and separate their soul not only from their earthly body but from every kind of body because of their great eagerness to be united with God' (*Mart.* 3). Origen's goal for Christians seems to be an afterlife close to God and in unity with Jesus Christ, and martyrdom is the best way to reach this goal. This does not mean that life on earth has become meaningless, but one's earthly life should be a life in anticipation of the post-mortem existence near God. This calls for the readiness to confess God even at the cost of one's life. This attitude will render the believer a superior knowledge already on earth, which is not only intellectual but also spiritual, and which will allow access to the full secrets of God after the fate of martyrdom (*Mart.* 13).[67] There may also be an autobiographical reason for Origen to highlight this motif, because one of the passages about it links it to the children of a

---

[ ] R. Ziadé, *Les martyrs Maccabées: de l'histoire juive au culte chrétien: Les homélies de Grégoire de Nazianze et de Jean Chrysostome*, VCS 80 (Leiden: Brill, 2007), 70-2, 91-4, 99, 227-33, 242-6, 253-6.
[63] Also *Mart.* 47.
[64] Origen characterizes the Maccabean brothers as 'athletes of or for εὐσέβεια' (*Mart.* 23 twice). See also *Mart.* 25 and 27.
[65] J.den Boeft and J. N. Bremmer, 'Notiunculae Martyrologicae IV', *VigChr* 45 (1991), 105-22, esp. 121 n. 33, suggest that this motif shows, among other things, Origen's Christian reinterpretation of the Maccabean martyrdoms. Also Ziadé, *martyrs Maccabées*, 98-9.
[66] Cf. *Mart.* 7; 10-11; 37-8.
[67] Cf. *Mart.* 4 and 6. Hartmann, 'Origène', 784 with n. 6, 792-6, 803, 820. Cf. W. Völker, *Das Volkommenheitsideal des Origenes*, Beiträge zur historischen Theologie 7 (Tübingen: Mohr, 1931); J. Lebreton, 'La source et la caractère de la mystique d'Origène', *Analecta Bollandiana* 67 (1949), 55-62.

martyr who are left behind 'out of love for God' (*Mart.* 38), a traumatic fate, which Origen himself experienced when he was less than 17 years old.[68]

The Maccabean martyrs as models

The Passion of Montanus and Lucius counts the mother of Flavianus among the old personal model figures of her group (*vetera exempla*) through the analogy with the Maccabean mother and the association with the patriarchs (Pas. Mont. 16). She equalled the patriarchs, proved herself to be a daughter of Abraham and is called a 'mother of Maccabees'. Her *pietas* and her self-denial by accepting her son's execution and even encouraging him is highlighted by references to a glorious past, including that of the Maccabean martyrs. Although this is not stated explicitly, that past belongs obviously to the history of her own group. The same line of thought underlies the even briefer passage about the mother of Marian in Passion of Marian and James 13.

The brief paraphrases of the Maccabean martyrdoms in Heb. 11.35–6 are part of an anonymous list of models (11.33–8), who acted in an exemplary way like the other old witnesses (cf. Heb. 11.2: ἐμαρτυρήθησαν οἱ πρεσβύτεροι) inspired by faith. The anonymous list follows upon a brief list of six models (11.32, the judges Gideon, Barak, Samson and Jephtah, followed by David and Samuel)[69] and a much more elaborate list of named witnesses in 11.2–31. The entire cluster of witnesses functions as models in the context of a larger parenetic section that offers consolation and encouragement to the intended readers (10.19–39; 12.4–15), who are confronted with a situation of persecution (10.32–4).[70] The cloud of witnesses forms together with Jesus Christ's crucifixion and vindication (12.1–3) an incitement of the readers to 'run with perseverance the race that is set before us' (12.1). Although at least some of the passages alluded to in Hebrews imply that these old witnesses were vindicated by God, the author states that they did not yet receive what was promised (11.39); they will be perfected together with the intended audience of the letter (the 'us' of 11.40), which must imply the salvation effected by Jesus Christ at the end of times (cf. 10.36–9).[71] All named 'witnesses' are figures of the past and, in fact, heroes from the history of Israel, but they have become part of another history that starts with and culminates in Jesus Christ. The cluster of witnesses leads anaphorically to Jesus as the one who founded faith and perfected it as well (12.2; cf. 5.8–9).[72] Jesus, therefore, encompasses and continues the trajectory exemplified by the witnesses from Hebrews 11, and he surpasses the

---

[68] Eusebius, *Hist. eccl.* 6.2. Oulton and Chadwick, *Alexandrian Christianity*, 172, 391.
[69] Eisenbaum, *Jewish Heroes*, 174.
[70] Attridge, *Epistle to the Hebrews*, 306; Rose, *Wolke der Zeugen*, 26, 79, 97; Eisenbaum, *Jewish Heroes*, 45, 137–8.
[71] Eisenbaum, *Jewish Heroes*, 177–8, with references.
[72] I. G. Wallis, *The Faith of Jesus Christ in Early Christian Traditions*, SNTSMS 84 (Cambridge: Cambridge University Press, 2005), 147–61. Also P. G. Müller, *ΧΡΙΣΤΟΣ ΑΡΧΗΓΟΣ, Der religionsgeschichtliche und theologische Hintergrund einer neutestamentlichen Christusprädikation*, Europäische Hochschulschriften Series 23, 28 (Frankfurt: Peter Lang, 1973), 309; G. Friedrich, *Die Verkündigung des Todes Jesu im Neuen Testament*, Biblisch-Theologische Studien 6 (Neukirchen-Vluyn: Neukirchener Verlag, 1982), 156–75.

witnesses by the beneficiary effect of his death and his immediate vindication (12.1–3). The Maccabean martyrdoms are radically reinterpreted as models in the Christocentric framework of salvation history in Hebrews. As noted already above, the ethnic and cultural-religious identities of the martyrs and the Jewish patriotic significance of the martyrdoms are completely ignored in Hebrews. Moreover, the martyrs have been anonymized and pluralized in order to suggest that many other heroes performed similar deeds. The focus of the paraphrases is not only on the suffering of the martyrs but also on their reward, reinterpreted as their resurrection at the end of times, as Heb. 11.35 indicates (above). They clearly support the parenetic argument about faith in the larger section 10.19–12.15 and the martyrs will be rewarded together with the believers in Christ when salvation comes (11.39–40). In this way the martyrs have become integrated with the community founded by Jesus Christ.[73]

Hippolytus too presents the Maccabean martyrs as well as Daniel and his companions in a framework of Christian reinterpretation (*Comm. Dan.* 2.20; 2.35). They seem to belong to the group of martyrs, or perhaps witnesses, of the past (τοὺς πάλαι μάρτυρας, 2.35.1), although they were not rescued as Daniel and his companions were, who were led on to the pit by the Holy Spirit (2.19.8; cf. 2.21.1–2). It was God's purpose that the Maccabees died as martyrs because they could function in this way as a model (ὑπογραμμός) for Hippolytus and his fellow Christians (ἵνα ἡμέτερος οὗτος γένηται ὑπογραμμός, 2.35.8).[74] This is also true for Hippolytus's other passage about the Maccabees (2.20). The quotation of 2 Macc. 7.6 in this passage probably refers to the Maccabean martyrs themselves, who will be comforted by God. The continuation of the commentary in 2.21 implies that contemporary martyrs can expect the same kind of comfort: 'You see how the Spirit of the Father cares for martyrs, he teaches, while urging and encouraging them, to despise this death and to hasten to what is better' (2.21.1). The Maccabees have become part of an ongoing chain of martyrs and function as models for Christian martyrs. Without any explanation they have become part of the Christian salvation history as imagined by Hippolytus. The model function works in two ways, highlighting both the proper attitude for the martyrs – remaining faithful to the word of God and taking up one's cross (2.21.3) – and their vindication by God.

Cyprian's *Ad Fortunatum* 11 also recreates the Maccabean martyrdoms in a Christian framework of interpretation that simply presupposes a continuity between the heroes of scripture, to whom the Maccabees also seem to belong, and the Christian martyrs of Cyprian's own period and the future up to the end of times. Cyprian argues that the afflictions of his fellow Christians and himself are nothing special, which he demonstrates with a cluster of heroes from the past and a great number of quotations from scripture. Abel as first model of this list implies that the entire human history is characterized by suffering or the violent death of righteous persons. A transition to a second series of heroes interprets the entire cluster as martyrdoms of the righteous (*martyria iustorum*) and models of faith and virtue (*fidei et virtutis exempla*). Cyprian expands the well-known Roman concept of personal models of virtue by combining

---
[73] Eisenbaum, *Jewish Heroes*, 131, 142, 153, 161, 165, 168, 173, 184–8.
[74] Cf. 1 Clem. 5.7 about Paul as the greatest model of steadfastness.

it with faith.[75] The introduction of the seven Maccabean brothers highlights that they were born from the same mother and shared the same virtues (*septem fratres et natalium pariter et virtutum sorte consimiles*), but these virtues are not elaborated. When Cyprian starts to paraphrase and quote 2 Macc. 6.18–7.42, he highlights the martyrdoms as manifestations of faith (*documenta fidei*). Both virtue and faith are mentioned again in Cyprian's reinterpretation of the first son: 'who [the Maccabean martyrs] had rather provoked the king by the constancy of virtue and faith (*virtutis et fidei constantia*)'.[76] Although Cyprian distinguishes former models (*vetera exempla*) from contemporary ones, as is apparent from the conclusion of this section, he presents the Maccabean martyrs as part of a one-dimensional history from the creation up to the end of time. The events of this history are interpreted from the perspective of Christian scripture. There is some sort of a superlative degree in this history, because if Christians will follow the example of the previous models, the number of Christian martyrs will be endless, which is, characteristically, pointed out with another passage from scripture:

> If, therefore, we too live dedicated and devoted to God, if we go on our journey along those ancient and sacred footsteps of the righteous, along the same evidence of tortures, the same testimonies of sufferings, we may take this into account as the greater glory of our time, that while the number of those former models (*vetera exempla*) may be counted, Christian martyrs (*martyres christiani*) will soon be without number by the abundant supply of virtue and faith (*exuberante postmodum copia virtutis ac fidei*); as the Apocalypse bears witness, and says, 'After these things I beheld a great multitude, which nobody could number'. (quotation of Rev. 7.9–15)

In short, if the Christian martyrs follow the lead of the Maccabees and other former models of faith, they will greatly surpass these old examples in number and enhance the glory of their time with their endless number of models of virtue and faith.

Finally, how do the Maccabean martyrs function in the context of Origen's *Exhortation*? Origen highlights the usefulness of the Maccabean examples by an *inclusio* at the beginning and end of the section about the martyrdoms. In *Exhortation* 22 he states, 'And this is useful for our purpose', and at the end he says, 'I think that in view of our present purpose it was most useful to give here this story from Scripture' (*Mart.* 27, above). The conclusion highlights at the same time Origen's reinterpretation of the martyrdoms as a death for the sake of proper worship and love for God (above). Obviously, Origen uses the Maccabean martyrs as models who illustrate his encouragement of Ambrose and Prototectus to embrace martyrdom. He invokes his intended readers to say words similar to those of Eleazar in 2 Macc. 6.30 (*Mart.* 22,

---

[75] H. W. Litchfield, 'National *Exempla Virtutis* in Roman Literature', HSCP 25 (1914), 1–71; H. Kornhardt, 'Exemplum: Eine bedeutungsgeschichtliche Studie' (PhD diss., Georg-August-Universität Göttingen, 1936), 13–24; A. Lumpe, 'Exemplum', RAC 6 (1966), 1229–57; M. B. Roller, 'Exemplarity in Roman Culture: The Cases of Horatius Cocles and Cloelia', CP 99 (2004), 1–56.

[76] Cf. also the fifth brother, who 'trampled by strength of faith (*fidei vigore*) upon the bloodshedding of the king', the mother's truth of faith (*in fidei veritate*) and Eleazar's sincere faith and perfect and pure virtue (*Sincera prorsus fides et virtus integra ac satis pura*).

above). He points to the exemplary function of the Maccabees by calling them a model (παράδειγμα), as the author of 4 Maccabees does (*Mart.* 23). He calls for the imitation of Daniel's companions in a similar way by actualizing the biblical story: 'Even now Nebuchadnezzar is saying the same words to us, the true Hebrews of the world to come. Let us imitate (μιμησώμεθα) those holy ones[77] in order to experience the heavenly dew extinguishing all fire around us and refreshing our mind.' Origen seems to transpose both the Maccabean martyrdoms and the execution of Daniel's companions to the contemporary reality of the persecution of Christians under Maximinus Thrax. His intended audience should follow the example of these heroes known from scripture. The introduction and conclusion of the section about the Maccabees include several quotations from scripture: Eccl. 4.2 ('I [Solomon] praised all those who have died more than the living, as many are alive until now'), Ps. 117.14LXX ('The Lord is my strength and my praise') and a combination of Phil. 4.13 and 1 Tim. 1.12 ('I can do all things through Christ Jesus, our Lord, who empowers me'). Together these quotations focus upon Jesus Christ as the one who supports and strengthens the martyrs in their situation of extreme suffering.[78] Scripture means clearly Christian scripture here. The Maccabean martyrs have become Christianized forerunners of and models for Christian martyrs.

Conclusion

What are the main outcomes of my analysis of the reinterpretations of the Maccabean martyrs in Hebrews 11, Hippolytus, Origen, Cyprian, the Passion of Montanus and Lucius and the Passion of Marian and James? There are several modes of reinterpretations: allusion to, paraphrase of and quotation from the martyrdoms as described in 2 Maccabees. Several writings show correspondences with 4 Maccabees, but without offering quotations of or allusions to this work. The Christian reinterpretations of the Maccabean martyrs lack clear indications of a Christian uneasiness about the ethnic and cultural-religious identities of the martyrs. These identities appear to be irrelevant at this stage of the Christian reception of the Maccabees, which shows no signs at all of a practice of continuous interaction between Jews and Christians. The Maccabees do not play a role of the 'Jewish other', who is used as legitimation for a partisan argument in support of one of the Christian denominations or a particular Christian ideology. Cyprian and Origen do refer to the Jewish law and Cyprian and Hippolytus mention the ancestral language of the Maccabees, but these issues are either unimportant or being reinterpreted from a Christian perspective. The Maccabees appear to have been totally 'historicized' (with Andrew Jacobs), that is, transferred to an embodied, living Christian past.[79] This 'historization' goes hand in hand with a second pattern of reinterpretation, which I would call the 'scripturalization' of the

---

[77] Cf. *Mart.* 35 and 4 Macc. 13.9.
[78] Cf. Eusebius, *Hist. eccl.* 5.1.22-4, 27-8, 56. Cf. Pas. Perp. 4.6; Origen, *Mart.* 4: the Spirit of Christ lives in Christians and incites them to trust God.
[79] This is also one of the results of the analysis of Knust, '"Who Were the Maccabees?"' (96).

Maccabees. The Maccabean martyrdoms are associated with Christian scripture or even integrated with it, implicitly at least in Cyprian and explicitly in Origen, who quotes from 2 Maccabees as scripture (ἡ γραφή, *Mart.* 23; 27).

The reinterpretations of the martyrs' motives confirm that they have become Christian heroes. The motive that is absent in 2 Maccabees but most frequently mentioned in the reinterpretations is faith (πίστις/*fides*), which is combined with virtue (*virtus*) in Cyprian. Another motive, which does link up with 2 Maccabees, is the expectation of divine vindication, mostly transferred to the end of times. In Origen εὐσέβεια ('proper attitude to God') and 'love for God' (ἡ πρὸς τὸν θεὸν ἀγάπη/τὸ πρὸς θεὸν φίλτρον) are prominent motives. All motives are interpreted from a Christian perspective, which implies that the Jewish motivations of the martyrs are replaced by Christian motivations. This makes it understandable that the Maccabees can function as role models for Christian martyrs in the framework of Christian salvation history, but in various ways. Sometimes they belong to a glorious past of Christian heroes, which implies that they contribute to constructions of Christian group identity. Their persuasive exemplary function suggests that many later heroes performed similar deeds. This is elaborated by Cyprian, who constructs a continuity between the Maccabees and Christian martyrs of his own period, but differentiates at the same time between the Maccabees as belonging to the previous models (*vetera exempla*) and the endless number of Christian martyrs who would follow their example. In this way former Jewish heroes enhance the glory of the Christian era.

What would be the implication of the Christianization of the Maccabees if one focuses on the imagined Christian community, in line with Benedict Anderson's felicitous phrase? The rhetoric of these martyrdom passages implies that the ideal community members would need to become 'Maccabees' in one way or the other. The actual historical circumstances are unimportant for the community; the crucial point is that they are perceived as a situation of a severe persecution that leads to a conflict of loyalties. The proper attitude in this conflict between the Christian way of life and obedience to the worldly authorities is highlighted by the previous self-sacrifice of the Maccabees. The re-enactment of the Maccabean attitude in this conflict by Christians would be a telling signal to the authorities that their time has come and that they will be defeated by the heirs of the Maccabees. These heirs deserve the same vindication as the Maccabees did, although this is postponed to the end of times. This community of martyrs is a key step towards a triumphant salvation history, and its attitude is determined by the faith and virtues exemplified by the Maccabean martyrs as well as by their rigorous lack of interest in a this-worldly life.

6

'The blind and the lame': An adapted category in early Christian communal self-understanding

Kylie Crabbe

In his commentary on Matthew's gospel, Ulrich Luz suggests that in Mt. 21.1–17, 'the blind and the lame' who approach Jesus in the temple represent the 'true people of God', in contrast to both the money changers who Jesus has just run out of the temple and the chief priests who stand by critically.[1] He intimates that early Christian readers would identify with these (ultimately healed) characters and recognize them as the new community of which they were themselves a part. In response to Luz's proposal, this essay considers key New Testament texts which refer to 'the blind and the lame' in light of the portraits of these groups in the Hebrew Bible, and various ways in which these are taken up in the Septuagint and sectarian literature from Qumran, to explore whether and how these terms might inform early Christian corporate identity.[2]

There are (at least) two senses in which early Christian self-understanding may appear to be shaped by these archetypal references to those with physical and sensory disabilities. First, in an approach we might call 'inclusion/exclusion', the community may construct itself in relation to a boundary, explicitly listing various conditions which are either included or excluded for group membership. Here there is scope for both literal and metaphorical application of the conditions 'the blind and the lame'. Or, secondly, group identity may itself be articulated in terms of communal identification with the impairments. This 'identification' approach necessarily incorporates a metaphorical sense, if the community as a whole is described as 'blind and lame'. However, the choice of this metaphor for self-understanding may still suggest a prominent place for the felt sense of weakness or affliction. I argue there is precedent for both approaches in the Hebrew Bible.

---

[1] I am grateful to Alma Brodersen, Candida Moss, and others at the ACU Rome seminar for discussion and insights related to this paper. Ulrich Luz, *A Commentary on Matthew*, trans. James E. Crouch, 3 vols, Hermeneia (Minneapolis, MN: Fortress, 2001–7), 3:14.

[2] 'The blind' and 'the lame' also make appearances together in some Graeco-Roman texts. See discussion in Louise A. Gosbell, *'The Poor, the Crippled, the Blind, and the Lame': Physical and Sensory Disability in the Gospels of the New Testament*, WUNT 1.469 (Tübingen: Mohr Siebeck, 2018), 52–5. My focus on the Jewish material here does not preclude the possibility that these other traditions also shape how some Jewish and early Christian writers portray these characters.

Key strands of 'the blind and the lame' in the Hebrew Bible

There are diverse strands within the Hebrew Bible's portrayal of those with physical and sensory impairments, but those which dominate relate to either restrictions on access and/or actions for those with such impairments or references within prophetic accounts of promised renewal or pilgrimage.[3] The following offers a brief survey, with particular attention to how the passages construct the Israelite community in relation to the groups listed.[4]

Before turning to these passages, however, a brief note on the language of 'disability' is warranted. This is of course a contemporary and not emic term in ancient texts.[5] However, I suggest two factors indicate that this contemporary language is appropriate. First, taking a social definition of disability (according to which the description of a person's physiology, morphology, and so on[6] is differentiated from the context-dependent social constructions around which aspects of human variation are deemed to be 'disabilities'),[7] it is clear that the Hebrew Bible sets out a suite of social ramifications for certain kinds of conditions. Without the term 'disability', the texts describe, for

---

[3] Texts such as Job and Isaiah 53 may encourage readers to identify with affliction in other ways, which there is not space to address here. Key biblical characters are also portrayed with impairments; see Gosbell on possible allusions to Moses's speech impediment (Gosbell, *'The Poor, the Crippled'*, 117–18).

[4] I focus particularly on the language of blind and lame which gains attention in each body of literature discussed here, though some attention to sensory and physical disability more broadly is occasionally helpful for making distinctions. This survey is necessarily limited. For more detail on Hebrew Bible texts, see Rebecca Raphael, *Biblical Corpora: Representations of Disability in Hebrew Biblical Literature*, LHBOTS 445 (New York: T&T Clark, 2008); Saul M. Olyan, *Disability in the Hebrew Bible: Interpreting Mental and Physical Differences* (New York: Cambridge University Press, 2008); and significant sections also in Gosbell, *'The Poor, the Crippled'*; and S. John Roth, *The Blind, the Lame, and the Poor: Character Types in Luke-Acts*, JSNTSS 144 (Sheffield: Sheffield Academic Press, 1997).

[5] Further discussion in Olyan, *Disability*, 12–13.

[6] This concept is often described with terms like 'impairment' or 'infirmity', in contrast to the category 'disability'. Raphael discusses a similar distinction between the 'biological body' and the 'ideological body' (Raphael, 'Disability, Identity, and Otherness in Persian-Period Israelite Thought', in *Imagining the Other and Constructing Israelite Identity in the Early Second Temple Period*, ed. Ehud Ben Zvi and Diana Vikander Edelman (London: T&T Clark, 2014), 278).

[7] Contemporary disability studies offers multiple models for defining disability. See discussion in Louise J. Lawrence, *Sense and Stigma in the Gospels: Depictions of Sensory-Disabled Characters* (Oxford: Oxford University Press, 2013), 4–5; Anna Rebecca Solevåg, *Negotiating the Disabled Body: Representations of Disability in Early Christian Texts* (Atlanta, GA: SBL Press, 2018), 4–9. Social, relational or cultural models are commonly distinguished from a medical model of disability, in which the claim is that assessments of disability arise from independent medical information through which certain traits can be classed uncontroversially as 'deficits'. Most contemporary theorists do not support this approach. The differences in *which* conditions might be labelled 'disabilities' in different social contexts highlight inadequacies in this approach. An additional model, the 'minority-group' approach, takes the lead from those who identify as having a disability and enables them to describe the disability in terms of the role it has in their lives, rather than describing their lives in relation to the disability (Lawrence, *Sense and Stigma*, 5). Raphael advocates adding a 'religious' element to models of disability in the ancient world, rather than reducing them to a medical/social distinction (Raphael, 'Disability, Identity', 279), which is a helpful reminder, though religious elements may be included in social and cultural frameworks.

instance, the social separation of those with skin conditions,[8] limitations on religious and social functions for those with damaged or unusual limbs or those with genital anomalies (whether congenital or acquired) and so on. Secondly, terms for particular conditions that frequently appear in close association with one another suggest a kind of categorization of thinking. 'The blind and the lame' is a good example; no necessary relationship between the conditions exists,[9] but their frequent appearance together in literary sources demonstrates a somewhat shared status we might label 'disability'.[10] By contrast, other exemplars of human variation, such as 'the tall', are not included in such lists or associated with the same categories. Recognizing the essentially social character of the categorization of disabilities also highlights that whether or not a community identifies with those with such impairments, corporate implications are never very far away.

Limitations on access or actions and purity considerations

Lev. 21.16–23

Lev. 21.16–23 communicates assessments of various conditions, which are categorized as 'blemishes' or 'defects' (מוּם, Gk μῶμος). The passage reports YHWH's instruction to Moses, stating that the presence of these conditions requires certain restrictions on priests' behaviour. 'One who is blind or lame' opens the list (the Septuagint reverses the order, but as in the Hebrew these conditions come first).[11] In some other texts, 'the blind and the lame' appears as a synecdoche, standing in as a short-hand descriptor for a range of other conditions.[12] Here, although the first position of these conditions may highlight a symbolic importance, the specificity of the other listed items suggests that the regulations relate to specific conditions. The further conditions which follow are:

> one who has a mutilated face or a limb too long, or one who has a broken foot or a broken hand, or a hunchback, or a dwarf, or a man with a blemish in his eyes or an itching disease or scabs or crushed testicles. (vv. 18–20)[13]

On each side of this list of exclusionary conditions, the text states twice that no descendant with a blemish may 'come near to offer the Lord's offerings' (v. 21; cf. vv. 17–18). However, it goes on to list tasks that *are* permissible: 'he may eat the food of his God, of the most holy as well as of the holy' (v. 22), before further specifying that

---

[8] See discussion in Raphael, 'Disability, Identity', 283.
[9] Though the parable of the blind and lame men in Apocryphon of Ezekiel moralizes about the need for the two to work together to complement their impairments. See Gosbell, 'The Poor, the Crippled', 134.
[10] Raphael, *Biblical Corpora*, 13–15.
[11] Throughout I have used Rahlf's text of the Septuagint for the Greek text (Rahlfs-Hanhart, 2006), and will generally refer to the Greek text as such, though I recognize that in some instances the manuscript and tradition history of the Greek text is more complex than this customary terminology indicates.
[12] Gosbell, 'The Poor, the Crippled', 134.
[13] MT has 'crushed testicle' (מְרוֹחַ אָשֶׁךְ), whereas the LXX has having a single testicle (μόνορχις, v. 20).

he may not 'come near the curtain or approach the altar', which would 'profane the sanctuaries' (v. 23).

Thus this influential passage does not restrict access to the temple for the wider community or even exclude someone from being a priest; it simply specifies particular cultic activities that they may not perform. Nonetheless, the listing of conditions remains shaping for corporate identity. By specifying bodily imperfections which alter one's ability to perform key cultic duties, it distances those with these impairments within the community and paves the way for more restricted applications of these regulations in some traditions which draw on this passage.[14] Although there is no consensus about the motivations for the particular conditions listed, most note the parallel stipulations in Lev. 22.17–33, where animals unsuitable for sacrifice are likewise excluded on the basis of a similar set of 'blemishes'.[15] Such associations indicate a hypersensitivity to norms which not only connect certain humans to imperfect animals in the cultic setting but also reshape their position within the community that gathers around these cultic practices.

2 Sam. 5.6–8

2 Sam. 5.6–8 suggests a more expansive exclusion; beyond the particular actions for priests in Leviticus 21, 2 Sam. 5.8b appears to restrict access to the temple for all those with mobility and visual impairments. The events narrated in this passage take place in the context of conflict between David (and his army) and the Jebusites, the residents of Jerusalem. In the MT, David's challenge to the Jebusites meets with the rebuff that 'even the blind and the lame' will fight off David's forces (v. 6).[16] David responds by invoking all to violence against the lame and the blind,[17] who are described as 'those whom he hates' (v. 8a). The military offensive is successful; David takes the city. The narrator then observes, 'Therefore it is said, "The blind and the lame shall not come into the house"' (v. 8b).

The blind and the lame are first mentioned in this story, then, as examples of opponents who, despite their weakened state, will keep David and his army out (v. 6); David's forces are so ineffective that they could not even defeat such as these (cf. Isa. 33.23). They then become the symbolic representatives of the Jebusites, whom David goes up against with rancour. The rhetoric only works because of the negative connotations of the labels 'blind' and 'lame' – both in terms of weakness, as in the Jebusites' initial comment, and as symbolic of Israel's enemy. Clearly the claim that David hates the blind and the lame indicates a negative portrayal in the MT. The LXX appears to adjust this, though arguably deepening the negative portrait while perhaps exonerating David from his negative emotional response, by stating that the blind and lame are those who hate David, not the reverse.

---

[14] As discussed in relation to 4QMMT below, some readers give functional explanations for excluding those with these impairments from priestly tasks.

[15] Olyan, *Disability*, 29–30.

[16] The LXX says 'for the blind and the lame resisted, saying "David shall not come in here"' (v. 6).

[17] The earlier order from v.6 is reversed in both the MT and LXX in v.8a.

However, the third reference to the blind and the lame involves an awkward transition. The conflict with the Jebusites is cast as an origin story for a particular practice: the exclusion of 'the blind and the lame' from 'the house'.[18] 'The house' most likely indicates the temple – a point which the LXX clarifies explicitly, referring instead to the house of the Lord (οὐκ εἰσελεύσονται εἰς οἶκον κυρίου) (v. 8). And here, given there is no mention of priestly roles, as Saul Olyan concludes, the prohibition is more akin to the exclusion from the full 'assembly of the Lord' in Deut. 23.1 than to the restrictions on priests within the temple in Leviticus 21, although the Deuteronomy reference excludes males with genital anomalies not those with visual or mobility impairments.

The references to 'the blind and the lame' in this passage are thus a mix of external and internal identities. Rebecca Raphael argues that those with disabilities in the HB reflect categories that are internal to Israel. She asserts, 'Disability is not mapped onto gentiles but onto non-compliant Israelites ... Thus it does not signify the cultural other, but rather the other inside – most intimately inside.'[19] This is part of the tension in this passage, at least in the form in which we have it, where the initial references associate the external enemy with the blind and the lame, but the conclusion drawn from the story is the exclusion of certain Israelite groups from the temple. Despite the differences, it reveals that the enemy 'other' could only be portrayed in such a way by playing on the stigmatization of those identified with the same conditions within Israel.

Although some raise questions about whether this exclusionary rule was ever practiced, as shown below, later texts suggest the passage was at least interpreted in this way. Olyan notes the consequences of being excluded from the temple, which extend to very practical daily realities. He observes, 'To be cut off from the sanctuary means to lose access to the primary context of meat consumption, the major locus for the shaping of social relations, the place of prostration and prayer, where vows are fulfilled, and where transgressions are expiated.'[20] He notes the cumulative effect over time, 'to the point where some texts cast persons suffering from skin disease as symbolically dead because of their separation from sanctuary and community'.[21] Even if 2 Sam. 5.8b were never applied in the community's life, readers would immediately appreciate these potential consequences of exclusion from the temple. In this and various ways, 2 Sam. 5.8b has implications for communal self-understanding: the blind and the lame are not at home at the heart of Israelite communal life.

---

[18] Olyan argues v. 8b was a popular adage that was grafted on here (Olyan, '"Anyone Blind or Lame Shall Not Enter the House": On the Interpretation of Second Samuel 5:8b', *CBQ* 60.2 (1998), 218). Schipper argues that in its context in 2 Samuel, this narrative plays on irony reflecting a rhetorical technique used across 2 Samuel's portrayal of disability and the royal dynasty (Jeremy Schipper, 'Reconsidering the Imagery of Disability in 2 Samuel 5:8b', *CBQ* 67.3 (2005), 423–4).

[19] Raphael, 'Disability, Identity', 296.

[20] Olyan, *Rites and Rank: Hierarchy in Biblical Representations of Cult* (Princeton, NJ: Princeton University Press, 2000), 62.

[21] Ibid.

Counter voices

Across HB texts, however, there are various voices which counter the more restrictive tendencies of these texts. First Samuel makes two references to Eli's vision in the context of his role as priest, observing his sightlessness in both cases – his 'eyesight had begun to grow dim so that he could not see' (1 Sam. 3.2; cf. 4.15).[22] The narrative offers no indication that he was no longer a priest, unable to enter the temple, or that his priestly activities were restricted. Indeed, the LXX includes a further statement reiterating that Eli is a priest at 3.1, before an extended account of the sudden deterioration of his eyesight in 3.2. It is worth noting that the failing eyesight is also mentioned in 2.33 as part of a prophecy of divine punishment as a result of the impiety of Eli's sons in their priestly offices; Eli's visual impairment is a consequence of this punishment.[23] Susan Ackerman notes numerous other legal requirements that the narrative about Eli fails to meet,[24] which indicates the need for caution in making claims about legal practice from this narrative. It is possible, however, that awareness of this legal tension led those responsible for the Greek text (or an alternative Hebrew text behind it) to reiterate Eli's status despite his sightlessness, by including the reference to his priestly status in 3.1.[25]

In a more direct challenge to exclusionary practices, Isa. 56.3-7 appears to be drawing on a stipulation such as that in Deut. 23.1.[26] It presumes a restrictive interpretation – that is, that a eunuch would not be permitted into the assembly – and at the same time forcefully *refutes* such a restriction. The passage presents negative self-assessments that might be made by 'the alien in the city' (v. 3a), and the eunuch – in the latter case: 'Do not let the eunuch say, "I am just a dry tree"' (v. 3b). It then responds with an affirmation towards each, this time with the eunuch first (vv. 4–5) and then the resident alien (vv. 6–7), so that the inclusion of both is woven together within the text. In the case of the eunuch, YHWH declares,

> To the eunuchs who keep my sabbaths, who choose the things that please me and hold fast my covenant, I will give, in my house and within my walls, a monument and a name better than sons and daughters; I will give them an everlasting name that shall not be cut off. (Isa. 56.4–5)

---

[22] See also discussion in Gosbell, *'The Poor, the Crippled'*, 148.

[23] There is not space to address the explanations for physical and sensory disabilities in the HB, but some texts, as with Eli here, explain the conditions as divine punishment. The words spoken by the Lord at the burning bush in Exod. 4.11 explicitly connect the power to disable to divine sovereignty.

[24] Susan Ackerman, 'The Blind, the Lame, and the Barren Shall Not Come into the House', in *Disability Studies and Biblical Literature*, ed. Candida R. Moss and Jeremy Schipper (New York: Palgrave Macmillan, 2011), 40. Ackerman focuses on Eli's interaction with Hannah, but it is also relevant here.

[25] This could also work in the reverse, with the LXX first naming Eli as priest before recounting events presumed to make him ineligible as a priest. However, the continuing narrative does not suggest Eli's priestly status has changed, and the final reference to his eyesight comes in 4.15 when he is 98 years old and approaching death, while his heart 'trembled for the ark of God' (v. 13).

[26] Deut. 23.1 reads, 'No one whose testicles are crushed or whose penis is cut off shall be admitted to the assembly of the LORD.' Olyan argues Isaiah 56 is a 'direct challenge to Deut. 23.2–9 (Eng 1–8)' (Olyan, *Disability*, 11).

While the Isaian writer is concerned to affirm the place of males with genital anomalies in the restored community, including in YHWH's 'house', there are other texts which affirm the need to show concern to vulnerable groups. For instance, Lev. 19.14 stipulates that 'you shall not revile the deaf or put a stumbling block before the blind', and Deut. 27.18 sets out a curse for misleading a blind person on the road. Such regulations suggest an interest in, and corporate sense of responsibility for, those with disabilities as a vulnerable group within the community. Nonetheless, Isaiah 56 is exceptional in its affirmation of a central place for the eunuch (indeed, even an elevated place),[27] and its focus on the person's piety and practices rather than an aspect of their physical condition.

Even where a list of conditions results in a claim to inclusion, however, the conditions listed are still important; not all forms of human variation attract attention. In Isaiah 56, the writer explicitly challenges other strands within the HB that describe certain physical conditions as beyond the scope of the community, reimagining the community as one in which such marginal characters, when pious, become central.[28] The promised action to gather 'the outcasts of Israel' then turns to the image of pilgrimage to YHWH's holy mountain (v. 7). This is also an important image for many of the references to 'the blind and the lame' in the HB, as discussed further below.

Place in an idealized future community

Transformation in the promised future

References to physical and sensory disabilities also appear in numerous passages which prophesy about an idyllic renewal in the future.[29] The references come in the context of a series of promises describing the transformation of the natural order. Alongside water in deserts, changes to those with disabilities demonstrate the kind of unnatural (or hyper-natural) transformation anticipated of the world. Several recent treatments of biblical texts from a disability perspective highlight ways in which texts use characters with disabilities as mere props in stories about something else, a technique David Mitchell and Sharon Snyder dub 'narrative prosthesis'.[30] This concept describes well the process here, where the implied author does not describe the events from the perspective of those whose bodies will be transformed, but orders them instead as part

---

[27] Olyan finds in this passage the only true example of a person with a condition identified as having a 'defect' being welcomed into the community without changing, rejecting stigma and cultic restrictions (Olyan, *Disability*, 85).

[28] The exclusion from the assembly relates most obviously to the eunuch in Deut. 23.1, but as noted above, it is also implied for those with visual and mobility impairments in 2 Sam. 5.8b. And of course, these conditions are all linked as bookends in Lev. 21.16–23, where 'the blind and the lame' open the list of 'defects', and those with damaged genitals close it.

[29] 'Eschatological' might be overstating the expectations in these texts, though that is certainly how these passages are interpreted in the early Christian texts which draw on them.

[30] David T. Mitchell and Sharon L. Snyder, *Narrative Prosthesis: Disability and the Dependencies of Discourse* (Ann Arbor: University of Michigan Press, 2000), 40–50. This concept is frequently taken up in biblical studies, e.g. by Raphael, *Biblical Corpora*; Solevåg, *Negotiating*.

of the material creation, whose alteration demonstrates divine power – and *that* is the real point of the passages.[31]

For instance, Isaiah 35 describes an anticipated transformation of the natural world. After outlining that the wilderness will be glad and the desert bloom, the centrality of divine power is underscored in the fierce 'vengeance' and 'swift recompense' by which YHWH will save 'you' (vv. 1–4). It continues: 'Then the eyes of the blind shall be opened, and the ears of the deaf unstopped; then the lame shall leap like a deer, and the tongue of the speechless sing for joy' (35.5–6).[32] Thus divine power not only enables these groups to achieve what might be expected of a norm but to *exceed* it. Here people will see or hear, who previously could not, but also the lame will move in ways that actually exceed the abilities of others (in terms that, through connections to Song 2.8–9, may allude to superlative beauty),[33] and the speechless will sing (not just speak) with *joy*. The affective term at the conclusion of the list introduces a more humanizing characterization of the speechless and their anticipated experience.

Similarly, and in keeping with the focus on divine power, Isaiah 29 begins by describing a series of negative events anticipated which are attributed to divine action – including YHWH *closing* the prophets' eyes:

> Stupefy yourselves and be in a stupor, blind yourselves and be blind! Be drunk, but not from wine; stagger, but not from strong drink! For the Lord has poured out upon you a spirit of deep sleep; he has closed your eyes, you prophets, and covered your heads, you seers. (Isa. 29.9–10)[34]

The reference to 'blinding' appears to be metaphorical, at least in v. 10's reference to YHWH's closing eyes[35] (though this does not preclude the audience from expecting YHWH to be responsible for causing literal blindness as well; cf. 1 Sam. 2.33, as discussed above, and Exod. 4.11).

But as the passage then describes the transformation of the world, it includes what seems most likely to be references to literal deafness and sightlessness: 'On that day the deaf shall hear the words of a scroll, and out of their gloom and darkness the eyes of the blind shall see' (Isa. 29.18). Like Isaiah 35, as also other texts like Isa. 42.7, Isaiah 29 presents an idyllic future in which these impairments have been removed.

As this passage deepens the portrait of the transformed people, however, it introduces concepts which explicitly connect to communal life. Indeed, the wider

---

[31] Olyan has an extended discussion of the centrality of divine power as the theme of these passages (Olyan, *Disability*, 78–89).

[32] Later, animals are mentioned – e.g. lions will not be near the pilgrims' travel route. Unclean people will also not be on that way.

[33] Olyan, *Disability*, 87. Olyan suggests this functions as a kind of reversal, so it plays in the assumption that people with disabilities are ugly.

[34] The first reference to blinding is altered in the LXX, instead: 'Be faint and amazed (ἐκλύθητε καὶ ἔκστητε)' (29.9).

[35] I am more cautious on the earlier reference to self-blinding, given Moss's instructive discussion of (literal) amputation as the context for interpreting decisive action to secure one's eschatological future in Mk. 9.43–48 (Candida R. Moss, *Divine Bodies: Resurrecting Perfection in the New Testament and Early Christianity*, ABRL (New Haven, CT: Yale University Press, 2019), 53–65).

frame situates transformation within Israel and as a corporate experience. The future promise to the deaf and blind comes in the context of inclusion and joy for other groups of vulnerable people (Isa. 29.19–20).[36] But those with disabilities, though seemingly included, are changed so that the ultimate community does not include them after all.[37] It seems even in the utopian setting, hearing is a necessary part of communal life. The specific activity that the previously deaf person is made able to do is to hear the scroll being read, thereby highlighting a concrete case of liturgical exclusion in the present and anticipated future.

Inclusion in a utopian future

Three pilgrimage texts, however, which provide an idyllic vision of a final return from exile, list the blind and/or the lame among those who will be gathered together. Here those with disabilities are described in parallels with other groups of humans, rather than features of the natural world as in Isaiah 35.

Jeremiah 31

As Jeremiah 31 sets out YHWH's promise of return, its focus is on a group identity, that of 'all the families of Israel' (v. 1). The statement about pilgrimage is introduced with instructions for shouting and praising and the citation: 'Save, O Lord, your people, the remnant of Israel' (v. 7). And then YHWH declares,

> See, I am going to bring them from the land of the north,
> > and gather them from the farthest parts of the earth,
> among them the blind and the lame,
> > those with child and those in labour, together;
> > a great company, they shall return here.
> With weeping they shall come,
> > and with consolations I will lead them back,
> I will let them walk by brooks of water,
> > in a straight path in which they shall not stumble;
> for I have become a father to Israel,
> > and Ephraim is my firstborn. (Jer. 31.8–9)[38]

The passage makes clear, in keeping with the emphases of Deuteronomistic theology, that it was YHWH who had scattered the people, and YHWH who will then facilitate their return. Unlike Isaiah 35, when nature terminology is used here it is as a metaphor

---

[36] The meek and 'the neediest people' will experience joy and offer praise, while the tyrant, scoffer and those seeking opportunities for evil are removed.
[37] Such ideas of transformation raise questions about whether someone would consider themselves the same 'self'. See Moss, *Divine Bodies*, 41–65.
[38] The gathering in Isa. 43.8–10 is similar (cf. William L. Holladay, *A Commentary on the Book of the Prophet Jeremiah*, 2 vols, Hermenia (Minneapolis, MN: Fortress, 1986–9), 2:156), though the language for impairments is metaphorical.

for human experience: 'Their life shall become like a watered garden, and they shall never languish again' (Jer. 31.12).

Moreover, the blind and the lame are listed among those included in the full gathering of Israel's return. Although it seems likely that the terms may function as a synecdoche here and thus represent a range of others whose disabilities may otherwise have led to their exclusion, this is not at the expense of possibly representing people with literal impairments.[39] Olyan observes a certain coherence between the non-ambulant groups which might particularly struggle to undertake such a pilgrimage, not only those with visual and mobility impairments but also those pregnant and labouring. For Olyan this is a source of frustration with the passage; he claims that it portrays those with disabilities as weak and without agency, having been 'normalized' by divine action.[40] He also suggests it feminizes these characters by aligning (male) people with disabilities with pregnant women.[41] However, I suggest the portrait of divine facilitation of their journey is less about normalizing and more about inclusion within the remnant of Israel. As Raphael quips, if one were in search for a biblical warrant for universal design, this passage provides it: it is the road which YHWH changes to enable their journey, not the people.[42]

Elements of communal identification with 'the lame'

Two further passages similarly describe a future utopian return. But here it is even clearer that the communal identity is not simply articulated in terms of inclusion of people with various disabilities, but that the group is itself explicitly *identified with* 'the lame'.

Thus, Mic. 4.6–7 states,[43]

> In that day, says the Lord,
> > I will assemble the lame
> and gather those who have been driven away,
> > and those whom I have afflicted.
> The lame I will make the remnant,
> > and those who were cast off, a strong nation;
> and the Lord will reign over them in Mount Zion
> > now and forevermore.

---

[39] By contrast, Raphael argues that there are no 'real' blind people in Jeremiah and that all references to disabilities are metaphorical (Raphael, 'Whoring after Cripples: On the Intersection of Gender and Disability Imagery in Jeremiah', in *Disability Studies and Biblical Literature*, ed. Moss and Schipper (New York: Palgrave Macmillan, 2011), 113; Raphael, *Biblical Corpora*, 119–30).

[40] Olyan argues, 'Texts that portray normalized disabled persons nonetheless function both to stigmatize disability and to exalt YHWH's incomparable abilities at the same time' (Olyan, *Disability*, 84).

[41] Olyan, *Disability*, 83.

[42] Raphael, *Biblical Corpora*, 129.

[43] The previous verse is about all the people *walking*.

The remnant is equated with 'the lame'. This is part of the group identity of those who are returning. BDB lists a possible meaning of צָלַע as a substantive 'of personification of Judah as flock', citing these references in Mic. 4.6, 7, and also Zeph. 3.19, as the evidence. This latter text sets out:

> I will deal with all your oppressors
>> at that time.
> And I will save the lame
>> and gather the outcast,
> and I will change their shame into praise
>> and renown in all the earth. (Zeph. 3.19–20)

Thus here, upon the return, the impairment is not removed, but the shame is. Notably, the passages identify this disability as the result of YHWH's action to punish in the exile.[44] For Raphael, this makes for an 'unsustained metaphor' – that is, 'the author easily shifts from exile-as-disability to return as simply wonderful'.[45] The choice of metaphor for communal identification remains important; it communicates the impact of the exile experience. At the same time as (potentially) justifying the place of those with mobility impairments in the community, by using the description metaphorically it appropriates the experience of particular people in claiming a shared identity and suffering. In the process, these passages present a quite different picture from the utopian transformation narratives of Isa. 29.18, 35.5–6 and 42.7. 'The lame' are not simply included in Israel, they *are* the remnant, constituting the returning community under YHWH's promise.

Adjustments in the Septuagint

Although some of the passages I have dealt with above are treated in slightly different ways in the LXX, and thus I have noted the differences along the way, here the differences in the Greek are more marked. In each of Jer. 31.8, Mic. 4.6–7 and Zeph. 3.19–20, the Greek includes none of the references to the blind and/or lame found in the Hebrew text.[46]

In Jer. 31.8, after describing the intention to gather the remnant, rather than the MT's references to the blind, lame, pregnant and labouring women, the LXX describes the gathering taking place 'at the feast of Passover, and you will breed a large crowd', before including the final phrase as in the MT 'and they shall return here'. Part of this difference could be explained by a possible reading, in which instead of עִוֵּר וּפִסֵּחַ בָּם ('with the blind and the lame'), the Hebrew is taken as בְּמוֹעֵד פֶּסַח, resulting in the Greek

---

[44] Olyan, *Disability*, 89–91.
[45] Raphael, *Biblical Corpora*, 130. Raphael concludes her short section on these passages: 'These three passages are similar in the use of disability imagery, especially terms of mobility impairment, to represent the scattered people' (130).
[46] In their detailed studies of passages that relate to disability in the Hebrew text, neither Olyan (*Disability*) nor Raphael (*Biblical Corpora*) refers to these differences in the Greek text traditions.

ἐν ἑορτῇ φασεκ ('at the feast of Passover'), though this does not explain the differences in the next part of the verse.

In Mic. 4.6, where there is a reference to 'the lame' (הַצֹּלֵעָה) in the MT, the LXX says συντετριμμένην, from συντρίβω, to crush or break. And where the MT describes 'those who have been driven away' and those whom YHWH 'afflicted', the LXX refers to those who have been rejected and whom YHWH drove away (οὓς ἀπωσάμην). Similarly, where Zeph. 3.19-20 refers to saving 'the lame', the Greek gives 'the one who has been rejected (τὴν ἐκπεπιεσμένην)'. And, rather than removing their shame, YHWH will 'welcome and make them objects of boasting'.

As always, the differences in the LXX could simply reflect different Hebrew textual traditions, though, significantly, 4Q72, which gives the text of Jeremiah 31, appears to preserve the same Hebrew text as that of the MT.[47] And although each text substitutes another word for 'the lame', in each case it is a different word, suggesting the differences do not simply track an alternative sense of a word used in translation. If the changes are intentional, or even simply (in the case of Jer. 31.8) an assumption that the Hebrew might better be read slightly differently, might they reflect a consistent discomfort with the idea that the blind and/or lame are a part of the gathered remnant or the identification of the remnant itself as 'the lame'? It seems possible that something in this image did not cohere with the communal self-understanding of at least some readers of the Hebrew Bible at this time.

Models of communal self-understanding

From among the diverse ways in which those with physical and sensory impairments are described, depicted and regulated in HB texts emerges a range of ways in which the images of 'the blind and the lame' may reflect communal self-understanding. Based on the discussion above, I suggest four key strands; the first three relate to the 'exclusion/inclusion' approach to group identity I noted above and the final to the 'identification' model. First, some texts specify a list of conditions that exclude a person from either priestly service (as in the case of Lev. 21.16-23) or access to key spaces (as in the case of 2 Sam. 5.6-8). Here the exclusions define the community, or a significant group within it, as importantly separate from those with these conditions. This is true even though, as Raphael rightly notes, disability is a category applied to others within the same community; the exclusions, whether practiced or not, function to highlight that subaltern status. In the second group, texts list the same conditions but, as a counter voice to the exclusion passages they implicitly bring to mind, focus instead on *inclusion* of these groups within the communal identity (e.g. Jer. 31.8-9; Isa. 56.3-7 and, possibly, 1 Sam. 3.2; 4.15). In the texts surveyed here, this can include claims about communal responsibility for the vulnerable (Lev. 19.14; Deut. 27.18). Thirdly,

---

[47] The second section of the verse, with the reference to the pregnant and labouring, is given as in the MT, whereas the LXX is very different there. There is a gap in the earlier section, showing ב[ם] עור ופסח (the underlined portions here show letters Tov is more tentative about in *DJD* XV: 197-8), but even here the presence of at least the vāv in the final term seems to confirm the same Hebrew reading as is evident in the MT.

some texts take a form we might consider 'inclusion *to* exclusion'. Here, as in texts such as Isa. 29.18, 35.5–6 and 42.7, apparent inclusion in the community leads to a promise of transformation, in effect resulting in exclusion of those with impairments from the ultimate community. In the final strand, group identity is itself articulated in terms of communal identification with impairments. Here texts use the imagery of these conditions as metaphors so that, for instance, the *whole* of the remnant who will return is identified with 'the lame' (Mic. 4.6–7; cf. Zeph. 3.19).[48] These four strands will be helpful in considering the portrait of 'the blind and the lame' in texts which build on Hebrew Bible traditions, both at Qumran and in the New Testament.

'The blind and the lame' at Qumran

A mixed portrait of those with impairments continues in the texts found at Qumran, where exclusionary regulations drawing on Hebrew Bible traditions *and* processes that indicate the ongoing presence of those with disabilities coexist. Given the nature of these texts, frequently setting out community regulations, they provide a particularly helpful insight into how these ideas relate to group identity.[49]

Several texts found at Qumran suggest that at least some readers of Lev. 21.16–23 and 2 Sam. 5.8b read these texts from the first, 'exclusion', strand identified above in a more restrictive sense. The Rule of the Congregation at the End of Days and the Damascus Document both appear to extend the regulations for priests in Leviticus 21 and apply them to other members of the community(ies). Without conflating the diverse contexts from which these two documents may have arisen, it is worth noting that they demonstrate some continuity in their treatment of those with disabilities. In both cases, a list of conditions renders someone ineligible for participation in a core community function, and it seems that the reason for the exclusion is the presence of the 'holy angels' in the community gathering. The Damascus Document states,

> And no one who is stupid [or de]ranged should enter; and anyone feeble-minded and insane, those with eyes too weak to see, [and] the lame or one who stumbles, or a deaf person, or an under-age boy, none [of] these [shall enter] the congregation, for the ho[ly] angels ... (4Q266 8 i 6–9=CD xv 15–17)[50]

The groups here do not appear to be excluded from the community in general,[51] but given that the previous regulations relate to an initiation process, it seems some further

---

[48] As noted above, 'the blind and the lame' can also be used metaphorically in other, 'exclusion/inclusion' texts. In 2 Sam. 5.8 David flips from alluding to his opponents as a *group* as 'the blind and the lame' to applying this reasoning to exclude certain people *within* Israel from Jerusalem.

[49] See Newsom on the rhetoric of rules in the formation of identity (Carol A. Newsom, *The Self as Symbolic Space: Constructing Identity and Community at Qumran*, STDJ 52 (Atlanta, GA: SBL Press, 2004), 149–52).

[50] Translations from the DSS are taken from Florentino García Martínez and Eibert J. C. Tigchelaar (eds), *The Dead Sea Scrolls Study Edition*, 2 vols (Leiden: Brill, 1997).

[51] Dorman argues that these groups cannot be excluded from community membership, because other parts of the Damascus Document describe a 'simple' priest (CD xiii 6), young boy (xiv 14–16)

council or event requiring initiation is in mind. Those with these conditions will never reach full initiation (that is, be permitted to 'come near').

In the Rule of the Congregation, the claim is:

> No man, defiled by any of the impurities of a man, shall enter the assembly of these; and no one who is defiled by these should be established in his office amongst the congregation: everyone who is defiled in his flesh, paralysed in his feet or in his hands, lame, blind, deaf, dumb or defiled in his flesh with a blemish visible to the eyes, or the tottering old man who cannot keep upright in the midst of the assembly; these shall not en[ter] to take their place [a]mong the congregation of the men of renown, for the angels of holiness are among their [congre]gation. (1QSa ii 3–9)

Although Anke Dorman claims the regulations of 1QSa seem out of place in an end-time scenario, the presence of holy angels here and in CD highlights the sense of continuity between the community's life and its imagination in relation to its imminent eschatological life. This highlights a tension in the portrayal of those with disabilities – they will be present at the end of days as they are already present in the community;[52] however, they cannot participate in settings where the holy angels are present.[53]

4QMMT also seems to draw on Leviticus 21, but in an even more restrictive way, extending the exclusion beyond priests to all 'blind' people and adding also all those who are 'deaf'. The reasons given are to do with defilement, and functional explanations for why people who are visually impaired or deaf would defile the sanctuary. The sightless risk being unable to discern when they have mixed those things which should not be mixed (4Q396 ii 1–3). And the deaf, not having heard the scripture, cannot implement its directions (ii 3–4): 'For whoever neither sees nor hears, does not [know] how to act' (ii 5). Though deaf people are not included in the exclusionary regulations in the Hebrew Bible, this does have an interesting similarity to Isa. 29.18, where the promised future involves the transformation of deaf people so that they can hear the scroll being read.

But of those found at Qumran, the text that presents the greatest extension of exclusion for those with physical and sensory disabilities is the Temple scroll,[54] where the blind and the lame are excluded from the city. This text appears to confirm that

---

and 'afflicted person' (xiv 14–16) in contexts where it is clear they are members of the community (Anke Dorman, 'The Other Others: A Qumran Perspective on Disability', in *Imagining the Other and Constructing Israelite Identity in the Early Second Temple Period*, ed. Ehud Ben Zvi and Diana Vikander Edelman (London: T&T Clark, 2014), 304). Responding to Wassen's implication that the exclusion would be reiterated each time there is an occasion that separates the full, initiated community members from others, Dorman also considers whether these regulations relate particularly to the celebration of the Feast of Weeks (305–6).

[52] Some scrolls texts also reflect a tradition of using sensory impairments as metaphors for negative attributes (also evident in the HB; and cf. Mt. 23.16–17). 1QS iv 11–12 offers what Olyan describes as innovation in extending the negative reach of these metaphors, associating sightlessness with wickedness, falsehood, opposition to God and 'destruction in a hell-like place' (Olyan, *Disability*, 106).

[53] Dorman argues against the idea that the concern is exposing the sanctuary to the evil/demon that caused the disability (Dorman, 'The Other Others', 302).

[54] Dorman, 'The Other Others', 308.

some readers of 2 Sam. 5.8b did in fact take it as indicating that those with visual and mobility impairments could not enter the 'house'.[55] But it extends the restriction even further, beyond the temple, to the whole of the city of Zion: 'No blind person shall enter it all their days, and they shall not defile the city in whose midst I dwell because I, YHWH, dwell in the midst of the children of Israel forever and always' (11QT^a (=11Q19) xlv 12-14).[56]

Despite the strong wording of this text as it sets out idealized expectations of Zion, the other documents which describe the life of their authors' community(ies) give a more mixed portrait. For all the interest in purity in Qumran sectarian literature, the kinds of regulations included in 1QSa and CD do suggest that people with disabilities were a part of the community. The provision is not the kind of generalized comments about 'the blind and the lame' that we see, for instance, in the stories of a promised pilgrimage in Jer. 31.8 but detailed and practical.

Some texts are more like the legal codes found in Deut. 27.18 or Lev. 19.14, where the focus is on caring for those with disabilities as part of a vulnerable subset. CD xiv 12-17 requires that financial provision be made for the,

> needy and poor, and to the elder who [is ben]t, and to the af[flic]ted, and to the prisoner of a foreign people, and to the girl who has [n]o re[dee]mer, [and] to the youth [w]ho has no one looking after him; everything is the task of the association, and [the house of the association shall] not [be deprived of] its [means]. (CD xiv 14-17)

And 1QSa specifies the process by which those who are excluded from the assembly on account of their disabilities or other sources of ineligibility may still be engaged: 'And if [one of] these has something to say to the holy council, they shall question [him] in private, but the man shall [n]ot enter in the midst of [the congregation,] because [h]e is defiled' (1QSa ii 9-10).

In the context of texts with such a strong sense of the boundary between the community and the outside world[57] and their own difference from other groups, it is

---

[55] Olyan notes a possible influence of Mal. 1.6-14, where blind animals pollute the altar, upon the interpretation of 2 Sam. 5.8b, such that humans with certain conditions might cause contamination, and Num. 5.3, where 'serious polluters' are expelled entirely from the 'desert camp' (Olyan, *Disability*, 105-6).

[56] The War Scroll also excludes those with certain conditions from participating in the eschatological war: 'And no lame, blind, paralysed person nor any man who has an indelible blemish on his flesh, nor any man suffering from uncleanness in his flesh, none of these will go out to war with them' (1QM vii 4-5). Although some in this list potentially indicate a pragmatic concern about efficacy on the battlefield (so Dorman, 'The Other Others', 309-11), some might relate more to questions of cultic purity (not to separate these concepts too starkly). The exclusion from military service does not necessarily relate to any exclusion from the eschatological community that will gather after this definitive defeat of evil; the membership of that community is not specified.

[57] See Newsom on how both polemical and non-polemical strategies contribute to this construction of identity in relation to those outside the community (Newsom, 'Constructing "We, You, and the Others" through Non-Polemical Discourse', in *Defining Identities: We, You, and the Other in the Dead Sea Scrolls*, ed. Florentino García Martínez and Mladen Popović, STDJ 70 (Leiden: Brill, 2008), 13-21).

noteworthy that those with disabilities remain clearly within the group. They remain among the 'sons of light'. Here there is a sense of strand 2 identified above, where people are included (even if these conditions remain central to their characterization and simultaneously set *limits* on their inclusion). This likewise reflects Raphael's concept, noted above, about disabilities being a way of describing Israelites not gentiles, and creating 'the other inside'.[58] Dorman describes this in terms of 'the other others', where those with disabilities are contrasted with the 'others' who come from outside, like the sons of darkness.[59]

The same texts which show that those with disabilities are included, at the same time make them a kind of underclass.[60] The financial provisions in CD indicate that those with disabilities would be among the worst off in a community following these regulations, despite the required financial commitment from other members. And as 1QSa indicates how people with disabilities should be consulted, it shows both how their interests would be protected, and their ongoing exclusion from the activity at the heart of the community, even in the end time and their communion with the holy angels. Thus the Qumran texts, in their use of the Hebrew Bible and their own regulations, give a sense of both exclusion *and* inclusion (strands 1 and 2), though without claims about future transformation or communal identification with the lame, as in strands 3 and 4.

Early Christian texts

'The blind and the lame' feature numerous times in the Gospels of Matthew and Luke. These references comprise examples, I suggest, of strands 2, 3 and 4, identified above, and contribute to portraits of communal self-understanding.[61]

Access and restriction: 'The blind and the lame' in the temple

The climax of the Matthean account of Jesus's entry into Jerusalem often goes unremarked.[62] After instructing his disciples to obtain the animals and then riding

---

[58] Raphael, 'Disability, Identity', 296.
[59] Dorman, 'The Other Others', 297.
[60] Ibid., 306. Dorman describes a relationship between community texts such as 1QSa and Leviticus 21:

> If it is assumed that the Qumranites regarded themselves as holy in the same way that priests are holy in Leviticus, then disabled members of the community were probably regarded as holy, too. By virtue of belonging to that community, disabled and nondisabled members were Othered from the rest of the world. However, within that self-proclaimed Othered community of holy people, disabled persons were further Othered. Parallel to disabled priests in Leviticus 21, they were accorded a special position: they were not holy enough or qualified enough to partake in a specific activity … they are a part of the holy community, but not holy *enough*. (302)

[61] There is no reference to the blind and lame together in Mark, only one in John at 5.3 and none elsewhere in the NT.
[62] This is the case even in studies of disability in the gospels. For example, the verse is not mentioned in the otherwise helpful study on this language by Gosbell (*'The Poor, the Crippled'*), or in the studies of disability in NT texts by Roth (Roth, *The Blind*), Lawrence (Lawrence, *Sense and Stigma*) or Solevåg

into the city, Jesus heads straight for the temple and acts immediately (like Luke, but of course unlike Mark). He removes those buying and selling, upending the money changers' and the dove sellers' furniture, and rebukes them, following which, Matthew writes, 'The blind and the lame came to him in the temple, and he cured them' (21.14). This single verse, unique to Matthew, is the only reference to these people in the passage. The interpretation then begins. All of these events are linked back together by the response of the chief priests and the scribes: they react to the 'amazing things (τὰ θαυμάσια)' Jesus has done and the refrain of 'the children crying out in the temple, "Hosanna to the Son of David"' (v. 15), thus reiterating the refrain that heralded Jesus on his way into Jerusalem (v. 9). The chief priests and scribes react with anger, and theirs is a response to all of these features: the removal from the temple, the inclusion and healing in the temple and the song of the children. They question Jesus about the children's singing, to which he responds,

> Yes; have you never read,
> 'Out of the mouths of infants and nursing babies
> you have prepared praise for yourself'?' (v. 16b)

On the basis of an assumption that no one ever implemented the restriction in 2 Sam. 5.8b, Luz claims that it is not significant that the blind and the lame are in the temple (though, he suggests, 'it probably is important, however, that [Jesus] healed them').[63] Luz's concern is to avoid an anachronistic interpretation that assumes Jewish practices were restrictive and Christian ones inclusive.[64] However, the above discussion has demonstrated that Hebrew Bible and Second Temple traditions are more diverse, as also I suggest are early Christian traditions. The grouping of 'the blind and the lame' with no other introduction or afterword, 'approaching Jesus (προσῆλθον αὐτῷ)' and 'in the temple (ἐν τῷ ἱερῷ)' enacts what is explicitly ruled out in 2 Sam. 5.8b. Whether or not the 2 Samuel passage provided a warrant for particular behaviours in practice in the Jerusalem temple, in the literary world of Matthew the reference would not be lost. The more restrictive interpretations in texts like CD, 1QSa and especially the Temple scroll indicate that at least some groups also drew on a restrictive interpretation of the 2 Samuel passage in their own literary portraits of their communities; diverse interpretations may also be familiar to Matthew's audience. As in strand 2 identified above, the text that excludes particular people is brought to mind, but in order (it seems at first) to assert their inclusion.

The structure of the Matthean passage also invites further reflection on the role of these groups. Jesus drives out the groups who he claims should not rightfully be in the temple, and immediately is approached by those who should be.[65] Such an

---

(Solevåg, *Negotiating*). On more general studies of the entry narrative, the conundrum of the two animals Jesus rides has attracted the lion's share of attention about the narrative.
[63] Luz, *A Commentary*, 3:12–13.
[64] Ibid., 3:13.
[65] I am grateful to Candida Moss for her response to an earlier draft of this essay, and particularly for her reflections in conversation on whether Matthew simply includes the blind and the lame among those, like the moneychangers, who should not be in the temple – but rather than ejecting them, Jesus changes them to make them fit. On balance, I think the combination of the climax of this

exchange emphasizes inclusion of 'the blind and the lame'. But readers may also find this motif of the movement into Jerusalem and straight to this activity at its heart in the temple (Matthew's change to Mark),[66] and the presence of the blind and lame, reminiscent of the promise of pilgrimage and restoration in Jer. 31.8, Mic. 4.6–7 and Zeph. 3.19–20. Indeed, given these connections, the central place of the blind and the lame here may also offer a reminder of the communal identity of Israel becoming impaired during the exile, with 'the lame' representing the returning remnant. This would involve a movement from simply inclusion to identification with those with these physical and sensory impairments, as in the fourth 'identification' strand; this is perhaps also in keeping with Luz's theorizing that the Matthean community might identify with these characters.[67] As noted above, when functioning to communicate a group identity, the reference to impairments is metaphorical. But even if symbolic, the text arguably works on another level to counter exclusion of those with literal impairments.

Nonetheless, the blind and the lame remain a literary device here. They are not real characters. We hear nothing of their interaction with Jesus or response of discipleship or otherwise. In a textbook version of Mitchell and Snyder's 'narrative prosthesis', the single verse about the blind and the lame simply functions to underscore the significance of what Jesus is doing and the eschatological time.[68] Like the children crying out hosanna, they are a plot device to reveal what is taking place. The reference to 2 Sam. 5.8b may be heard in the careful ordering of the verse: first they approach Jesus in the temple, and then Jesus heals them. In this way the challenge to a restrictive reading of 2 Sam. 5.8b may be called to mind. But as the healing takes place, another series of texts comes to the fore: the healing of the blind and the lame is a sign of eschatological fulfilment.

Presence in the eschatological community

Transformation as eschatological sign

The bulk of Matthew's and Luke's references to 'the blind' and 'the lame' present healings as a sign of eschatological fulfilment, drawing on traditions like Isa. 29.18,

---

pilgrimage to the heart of Jerusalem (see below) and the celebratory singing of the children ensures the passage celebrates this encounter, but as I note below, it does ultimately lead to an 'inclusion to exclusion' dynamic through the healing (strand 3), even if it also invites the reader to identify with these groups of included and healed people (strand 4).

[66] A redaction-critical approach based on the assumption that Matthew used Mark (and Luke in turn most likely used Matthew) also shows the important intervention Matthew makes in taking the entry narrative straight into Jerusalem and then to its heart in the temple where he immediately acts, rather than looking around and leaving until the next day as in Mark. This makes the place of those with disabilities more obviously a climax of this whole journey.

[67] Luz, *A Commentary*, 3:14; see above.

[68] See n. 30.

35.5-6 and 42.7.[69] Here the approach is one of apparent 'inclusion to exclusion', as in strand 3 above. Mt. 11.5 and 15.30-1 describe the healing of people with a range of disabilities, including 'the blind' and 'the lame' in both passages. Both present the healings as evidence of the fulfilment of eschatological prophecy, though without specific citations. François Bovon suggests the episode with John the Baptist's disciples in Mt. 11.5 and Lk. 7.22 is based on a general Isaianic sense of prophecy, drawing on Isa. 26.19, 29.18-19, 35.5-6 and 61.1.[70] Luz points out examples of healing for each of the groups in the preceding chapters in Matthew.[71]

In the parallel account, Luke inserts a summary verse between the challenging question from John's disciples and Jesus's response: 'Jesus had just then cured many people of diseases, plagues, and evil spirits, and had given sight to many who were blind' (v. 21). It is this that prompts the interpretation:

> Go and tell John what you have seen and heard: the blind receive their sight, the lame walk, the lepers are cleansed, the deaf hear, the dead are raised, the poor have good news brought to them. And blessed is anyone who takes no offense at me. (vv. 22-3)

Thus the immediate literary framing goes even further in emphasizing that these characters are healed in order for a different narrative purpose. The Isaian introduction to Jesus's ministry at Nazareth in Lk. 4.18-19, with its reference to the blind receiving sight (cf. Isa. 42.7) and the poor having good news brought to them, confirms that this is the fulfilment of the ministry that Jesus had announced.

Each of these passages thus aligns the healing accounts, through the connections to earlier traditions, with an interpretation of the messianic significance of Jesus's work. In this way they create again the sense that these are not real characters, especially in the summary verse in Lk. 7.21. Rather, those with impairments are mentioned in generic category lists as objects of Jesus's healing ministry to make a plot point, and as evidence to settle a dispute with John's disciples.[72] These groups have no place in communal identity. Instead, the picture the passages supply is again that of an ideal, restored community without impairments.

---

[69] Roth examines 'the blind', 'the lame' and 'the poor' as literary character types in Luke and Acts, based on a study of these and various character types with impairments in the LXX. His chief concern is the disparity in references in Luke and Acts (Roth, *The Blind*).

[70] François Bovon, *A Commentary on the Gospel of Luke*, trans. Christine M. Thomas, Donald S. Deer and James Crouch, 3 vols, Hermeneia (Minneapolis, MN: Fortress, 2002-13), 1:282.

[71] The 'blind' in Mt. 9.27-31, 'lame' in 9.2-8, a 'leper' in 8.1-4, 'deaf' in 9.32-4 and raising the dead in 9.1-26 (Luz, *A Commentary*, 2:130).

[72] From the perspective of a disability studies reading, such passages promote the 'terror' of healing narrative traditions (see Sharon V. Betcher, 'Disability and the Terror of the Miracle Tradition', in *Miracles Revisited: New Testament Miracle Stories and Their Concepts of Reality*, ed. Stefan Alkier and Annette Weissenrieder (Berlin: de Gruyter, 2013), 161-81). This language evokes Phyllis Trible's influential identification of *Texts of Terror* from a feminist perspective (Philadelphia, PA: Fortress, 1984). Here the miracles evoke terror because they imply the need for radical change to some people, in order for their inclusion in the discipleship or ultimate community, raising questions about people's inherent value and continuity of identity (see Lawrence, *Sense and Stigma*; Solevåg, *Negotiating*; Moss, *Divine Bodies*).

Inclusion in the current and eschatological community

However, two references to 'the poor, the crippled, the lame, and the blind' in quick succession in Lk. 14.13 and 14.21 suggest a different communal self-understanding from the reference in 7.21–2.[73]

The meal setting in Luke 14, which incorporates Jesus's advice to guests and hosts (vv. 7–11; 12–14) and the parable of the great banquet (vv. 15–24), describes inclusion of the 'poor, the crippled, the blind, and the lame' in both the community's current life and in an eschatological setting.[74] Louise Gosbell criticizes the common practice of reading the staged adjustments to the invitation list in the banquet parable allegorically, despite the literal reference only a few verses earlier.[75] And, as David Moessner points out, the repeated phrases function so that the parenetic material helps to interpret the parable. Like Jesus's advice to hosts, the parable's list of new invitees from increasingly marginalized groups,[76] including those with impairments in the second round of invitations,[77] exhorts the reader to an inclusive communal identity.[78]

In support of her argument for a literal reading of the poor, crippled, blind and lame in the parable, Gosbell provides numerous examples in Graeco-Roman literature of those with impairments being used as an entertaining spectacle in private and public settings, including at meals.[79] She recognizes this as both a literary tradition (reflecting the wider influence of sympotic literature on Luke's meal scenes) and a social practice, judging by examples in historiographical texts such as those by Suetonius and Tacitus.[80] Moreover, some interpreters take issue with the behaviour of the host,

---

[73] Although Luke Timothy Johnson discusses the parallels between the references in Lk. 7.22 and 14.21, as 'special targets for the proclamation of the good news', he fails to notice a significant difference in relation to the transformation (7.22) or inclusion (14.21) of these characters (*The Gospel of Luke*, SP 3 (Collegeville: Liturgical Press, 1991), 232).

[74] The alignment of this sense of contemporary and eschatological communal experience is in some senses reminiscent of that in 1QSa.

[75] Gosbell, 'The Poor, the Crippled', 223. The allegory frequently mapped onto the parable is the salvation-historical extension of divine mission to the gentiles; Gosbell helpfully lists numerous problems with putting this framework onto the parable (165). (Though note that her criticism that gentiles cannot be identified with the characters with disabilities given their status as those othered within the community does not address some versions of this allegorical interpretation, such as Johnson's argument that the second round of invitations is to marginalized Jewish groups and the third round extends to gentiles; Johnson, *The Gospel of* Luke, 232). Even if the reference in v. 13 is not limited to those literally 'poor, blind, crippled, and lame', it nonetheless relates to marginalized characters including those with non-metaphorical impairments.

[76] See Rohrbaugh on the social structure of the city and those outside, as informative for interpreting the further rounds of invitations (Richard L. Rohrbaugh, 'The Pre-Industrial City in Luke-Acts: Urban Social Relations', in *The Social World of Luke-Acts: Models for Interpretation*, ed. Jerome H. Neyrey (Peabody, MA: Hendrickson, 1991), 125–49).

[77] Unlike the similar parables in Mt. 22.1–14 and the Gospel of Thomas 64 (where the later invites are to whoever can be found – Matthew specifies all, 'the bad and the good' (Mt. 22.10)).

[78] Moessner suggests that these connections across the passage lead to 'an ultimate warning' for readers (David P. Moessner, *Lord of the Banquet: The Literary and Theological Significance of the Lukan Travel Narrative* (Harrisburg: Trinity Press International, 1989), 158). Tannehill notes the 'multivalence' of the parable, arguing that the immediate literary context provides a warning to lawyers and Pharisees, but that the wider setting shows how this dynamic 'is working itself out in Jesus's ministry' (Robert C. Tannehill, *The Narrative Unity of Luke-Acts: A Literary Interpretation*, 2 vols, FF (Minneapolis, MN: Fortress, 1986–90), 1:185).

[79] Gosbell, 'The Poor, the Crippled', 204–8.

[80] Ibid., 207.

who only considers extending the invitations to further groups when the original invitees decline.[81] However, as elsewhere with Lukan parables, the stock images from everyday life serve to make a key point, here: eschatological reversal. In calling to mind the sympotic traditions, the parable subverts expectations about the role impaired characters would play at a meal, and instead makes them reclining guests while others are excluded. The contrast to the meal and assembly in 1QSa ii 3–9 is notable.[82]

The references across Luke 14 project the community as one in which people like those with visual and mobility impairments are included. Moreover, when turning to an eschatological setting, the same groups remain explicitly included without the transformation required elsewhere. But there is also a sense in which the parable invites the reader to identify the eschatological community with all of the marginalized groups listed, including 'the blind and the lame'. Given the starkness of the reversal, with the original invitees ultimately excluded ('For I tell you, none of those who were invited will taste my dinner' (v. 24)), regardless of their social position, readers who wish to imagine themselves as participants in the great banquet must also identify with those included in the further rounds of late invitations.

Conclusion: Communal self-understanding and impairment

The approaches to those with physical and sensory impairments in the Hebrew Bible and texts found at Qumran demonstrate a diversity which is also evident in the Gospels of Matthew and Luke. The majority of the gospels' references to 'the blind' and 'the lame' occur in the context of the fulfilment of eschatological expectation in the healing of these groups, in which they function as narrative props with no or minimal impact on communal identity – except perhaps to imply that those with impairments are not expected as part of the eschatological community (the 'inclusion to exclusion' move I described as strand 3 above).

But there are also other strands of tradition. Several of the texts explicitly assert inclusion, as in strand 2 above. Where passages suggest a self-understanding in which the discipleship community inherently includes those with impairments, sometimes this leads to an image of social (and financial) responsibility for the other. As in Lev. 19.14, Deut. 27.18 and CD xiv 12–17, Jesus's advice about whom to invite for dinner has this quality (Lk. 14.13), framed with eschatological reward through inviting those who cannot repay the favour. Some passages affirm a communal self-understanding for the discipleship community where those at the margins are put at the centre, as in Isa. 56.4–5, Lk. 14.13 and, in some ways, Mt. 21.14. When the focus turns to a restored or eschatological community, likewise there are examples of explicitly including 'the blind' and 'the lame' in the communal identity, as in Jer. 31.8 and Lk. 14.21.

---

[81] See discussion of these concerns about the 'snubbed host' in Gosbell, *'The Poor, the Crippled'*, 178.
[82] Tannehill notes that the reasons given by the original invitees align with standard exemptions from war service, noting the exclusions from holy war in 1QM (Tannehill, *Narrative Unity*, 1:231–2; see also n. 56).

However, even where the texts describe various conditions in order to affirm their inclusion in the community, those listed are still significant. The passages interact with traditions of exclusion, as Isa. 56.4–5 relies on traditions like that in Deut. 23.1. And this is a key consideration, I suggest, when contemplating those texts which reflect not only the *inclusion* of those with impairments in the community but the *identification* of the community as a whole with the impaired (as in strand 4). Here the potentially interesting parallels between pilgrimage texts like Mic. 4.6–7 and Zeph. 3.19–20 and Mt. 21.14 and Lk. 14.21–4 highlight a metaphorical use of impairment. But the *choice* of metaphor for self-understanding is striking. Recognizing the risks it runs of appropriating, and even eclipsing, the experience of people with such (non-metaphorical) impairments, it places at the heart of corporate identity a role for impairments known for their disabling social consequences. It highlights a lived reality in early Christian communities, behind the miracle stories of their literature. Arguably in keeping with Judith Perkins's renowned observations about the role of suffering and pain in early Christian identity,[83] these images perhaps provide a way to frame Christian experience – in a similar manner to Micah's portrait of the limping remnant's return.

---

[83] Judith Perkins, *The Suffering Self: Pain and Narrative Representation in the Early Christian Era* (London: Routledge, 1995).

7

The ethics of Eden: Luxury, banqueting and the New Jerusalem

Candida R. Moss

It is common in Jewish and Christian prophetic and apocalyptic thought to find heaven described in familiar materialistic terms. The heavenly temple of Ezekiel is patterned on the typical four-roomed house of ancient Israel; only it is much larger and considerably grander. Merely the language of temples, throne rooms and gates recalls the decorative and architectural features of elite social spaces in the ancient Near East. Revelation is no exception to this pattern; drawing upon ancient Jewish apocalyptic traditions about heavenly space and eschatological expectations, it describes the New Jerusalem in thoroughly materialistic terms. Indeed, as has been observed in the past, Revelation's eschatological framework 'has no parallel in the New Testament' and instead 'depends ... upon Jewish tradition'.[1]

The purpose of this essay is to look at the reception of shared Jewish and Christian traditions about the wealth of the heavenly city as mediated through interpretations of the New Jerusalem in Revelation. As we will see early Christians, like many ancient Greeks, Romans and Jews, advocated for earthly self-restraint on questions relating to luxury and hedonistic self-indulgence. For Christians, as for some Second Temple Jews, this ascetic ethos was related to the anticipation of eternal rewards that were themselves arguably hedonistic. In contrast to, for example, Stoic displays of heroic

---

[1] I am grateful to Liane Feldman, Christa Grace Watkins, Meghan Henning, Stephen Carlson, Simon Gathercole, Francis Watson and the editors of this volume for their suggestions and recommendations. J. W. Bailey, 'The Temporary Messianic Reign in the Literature of Early Judaism', *JBL* 53 (1934), 170, 87. A great deal of the evaluation of Revelation's eschatological heritage as Jewish rests on the distinctiveness of the thousand-year reign in Rev. 20.1–6. The association of the thousand-year reign with Jewish exegetical tradition rests in large part on certain sets of assumptions: first, how scholars understand the framework of 1 Thessalonians 4 and 1 Cor. 15.23–8 and whether or not one identifies an 'interim' period in Paul's schema of the resurrection. Second is the subtly anti-Jewish alignment of the 'baser' understanding of bodily afterlife exclusively with Jewish tradition. On the presence of a 'first resurrection' in Pauline thought see the overview in Candida R. Moss and Joel S. Baden, '1 Thessalonians 4.13–18 in Rabbinic Perspective', *NTS* 58.2 (2012), 199–212. For the scholarly idea that the rejection and denigration of bodily resurrection is anti-Jewish see Candida R. Moss, *Divine Bodies: Resurrecting Perfection in the New Testament and Early Christianity* (New Haven, CT: Yale University Press, 2019), 5–11.

self-control, Christians saw their own practices of bodily asceticism and embrace of suffering both as temporary and as eschatologically focused. The practical exercise of Christian identity reflects an anticipated participation in heavenly affairs and is part of a broader complex of identity-shaping beliefs that positions early Christians as 'citizens of heaven' (Phil. 3.20).

There were many ways in which early Christians related their earthly conduct to the eschatological expectations and rewards laid out in Revelation. Prayer, fasting, feasting, attire and martyrdom are all arenas in which Christian identity is sculpted in relation to post-mortem expectations.[2] For the purposes of this essay we will focus on two: eschatological dining and interpretations of the heavenly banquet among second- and third-century Christians, and the rejection of literalist interpretations of Revelation's description of heaven among some second-century Christians. While these foci may seem distinct, they are, as we will see, more integrated in early Christian anxieties than it might initially appear. The essay will begin, however, with a discussion of recent academic conversations about wealth in Jewish and Christian tradition and an overview of the ambiguous status of luxury among Greek-speaking Jewish authors.

It is appropriate to offer several important caveats at the outset of this endeavour. First, ancient reading practices do not separate verses, themes or even epochs in a hermetic fashion. In offering his particular brand of chiliasm, for example, Irenaeus essentially collapses the sharp distinction between the restored paradise of the thousand-year reign (Revelation 20) and the new creation (Revelation 21–2). Evil is essentially destroyed prior to the first resurrection and the last judgement occurs when the saints reach a state of preparedness for incorruptibility.[3] In the same way that Irenaeus elides the distinction between the reign of the saints and the heavenly Jerusalem, our analysis will include some discussion of the temporary kingdom as well as the eternal one.[4]

Second, in approaching this subject from the perspective of luxury, food, identity and constructions of heaven, we are trespassing into several much-debated areas of scholarship that will not be fully discussed here: the canonical status of Revelation; early Christian definitions of orthodoxy and heresy; chiliastic thought in the early church; and debates over the resurrection of the body. It is hoped that approaching the question in another way will be interesting enough to compensate the reader for these oversights.

---

[2] In recent scholarship a number of studies have examined the ways in which certain practices and identities rhetorically served to craft Christian identity as distinct from other groups, including Jewish ones. See, e.g. Judith M. Lieu, *Neither Jew nor Greek?: Constructing Early Christianity* (London: T&T Clark, 2005).

[3] Christopher R. Smith, 'Chiliasm and Recapitulation in the Theology of Irenaeus', *VC* 48.4 (1994), 313–31.

[4] For a general introduction to the thousand-year reign in Revelation see Charles E. Hill, *Regnum Caelorum: Patterns of Millennial Thought in Early Christianity*, 2nd edn (Grand Rapids, MI: Eerdmans, 2001). Curiously Irenaeus does not utilize Revelation 20 in his description of the millennial kingdom. Instead the general resurrection takes place 'after the times of the kingdom' (*Haer.* 5.33.2).

Wealth, heavenly praxis and identity

In the past ten years a cluster of innovative and important books on early Christian concerns about wealth, altruism and eschatology have been published. These studies have sought to locate the origins of early Christian discomfort with earthly wealth within biblical tradition and Second Temple Judaism; to highlight the importance of charitable giving as a path of access to the afterlife; and to map the social structures that undergird and support the practice of giving in the Roman world.

In late antique studies, Peter Brown's rich *Through the Eye of a Needle* elaborated on the social and intellectual shifts that allowed late antique Christians to come to terms with the problem of wealth.[5] Brown's work in this area draws heavily upon a parallel argument, most prominently advanced by Hebrew Bible scholar Gary Anderson, that ancient and medieval Jews and Christians engaged in almsgiving as a means of earning salvation.[6]

Between Anderson and Brown lies something of a gap: the conceptualization of wealth from the mid-first to early fourth century. Anderson's work uses the Judeo-Christian concept of 'sin' to analyse the problems inherent in the possession of wealth. Brown's study is a social history focused on regional social networks and practices. What remains untreated in these works are the various and highly theorized discussions of wealth that took place in what might approximately be described as 'the early church'.

For Brown the parameters of the study are drawn clearly by the profound difference he detects in Christian and Roman concepts of the afterlife: 'Certain aspects of Christian giving', he writes, 'represented a novelty not only in the professed aim of this giving – to give to the poor – but in the motivations ascribed to the giver … The notion of the working of the gift itself was different. In some way or another, for early Christians to give was to open a path to heaven.'[7] While we might contest Brown's flat characterization of the Roman motivations for giving, he, following Anderson, strikes upon a central difference between constructions of charitable giving among many in the early church and constructions of charitable giving among many of their contemporaries. For Christians, like Jews, the target of these practices lay in the distant future.

What lies unexplored in these studies is the manner in which a number of other wealth and status-related practices function similarly. Anderson is clear that the classic 'triad' of practices are fasting, prayer and almsgiving. For early Christians, the range of eschatologically oriented practices was broader, even if they derive from similar principles. Early Christians expected to be eschatologically rewarded not only for

---

[5] Peter Brown, *Through the Eye of a Needle: Wealth, the Fall of Rome, and the Making of Christianity in the West, 350–550 A.D.* (Princeton, NJ: Princeton University Press, 2012). See also Brown, *Ransom of the Soul: Afterlife and Wealth in Early Western Christianity* (Cambridge, MA: Harvard University Press, 2015), 83–114.
[6] Gary A. Anderson, *Sin: A History* (New Haven, CT: Yale University Press, 2009), 228; Anderson, *Charity: The Place of the Poor in the Biblical Tradition* (New Haven, CT: Yale University Press, 2013).
[7] Brown, *Through the Eye of a Needle*, 83–4. For Anderson, whose aim is to carve a monolithic tradition from Jewish scriptural testimony to Christian tradition, the machinations of Roman society are never in view.

almsgiving but also for displays of hospitality, for their experience of alienation, for leaving their families and for embracing martyrdom. Other practices like prayer, bathing, dress and diet focused on pre-emptively transforming the body into one suitable for heaven. Expectations of reward relied not only upon the idea of exchange (or, in some formulations, debt) but on specific understandings of the topography, architecture and activities of heaven. It was the understanding of heaven as a space of great luxury, wealth and gastronomic delight that informed and gave meaning to practices of self-denial in the present. The heavenly treasury features prominently in Anderson's understanding of almsgiving, but for early Christians the heavenly banquet loomed much larger.[8] The ways in which heaven was imagined could shape practices in the lived present.

Secondary literature on tours of heaven has primarily located the source of the descriptions of heavenly banqueting and architecture in Second Temple Jewish ascents to heaven. But these concepts are more than a rusty iconographic inheritance or neutral framework for cosmological speculation; they do important theological work. A variety of scholars has noted the ways in which heavenly affairs shaped the valuation of earthly affairs. How does our consideration of Christian abstemiousness change when that self-discipline is both preparatory and temporary? How are luxury-related Christian practices of dieting reconfigured in the context of eschatological reward? And, by extension, how do these reimagined practices alter our understanding of early Christian identity?

The literature on the construction of wealth and poverty; the practices of almsgiving; and attitudes towards the poor in the ministry of both the historical Jesus and the kerygma of the early church is vast. What follows is an analysis of two ways in which second-century Christians receive shared Jewish and Christian apocalyptic traditions about heaven as a place of luxury, wealth and decadence. Independent from the question of post-mortem hopes, diet was a means by which social groups created and regulated their sense of identity. Much more could be said about this tradition; but the purpose here is to highlight the ways in which Christians conceived of interpretations of heavenly wealth as relevant to everyday praxis and, thus, socially defining.[9]

Part of this project is to highlight an apparent tension between the expectations of luxury and rewards found in heavenly space and broader attitudes towards wealth. The decadent lifestyles of the wealthy were condemned by ancient Jews, Romans and Christians alike. Everyone, it seems, worried about the sharp divide between rich and poor, as well as the socially and morally corrosive effects of greed. Alongside the broader Christian condemnation of acquisitiveness runs a second, almost perversely contrarian tradition: heaven itself is a place of exorbitant wealth and – what would be in other contexts ruinous – gluttony.

---

[8] Between the New Testament and the fourth century there are precious few references to the heavenly treasury. The clear exception is Irenaeus who quotes Prov. 19.17: 'He who is generous to the downtrodden, makes a loan to the Lord' in *Haer.* 4.18. Irenaeus construes the loan in liturgical rather than financial terms. See discussion in Anderson, *Charity*, 151. Charitable giving is discussed in Justin Martyr, *1 Apol.* 67; Clement of Alexandria, *Strom.* 3.6.

[9] By relevant I mean more direct than the simple assumption that one's behaviour now determines one's post-mortem destiny.

We will begin, therefore, with a small yet important distinction between Jews and Christians, on the one hand, and first-century pagans, on the other – that is, the particular ways in which the language of luxury was discussed in Septuagintal tradition.[10] The purpose of this examination is to draw out the ways that the construction of heavenly space circumvented accusations of immorality that otherwise encompassed extravagant displays of wealth.

Luxury, Eden and heavenly space

By the second century CE, *luxuria* and its Greek equivalent τρυφή had become bywords for moral corruption in the writings of the moralists. According to the Roman historians, it was the infectious contagion of Persian *luxuria* that had led to the collapse of the Republic. Josephus rehearses the same narrative in his retelling of Judges 1–2 in which τρυφή emerges out of peacetime and leads to the softening of the people and moral decline: 'And after these things, the Israelites became soft regarding wars, and they devoted themselves to the land and its labors. When they thereby gained wealth, because of τρυφή and pleasure they neglected order and their constitution, and they were no longer exact disciples of the laws.'[11]

In comparison to the emerging philosophical consensus, the scriptural tradition was more ambiguous. In the biblical creation story, Eden is described as ὁ παράδεισος τῆς τρυφῆς (Gen. 3.23, 24). English translations of the Septuagint tend to render this phrase as 'the garden of delights', but as Gorman and Gorman have noted, 'this seems to … [be] somewhat imprecise'.[12] The expectations of paradise, and the meaning of τρυφή, here seems to connote something more like the fulfilment of one's expectations of comfort than outright luxury. Throughout the Septuagint there are numerous places in which the provisions that God provides for the righteous are labelled τρυφή.[13] Take for example Ps. 36.4, in which humans are commanded 'κατατρύφησον τοῦ κυρίου, καὶ δώσει σοι τὰ αἰτήματα τῆς καρδίας σου', a phrase that seems to imply that people should look to the Lord to take care of them 'and he will give you the requests of your heart'. Similarly in Ezekiel 34, as God searches for his sheep in order to give them rest, he promises to 'feed them in a good pasture; their folds shall be on the lofty mountain

---

[10] A number of scholars discuss the influence of Jewish apocalyptic thought upon the development of more 'materialistic' early Christian views of the afterlife (by materialistic I mean the resurrection of the body or the existence of an earthly millennial kingdom). See, e.g. the statement of Emil Schurer that 'chiliasm, inherited from Jewish political messianism, governed religious thinking' in the second century in Emil Schürer, *The History of the Jewish People in the Age of Jesus Christ (175 B.C.–A.D. 135)* (Edinburgh: T&T Clark, 1973–87), 2.547. My purpose here is to observe that the 'luxurious' qualities of heaven that would come by later patristic commentators to be identified as Jewish are a common part of biblical tradition.

[11] Josephus, *Ant.* 5.132. Cf. 6.34, where the children of Samuel abandon justice in favour of profit and, 'inclining toward luxury and an opulent lifestyle' (πρὸς τρυφὴν καὶ πρὸς διαίτας πολυτελεῖς πονενευκότες), oppose God and Samuel.

[12] Robert J. Gorman and Vanessa B. Gorman, *Corrupting Luxury in Ancient Greek Literature* (Ann Arbor: University of Michigan Press, 2014).

[13] 2 Esd. 19.25; Ps. 35.9, 36.11, 138.11; Prov. 4.9; Wis. 19.11; Isa. 55.2, 58.13, 66.11; Ezek. 36.35.

of Israel; there also shall they lie down, and there they shall rest in fine luxury (ἐν τρυφῇ αγαθῇ), and they shall be fed in a rich pasture on the mountains of Israel' (34.15).

The experience of receiving provisions, however, is not wholly positive or even neutral. We might compare Ezekiel's insistence that his people look to him for rest, food and provisions to Isaiah 57's indictment of the people for looking elsewhere: 'In what have you indulged (ἐνετρυφήσατε)? And against whom have you opened your mouth wide?' (Isa. 57.4). Those who are wicked, Micah tells us, will be 'cast out of their luxurious houses (ἐκ τῶν οἰκιῶν τρυφῆς αὐτῶν)' (Mic. 2.9). Self-indulgence and luxury are associated in prophetic tradition with sinfulness and impending judgement.

Philo regularly picks up on the association of Eden and τρυφή. In *De Cherubim* 12 he writes,

> 'Now Nod is interpreted as a disturbance, while Eden is τρυφή, so the one is a symbol of evil agitating the soul, and the other of virtue, which preserves comfort for the soul and τρυφή, not the shattering that comes from the irrational experience of pleasure (δι' λόγου πάθους ἡδονῆς θρύψιν), but a joy that comes with much comfort, free from toil and hard work.'[14]

Here τρυφή is a cipher for virtue and one that stands in distinction to the evil of agitation. It is clearly distinguished from irrational pleasure and instead denotes a life free from toil and anxiety.[15] That Philo feels the need to distinguish different forms of luxury and defend one indicates a recognition of the overarching assumption that τρυφή can be highly negative. Certainly, the idea of a return to a state of luxury reappears, as we will see, among certain branches of early Christianity.

Simultaneously, Philo reflects broader Hellenistic philosophical conventions and attitudes to luxury when he writes that '[Moses] does not think it right that the man who is concerned with virtue should enjoy an easy life and pursue τρυφή' (*Somn.* 1.121).[16] Men should instead seek the harder life and be content with few possessions while women busy themselves with the soft trappings of luxury.[17] He censures the lifestyle of those accustomed to τρυφή – describing it as the 'flabby life' that will ultimately lead to the breakdown of society.[18]

Philo's writings reflect several different thematic treatments of τρυφή. On one hand, τρυφή is a gift of abundance, rest and pleasure that comes from God and is often explicitly connected to descriptions of Eden and paradise. On the other, he invokes a philosophical commonplace: that τρυφή, while appropriate for women, softens

---

[14] Philo, *Cher.* 12.
[15] See also Philo, *Flacc.* 184; *Poster. C.* 32 (where it is tied to divine wisdom); *Migr. Abr.* 204 (as the abundant satiation of each of the five senses); *Spec. Leg.* 1.134 (with respect to the lifestyle of priests); *Spec. Leg.* 1.303–4 (as a gift of God).
[16] Philo's indebtedness to Greek philosophy was recognized as early as Goodenough who labelled him 'unoriginal'. Erwin R Goodenough, *An Introduction to Philo Judaeus*, 2nd edn (Lanham, MD: University Press of America, 1962, repr. 1986), 94–5.
[17] Philo, *Somn.* 1.123–4.
[18] Philo, *Spec. Leg.* 2.240; cf. 2.99; *Jos.* 44; *Vit. Cont.* 48; *Leg. Gai.* 168; *Vit. Mos.* 2.12–13; *Virt.* 161–3. We might compare his famous description of the corruption of Sodom; see *Abr.* 133–6.

and corrupts the nature of men (and whole peoples) who seek virtue.[19] The return to Eden, or the ascent to heaven, we might expect would (to readers of the Septuagint) naturally involve a return to luxury. For many in the ancient world, earthly luxury was ethically problematic when it was out of place or excessive. This sense of propriety was intimately tied to status, and thus, the presence of luxury in heaven was unproblematic in the sense that no one could be more deserving of luxury than God. Whether or not we identify the Septuagintal construction of luxury to be the by-product of broader Hellenistic usage, the result was the construction of heaven as a space of luxurious provision in which one's physical needs are constantly met. Even beyond and outside of the apocalyptic tradition there was an understanding of paradisaical space that utilized the morally ambiguous language of luxury to describe the rewards of fidelity to God.

Feasting in the temporary and eternal kingdoms

In the same way that the Septuagint defines divinely originating τρυφή as luxurious provision, early Christian descriptions of heaven regularly describe it as a place of physical sustenance. The gospels record a number of occasions upon which Jesus speaks of the 'eating and drinking' that would take place in heaven; the Gospel of Matthew regularly uses the marriage celebration in its parables of the kingdom; and Revelation refers to the marriage supper of the lamb.[20] The use of feasting imagery in Roman catacomb art may offer further support for the idea that Christians expected an afterlife characterized by feasting.[21] The idea of heavenly festivities was hardly unique to Christianity. As Stein summarizes, 'We find this metaphorical use of a supper in the Apocrypha (2 Esdras 2:38), the Pseudepigrapha (1 Enoch 60:7f; 62:14), the Dead Sea Scrolls (1QSa ii 11–23), as well as in the rabbinic literature (Midrash Genesis 62:2; b. Sanhedrin 153a).'[22] Heaven is a space in which food is implicitly and explicitly supplied and that food is, upon occasion, the source of immortality and even transformation.[23]

---

[19] E.g. Aeschylus, *Pers.*; Livy 39.6. See discussion in Jennifer Eyl, 'The Apocryphal Acts of the Apostles', in *The Oxford Handbook of New Testament, Gender and Sexuality*, ed. Benjamin Dunning (Oxford: Oxford University Press, 2019), 387–406, 398.

[20] Lk. 13.29; 14.15; 23.20; Mt. 22.1–14; 25.1–13; Rev. 19.1–6. For the view that the Apocalypse envisions the eucharist as a proleptic participation in heavenly banquets see Jürgen Roloff, *Die Offenbarung des Johannes* (Zürich: Theologischer, 1984), 203. To be read with criticisms in Jens-W. Traeger, *Johannesapokalypse und johanneischer Kreis* (Berlin: de Gruyter, 1988), 50–4.

[21] For examples of this see the meal scene in the Capella Graeca of the Catacomb of Priscilla, banquet scenes in the Catacombs of Callistus, the depiction of a banquet on a sarcophagus fragment now in the Vatican Museo Pio Cristiano and a banquet scene found in the small catacomb of Vibia on the Via Appia Antica in Rome.

[22] R. H. Stein, *An Introduction to the Parables of Jesus* (Philadelphia, PA: Westminster, 1981), 86.

[23] E.g. see the scent of food and streams of honey, milk, oil and wine in 2 En. 8.1–5. For a recent review of this theme see discussion in David Hellholm, 'Ailments of Immortality in the Afterlife: Apocalyptic and Eschatological Notions of Eternal Life', in *The Eucharist – Its Origins and Contexts: Sacred Meal, Communal Meal, Table Fellowship in Late Antiquity, Early Judaism, and Early Christianity*, ed. David Hellholm and Dieter Sanger (Tübingen: Mohr Siebeck, 2017), 1851–910. For transformative acts of eating see, e.g. the bittersweet honey of the heavenly scroll in Rev. 10.10 and Perpetua's consumption of cheese in her vision of heaven (Passion of Perpetua 4.10). On the transformative effects of heavenly eating see Meredith J. C. Warren, *Food and Transformation in Ancient Mediterranean Literature*, ed.

In the same way, a number of chiliast early Christian writers refer to food and dining during the thousand-year reign.[24] One fragment, preserved in Irenaeus, uses biblically styled language of superabundant harvests in the kingdom: 'The days are coming when vines will come forth, each with ten thousand boughs; and on a single bough will be ten thousand branches ... every grain will yield ten pounds of pure, exceptionally fine flour.'[25] Maximus the Confessor writes, 'Papias ... spoke about the pleasures of food in the resurrection (τὰς διὰ βρωμάτων εἶπεν ἐν τῇ ἀναστάσει ἀπολαύσεις).'[26] He adds, 'Irenaeus of Lyons says the same thing in the fifth book of his work.' Irenaeus's arguments about eating in the millennium refer more to a return to an idyllic pre-lapsarian state than the sensual enjoyment of food. Nevertheless, the presence of gastronomic delights and divine provision is an element of Irenaeus's picture of the thousand-year reign.[27] Justin Martyr more opaquely references 'rejoicing' in the 'adorned and enlarged (καὶ κοσμηθείσῃ καὶ πλατυνθείσῃ)' Jerusalem but does not discuss banqueting or gastronomy.[28]

In scholarship on the relationship between dining practices and the eschaton, the focus has often been placed upon the ways in which eating in the present (when properly regulated) anticipates banqueting in the future.[29] With respect to the Qumran community, some have argued that belief in an eschatological messianic banquet played a significant role in the day-to-day life of the sectarian Qumran community and shaped their dining practices.[30] Similar arguments have been advanced for eucharistic serves and *refrigeria* meals in the catacombs: ritual dining collapses the boundaries between heaven and earth and allows participants to briefly experience the heavenly idyll. For Christians, therefore, the existence of the eschatological banquet reconfigured practices of eating that Christians had inherited from pagan culture: *refrigeria* meals at the tombs of the saints were now no longer an opportunity to feed one's loved ones, but rather a chance to participate in the ongoing heavenly banquet.[31]

Clare K. Rothschild, Writings from the Greco-Roman World Supplement Series, vol. 14 (Atlanta, GA: SBL Press, 2019).

[24] For a survey of early Christian chiliast views see Walter Bauer, 'Chiliasmus', *RAC* 2 (1954), 1073–8. Not discussed here: Victorianus's reference to drinking 'the fruit of the vine in the kingdom' in *Commentary on the Apocalypse*, 215–16.

[25] Irenaeus, *Haer.* 5.33.3–4; (Greek) Eusebius, *Hist. eccl.* 3.39.1 (trans. Ehrman).

[26] Maximus the Confessor, *On the Ecclesiastical Hierarchy*, 7. Maximus here augmented a testimonium from John of Scythopolis, who may not have been familiar with Papias's writings himself. It is possible that John was extrapolating from Irenaeus and Eusebius. For this observation I am greatly indebted to Stephen Carlson.

[27] Irenaeus, *Haer.* 5.33.2. See discussion in Smith, 'Chiliasm and Recapitulation in the Theology of Irenaeus', 315–17.

[28] Justin Martyr, *Dial.* 80.4, 1.

[29] Despite the fact that he refers to fasting as meritorious action that stores up rewards in heaven, Anderson does not discuss the breaking of the fast in heaven. He only once refers to the heavenly banquet, and then obliquely, as a euphemism for salvation (201 n. 14).

[30] Lawrence H. Schiffman, *The Eschatological Community of the Dead Sea Scrolls: A Study of the Rule of the Congregation* (Atlanta, GA: Scholars Press, 1989), 53–67. Schiffman refers primarily to 1QSa ii 11–22 and 1QS xi 2–6. Schiffman's analysis of this material and particularly his categorization of the meal as 'messianic' have been challenged. See the review by Ben Zion Wacholder in *JBL* 110 (1991), 147–8.

[31] Candida R. Moss, 'Christian Funerary Banquets and Martyr Cults', in *The Eucharist – Its Origins and Contexts: Sacred Meal, Communal Meal, Table Fellowship in Late Antiquity, Early Judaism, and Early Christianity*, ed. David Hellholm and Dieter Sanger (Tübingen: Mohr Siebeck, 2017), 819–28.

What has been neglected in the work of Brown and Anderson is the manner in which Christian fasting, like almsgiving, anticipates the eschatological banquet. Fasting stands in distinction to indulgence and, as such, opposes the morally and physiologically corrupting effects of surfeit.[32] As a habit, fasting was both medically and religiously prescribed, and was widely practiced across numerous groups for a variety of reasons. Among these was the role fasting practices played in distinguishing early Christians from others. The Didache prescribes that Christians should not fast on Mondays and Thursdays 'like the hypocrites', but should instead choose Wednesdays and Fridays.[33] At least to an extent, Christians self-consciously tailored their fasting in opposition to those of Jews even as they followed the same practices and scheduling.[34]

One such social function I would like to draw attention to is the notion that fasting in the present is related to expectations of post-mortem revelry. A number of early Christian martyrdom accounts portray the martyrs both as expecting to participate in the heavenly banquet and of fasting in anticipation of this event.[35] James, one of the eponymous characters in the North African Martyrdom of Marian and James, sees a vision of the martyr Agapius and exclaims in its aftermath, 'I am on my way to the banquet of Agapius and the other blessed martyrs!'[36] Bishop Fructuosus of Tarragona delays eating while imprisoned in anticipation of the heavenly feast.[37] These references undoubtedly reflect the nascent cult of the saints and its attendant food culture, but at the same time they direct us to the idea of heavenly feasting.[38]

It was not only martyrs who fasted in preparation for the resurrection. Having assembled a host of biblical exemplars for fasting, Tertullian then argues that deprivation in the present actually facilitates the mechanics of the resurrection; 'emaciation does not displease us; for it is not by weight that God bestows flesh any more than he does the spirit by measure. More easily through the "straight gate" of

---

[32] On the corrupting effects of surfeit see Clement, *Strom.* 2.1.14.4. He criticizes agape meals that too closely resemble symposia in *Paed.* 2.1.4.3-4; 2.1.5.3. Musonius Rufus also criticizes eating for pleasure in *Dissertations* 18b.55-65. A number of medical authors exhibit a concern about surfeit; see e.g. Galen, *On the Diagnosis and Cure of the Errors of the Soul* 1.9, K45. The concerns about excessive eating formed part of sumptuary legislation: the Aemilian law of 115 BCE, for example, specified the type of foods consumed at banquets. See Gellius, 2.24.12; Pliny, *Nat.* 8.82; Macrobius, *Saturnalia* 3.17.13. See discussion in Emanuela Zanda, *Fighting Hydra-Like Luxury: Sumptuary Regulation in the Roman Republic* (London: Bloomsbury, 2011), 51.

[33] Did. 8.1.

[34] On the identity of the hypocrites as Pharisees in particular and the relationship to Judaism see H. W. M. Sandt and David Flusser, *The Didache: Its Jewish Sources and Its Place in Judaism and Christianity*, Compendia Rerum Iudaicarum Ad Novum Testamentum (Assen: Royal Van Gorcum; Minneapolis, MN: Fortress, 2002), 291.

[35] The evidence is not purely literary; for a discussion of the archaeological data for feasting in the catacombs in Rome see David L. Eastman, *Paul the Martyr: The Cult of the Apostle in the Latin West* (Atlanta, GA: Society of Biblical Literature, 2011). Arguably the earliest evidence of dining at the tomb of a martyr is Martyrdom of Polycarp 18.3.

[36] Martyrdom of Marian and James 11.3: 'ad Agapii ceterorumque martyrum beatissimorum pergo conuiuium'. Later in the account the martyrs are told by another martyr, this time a young boy, that they will 'dine' with him in heaven the next day (11.6).

[37] Martyrdom of Fructuosus 3.3.

[38] On food culture and the cult of the saints in the third century see Eliezer Gonzalez, *The Fate of the Dead in Early Third Century North African Christianity* (Tübingen: Mohr Siebeck, 2014).

salvation will slender flesh enter; more speedily will lighter flesh rise; longer in the sepulcher will drier flesh retain to firmness.'[39] Gastronomic self-restraint is often linked by Tertullian to sexual renunciation and together these practices serve to dry out the body in preparation for the resurrection.[40] The preferability of the 'dry' body gestures to ancient Greek and Roman medicine, in which male bodies were drier than the naturally soft and weak bodies of women. But the goal of fasting here is neither the medicinal nor psychological rewards described by Galen, but rather the anticipation of the heavenly banquet.[41] What was a lifestyle for the philosophers was, instead, a diet for some Christians.

Rejections of materialistic heaven by early Christians

As is well documented and much discussed, Revelation began to be met with more scepticism and concern by early Christian readers in the third century.[42] Prior to this point, most acknowledge, it was broadly accepted. Surveys of opposition to the scriptural and canonical status of the Book of Revelation ordinarily begin with Dionysius of Alexandria, whose work was the first to seriously question the apostolic authorship and canonicity of the Book of Revelation. The reason for this is clear: Dionysius opposed the canonical status of the book. Our purpose is somewhat different; we are interested only in the ways in which early Christian writers, regardless of whether or not they deemed the book 'canonical', were concerned about the materialism of the book's description of heaven and morally problematic descriptions of gluttony and wealth described therein.[43]

---

[39] Tertullian, *Jejun.* 17.7. See Taylor Petrey, *Resurrecting Parts: Early Christians on Desire, Reproduction, and Sexual Difference*, Routledge Studies in the Early Christian World (London: Routledge, 2015), 93–4. Here Tertullian discusses the mechanics of the resurrection. Elsewhere Tertullian indicates a belief in a millennial kingdom that will serve as a reward to the saints (*Marc.* 3.24).

[40] Tertullian, *Res.* 61.5–7. See discussion in 'We are Called to Monogamy: Marriage, Virginity, and the Resurrection of the Fleshly Body in Tertullian of Carthage', in *Coming Back to Life: The Permeability of Past and Present, Mortality and Immortality, Death and Life in the Ancient Mediterranean*, ed. Fred Tappenden and Carly Daniel-Hughes (Montreal: McGill University Library, 2017), 239–65.

[41] For a more traditional assessment of diet and surfeit among Christian authors see Clement of Alexandria, *Paed.* 2.1.7.3. Jerome appears to appreciate the notion of exchanging poverty for excess when he writes, 'The Jews and the Ebionites heirs of the Jewish error, who have taken the name "poor" through humility, understand all the delights of the thousand years in a literal sense' (*Comm. Jer.* 66.20).

[42] On the larger question of canonization see Lee Martin McDonald, *The Formation of the Christian Biblical Canon* (Peabody, MA: Hendrickson, 1995), 228–49; William Farmer and Denis Farkasfalvy, *The Formation of the New Testament Canon* (New York: Paulist, 1983).

[43] For a survey of anti-millenarianism see Everett Ferguson, *The Early Church at Work and Worship: Volume 2. Catechesis, Baptism, Eschatology, and Martyrdom* (Cambridge: James Clarke, 2014), 216–31. For a discussion of the problems with wealth in Jerusalem see discussion in Candida R. Moss and Liane M. Feldman, 'The New Jerusalem: Wealth, Ancient Building Projects and Revelation 21–2', *NTS* 66.3 (2020): 351–66. The rejection of wealth and materialism was not solely linked to concerns about Revelation. Marcion omits Lk. 13.29, which refers to the feast in the kingdom of God, and the passage in the last supper pericope which refers to eating in the kingdom of God (Lk. 22.16). I am grateful to Simon Gathercole for both of these observations.

The second-century Asian Epistula Apostolorum staunchly rejects any notion of heavenly consumption as was sometimes inferred from Rev. 20.4.[44] Positioning itself against the teachings of Cerinthus, it insists not only on the absence of an earthly millennium (21) but also on the erasure of 'eating or drinking' (19) in the place 'above'. The Ethiopic interprets food as part of the corrupted order and adds, 'You will not have part in the lower creation, but in that which is incorruptible of my Father' (19.14–15).[45]

Around the turn of the third century, Clement of Alexandria took issue with the rather materialistic vision of heaven described in Revelation 21. In rejecting a literalist reading of the eschatological city, Clement argued that the gold and gems of Rev. 21.18–21 were mere metaphors: '[by] the incomparable brilliance of gems is understood the spotless and holy brilliance of the substance of the spirit'. Only the foolish and ignorant Christian exegete would read these passages as a literal description of heaven.[46] Clement's statement inaugurates a trend even among the more literal millenarian commentators on Revelation in which the heavenly city is understood symbolically as a cipher for the church and her virtues.[47]

Similar objections were voiced by Clement's ecclesiastical descendent, Dionysius of Alexandria. In writing against Nepos's deeply materialistic millennial views, Dionysius produces his now famous arguments against the canonical status of Revelation, which are preserved in edited form in Eusebius, *Hist. eccl.* 6.24–5. Less frequently noted among these arguments are his views, greatly abbreviated by Eusebius, that millennialists lead people to 'hope for things that are trivial and corruptible' (6.24.1) and that the book 'cannot be understood in the bald, literal sense' (6.24.4). Though he is somewhat opaque here, the reference to corruptible things appears to refer to superficial delights of wealth and luxury. To amplify the association, he follows others in arguing that Revelation be attributed to Cerinthus, 'a man devoted to the pleasures of the body ... the belly; and what comes beneath the belly' (6.24.3).[48] It is precisely the decadence of 'the marriage feast [that lasts] a thousand years' that Eusebius elsewhere identifies as base and deceptive (3.28.2). The reference to gluttony is somewhat predictable; at risk of undervaluing the corrosive effects of lust, it was gluttony that most troubled ancient moralists.[49] It here stands as

---

[44] On the provenance of this text see Charles Hill, 'The "Epistula Apostolorum": An Asian Tract from the Time of Polycarp', *JECS* 7.1 (1999), 1–53.

[45] Francis Watson (trans.), 'The Epistula Apostolorum: English Translation from Coptic and Geʽez', in *An Apostolic Gospel: The 'Epistula Apostolorum' in Context* (Cambridge: Cambridge University Press, 2020), 55.

[46] Clement, *Paed.* 3.2.12–13, 2.12.119. The example from Clement is cited by and discussed in Kristi Upson-Saia, *Early Christian Dress: Gender, Virtue and Authority*, Routledge Studies in Ancient History (New York: Routledge, 2011), 39–40.

[47] See, e.g. Tyconnius of Carthage, *Exposition of the Apocalypse*, 7.21.

[48] Writing around 200 CE, Gaius of Rome seems to have been the first to attribute the authorship of Revelation to Cerinthus (Eusebius, *Hist. eccl.* 3.28.2). On the origins of Cerinthus see Charles E. Hill, 'Cerinthus, Gnostic or Chiliast? A New Solution to an Old Problem', *Journal of Early Christian Studies* 8.2 (2000), 135–72. On the association of the belly and loins in ancient thought see, e.g. the writings of first-century medical writer Rufus of Ephesus, *On Satyriasis and Gonorrhea 19-20*, ed. Charles Daremberg, Oeuvres de Rufus d'Éphèse (Paris: Imprimerie nationale, 1879), 72, lines 4–21.

[49] Ismo Dunderberg, 'Moral Progress in Early Christian Stories of the Soul', *NTS* 59.2 (2013), 247–67.

a cipher for a whole host of wealth-related sins.[50] Revelation's association with and tacit support for gluttony and hedonism seems to be one reason for its rejection by Dionysius.

These complaints may date earlier than Clement. Eusebius mentions that Gaius of Rome offered the earliest complaint at the turn of the third century.[51] And, according to Epiphanius, objections about the moral character of Revelation may have been lodged as early as the second century. A group known as the 'Alogi' objected to factual inaccuracies in the book – the lack of a church at Thyatira – and the 'sensuous symbolism' in the book.[52]

In scholarship, concerns about the sensualism of literal readings of the thousand-year reign (Revelation 20) and the New Jerusalem (Revelation 21–2) are linked to anxieties about two related early Christian 'heresies': 'Asiatic chiliasm' in general and the New Prophecy movement in particular.[53] While belief in the millennium (unlike belief in resurrection of the body) seemed to be a negotiable part of Justin's definition of orthodox Christianity, from the third and fourth centuries onwards others would reject it outright.[54] Those who did, rhetorically linked it to Judaism. There is, of

---

[50] As a social practice, banqueting was one of the cornerstones of elite Greek and Roman society. Banquets were occasions for celebrations and symposia during which the exchange of ideas and pleasantries could cement social ties even of the highest order. Simultaneously, however, ritualistic meals, especially those organized and attended by the social elites, occupied a precarious space between socially important displays of power and morally corrosive displays of luxury, such that attendance at banquets was always a potential occasion for personal moral corruption. Cicero claims that abstaining from banquets could clear a man of charges of immorality (Cicero, *Rosc. Amer.* 39). Philo writes that it was gluttony that led to the downfall of Sodom (Philo, *Abr.* 133–6). The connection between excess food and drink and sexual impropriety was well established: we need only look to the rumours about Caligula and his sisters for evidence that indulgence in foods could lead to incest during banquets (Suetonius, *Cal.* 24.1). Banqueting, thus, was socially elevating and morally unsettling. Jesus himself was well-known for his love of dinner parties. He appears to have scandalized a Pharisee named Simon by allowing a woman to touch him during one such meal (Lk. 7.36–50). The reputation would haunt him: according to a section of Origen's *De Resurrectione* referred to in Pamphilus's *Apology for Origen*, Jesus's fondness for dining led to the accusation that he was a 'winebibber and glutton'. Pamphilus, *Apology for Origen*, 113, in St. Pamphilus, *Apology for Origen*. Rufinus, *On the Falsification of the Books of Origen*, trans. Thomas P. Scheck, The Fathers of the Church 120 (Washington, DC: Catholic University of America Press, 2010), 90.

[51] Eusebius, *Hist. eccl.* 3.28.2.

[52] Epiphanius, *Pan.* 51.3.1. The so-called 'Alogi' objected to more than Revelation; they also rejected the Johannine corpus in its entirety. For a discussion of the arguments of the Alogi together with an appraisal of their existence outside of the work of Epiphanius see T. Scott Manor, *Epiphanius' Alogi and the Johannine Controversy: A Reassessment of Early Ecclesial Opposition to the Johannine Corpus* (Leiden: Brill, 2016).

[53] On the descent of heavenly Jerusalem in Montanist thought see Eusebius, *Hist. eccl.* 5.18.2; Epiphanius, *Pan.* 48.14; and William Tabernee, *Fake Prophecy and Polluted Sacraments* (Leiden: Brill, 2007). For the debate over Montanist use of Revelation see Christine Trevett, *Montanism: Gender, Authority, and the New Prophecy* (Cambridge: Cambridge University Press, 1996), 130–9. The relationship between Montanism and Judaism was first raised in Karlfried Froehlich, 'Montanism und Gnosis', *Orientalia Christiana Analecta* 195 (1973): 109.

[54] Justin Martyr, *Dial.* 80.1. I am ignoring here those Christians who necessarily rejected the thousand-year reign based on their rejection of the resurrection of the body in general. It is noteworthy that a number of Nag Hammadi texts dealing with the ascent of the soul exhibit grave concerns about the consumption of food. See discussion in Dunderberg, 'Moral Progress', 265. The place of millenarian ideas in emerging debates about orthodoxy is not the purpose of this essay; for more on this see Outi Lehtipuu, *Debates over the Resurrection of the Dead: Constructing Early Christian Identity* (Oxford: Oxford University Press, 2015), 7–8, 70–1.

course, evidence for millenarianism among ancient Jewish authors and some of these authors and thinkers had concrete political ambitions in mind.[55] Justin and Irenaeus both grounded their ideas about the millennial kingdom in biblical prophecies about the restoration of Israel that featured with equal prominence among Jewish chiliasts, especially around the time of the Bar Kokhba revolt.[56] But it was hardly because of the citation of texts from the Hebrew Bible that millenarianism would be designated as a 'Jewish' idea. Cerinthus, the antagonist of the Epistula Apostolorum, was labelled a Judaizer by Epiphanius and Hippolytus.[57] Accusations of 'Jewishness' were intended to distance chiliasm from orthodox Christianity. Jerome, for example, charged Papias with 'propagating the Jewish tradition of the millennium'.[58] Origen, too, presented Christian chiliasm and Jewish messianism as essentially the same phenomenon. He described chiliasts as 'men who believe in Christ' but understand the scriptures in a 'Jewish fashion'.[59] In this way, the construction of millenarians as a kind of 'Jewish other' whose errors are grounded in a particularly 'Jewish' mode of reading and interpreting scripture is used to divorce chiliasts from Christianity proper. The argument that they should more properly be seen as 'Jews' rather than 'Christians' does a great deal of rhetorical work, work that obscured the shared cultural and conceptual heritage of both groups.

What is of relevance for our purposes is that critics of both the millenarian position and the literalist interpretation of the heavenly city refer to concerns about materialism, luxury and gluttony. Clement's anxieties about literalist readings of the heavenly city and Dionysius's worries about millenarianism are of a piece. Methodius would attempt to sanitize the millennium by eliminating the need for physical punishment and the possibility of repopulation.[60] Reservations about how

---

[55] 1 En. 93.3–10; 93.11–17; 4 Ezra 7.26–44; 12.31–34; 2 Bar. 29.3–30.1; 40.1–4; 72.2–74.3. For a discussion of the thousand-year reign in ancient Jewish apocalyptic literature see Bailey, 'Temporary Messianic Reign', 172–84; David E. Aune, *Revelation 17–22*, Word Biblical Commentary, vol. 52C (Nashville, TN: Thomas Nelson), 1104–8; H.-A. Wilcke, *Das Probleme eines messianischen Zwischenreichs bei Paulus*, Atant, vol. 51 (Zürich: Zwingli, 1967). For the relationship between Jewish and Christian chiliasm see Robert L. Wilken, 'Early Christian Chiliasm, Jewish Messianism, and the Idea of the Holy Land', *HTR* 79.1 (1986), 298–307. Practically speaking, there is evidence of significant personal interaction between Christians and Jews throughout the first and second centuries and Bar Kokhba, in particular, was attractive to some Christians. See Justin, *1 Apol.* 31; *Dial.* 42.4–5 and, potentially, Apoc. Pet. 2. For discussion see William Horbury, 'Messianism among Jews and Christians in the Second Century', *Augustinianum* 28 (1988), 83–4.

[56] Justin appears to refer to Ezek. 36–39 and cited Isa. 65.17–50 in *Dial.* 80. Irenaeus relies on Ezekiel 37, a collection of passages from Isaiah and Genesis. Irenaeus, *Haer.* 5.35, compare Gen. 13.13, 14, 17; Isa. 31.9; 32.1; 54.11–14; 65.18. The same group of texts used by Justin and Irenaeus would be used in the fourth century to support the notion of a return to the land of Israel. See Robert L. Wilken, 'The Restoration of Israel in Biblical Prophecy: Christian and Jewish Responses in the Early Byzantine Period', in *To See Ourselves as Others See Us: Christians, Jews, and Others in Late Antiquity*, ed. Jacob Neusner and Ernest D. Frerichs (Chico, CA: Scholar's Press, 1985), 443–71.

[57] Hill, 'Cerinthus, Gnostic or Chiliast?', 143–9. Compare Irenaeus's assessment of Cerinthus as a 'Gnostic' in *Haer.* 3.3.4.

[58] Jerome, *Vir. ill.*, 18. A whole host of scholars labour to free Irenaeus and Justin from the label 'chiliast'.

[59] Origen, *Princ.* 2.11.1. For his figurative interpretation of the New Jerusalem see *Cels.* 7.29.

[60] Methodius, *Symp.* 9.1–5. Hill, *Regnum Caelorum*, 40–1. Danielou argues that Methodius is developing a millenarian position found in Sib. Or. 8.145–9 when all 'will eat the dewy manna with

Conclusion

For early Christians, images of heaven could provide an aspirational ideal for daily life. Some, like Tertullian, hypothesized that shaping the body through sexual and digestive restraint would enable it to rise more quickly. Others saw mimesis as a way to anticipate the heavenly life, to draw it to oneself and live already like an angel. We can imagine that for others still the heavenly life did not obligate straightforward imitation but, rather, provided a kind of purpose. The potential for resurrection endowed the body with an end, an ethical goal.

For some authors, like Clement and Dionysius, the materialism and superficiality of Revelation's description of heaven was the source of concern. It was not the potential debauchery in the eschaton but rather the effects of this expectation on those in the present that were of concern. It was precisely because expectations of banqueting and wealth might affect early Christian conduct and self-definition in the present that Dionysius worried about these views.

The relationship between present conduct and future conduct need not be understood as inherently self-contradictory. What made *luxuria* ethically problematic was not its existence but the manner in which it might corrupt the individual and lead them to acquisitiveness and envy.[61] For writers like Papias and Irenaeus, the causative relationship between the two would not exist in the kingdom and, thus, the opulence of the kingdom did not provoke fears about greed. In keeping with the Septuagintal descriptions we have examined, luxury was construed in both positive and negative terms. For Irenaeus, who understood the first resurrection as a kind of return to the primordial state, it was only logical that the resurrected body share in the luxury of paradise.

In his work on almsgiving, Anderson argued that for ancient Jews and the authors of the New Testament charity in the present was a loan to God that anticipated repayment from the heavenly treasury in the future. As we have seen, if only in part, in early Christian circles the relationship between almsgiving and the heavenly treasury is one instance of a broader pattern in which the exercise of moderation and self-denial in the present are related to the expectations of future rewards. To almsgiving we can add dress, diet and even martyrdom. All of these practices anticipate post-mortem restitution, repayment and reward and each of them is, in turn, reshaped by the heavenly ideal and goal.

The trappings of wealth and the life of luxury found in early Christian descriptions of heaven are surely not, as some have argued, the ruins or aesthetic detritus of the

---

white teeth'. See discussion in Jean Danielou, *The Theology of Jewish Christianity* (London: Darton, Longman and Todd, 1964), 395.

[61] Catharine Edwards, *The Politics of Immorality in Ancient Rome* (Cambridge: Cambridge University Press, 1993), 24–32.

Jewish eschatological or linguistic traditions from which they draw. They function as models of a range of identity-forming, scripturally grounded practices. Practices of moderation and self-denial would have been intelligible to most people in the ancient world, but within the context of the longer reach of immortality Christian expectations find new shape and purpose.

8

Scribes, Pharisees, Sadducees and Trypho: Jewish leadership and Jesus traditions in Justin's construal of Christian and Jewish identity

Benjamin A. Edsall

In discussions of Jewish traditions in the second-century Christian imagination, Justin Martyr's *Dialogue with Trypho* remains an important touchstone. It is a work rife with passages from Jewish scriptures and elements of Jewish tradition, which Justin's literary avatar attempts to appropriate as symbols within his Christian theological and social vision. Throughout, Justin is concerned to present Christianity as coherent and unified, construing Trypho's Jewish identity as a foil to his own. One important aspect of this is seen in his representation of Jewish leadership groups such as the scribes, Pharisees and Sadducees. Far from this being a simple question about Justin's knowledge or ignorance of contemporary Judaism, it becomes immediately clear that Justin's representation of these groups is closely related to his reception of early Christian gospel traditions, the '*Memoirs* of the apostles', in his well-known formulation.[1] In his reception of these traditions, Justin demarcates the boundaries of his contemporary Jewish and Christian communities, and thus makes the story of Jesus constitutive of the social identity of second-century Christianity.

Much has, of course, been written about Justin Martyr, Judaism and Christian identity. Amidst the numerous (and erudite) arguments, the goal of the present contribution is not to uncover some new evidence about Justin's knowledge but rather to focus on one small feature of the *Dialogue* that has previously been taken to signify *both* his knowledge *and* his ignorance about Judaism, depending on whether the potential for external referents or the role of gospel mediation is emphasized. My argument, in short, is that Justin's reception and presentation of scribes, Pharisees, Sadducees and other leadership groups *is* markedly indebted to gospel traditions *even while* it pushes at the limits of that early Christian tradition in the Apologist's broader claims about contemporary Christian and Jewish identities and their communal attempts to demarcate their boundaries.

---

[1] On the '*Memoirs* of the apostles' (τὰ ἀπομνημονεύματα τῶν ἀποστόλων; *1 Apol.* 66–7; *Dial.* 100–7), see further below.

With that destination in view, the itinerary for this journey is relatively simple. After raising a few general considerations about Justin's *Dialogue*, the argument will turn to a survey of Justin's characterization of various Jewish leadership groups: scribes and Pharisees, chief priests and elders, Sadducees and other 'heresies'. These will be taken up in two parts: first, those passages which can be explained with reference to Justin's appropriation of gospel material; and second, those which escape simple 'gospel' explanations. With Justin's descriptions of these groups in place, I will conclude with a (very) brief attempt to explain the phenomena of those Jewish groups we see in Justin's *Dialogue* with a few tools gleaned from Paul Ricoeur and Bruno Latour.

General considerations: Justin Martyr's *Memoirs* and knowledge of Judaism

The above framing and the shape of the subsequent argument raise three preliminary issues: the audience of Justin's *Dialogue*, his knowledge of contemporary Judaism and the identity of Justin's gospel *Memoirs*. Rather than attempt any comprehensive account of these matters, it is sufficient for the present simply to mark out the space within which my argument unfolds.

Despite much ink being spilled over the question of Justin's intended audience, the fact remains that there is no clear internal or external evidence available to help settle it.[2] Arguments for a principally Christian audience, which currently appear to hold the field, have several strong points in their favour – from the often self-justifying, internal aim of much apologetic writing to the practical point that ancient textual publication was primarily accomplished through networks of friends and patrons.[3] Nevertheless, it remains difficult to exclude entirely some 'external' audience, particularly insofar as it is impossible to delineate which group constitutes the 'internal' audience: Christianity and Judaism were both variegated phenomena in the second century.[4] The concrete

---

[2] The appeal to a certain Marcus Pompeius in *Dial.* 141 unfortunately does not clarify matters since we know nothing about him, aside from his Roman name.

[3] See especially the recent work of Matthijs den Dulk, *Between Jews and Heretics: Refiguring Justin Martyr's Dialogue with Trypho* (London: Routledge, 2018), 43–54, building on the classic work of Harry Gamble; Harry Y. Gamble, *Books and Readers in the Early Church: A History of Early Christian Texts* (New Haven, CT: Yale University Press, 1995); and Harry Y. Gamble, 'The Book Trade in the Roman Empire', in *The Early Text of the New Testament*, ed. Charles E. Hill and Michael J. Kruger (Oxford: Oxford University Press, 2012), 23–36. Other works arguing in this vein include Daniel Boyarin, *Border Lines: The Partition of Judaeo-Christianity* (Philadelphia: University of Pennsylvania Press, 2004); David Rokeah, *Justin Martyr and the Jews*, Jewish and Christian Perspectives (Leiden: Brill, 2002); and Adam Gregerman, *Building on the Ruins of the Temple: Apologetics and Polemics in Early Christianity and Rabbinic Judaism*, TSAJ (Tübingen: Mohr Siebeck, 2016), 22–4. Arguments about audience are closely related to those of Justin's knowledge of Judaism in the scholarly literature; cf. the arguments in Miriam S. Taylor, *Anti-Judaism and Early Christian Identity: A Critique of the Scholarly Consensus* (Leiden: Brill, 1995), against Justin's knowledge of Judaism and the more nuanced treatment in Marc G. Hirshman, *A Rivalry of Genius: Jewish and Christian Biblical Interpretation in Late Antiquity* (Albany: State University of New York Press, 1996).

[4] Cf. the comments on this point in Michael Slusser, 'Justin Scholarship: Trends and Trajectories', in *Justin Martyr and His Worlds*, ed. Sara Parvis and Paul Foster (Minneapolis, MN: Fortress, 2007),

social or institutional contexts that elicited and enabled the production and circulation of Justin's *Dialogue* are likewise unclear.[5] The upshot of this, then, is that one should consider the *Dialogue* against a broad set of possible readers in the second century: Christians (of various stripes), Jews and even other interested Greek-speaking inhabitants of the Roman Empire.[6] Justin's literary construction of Judaism and Christianity in his *Dialogue* can, therefore, be considered in relation to both its reception of early Christian texts and traditions and its *claims* about contemporary groups.

This leads to a question that will accompany most of what follows: what did Justin know about his contemporary Jews? Scholars have long debated the significance of his apparent knowledge of some (proto-)Rabbinic traditions, whether he had gleaned them from contact with contemporary Jews or whether they are largely illusory, resulting from broader shared interpretive contexts.[7] One of the issues at stake in this debate is the role of scripture (Jewish and Christian) in mediating Justin's knowledge of Judaism. In other words, the question is whether Justin actually had contact with Jews or whether he is merely cribbing inherited scriptural accounts. As I hope will become clear, in the case of Justin's references to Jewish leadership groups, scriptural mediation and Justin's claims about contemporary Jewish communities go hand in hand: one need not cancel out the other. On this point, Paul Ricoeur's language of 'standing for' can be a helpful framing, to which I will return below. Put briefly here, the world presented

---

19-20. While den Dulk acknowledges this point (den Dulk, *Between Jews and Heretics*, 40-1), he nevertheless pushes very hard for an 'internal' Christian polemic in Justin's *Dialogue*. The presence of an internal polemic, however, does not settle the question of audience, intended or otherwise.

[5] den Dulk, *Between Jews and Heretics*, 45, has suggested Justin's philosophical school as the initial location for dissemination, though Justin's school context should not encourage scholars to draw strict boundaries, given the evidently open and protreptic quality of Justin's pedagogical work, teaching any who came to him the 'words of truth' (*Acta Iust.* 3.3); see the evidence from Justin's writings discussed in Jörg Ulrich, 'What Do We Know about Justin's "School" in Rome?', *ZAC* 16.1 (2012), 62-74. The presentation of Justin's school in the *Acta Iustini* is notably consonant with this; cf. Tobias Georges, '"... herrlichste Früchte echtester Philosophie." - Schulen bei Justin und Origenes, im frühen Christentum sowie bei den zeitgenössischen Philosophen', *Millennium* 11.1 (2014), 25-31, who also notes analogues with other philosophical teachers in the first and second centuries.

[6] This is, essentially, the conclusion of Judith Lieu, *Image and Reality: The Jews in the World of the Christians in the Second Century* (London: T&T Clark, 1996), 108, lightly updated to include the more recent arguments of Rokeah and den Dulk. Note also the comments in Benjamin L. White, 'Justin between Paul and the Heretics: The Salvation of Christian Judaizers in the *Dialogue with Trypho*', *JECS* 26.2 (2018), 182: 'The *Dialogue*, as it turns out, has multiple expressed audiences and Justin is doing a variety of things at once in it.'

[7] Some (unquantifiable but significant) contact with Judaism: Lieu, *Image and Reality*, 104 (cf. Judith Lieu, *Christian Identity in the Jewish and Graeco-Roman World* (Oxford: Oxford University Press, 2004), 43); Hirshman, *Rivalry of Genius*; Daniel Boyarin, 'Justin Martyr Invents Judaism', *Church History* 70.3 (2001), 427-61; S. J. G. Sanchez, 'Justin Martyr: un homme de son temps', *Sacris Eruditi* 41 (2002), 12-17; Boyarin, *Border Lines*, 37-73; Antti Laato, 'Justin Martyr Encounters Judaism', in *Encounters of the Children of Abraham from Ancient to Modern Times*, ed. Antti Laato and Pekka Lindqvist (Leiden: Brill, 2010), 97-123. Little to no actual contact with or knowledge of contemporary Judaism: Taylor, *Anti-Judaism and Early Christian Identity*; Tessa Rajak, *The Jewish Dialogue with Greece and Rome: Studies in Cultural and Social Interaction* (Leiden: Brill, 2001), 511-31; Rokeah, *Justin Martyr and the Jews*.

by Justin's *Dialogue* 'stands for', represents, implicitly refers to the world in which Justin lived and wrote.[8] Justin's claims about Judaism happen invariably within the world of the text, and their symbolic function within that world is precisely what grounds their referential possibility.[9]

Finally, there is the question of what kind of texts were at work in mediating Justin's account of different Jewish groups. Leaving aside the question of Justin's use of and witness to the Greek Jewish scriptures,[10] the more relevant matter here are the 'gospels', which he sometimes refers to as the 'apostolic *Memoirs*'.[11] Despite the fact that we have no clear evidence in Justin for the distinct qualities of the individual *Memoirs*, there is widespread agreement that he regularly relied on Matthean-like synoptic gospel traditions.[12] It is worth adding to this, moreover, that while Justin typically refers to 'gospels' and 'memoirs' in the plural, he can also refer to a singular gospel which Trypho has read and which provides support for some of Justin's arguments.[13] This implies that, even lacking further clarity on the text or identity of Justin's *Memoirs*, the category does appear to include multiple discrete texts which are attributed to certain apostles. With these three points in mind, then, we turn to Justin's presentation of Jewish leadership groups in his *Dialogue*. We begin with those references that most strongly depend on gospel traditions before turning to points that escape easy reduction to such early Christian traditions.

---

[8] See the discussion below, with bibliography, in n. 60.

[9] Cf. Bobichon's conclusion:

> Fiction et vérité ne sont peut être pas les catégories les mieux appropriées pour l'examen du Dialogue, et l'appréciation de sa valeur comme témoignage historique. Justin lit l'Écriture et pense la réalité selon d'autres schémas qui en gouvernent la perception et la restitution. Sa vision du monde est essentiellement théologique, et une analyse critique de ses affirmations doit prendre en compte cette priorité. Il faut adopter son regard pour mieux voir ce qu'il montre.

Philippe Bobichon, *Justin Martyr, Dialogue avec Tryphon: Édition critique, traduction, commentaire*, 2 vols, Paradosis (Fribourg: Éditions universitaires de Fribourg, 2003), 74.

[10] On this, the work of Oskar Skarsaune, *The Proof from Prophecy: A Study in Justin Martyr's Proof-Text Tradition: Text-Type, Provenance, Theological Profile*, NovT Sup (Leiden: Brill, 1987), remains unsurpassed.

[11] The equation between the two is found in *1 Apol.* 66. On the relation between such 'memoirs' and Justin's philosophical context, cf. Oskar Skarsaune, 'Justin and his Bible', in *Justin Martyr and His Worlds*, ed. Parvis and Foster, 71–2; and Katharina Greschat, '"Worte Gottes, verkündigt von den Aposteln": Evangelienzitate bei Justin', in *Gospels and Gospel Traditions in the Second Century: Experiments in Reception*, ed. Jens Schröter, Tobias Nicklas and Joseph Verheyden, BZNW (Berlin: De Gruyter, 2019), 177, 179–80, with further bibliography there.

[12] Cf. classic works like Édouard Massaux, *The Influence of the Gospel of Saint Matthew on Christian Literature before Saint Irenaeus: Book 3, the apologists and the Didache*, trans. Norman J. Belval and Suzanne Hecht, New Gospel Studies (Leuven: Peeters; Macon: Mercer, 1990); Skarsaune, *Proof from Prophecy*; and the more recent discussion in Joseph Verheyden, 'Justin's Text of the Gospels: Another Look at the Citations in 1 Apol. 15.1–8', in *The Early Text of the New Testament*, ed. Charles E. Hill and Michael J. Kruger (Oxford: Oxford University Press, 2012), 313–35. The list in Craig D. Allert, *Revelation, Truth, Canon and Interpretation: Studies in Justin Martyr's Dialogue with Trypho*, VC Sup (Leiden: Brill, 2002), 255–76, conveniently shows the dominance of Matthew in Justin's gospel citations.

[13] See *Dial.* 10 and 100 for Justin's discussion of 'the gospel'.

Describing Jewish leadership groups in Justin's *Dialogue*

Jewish groups mediated by the *Memoirs*

There are five Jewish leadership groups presented by Justin that show evidence of being mediated by Matthean gospel traditions, though none of Justin's citations match known gospel texts exactly:[14] Pharisees and scribes, (chief) priests and elders, and Sadducees. I will take these in turn.

Pharisees and scribes

The first mention of both scribes and Pharisees in the *Dialogue* demonstrates Justin's clear debt to gospel traditions.

> 'Then he even overturned the money-changers' tables in the temple', and exclaimed, 'Woe to you, Scribes and Pharisees, hypocrites! because you pay tithes on mint and rue, and never think of the love of God and justice. You are whited sepulchers, which outwardly appear beautiful, but within are full of dead men's bones.' And to the Scribes he said, 'Woe unto you, Scribes, for you have the keys, and you do not enter in yourselves, and you hinder them that are entering; you blind guides!'[15]

Justin's 'woes' here closely parallel the woes in Matthew, also found in the parallel Lukan passages. The first appears to be a conflated citation of Mt. 23.23, 27, bringing together two criticisms levelled against the scribes and Pharisees under the epithet 'hypocrites'.[16] The latter is a rather loose citation of the material in Mt. 23.13 and Lk. 11.52,[17] with the image of 'blind guides' from Mt. 23.16, 24 brought in to cap off this composite citation.[18] In context, the purpose of these citations is to establish the long-standing errors of the Jews, for whom Trypho is the literary spokesman. This is established first with reference to the prophets, whom Trypho acknowledges to be inspired, and secondarily with reference to Jesus's own actions and teaching, with which Justin claims Trypho is familiar (*Dial.* 18.1). The apparent sting of this critique is closely related to the link he draws elsewhere between Trypho's 'teachers' and the Pharisees, a point developed further below. This example, though, nicely illustrates

---

[14] So, among others, Greschat, '"Worte Gottes"', 178 n. 19, who builds on this point to criticize the tendency to attempt to identify the precise origin of Justin's citations (variant manuscripts, a gospel-harmony, inexact quotation from memory, etc.).

[15] *Dial.* 17.3–4. Greek text in Bobichon, *Dialogue avec Tryphon*. Unless otherwise noted, translations are drawn from Thomas B. Falls and Thomas P. Halton (trans.), *St. Justin Martyr: Dialogue with Trypho*, Selections from the Fathers of the Church 3 (Washington, DC: Catholic University of America Press, 2003), 29.

[16] Cf. also Lk. 11.42.

[17] Mt. 23.13 includes both 'scribes and Pharisees', rather than singling out the former, while Lk. 11.52 identifies 'lawyers' (νομικοί) as the target.

[18] On this phenomenon in Justin, see recently Philippe Bobichon, 'Composite Features and Citations in Justin Martyr's Textual Composition', in *Composite Citations in Antiquity Volume 1: Jewish, Graeco-Roman, and Early Christian Uses*, ed. Sean A. Adams and Seth M. Ehorn, LNTS (London: Bloomsbury, 2016), 158–81.

the way in which gospel traditions provide a basis for Justin's portrayal of the scribes and the Pharisees: drawing on a pastiche of citations, Justin constructs 'Jews' for his interlocutor.

Other comments in the *Dialogue* further complicate this relatively simple account. One particularly important gospel passage (or group of passages), which recurs throughout the *Dialogue*, helps Justin in his efforts to establish the prophetic power of Jesus.

> Christ came and brought to a close John's prophesying and baptising at the river Jordan, and preached the gospel in person, affirming that the kingdom of heaven is at hand, and that he had to suffer much at the hands of the scribes and Pharisees, and to be crucified and to rise again on the third day, and to appear again at Jerusalem to eat and to drink with his disciples; and if he predicted that in the meantime before his second coming there would arise ... heresies and false prophets in his name (which has been verified), how can there be question of ambiguity when the facts speak for themselves.[19]

Jesus's preaching about the Son of Man – that he would suffer, be crucified and rise again – is present in all three synoptic gospels, with little variation.[20] Justin's version of this passage, however, differs notably from the extant synoptic versions: where the synoptic accounts unanimously attribute the suffering to the hands of 'the elders, chief priests and scribes', Justin replaces the first two on the list with Pharisees.[21] Given the noted lacunae in our knowledge about Justin's gospel texts, it is hard to say with certainty whether he is altering them or simply citing versions otherwise unknown to us. Even with this caveat in mind, however, the present instance appears to be a simplification of the Jewish leadership groups in view and an inflation of the place of the Pharisees in Justin's presentation of Judaism.

This same process of inflation can be seen elsewhere in the *Dialogue*. In *Dial.* 103.1, during his extended exposition of Psalm 22 (*Dial.* 98–106), Justin offers a loose paraphrase of Jesus's arrest, as narrated in Mt. 26.3–4, 47, as evidence that Ps. 22.15–18 should be applied to Christ. As in the citations of Mt. 16.21 (and parr.) noted earlier, however, there is a disparity between Justin's version and that present in the extant versions of the gospel material. Where earlier Justin replaced 'elders and chief priests' with Pharisees, here he replaces them with 'the Pharisees and scribes'. This continued inflation of the role of the Pharisees is curious. If it is due to a change to the gospel traditions introduced by Justin himself, then one must ask what significance this

---

[19] *Dial.* 51.2; trans. lightly modified from Falls and Halton *ad loc.*; cf. also *Dial.* 76.7; 100.3.

[20] This is according to the apparatus in the NA²⁸; cf. Mt. 16.21; Mk 8.31; Lk. 9.22; alluded to in the present passage, cited in *Dial.* 76.7; 100.3.

[21] Mt. 16.21: ... δεῖ αὐτὸν ... πολλὰ παθεῖν ἀπὸ τῶν πρεσβυτέρων καὶ ἀρχιερέων καὶ γραμματέων ...; Mk 8.31 and Lk. 9.22 read: ...δεῖ τὸν υἱὸν τοῦ ἀνθρώπου πολλὰ παθεῖν καὶ ἀποδοκιμασθῆναι ὑπὸ τῶν πρεσβυτέρων καὶ τῶν ἀρχιερέων καὶ τῶν γραμματέων. Massaux, *Influence*, 87, notes the synoptic parallels in *Dial.* 76.7 and suggests that Justin is being rather loose in his citation. Bobichon notes simply, and somewhat laconically, 'Citation approximative: les Pharisiens ne sont mentionnés dans aucun des versets de référence' (Bobichon, *Dialogue avec Tryphon*, 722).

intervention holds for Justin's argument. Why do the Pharisees loom so large in Justin's representation of Jewish leadership groups?

One possible answer to this question emerges in *Dial.* 102.5. There, Justin interprets Ps. 22.10–16 by way of a brief précis of Jesus's teaching ministry. If the Psalmist writes, 'My strength is dried up like a potsherd, and my tongue is stuck fast in my throat', Jesus's ministry also demonstrates just such a desiccated speechlessness. Initially, Jesus was filled with God's power, which he used to refute the 'Pharisees and scribes', but later he remained silent before Pilate in the face of his accusers, 'as recorded in the writings of the apostles'. Justin's summary interpretation, however, not only establishes links with gospel traditions but also explicitly includes Trypho and other Jews: 'the power of his mighty word with which he always refuted the Pharisees and Scribes, and *indeed all the teachers of your race* who disputed with him' (*Dial.* 102.5). Justin's link between Trypho's Jewish teachers and the scribes and Pharisees helps to explain the inflated role of the Pharisees elsewhere in Justin's gospel citations and allusions. Insofar as Justin's criticisms of Trypho are grounded in the apostolic *Memoirs*, his argument requires a link between the Pharisees/scribes and Trypho's teachers. If Trypho's teachers could be identified as 'pharisaic', then their genealogical connection with the Pharisees encountered by Jesus establishes the long error of their intellectual tradition.[22]

Chief priests and elders

When one turns to the portrayal of chief priests in Justin's *Dialogue*, the locus of mediation shifts significantly. In the case of the 'elders', they are twice included in scriptural citations[23] but they appear more often in Justin's appeal to the legend of the seventy elders in the court of Ptolemy II Philadelphus in the third century BCE.[24] Justin's presentation of the chief priests, on the other hand, is mediated principally through the presentation of their role in scripture, which may perhaps be expected since there is no evidence that Justin had spent any time in Jerusalem nor was there a Jerusalem temple in the second century where he could witness their activities. Justin, then, refers to such elements as their enactment of the Jewish laws around offerings and Sabbath, and their priestly garments.[25] Also important for Justin is the role of Melchizedek as a priest in Ps. 109.4, thanks to his reliance on the Christological interpretation of this passage in Heb. 5.10 and 6.20.[26]

Even so, despite the dominant mediating role of the scriptures, there remains here too a mediating role for the gospels. As we have already noted, Justin appropriates several gospel passages in which the chief priests or elders are mentioned but shifts

---

[22] *Pace* Philippe Bobichon, 'Autorités religieuses juives et «sectes» juives dans l'œuvre de Justin Martyr', *Revue des Études Augustiniennes* 48 (2002), 7; the term 'scribes' here (along with Pharisees) is not simply a generic reference to teachers of the Law, nor does his later comment, that the term Φαρισαῖοι does not clearly signify 'une réalité contemporaine de Justin' (11), address the genealogical significance the scribes and Pharisees play within Justin's construal of Trypho's Judaism; see further below.
[23] See *Dial.* 131.1/Deut. 32.7–9; *Dial.* 133.2–3/Isa. 3.9–15.
[24] *Dial.* 68.7; 71.1–2; 84.3; cf. the discussion in Bobichon, 'Autorités religieuses', 10.
[25] *Dial.* 27.5; 29.3; 37.4.
[26] *Dial.* 33.1–2; cf. 86.3; 116.2; cf. Bobichon, 'Autorités religieuses', 5.

the emphasis onto the Pharisees and scribes. Elsewhere in the *Dialogue*, however, he maintains a role for the 'elders and chief priests' in handing Jesus over to be crucified, though Justin simply identifies the latter as 'priests' (*Dial.* 40.4; Mt. 26.47). Perhaps more notably, in *Dial.* 78.1 Justin recounts Herod's interrogation of his advisors concerning the Magi's message, replacing the 'chief priests and scribes of the people' from Mt. 2.4 with a simplified 'the elders of the people'.[27] The significance of this shift is difficult to assess, though it may mean that the term 'elder', in Justin's work, refers to a general category of Jewish leadership involving a variety of different roles within it (rather than a specific reference to a formal institution such as the *gerousia*).

These two Jewish leadership groups, then, the chief priests and elders, are important to Justin for different reasons. The former supports various arguments, from highlighting the tensions in the Law to supplying a Christologically significant category. The latter group helps to establish the role of Jewish leaders in Jesus's death and the recalcitrance of Trypho in his scepticism regarding the LXX. Both groups are mediated principally through the scriptures and related interpretive traditions, but both also appear to be partially shaped in presentation by their roles in the *Memoirs*.

Sadducees

The final group to assess under the rubric of mediation via gospel traditions are the Sadducees, whom Justin mentions only a single time across his extant works, in the somewhat perplexing list of Jewish *haireseis* in *Dial.* 80.4. Even on such a sparse showing, however, there is still an evident link with gospel traditions. Quite apart from their designation as a *haireseis*, a term with clear negative connotations for Justin,[28] his mention of the Sadducees in *Dial.* 80.4 is notable for its pride of place in the list of Jewish groups who do not (in his view) have a proper claim to the title 'Jew'. In the immediate context, after affirming his genuine belief in the eschatological restoration of Jerusalem, Justin tells Trypho that any self-proclaimed Christian who does not believe in the resurrection does not deserve the name: 'Do not consider them to be Christians; just as one, after careful examination, would not acknowledge the Sadducees as Jews.'[29] It is important to note that, despite the fact that the Sadducees appear with some regularity in Matthew, the gospel tradition closest to Justin's own, they are only singled out for comment in one vignette: their debate with Jesus over the resurrection. There the reader is informed by the gospel

---

[27] Note also Justin's appeal to a functioning high-priestly office under Herod (*Dial.* 52.3), which may be linked with Justin's evident knowledge of this tradition from Matthew.

[28] The work of Alain Le Boulluec, *La notion d'hérésie dans la littérature grecque, IIe-IIIe siècles*, 2 vols (Paris: Etudes augustiniennes, 1985), remains of fundamental importance on this, though some have pushed back on his designation of Justin as marking the beginning of the concept of 'heresy' in Christianity. On the role of his *Syntagma* in the conversion of philosophical doxography into a heresiological tool, see esp. Le Boulluec, *La notion*, 1.41–51, followed recently by Matthijs den Dulk, 'Justin Martyr and the Authorship of the Earliest Anti-Heretical Treatise', *VC* 72.4 (2018), 483, who is arguing against Geoffrey S. Smith, *Guilt by Association: Heresy Catalogues in Early Christianity* (Oxford: Oxford University Press, 2014).

[29] *Dial.* 80.4; trans. modified from Falls and Halton *ad loc.*

writers that the Sadducees deny the resurrection (Mt. 22.23/Mk 12.18/Lk. 20.27).[30] In Justin's view, on the contrary, 'real' Jews believe in the resurrection and so it is fitting that the group marked out in the gospel materials specifically for their denial of this belief becomes the first example of Jewish sects which are theologically beyond the pale.[31]

This passage, however, continues with Justin's famous list of *haireseis* which, already in the discussion of the Sadducees, operates on certain assumptions about what kind of beliefs someone like Trypho would admit to be true. These points move the discussion towards the next stage of the argument, following up the subtle indications that Justin is not merely constructing his Jewish leadership groups from scratch out of information gleaned from the *Memoirs*.

Jewish groups beyond the *Memoirs*

Despite the fairly obvious role the gospel material plays in Justin's construal of various Jewish leadership groups, there are aspects of his portrayal that escape easy explanation in terms of previous Christian traditions. These raise questions about the way in which Justin's construction of Jewish groups 'stands for' a contemporary reality, though they are questions difficult to answer on all accounts. We will revisit this problem in the conclusion.

As noted above, Justin appears to inflate the role of the Pharisees in his appeals to gospel material. Given the uncertainty that surrounds the state of Justin's gospel texts – and his use or otherwise of a gospel harmony – confident conclusions about the significance of this inflation are hard to come by.[32] In a recent discussion of Justin's composite citations, though, Philippe Bobichon argues that their arrangement and subtle textual details/alterations *are* important to the outworking of the apologist's arguments in both his first *Apology* and the *Dialogue*. He concludes,

> I could not find one single composite citation whose composition is not fully justified by its place and function ... In many cases, Justin's scriptural citations are composite only in terms of their deviances from the textual traditions of the Old and New Testaments. Some of these deviances can be attributed to the apologist himself and, upon analysis, one is forced to admit that they amount to a form of textual 'hijacking', particularly in the *Apology*.[33]

---

[30] Sadducees' denial of resurrection is also famously attested in Acts 23.6 and by Josephus, *War* 2.164–5.
[31] Cf. the comments in Le Boulluec, *La notion*, 1.71–2; and den Dulk, *Between Jews and Heretics*, 130 n. 88, among others.
[32] For a recent defence of Justin's access to an existing gospel harmony, see esp. Nicholas Perrin, 'What Justin's Gospel Can Tell Us about Tatian's: Tracing the Trajectory of the Gospel Harmony in the Second Century and Beyond', in *The Gospel of Tatian: Exploring the Nature and Text of the Diatessaron*, ed. Matthew R. Crawford and Nicholas J. Zola, The Reception of Jesus in the First Three Centuries (London: Bloomsbury, 2019), 93–109. Despite the careful arguments of Perrin et al., Katharina Greschat's observation about the limits of the evidence remains appropriate; see n. 14.
[33] Bobichon, 'Composite Features', 181.

If this holds true, it carries implications for Justin's portrayal of the Pharisees and scribes.[34] As we saw above, this group is subtly linked in *Dial.* 102.5 with Trypho's Jewish teachers, establishing a sort of theological genealogy by which Justin is able to implicate his Jewish interlocutor in the critiques of the Pharisees and scribes offered by Jesus in the *Memoirs*.

The inflated critique of Pharisees and the subtle link established with Trypho and his group is given more explicit formulation towards the end of the *Dialogue*. In his final appeal to his interlocutors to put off their 'hardness of heart' and accept that Jesus is the beloved son of God, Justin urges Trypho and his companions, 'Do not revile the Son of God nor, trusting your Pharisaic teachers, scorn the king of Israel (as your synagogue leaders teach you to do after prayer).'[35] This short statement contains many interesting elements, only a few of which are directly relevant here.[36] The first is that where previously the link between Trypho's teachers and the Pharisees was somewhat attenuated, here it is direct: the teachers whom Justin has been critiquing throughout the *Dialogue* are identified as Φαρισαῖοι διδάσκαλοι. Moreover, the contemporary institutional locus of these 'Pharisaic teachers' is found in the synagogue; these teachers are, specifically, ἀρχισυνάγωγοι. If we can bracket, momentarily, our scholarly reservations about a clear relationship between the Rabbinic tradition and Pharisaism,[37] we may be able to appreciate the force of this connection within Justin's argument. Given the multifaceted quality of 'Judaism' in the second century – a quality about which Justin himself is manifestly aware – and the historical, geographical and (potential) theological distance between Trypho and first-century Jewish groups portrayed in the gospel traditions, it is important for Justin to establish a clear line of Jewish tradition running from the *Memoirs* to Trypho.[38] Further, his identification of the institutional

---

[34] Bobichon, 'Composite Features', 181. Bobichon's conclusion carries implications further for the reliability of the exceedingly sparse manuscript tradition for Justin's works.

> This feature represents an additional piece of evidence in favor of the accuracy of Justin's thought and method and of that of the scribes. This goes against an entire established tradition. The text preserved in the manuscript is indeed, almost invariably, infinitely more satisfying than the conjectures and corrections that have been put forth since the sixteenth century, in most of the editions.

[35] *Dial.* 137.2, my translation.

[36] I leave aside, for instance, the matter of the *Birkat ha-minim* to which Justin apparently alludes here. If scholars once took Justin's witness to this phenomenon for granted, such is no longer the case; see Taylor, *Anti-Judaism and Early Christian Identity*; Judith Lieu, 'Accusations of Jewish Persecution in Early Christian Sources, with Particular Reference to Justin Martyr and the *Martyrdom of Polycarp*', in *Tolerance and Intolerance in Early Judaism and Christianity*, ed. Graham N. Stanton and Guy G. Stroumsa (Cambridge: Cambridge University Press, 1998), 279–95; Rokeah, *Justin Martyr and the Jews*, 16–17; Boyarin, *Border Lines*, 67–8.

[37] See the incisive and critical discussion in Boyarin, *Border Lines*, 41–3, who is following the work of Shaye Cohen; cf. Shaye J. D. Cohen, 'Yavneh Revisited: Pharisees, Rabbis and the End of Jewish Sectarianism', in *Society of Biblical Literature 1982 Seminar Papers*, ed. Keith Harold Richards, SBL Seminar Papers (Chico, CA: Scholars Press, 1983), 45–61; Shaye J. D. Cohen, 'Were Pharisees and Rabbis the Leaders of Communal Prayer and Torah Study in Antiquity? The Evidence of the New Testament, Josephus, and the Early Church Fathers', in *Evolution of the Synagogue: Problems and Progress*, ed. Howard Clark Kee and Lynn H. Cohick (Harrisburg: Trinity Press International, 1999), 89–105.

[38] Bobichon, 'Autorités religieuses', 6, notes that the formulation Φαρισαῖοι διδάσκαλοι is likely Justin's own rather than being culled from the New Testament and that there is an equivalence being drawn between the 'teachers' and the *archisynagogoi*.

setting for Trypho's teachers provides a location where his readers – Jewish, Christian or otherwise – could find or encounter such teachers, if they so desired. This passage, then, constitutes a direct claim about contemporary Jewish leaders, Pharisaic teachers in the synagogues, framed in terms of a category drawn from the gospels, which holds an important symbolic place in Justin's argument.

Justin offers a rhetorically similar link between Trypho's teachers and the 'chief priests' earlier in the *Dialogue*. Beginning in *Dial.* 115, Justin turns to a passage from Zechariah (3.1–7) to support his argument that Jesus's role as high priest was already foretold in scripture by the Holy Spirit. The sacrifice offered by Christians in the name of Jesus is, of course, the Eucharist with its attendant prayers and commemoration. In this context, Justin returns to the theme of blasphemy, which he introduced in *Dial.* 17,[39] claiming that the name of Jesus is 'profaned and blasphemed' because of the actions of 'the chief priests and teachers of your people' (*Dial.* 117.3). On one hand, this appears to be a general charge, bringing together the priests and teachers as a vague reference to Jewish leaders, without claims about any contemporary or historical reality.[40] Furthermore, the plural ἀρχιερεῖς is curious since there was usually only one chief priest at a time and so it is tempting to see the influence of gospel traditions here.[41] On the other hand, Justin's claim, in context, places the point of contention in the present: Trypho's intransigence towards Justin's argument 'even now' (μέχρι νῦν; 117.2) is an instance of this continuing opposition between Jewish leadership groups and Jesus. The current 'teachers of the people' stand in continuity with the high priests, whether taken in succession or treated in general terms.[42] Unlike Justin's discussion of Pharisees, however, there is no direct claim that Trypho's teachers are priestly in any meaningful sense, only that they function as related examples of leadership groups.

To close this section, let us return to the famously vexing 'heresy catalogue' in *Dial.* 80.4. For present purposes, there are three issues to address: the symbolic function of the Sadducees, the problem of the Pharisee-baptists and the wider function of the 'heresy catalogue' in Justin's portrayal of Judaism.[43] The passage runs as follows.

> If you have ever encountered any so-called Christians who do not confess this doctrine [*viz.* of the physical resurrection] … do not consider them to be Christians; just as one, after careful examination, would not acknowledge as Jews the Sadducees or the similar sects of the Genistae, Meristae, Galileans, Hellenians and the Pharisee-Baptists (please take no offence if I say everything that I think),

---

[39] Cf. *Dial.* 17, citing Isa. 52.5; the Greek version of this verse was influentially put to similar use by Paul in Rom. 2.24.
[40] Such is the impression given by Bobichon, 'Autorités religieuses', 5.
[41] The plural ἀρχιερεῖς occurs eighteen times in Matthew, fourteen times in Mark, twelve times in Luke and ten times in John.
[42] Cf. the use of the plural ἀρχιερεῖς as a collective reference to the succession of high priests or as a general reference to the group; Josephus, *Ant.* 13.78 (τῶν διαδοχῶν τῶν ἀρχιερέων); *Ant.* 8.93.
[43] See the important recent discussion of this in den Dulk, *Between Jews and Heretics*, who offers a critique of the arguments offered in Smith, *Guilt by Association*; and Boyarin, *Border Lines*. Still helpful is the summary discussion in Bobichon, 'Autorités religieuses'; and the now classic work of Le Boulluec, *La notion*, 1.70–7.

but would realise that they are Jews and children of Abraham in name only, paying lip service to God, while their heart, as God himself declared, is far from him.[44]

(1) The standard view that Sadducees as a group ceased to have any real existence after the destruction of the temple in 70 CE has been taken to indicate that their inclusion in a list of Jewish sects in the mid-second century is patently false.[45] This is not as clear as one might suppose, though. In the first place, as Martin Goodman has argued cogently, there is no evidence apart from a certain (proto-)Rabbinic silence that the Sadducees disappeared with the temple.[46] However one decides on the plausibility that Justin could be aware of a Sadducean group continuing in his period, though, the literary context for the catalogue gives Justin's claim an ostensibly contemporary reference. At the very least, the figure of Trypho is constructed as a Jew to whom the Sadducees are a familiar entity.

(2) The final 'heresy' in Justin's list appears as ΦαρισαίωνΒαπτιστῶν, attended by a subscript ligature in manuscript A.[47] This has caused numerous difficulties for editors and interpreters through the years, being rendered as Φαρισαίων Βαπτιστῶν (Stephanus), Φαρισαίων, Βαπτιστῶν (Migne) and Φαρισαίων καὶ Βαπτιστῶν (Lange, Grotius, Otto, Goodspeed, Marcovich).[48] In favour of reading them as separate groups is the view that the catalogue is rendered complete with seven, rather than six, heresies.[49] Boyarin, further, argues that this list originated as a catalogue of Jewish heresies that reflects the fact that Rabbinic authorities never named Pharisees *as such* as their predecessors in Orthodox Judaism.[50] As den Dulk has recently noted, however, Boyarin's view is somewhat hard-pressed to account for the fact that Justin presents his interlocutor as a direct heir to the Pharisaic tradition on multiple occasions, as we have seen.[51] In what way, then, is Trypho supposed to accept that Pharisees were not properly entitled to the name 'Jew'?[52]

---

[44] *Dial.* 80.4, trans. lightly modified from Falls and Halton *ad loc.*
[45] Cf. Matthew Black, 'The Patristic Accounts of Jewish Sectarianism', *BJRL* 41 (1959), 290; Lieu, *Image and Reality*, 144; Günter Stemberger, 'The Sadducees – Their History and Doctrines', in *The Cambridge History of Judaism*, ed. William Horbury, W. D. Davies and John Sturdy (Cambridge: Cambridge University Press, 1999), 428–43.
[46] Martin Goodman, *Judaism in the Roman World: Collected Essays* (Leiden: Brill, 2007), 160; cf. Gary G. Porton, 'Diversity in Postbiblical Judaism', in *Early Judaism and Its Modern Interpreters*, ed. Robert A. Kraft and George W. E. Nickelsburg (Atlanta, GA: Scholars Press, 1986), 66–8.
[47] See Bobichon, *Dialogue avec Tryphon*, 406 n. 5; note that manuscript A (*Parisinus graecus* 450) is the only independent manuscript of the *Dialogue* extant today (167–8, 172).
[48] These are noted in Bobichon's apparatus *ad loc.*
[49] den Dulk, *Between Jews and Heretics*, 113, suggests that Justin adds Pharisees to a list of his own making, *despite* the fact that it is in tension with his presentation of them elsewhere, because it was so important for him to arrive at a seven-group list.
[50] See n. 37.
[51] den Dulk, *Between Jews and Heretics*, 111; cf. the earlier statement of this point already by Adolf Harnack, *Ist die Rede des Paulus in Athens ein ursprünglicher Bestandteil der Apostelgeschichte? Judentum und Judenchristentum in Justins Dialogue mit Trypho, nebst einer Collation der Pariser Handschrift Nr. 450*, TU (Leipzig: Hinrichs, 1913), 57.
[52] The comments of Black, 'Patristic Accounts', 288, are still relevant, insofar as one needs to consider Justin's argument against the broadest possible readership in the second century, a matter of rhetorical effectiveness which is matched by the internal logic of Justin's argument.

Bobichon's text for this passage – rendering it simply as ΦαρισαίωνΒαπτιστῶν in line with the manuscript evidence, such as it is – offers a better solution, one which does not need to suppose Justin either incorporated a pre-circulated Jewish heresy catalogue or added Pharisees to a list of his own without recognizing the tensions it introduced into an important line of argument running throughout the *Dialogue*. There is no reason to suppose that Justin needed or desired a seven-sect list;[53] its completeness or otherwise is not a feature of his argument either explicitly or implicitly. His argument moves forward on the basis of an analogy (ὥσπερ) rather than on the basis of having provided such a symbolically complete list of Jewish heresies. In the absence of compelling external or internal evidence, there is little reason to emend the text of the manuscript in its linking of Φαρισαίων and Βαπτιστῶν directly, that is, without the καί that separates the other elements in the catalogue.[54]

The question then arises: who are these Pharisee-baptists? Do they correspond roughly with the Pharisees or *hemerobaptists* in Heggesippus's list?[55] Does the term designate a particularly stringent group of 'Pharisaic' ascetics?[56] In the absence of any clarifying remark from Justin, this must remain an intractable issue, subject to speculation but not much more.

(3) Reading with the manuscript witness, then, presents a list of six Jewish 'heresies' that bear only the slightest resemblance to anything in the gospel traditions or elsewhere in the emerging Christian scriptures: Sadducees, Genistae, Meristae, Galileans, Hellenians and Pharisee-Baptists.[57] Whether and how one might be able to correlate these names with Jewish groups known from other sources remains difficult.[58] Indeed, den Dulk makes the compelling point that Justin's list is prescriptive rather than descriptive on its own terms.[59] Even so, in the dramatic context, Justin's literary avatar presumes that a plurality (*this* plurality?) of Jewish sects would be familiar to Trypho *and* that distinguishing between true and false 'Jews' is a possibility he could recognize. In other words, it portrays heresiological discourse as already at work among Jewish communities in the mid-second century. Justin's construal of Jewish

---

[53] Lieu, *Image and Reality*, 145, notes that despite some attraction of finding a 'formulaic' list of seven, 'it might be better to take the last two terms together'.

[54] Cf. the comments in Smith, *Guilt by Association*, 96 n. 28. It is worth noting that the structure of this sect name mirrors the adjectival use of Φαρισαῖοι in *Dial* 137.2.

[55] Heggesippus *apud* Eusebius *Hist. eccl.* 4.22.7. Correlating these two lists is more difficult than den Dulk, *Between Jews and Heretics*, 133, admits. The similarity noted in Smith, *Guilt by Association*, 108, is not entirely compelling: 'Justin's catalogue of Jewish heresies resembles Hegesippus's in that it is a list of Jewish heresies assembled (or possibly appropriated) by a follower of Jesus.' Given the better reading of Justin's list in Bobichon's text, there are only two points of clear overlap between the two (Sadducees and Galileans). Whether the ΦαρισαίωνΒαπτιστῶν should be linked with Ἡμεροβαπτισταί or Φαρισαῖοι is impossible to say, given the lack of exposition by either author.

[56] This view is canvassed in Bobichon, 'Autorités religieuses', 19; cf. the earlier arguments in favour of this in Black, 'Patristic Accounts', 289.

[57] *Pace* den Dulk, *Between Jews and Heretics*, 145–53, the list as we have it correlates poorly with Jewish groups culled from the book of Acts. Of the six mentioned by Justin, only the Sadducees are directly mentioned.

[58] On efforts at correlation, see e.g. Black, 'Patristic Accounts'; Le Boulluec, *La notion*, 1.76; Boyarin, *Border Lines*, 58–63; Bobichon, 'Autorités religieuses'; den Dulk, *Between Jews and Heretics*, 110.

[59] den Dulk, *Between Jews and Heretics*, 143, cf. 112; Trypho, Justin admits, would need to 'consider the matter carefully' rather than operating already with such heresiological categories.

groups, as an analogy for divergent Christian groups, claims a common 'heresiological' reasoning for both.

Conclusion: Towards explaining Jewish leadership groups in Justin's *Dialogue*

From the above discussion a twofold pattern has emerged. On one hand, Justin's accounts of the Pharisees, scribes, chief priests and Sadducees are shaped by the gospel traditions available to him – that is, they are mediated by the *Memoirs*. On the other hand, in both subtle and explicit ways, Justin's reception of these Jewish groups functions as a claim about contemporary Jewish identity and discourse relative to his own Christian views. The Pharisees in particular, for Justin, play an inflated role in his gospel traditions, by which he emphasizes their role as Jewish teachers, thereby strengthening the link between Trypho, his teachers and the critiques of the Pharisees by Jesus. As noted in the introduction, I will close here with a reflection on theoretical resources to help clarify what is at stake in this analysis and framing.

The literary world of Justin's work, in which the Christian philosopher and his Jewish interlocutor inhabit substantially overlapping discursive spaces and can debate for days over detailed exegetical points, offers itself to readers (past and present) as an ostensible representation of possible events in the world. Without taking the dialogue as a historical account or being able to identify Trypho as a historical figure, there remain the gestures towards contemporary Jewish groups – in Justin's presumption that heresiological discourse would be intelligible; in the claim that the opposition to Christianity which began with Jesus happens still now in the synagogues; and so on. This literary world, then, in Ricoeur's terms, 'stands for' a conversation between Justin and an educated Jewish interlocutor (and his companions).[60] The precise relation of the Jewish leadership groups, of Trypho and his companions, and of Trypho's teachers, to historical persons who lived in the second century will always remain obscure. But, as I noted above, rather than eliminating the possibility of external reference, the symbolic and rhetorical function of these Jewish groups within Justin's work in fact underwrites the very possibility for them to represent the world in which dialogues between Jews and Christians could and did take place.[61] Put differently,

---

[60] This is closely related to Ricoeur's mimetic account of writing and reading. The relationship between the two 'worlds' is worked out with relation to historiography and fiction in particular detail in Paul Ricoeur, *Time and Narrative*, trans. Kathleen McLaughlin and David Pellauer, 3 vols (Chicago: University of Chicago Press, 1984), vol. 3, chapter 7; cf. also the later development of this discussion in Paul Ricoeur, *Memory, History, Forgetting* (Chicago: University of Chicago Press, 2004), 274–80. There is an important distinction between the modern historiographical genre of writing and the ancient genre of philosophical dialogue, particularly around what Ricoeur refers to as the implicit 'contract' with the reader of historical writing (Ricoeur, *Memory*, 275). This is less relevant with regard to fiction, however. I am rearranging Ricoeur's terminology somewhat by applying his historical 'standing for' to a non-historical mode of writing.

[61] This is one of the principal difficulties with Taylor's appeal to the 'symbolic' function of Jews in Justin and other early Christian authors (Taylor, *Anti-Judaism and Early Christian Identity*). Being 'symbolic' does not close down referential possibilities (they only function within Christian theological structures *rather than* reflecting Jews in the world) but enables them. Among others,

considering Jewish leadership groups in relation to an external reality of Jewish groups contemporary with Justin does not obviate their significance as symbols within Justin's construal of Christian identity, symbols that must be interpreted and whose meaning is enmeshed in a network of other symbols.[62] Perhaps one of the reasons for the evidently intractable disagreement over the historicity of Trypho is that, quite apart from limitations of evidence, the underlying problem is primarily philosophical. After all, what would a historical Trypho get us, if we knew that he in fact existed? Scholars would still be faced with his symbolic function and with the problems that attend every discussion of text and world, or sense and reference. The Jewish leadership groups in the *Dialogue*, then, function both as received symbols in a project oriented towards shaping Christian identity *and* as a claim about religious and social identities of, and interactions between, Jews and Christians.

Finally, I have spoken above about the gospels *doing* things for Justin – enabling, shaping, constraining and so on – but is this legitimate? Is not Justin doing all the work himself? What agency can be ascribed to inanimate objects like the gospels? For questions such as this, a second set of tools needs to be introduced, this time from sociology. In his development of what is infelicitously called 'actor-network theory', Bruno Latour has attempted to conceptualize the impact that non-human objects can have on any given action.[63] For Latour, these non-human objects 'are actors, or more precisely, *participants* in the course of action waiting to be given a figuration'.[64] Even the term 'object', for Latour, does not denote a pure passivity but, on the contrary, highlights a thing's ability 'to object to what is said' about it.[65] To call objects such as the apostolic *Memoirs* 'actors' does not simply reverse the order of interpretive causality; the gospel traditions did not simply 'cause' Justin to say anything. 'Rather it means that there might exist many metaphysical shades between full causality and sheer inexistence … things might authorize, allow, afford, encourage, permit, suggest, influence, block, render possible, forbid and so on.'[66] Agents in a given course of action must accommodate themselves to the other participants. From this perspective, the

---

Hirshman, *Rivalry of Genius* makes a strong case that both Rabbinic and early Christian texts bear witness to these dialogues. The Jewish source cited by Celsus (Origen, *Cels.* 1–2) may similarly represent Jewish/Christian interaction in the mid-second century, though perhaps on less collegial terms than those scripted by Justin Martyr.

[62] Ricoeur, again, offers help: reading, as the final movement of a threefold mimetic process, 'cannot take up the problem of communication without taking up that of reference, inasmuch as what is communicated is, in the final analysis, beyond the sense of the work, the world the world projects, the world that constitutes the horizon of the work'; Ricoeur, *Time and Narrative*, 3.178.

[63] See his systematic account of the theory and practice associated with ANT in Bruno Latour, *Reassembling the Social: An Introduction to Actor-Network-Theory*, Clarendon Lectures in Management Studies (Oxford: Oxford University Press, 2005), where he also notes his own dissatisfaction with name 'actor network theory'. I am indebted to the work of Rita Felski for repurposing the work of Latour for literary studies; cf. Rita Felski, *The Limits of Critique* (Chicago: University of Chicago Press, 2015).

[64] Latour, *Reassembling*, 71.

[65] Latour, *Reassembling*, 125 – 'and there are those [sociologists] that try to be objective because they track objects which are given a chance to *object* to what is said about them.' Note also his earlier comments on the constraining factors that attend different objects (under his preferred terminology, 'matters of concern') on p. 114.

[66] Latour, *Reassembling*, 72.

Memoirs affect Justin; they participate in the activity of receiving and representing these Jewish leadership groups. Furthermore, other human actors in the network of second-century relations, including his contemporary Jews, *also* participate in this reception and representation activity. As it turns out, this latter group – contemporary Jews – is the more difficult one to see clearly, even though his claims about them and their religious heritage consistently attend his efforts to appropriate gospel materials and Jewish symbols within his apologetic vision.

Part 3

The reception of Jewish practices

9

Denial of forgiveness and the Spirit: 'Anxiety of influence' and the Christian demotion of John's baptism

Joel Marcus

The Baptist's denial of the Spirit

'I have baptized you with water, but he will baptize you in the Holy Spirit.'[1] So says John the Baptist in our earliest Gospel (Mk 1.8). The Q form of this saying (Mt. 3.11// Lk. 3.16) mixes fire with Spirit on the right-hand side of the equation but leaves the same basic impression: John viewed his water baptism as a limited rite, which explicitly did *not* impart the Spirit. That would be the job of the 'Stronger One', the 'Coming One' – presumably the Messiah, who, according to the continuation in Q, will purge the threshing floor of the world, gather the 'grain' into the barn and burn the 'chaff' with fire.[2] The Fourth Evangelist gives his own version of the contrast between John's water baptism and the Coming One's Spirit baptism when he has John recount a private screening of coming attractions: 'The one who sent me to baptize in water said to me, "The one upon whom you see the Spirit descending and remaining, he is the one baptizing in the Holy Spirit"' (Jn 1.33). For the Fourth, as for the first three Evangelists, this messianic baptizer-in-the-Spirit is, of course, Jesus.

It is doubtful that John himself would have sanctioned this identification. Though it serves a key agenda of the Evangelists, it is achieved in the Synoptics only through the editorial juxtaposition between John's prophecy and the immediately subsequent account of his baptism of Jesus, which itself contains legendary elements that grew over

---

[1] Unless otherwise noted, biblical translations are my own, though I have often consulted the RSV.
[2] This is very similar to the description of the judgement to be executed by the Son of David, the 'Anointed One of the Lord' (χριστὸς κυρίου), in Pss. Sol. 17.21–46: he will gather a holy people, purge (καθαριεῖ) the Holy Land of sinners and destroy the latter. He will, moreover, be 'powerful in the Holy Spirit' (δυνατὸν ἐν πνεύματι ἁγίῳ 17.37; cf. further references to his 'strength' [ἰσχύς] later in 17.37 and ἰσχυρός in 17.22, 36, 38, 40). On the 'Coming One' = 'Stronger One' in Mk 1.7–8//Mt. 3.11//Lk. 3.16 as the Messiah, see further Joel Marcus, *Mark: A New Translation with Introduction and Commentary*, AYB 27/27A (New Haven, CT: Yale University Press, 2000–9), 1.151–2.

time.³ Nothing in the Q passage itself points towards Jesus; it reflects, rather, a standard Jewish expectation about the role of the Davidic Messiah.⁴ And the notion that John identified Jesus as this Messiah near the beginning of Jesus's career is challenged by a later Q passage, Mt. 11.2-6//Lk. 7.18-23. Here John, in prison at the end of his life,⁵ seems to be considering for the first time the possibility that Jesus might be the Messiah. He dispatches messengers to investigate the possibility, and Jesus responds by relating classic eschatological texts from Isaiah to his own ministry. Significantly, however, the passage concludes without John being convinced.

Thus Christian theology – namely the core conviction of Jesus's messiahship – has mixed with historical memory in shaping the Gospels' account of John's relationship to Jesus. But how far does this influence reach? Specifically, I want to ask, was John himself responsible for the contrast between his water baptism and the Coming One's Spirit baptism, or does this contrast, like the identification of Jesus with the 'Coming One' prophesied by John, reflect the influence of the early church?

Since the contrast is found only in Christian documents (the Gospels and Acts), and since we lack contemporary or near-contemporary accounts of John's ministry from inside his movement,⁶ it is worth noting that the contrast fits into a tendency for early Christian authors to exalt the Christian community's unique possession of the Spirit and link it with Christian baptism. In Romans alone, for example, Paul connects endowment with the Spirit with the life Christ brings (Rom. 8.10-11), with the liberation from the Law he effects (Rom. 8.2-4) and with the piety and good works he inspires (Rom. 5.5; 7.6). In the same letter, Paul explicitly equates God's Spirit with Christ's (8.9-11) and distinguishes Christians as those who have 'the first fruits of the Spirit' (Rom. 8.23) and possess the kingdom of God through their 'righteousness, peace, and joy in the Holy Spirit' (Rom. 14.17).

As for the connection between the Spirit and Christian baptism in particular, Ernst Käsemann points out that several Pauline passages (1 Cor. 6.11; 12.13; 2 Cor. 1.22) 'explicitly characterize the πνεῦμα as the baptismal gift,'⁷ and a couple of others may imply the same connection.⁸ A Deutero-Pauline text, Tit. 3.5, continues this trajectory

---

³ In Mk 1.10-11, the opening of the heavens, the descent of the Spirit and the voice from heaven are observed only by Jesus. In Mt. 3.16-17, and probably in Lk. 3.21-2, they are public events observed by all.
⁴ In addition to Pss. Sol. 17, see e.g. Isa. 11.1-5; 1 En. 45.3, 6; 48.10; 55.3-4; 62.3-5; 4Q285; 4 Ezra 11.37-12.3; 13.8-11; Sib. Or. 3.651-64.
⁵ This is said explicitly in Matthew, not in Luke, but, in Luke, John has been in prison since 3.20, and the next time he is mentioned in that Gospel, he is dead, and Herod is speculating that Jesus may be him returned from the dead (Lk. 9.7-9). The prison setting provides a plausible historical context for the question; if John had been at liberty when he began to consider the possibility that Jesus might be the Messiah, he could have tried to reunite with him in order to check the hunch out personally.
⁶ On Josephus's account of John, see below, 171-3.
⁷ Ernst Käsemann, 'The Pauline Doctrine of the Lord's Supper', in *Essays on New Testament Themes* (Philadelphia, PA: Fortress, 1964), 113; cf. Volker Rabens, *The Holy Spirit and Ethics in Paul: Transformation and Empowering for Religious-Ethical Life*, Wissenschaftliche Untersuchungen zum Neuen Testament. 2. Reihe 283 (Tübingen: Mohr Siebeck, 2010), 6.
⁸ In Rom. 6.3-4, dying and rising with Christ in baptism is linked with walking 'in newness of life' (cf. 'newness of the Spirit' in Rom. 7.6). Peter Stuhlmacher also sees Rom. 8.10-11 as a reference to baptism (see Rabens, *Holy Spirit*, 11).

by speaking of 'the washing of regeneration and renewal in the Holy Spirit'.[9] Nor are these connections restricted to the Pauline orbit. In Jn 7.38-9, for example, the Evangelist links Jesus's prophecy about the rivers of water flowing from his belly, which is very likely a baptismal allusion,[10] with the Spirit that those who believed in him would receive after his 'glorification', that is, his death and resurrection, 'for as yet the Spirit had not been given, because Jesus was not yet glorified'.[11] Throughout the New Testament, then, the Spirit is a gift that is especially connected with Christian baptism and that is bestowed by God in the Christ-event – and not before.

The Spiritless Baptists of Ephesus

Of all New Testament passages, the one that emphasizes most sharply the distinctiveness of Christian possession of the Spirit, to the exclusion of any other group – including the Baptist and his followers – is Acts 19.1-7. Here Paul encounters Ephesian adherents of the Baptist who are unacquainted either with the Spirit or with Jesus,' but who receive the Spirit when Paul baptizes them 'in the name of the Lord Jesus.' In the sermon that precedes this act of baptism, Paul emphasizes that *John's* baptism was only one of repentance, but that John himself pointed forward 'to the one coming after him – that is, to Jesus' (v. 4). The Ephesians' reception of the Spirit confirms this point and, in the context of Luke's two-volume work, fulfils John's prophecy about the 'Coming One' who will baptize in the Spirit.[12]

This important story probably rests on a historical memory, since it goes against the grain of the early Christian tendency to portray the Baptist movement quickly and naturally evaporating into early Christianity.[13] But other aspects of the narrative, including those connected with what we may call the 'denial of Spirit' motif,[14] strain

---

[9] See also the link between the Spirit and the 'sealing' terminology in Eph. 1.13; 'one Spirit, …one faith, one baptism' in Eph. 4.4-5; and the reclothing imagery in Eph. 4.22-4, which is linked with renewal 'in the spirit of your minds'. See also 2 Thess. 2.13; Heb. 6.1-6; 1 Jn 5.6-8.

[10] See Raymond E. Brown, *The Gospel according to John*, AB 29 & 29A (Garden City, NY: Doubleday, 1966-70), 1.329, pointing to the close connection between 7.38-9 and 19.34, which has strong baptismal significance; the background of the reference to 'scripture' in 7.38 in the wandering rock tradition of Exodus, which is interpreted baptismally in 1 Cor. 10.4; and the use of Jn 7.38-9 in the early baptismal art of the catacombs. As Martinus C. de Boer, *Johannine Perspectives on the Death of Jesus*, Contributions to Biblical Exegesis and Theology 17 (Kampen: Kok Pharos, 1996), 297, points out, moreover, 'water/Spirit symbolism is closely associated with baptism in the early chapters of John (cf. 1.33; 3.5, 22-6)', and 'baptismal themes and imagery underline the Johannine symbolism of "living water" (4.4-15)'.

[11] See also Acts 2.38: 'Repent, and be baptized every one of you in the name of Jesus Christ for the forgiveness of your sins; and you shall receive the gift of the Holy Spirit' (RSV).

[12] See already Martin Dibelius, *Die urchristliche Überlieferung von Johannes der Täufer*, FRLANT 15 (Göttingen: Vandenhoeck & Ruprecht, 1911), 43, on the way in which the Holy Spirit in this story becomes 'a shibboleth in the controversy of the Christians with the disciples of the Baptist'.

[13] See e.g. the transfer of allegiance by the Baptist's disciples in the paradigmatic tale in Jn 1.35-42.

[14] See Otto Böcher, 'Wasser und Geist', in *Verborum Veritas: Festschrift für Gustav Stählin zum 70. Geburtstag*, ed. Otto Böcher and Klaus Haacker (Wuppertal: Theologischer Verlag Rolf Brockhaus, 1970), 203, who refers to the tendency 'der Johannestaufe die Kraft der Geitsmitteilung abzusprechen'. I am indebted to Böcher's little-noticed essay for pointing to OT and Qumran texts that render this tendency questionable; Böcher is, so to speak, my John the Baptist.

credulity. Ernst Käsemann, for example, scoffs that Luke's Ephesian disciples 'seem to be living in a vacuum', and John Meier points out the dubiousness of disciples of the Baptist who have 'never heard about the "spirit of holiness" spoken of in the Old Testament and reflected upon further in intertestamental literature and the documents of Qumran'.[15] Luke probably shaped the tradition about the Ephesian followers of the Baptist in this improbable way because he knew that, even in in his own day, there were adherents of the Baptist who did not follow Jesus. In Acts 19 he acknowledges this group's existence but demonstrates the error of its ways; indeed, part of the purpose of his Gospel in general may be to lead followers of the Baptist gently to faith in Jesus.[16]

The 'denial of Spirit' motif, then, nests comfortably within early Christian theology. This does not necessarily mean that it is unhistorical; in research into the historical Jesus and related subjects, discontinuity with the thought of the later church may point in the direction of historicity, but continuity with the church does not necessarily suggest the opposite. It is *possible* that John denied that his baptism conveyed the Spirit. It is *possible* that he looked for Spirit baptism to come from another source, namely a messianic successor figure. It is *possible* that the church merely picked up John's 'denial of Spirit' motif and used it for its own ends.

All that is possible – but I think unlikely. Rather, I will argue, John probably saw his baptism as an eschatological rite that ushered its recipients into the new age, where they experienced both forgiveness of sins and the interrelated boon of the Spirit. One initial indication of this is that, even in the Synoptic tradition, Jesus receives the Spirit during, or immediately after, his baptism in the Jordan at John's hands (Mk 1.10// Mt. 3.16//Lk. 3.21–2). As Jerome asks rhetorically, acknowledging the difficulty this passage poses for the 'denial of Spirit' motif, 'What do we mean by saying that John in his baptism could not give the Holy Spirit to others, yet gave it to Christ?'[17]

To further strengthen the case that John linked forgiveness and the Spirit with his own baptism, I will first turn to Old Testament and Second Temple Jewish texts and institutions that present water rites, forgiveness and reception of the Spirit as part of an unbreakable gestalt. The Christian adaptation of this gestalt shattered the connection between John's baptism, on the one hand, and forgiveness and the Spirit, on the other, reconfiguring the gestalt instead around *Christian* baptism. It is thus a premier example of 'the ways in which Jewish texts and traditions (including social practices) were received (selected, adopted, interpreted, reframed …) in the early Christians' definitions of themselves as a community'.[18]

---

[15] John P. Meier, *A Marginal Jew: Rethinking the Historical Jesus*, 5 vols, ABRL (New Haven, CT: Yale University Press, 1991–2016), 2.82 n. 95; Ernst Käsemann, 'The Disciples of John the Baptist in Ephesus', in *Essays on New Testament Themes*, NTL (Philadelphia, PA: Fortress Press, 1964, original 1952), 138.

[16] This may help to explain Luke 1, where not only John (1.15, 80) but also his mother Elizabeth (1.41) and his father Zechariah (1.67) are filled with the Holy Spirit. These passages may come from a Baptist source that Luke incorporated with a missionary intention; cf. Peter Böhlemann, *Jesus und der Täufer. Schlüssel zur Theologie und Ethik des Lukas*, SNTSMS 99 (Cambridge: Cambridge University Press, 1997), 69–70; Joel Marcus, *John the Baptist in History and Theology*, Studies on Personalities of the New Testament (Columbia: University of South Carolina Press, 2018), 67, 133–4.

[17] Jerome, *Lucif.* 7 (PL 23.161C); cf. Böcher, 'Wasser', 203 (without quoting Jerome).

[18] From the framing document of this conference.

Denial of forgiveness

A crucial step in this argument is attention to the text and afterlife of the earliest Christian elaboration of the purpose of John's baptism: it was, according to Mk 1.4, a 'baptism of repentance unto forgiveness of sins' (βάπτισμα μετανοίας εἰς ἄφεσιν ἁμαρτιῶν; cf. Lk. 3.3). In this summary, the compressed and cryptic nature of which suggests a genuine slogan going back to John, baptism, repentance and forgiveness all cohere, and there is no indication that any of them takes place at a different time from the others. John's adherents confess their sins as they enter the waters to be baptized by him (see Mk 1.5); they emerge from those waters with their sins absolved.

This is what we would expect from history-of-religions parallels in general and the Jewish texts and institutions that John drew upon in formulating his baptismal rite in particular. Water rites are designed for ritual cleansing, and there is considerable overlap in the Old Testament itself between ritual cleansing and cleansing from sin.[19] In Num. 8.5–12, for example, Aaron is commanded to sprinkle 'waters of expiation' (מֵי חַטָּאת, lit. 'waters of sin') on the Levites 'to cleanse them' (לְטַהֲרָם), as part of a ritual that is designed to 'make atonement for the Levites' (לְכַפֵּר עַל־הַלְוִיִּם). So firm is this connection between water rituals, cleansing and forgiveness that the combination can be used in a metaphorical sense in later OT texts, where it is often joined with a call to repentance (see e.g. Isa. 1.16–18; 4.4; Ps. 51; Ezek. 36.25–33; Zech. 13.1). This combination continues in Second Temple Jewish texts in general[20] and the Qumran literature in particular (see e.g. 1QS 3.1–9; 4.20–2).

The seemingly obvious connection between John's water rite and forgiveness of sins, however, has caused unease for Christian interpreters from a very early period of Christian history. In fact, we notice this unease already in the two earliest interpreters of Mark – namely Luke and Matthew. Although Luke retains the Markan formula 'a baptism of repentance unto forgiveness of sins' in 3.3, he shortens it to 'a baptism of repentance' in Acts 19.4, an important passage, in which, as we have seen, he is concerned to put John in his place (below Jesus). Similarly, Matthew removes the phrase 'unto forgiveness of sins' from the account of John's baptism (Mt. 3.1, 11) and instead inserts it into the 'cup word' at the Last Supper (Mt. 26.28; cf. Mk 14.24) – presumably because he wishes to associate forgiveness with Jesus's death rather than John's baptism. The motivation seems obvious: if John's baptism already accomplished forgiveness of sins, what need was there for Jesus to die?

In fact, this is precisely the sort of retrospective thinking that we see in a fascinating passage from St Jerome, in which he interprets the Markan formula as a reference to a *future* remission of sins – an interpretation that goes back at least

---

[19] Jonathan Klawans, *Impurity and Sin in Ancient Judaism* (Oxford: Oxford University Press, 2000), draws an overly sharp distinction between the two concepts, though he acknowledges that there is a great deal of overlap between them both in the Tanach and in the Qumran literature. He is perhaps overly influenced by his careful study of the rabbinic literature, in which the two categories are more distinct.

[20] See, e.g. Philo, *Deus Imm.* 7; and *Spec. Leg.* 1.257–60, cited by Robert L. Webb, *John the Baptizer and Prophet: A Socio-Historical Study*, JSNTSup 62 (Sheffield: JSOT Press, 1991), 111.

to Tertullian and can still be found in modern exegesis.[21] The passage appears in Jerome's Dialogue Against the Luciferians, a group of Christian rigorists, followers of the fiercely anti-Arian bishop Lucifer of Cagliari (d. 370 or 371), who insisted on rebaptizing people who had been baptized by Arian bishops. Lucifer justified this rebaptism by comparing his baptizands to the Ephesian disciples of John, who were rebaptized by Paul in Acts 19; Jerome counters by arguing that the Ephesian disciples had received only John's baptism, which was merely provisional, not Christian baptism, as the Luciferians had. What is especially revealing is the tortuous and frankly Christological nature of the logic Jerome uses to justify his conclusion about the provisionality of John's baptism:

> The baptism of John did not so much consist in the forgiveness of sins as in being a baptism of repentance for the remission of sins, that is, for a future remission (*in futuram remissionem*), which was to follow through the sanctification of Christ ... But if John, as he himself confessed, did not baptize with the Spirit [cf. Mk 1.8 pars.], it follows that he did not forgive sins either, for no one has their sins remitted without the Holy Spirit. Or if you contentiously argue that, because the baptism of John was from heaven, therefore sins were forgiven by it, show me what more (*quid amplius*) there is for us to get in Christ's baptism. Because it [John's baptism, according to the contrary argument] forgives sins, it releases from Gehenna. Because it releases from Gehenna, it is perfect. But [I say that] no baptism can be called perfect except that which depends on the cross and resurrection of Christ ... In your perverse scrupulosity you give more than is due to the baptism of the servant and destroy that of the master, to which you leave no more than to the other (*cui amplius nihil relinquis*; Dialogue Against the Luciferians 7 [PL 23.162C-163A]; trans. alt. from NPNF).

Note the retrospective nature of Jerome's logic: the baptism of John could not have imparted forgiveness of sins, since, if it had, it would have been perfect – but only the redemption wrought by Christ's death and resurrection is perfect. To say the contrary is to ascribe to John a status and office equal to Christ's, but that cannot be; for if John's baptism had already imparted forgiveness, what more (*quid amplius*) was to be obtained from Christ's death and resurrection, and the baptism that flows from them? John's baptism, then, could not have imparted forgiveness of sins, and 'unto forgiveness of sins' in Mk 1.4 must be interpreted as a reference, not to John's baptism, but to Christ's future one. And this is probably the same retrospective logic that led Matthew and Luke to remove 'unto forgiveness of sins' from their accounts of John's baptism, and for Matthew to insert it instead into the cup-world at the Last Supper.

---

[21] In *Bapt.* 10.5-6, Tertullian says that John's baptismal preaching of forgiveness of sins 'was an announcement made in view of a future remission' (*in futuram remissionem enuntiatum est*); for other patristic and medieval examples, see Marcus, *John the Baptist*, 71, and the notes on pp. 201-2. A modern example of this interpretation is James D. G. Dunn, *Baptism in the Holy Spirit* (London: SCM, 1970), 15-17, 22.

The movement from the Markan version of the purpose for John's baptism to the Matthean and Lukan ones, then, is an example of the way in which a Jewish text and tradition – namely the tradition about John's baptism and the social practices connected with it – was received and reframed in the early Christians' definitions of themselves as a community – indeed, as *the* elect community.

Forgiveness and the Spirit

This reframing relates not only to the forgiveness of sins but also to the Holy Spirit. For as Jerome himself remarks, 'No one has their sins remitted without the Holy Spirit.' If John, then, remitted sins, he also imparted the Spirit. But that, in Jerome's view, cannot be: only Christ gives the Spirit.

Jerome had good biblical precedent for connecting forgiveness of sins with the Spirit. In the Old Testament, forgiveness is strongly associated with the action of God's רוח (e.g. Ps. 51.1–2, 10–12; Ezek. 11.18–20; 18.30–1; 36.25–31; cf. Jer. 31.31–4). This association continues in the Qumran literature (e.g. 1QS 3.6–7; 4.20–3; 9.3–5; 1QH^a 17[9].32–4; frag 2 1.13; 4Q506 frags 131–2 11–14) – a significant connection because, as I argue at length elsewhere, John probably belonged to the Qumran community before striking out on his own.[22] Particularly important for our purposes are Ezek. 36.25–7 and its echo in 1QS 4.20–3. Here is the Ezekiel passage in its larger context:

> [24]For I will take you from the nations, and gather you from all the countries, and bring you into your own land. [25]I will sprinkle clean water upon you, and you shall be clean from all your uncleannesses, and from all your idols I will cleanse you. [26]A new heart I will give you, and a new spirit I will put within you; and I will take out of your flesh the heart of stone and give you a heart of flesh. [27]And I will put my spirit within you, and cause you to walk in my statutes and be careful to observe my ordinances. [28]You shall dwell in the land which I gave to your fathers; and you shall be my people, and I will be your God. (RSV trans.)

Here, in a vision of eschatological restoration to the land and covenant renewal, the revived holiness of the people is suggested by the conjoined images of sprinkling with water and creating a new heart and spirit. The basic elements found in the summary of John's baptism in Mk 1.4 – human repentance, divine forgiveness and water imagery – are combined with a reference to endowment with God's eschatological spirit.

These linkages are preserved and extended in a significant way in an important passage from the foundational Qumran document, the Community Rule. Here, in an

---

[22] See chapter 2, 'Qumran', in Marcus, *John the Baptist*. Key arguments here include the centrality of water rites in the Qumran community and the Baptist's ministry, the similar eschatological horizon of those rites, the common linkage of Isa. 40.3 with the water rites and with the community's location in the Judean Wilderness, and the 'brood of vipers' terminology. Most of these features are rare to non-existent in Second Temple Jewish texts outside the Qumran community and the tradition about John the Baptist.

ecstatic eschatological vision near the conclusion of the Discourse on the Two Spirits, we read:

> By His truth God shall then purify (יברר) all the deeds of man, and refine some of the children of man so as to extinguish every perverse spirit from the inward parts of his flesh, cleansing him from every wicked deed by a holy spirit (לטהרו ברוח קודש מכול עלילות רשעה). Like purifying waters, He shall sprinkle him with a spirit of truth (ויז עליו רוח אמת כמי נדה), effectual against all the abominations of lying and sullying by an unclean spirit. (1QS 4.20–22; DSSEL trans. alt.)

The imagery here is obviously indebted to Ezekiel 36, in which, as we have seen, it is prophesied that God will sprinkle clean water on Israel, cleanse them from their sins and put a new spirit within them. Significantly, however, in 1QS 4 the 'new spirit' becomes a 'holy Spirit', drawing it closer to John the Baptist's prophecy of 'the Coming One', and it is clearer than it is in Ezekiel that this Spirit, which is likened to purifying water, is the agent of eschatological cleansing. This is, to be sure, a preview of the eschatological future, not in the first instance a description of the Qumranian present, and the 'sprinkling' is metaphorical rather than literal. But the members of the Qumran group felt themselves already, in a sense, to be living in the dawning eschaton,[23] and it is hard to imagine that they could have read the description of 'purifying waters' here without thinking of their thrice-daily ablutions in the miqvaot that are such a prominent feature of Qumran architecture.[24]

In view of these linkages, it may be asked whether John would have proclaimed a baptism that brought forgiveness of sins without associating it with the eschatological action of the Spirit. The answer is probably no – especially in view of John's Qumran connection. The contrary case would be that John for some reason removed the Spirit from relation to his own baptismal ministry, only to have it be reinstated by the early Christians. It makes more sense to think that, with regard to the gestalt of water, forgiveness and endowment with the Spirit, there was continuity between John's predecessors (Ezekiel and the Qumranians), John, and John's successors, the early Christians.[25]

---

[23] On the element of realized eschatology in the Qumran literature, see Heinz-Wolfgang Kuhn, *Enderwartung und gegenwärtiges Heil. Untersuchungen zu den Gemeindeliedern von Qumran mit einem Anhang über Eschatologie und Gegenwart in der Verkündigung Jesu*, SUNT 4 (Göttingen: Vandenhoeck & Ruprecht, 1966); David Edward Aune, *The Cultic Setting of Realized Eschatology in Early Christianity*, NovTSup 28 (Leiden: E. J. Brill, 1972), 29–44; E. P. Sanders, *Paul and Palestinian Judaism: A Comparison of Patterns of Religion* (Philadelphia, PA: Fortress, 1977), 280–1.

[24] On the prominence of miqvaot at Qumran, see Jodi Magness, *The Archaeology of Qumran and the Dead Sea Scrolls*, Studies in the Dead Sea Scrolls and Related Literature (Grand Rapids, MI: Eerdmans, 2002), 158; and Eric M. Meyers, 'Khirbet Qumran and Its Environs', in *The Oxford Handbook of the Dead Sea Scrolls*, ed. Timothy H. Lim and John J. Collins, Oxford Handbooks in Religion and Theology (Oxford: Oxford University Press, 2010), 34.

[25] The reasoning here is similar to Dale Allison's argument that John the Baptist's theology was apocalyptic and so was that of the early church; it therefore makes more sense to assume that Jesus, the middle term between the two, was also apocalyptic in orientation than that Jesus de-apocalypticized and then the church re-apocalypticized; see Dale C. Allison, 'A Plea for Thoroughgoing Eschatology',

A problem: 1QS 3.6–9 and Josephus, *Antiquities* 18.116–17

I have to admit, however, that there are a couple of problems with the argument I have developed so far that John thought that his baptism imparted forgiveness of sins through the power of the Spirit. The first is that this is what Josephus explicitly *denies* in *Ant.* 18. The second is the way in which this denial seems at first to cohere with an earlier passage from the Qumran Community Rule which, like 1QS 4.20–2, echoes Ezekiel 36.

Here is the Josephus passage:

116) For Herod had killed this John, although he was a good man, and had exhorted the Jews to exercise virtue by practicing righteousness towards each other and piety towards God, and thus to be joined together by baptism (βαπτισμῷ συνιέναι). 117) For in his eyes baptism was unacceptable as a way of gaining remission of sins (μὴ ἐπί τινων ἁμαρτάδων παραιτήσει χρωμένων), but [acceptable] as a way of obtaining cleanliness of the body, inasmuch as the soul had already in fact been purified by righteousness (ἀλλ' ἐφ' ἁγνείᾳ τοῦ σώματος ἅτε δὴ καὶ τῆς ψυχῆς δικαιοσύνῃ προεκκεκαθαρμένης; my trans.).

And here is the Qumran passage:

For through the Spirit of the counsel/council of truth (כיא ברוח עצת אמת) pervading all the ways of man will atonement be made (יכופרו) for all his iniquities (כול עוונותו); only thus can he gaze upon the light of life and so be joined to His truth by a Spirit of holiness (ברוח קדושה), purified from all iniquity (יטהר סכול עוונותו). Through an upright and humble attitude his sin will be covered (תכופר חטתו), and by humbling himself before all God's laws his flesh will be made clean (יטהר בשרו). Only thus can he receive the purifying waters (להזות במי נדה) and be sanctified by the cleansing water. (להתקדש במי דוכי; 1QS 3:6–9; DSSEL trans. alt.).

Josephus specifically denies that John's baptism cleansed people from their sins, or was intended to do so. It was the repentance preceding the baptism that accomplished purification; baptism itself only washed the body, confirming in a physical way the spiritual cleansing that had already occurred. Similarly, 1QS 3 seems to make purification from sin through the Spirit the prerequisite for rather than the result of entering the miqveh, the function of which, it might seem, is merely to cleanse the flesh.

It is important, however, to ask what these two passages are aiming for in their contexts. Both are concerned to combat a view of immersion as an *ex opere operato* rite. The Qumran passage concerns the person who attempts to join the elect community but refuses to do so in the right way, humbly and repentantly, trying instead to sneak

---

JBL 113 (1994), 654–5; Dale C. Allison, *Constructing Jesus: Memory, Imagination, and History* (Grand Rapids, MI: Baker Academic Press, 2010), 54–5.

in 'in the stubbornness of his heart' (2.25–3.1). Unworthy candidates of this sort will not be granted permanent entry, despite all the knowledge, power and wealth at their disposal, because they have not truly repented of their sins (3.2–3). It is of this sort of insincere candidate, not of candidates in general, that it is said that 'ceremonies of atonement cannot restore his innocence, neither cultic waters his purity; he cannot be sanctified in oceans and rivers, nor purified by ritual bathing' (3.4–5, DSSEL trans. alt.). The warning, then, is similar to the one John issues to the 'brood of vipers' coming to his baptism in Mt. 3.7–8//Lk. 3.7–8a.

But for the candidate who comes to the Yaḥad with the right attitude, who is moved by the Spirit to submit humbly to the laws of the community, the waters truly *are* purifying, and his sin is covered as his flesh is made clean (3.6–9). Thus, the DSSEL is right to translate להזות במי נדה ולהקדש במי דוכי in 1QS 3.9 as 'only thus can he *really* receive the purifying waters and be purged by the cleansing flow' (emphasis added). Not everyone who enters the miqveh is spiritually cleansed by it; but some – the sincerely repentant – are. For them, the rite *is* efficacious, and the Spirit that has led them to the waters with a repentant attitude will also purify them in those waters, as we can infer from 1QS 4.20–2. The passage from the previous column, then, is not evidence that the Qumranians separated their immersions from the Spirit and forgiveness of sin, but only that they thought unworthy aspirants would not receive those gifts. And even in this passage, where the vagueness of Qumran syntax makes it impossible to pin down a precise order of events, forgiveness and endowment with the Spirit are portrayed as happening in the same general time frame as immersion, not at some indefinite future time.

It is similarly necessary to ask how the passage in *Ant.* 18 fits into Josephus's overall theological programme. His worry seems to be that Judaism in general, and John's theology in particular, will be misunderstood as encouraging the sort of magical interpretation of religious rites that was despised by Greco-Roman intellectuals. This is in line with the apologetic note that Josephus often strikes in defending Judaism before his Greco-Roman audience (and before Jews who are influenced by that environment or have to answer to it).[26]

But the sort of rationalizing interpretation Josephus offers in combating an *ex opere operato* understanding reduces John's baptism itself to an unnecessary feature and thus proves inadequate to the task of explaining what it meant to him and his followers. John was remembered primarily as John *the Baptist*, not as John the Preacher of Repentance.[27] It is hard to imagine that so many people would have made the long trek out to the desert to be baptized by him if they thought that they had *already* been

---

[26] On Josephus's frequently tendentious polemics, see Martin Hengel, *The Zealots: Investigations into the Jewish Freedom Movement in the Period from Herod I Until 70 A.D.* (Edinburgh: T&T Clark, 1961, repr. 1989), 15–16, 237–44; John M. G. Barclay, *Jews in the Mediterranean Diaspora from Alexander to Trajan (323 BCE–117 CE)* (Edinburgh: T&T Clark, 1996), 352–3, 358; Steve Mason, 'Fire Water and Spirit: John the Baptist and the Tyranny of Canon', *SR* 21 (1992), 179; John M. G. Barclay, *Against Apion*, Flavius Josephus, Translation and Commentary 10 (Leiden: Brill, 2007), xxx–xxxvi, li–liii. On Josephus's indirect apologetic, see John Barclay, 'Apologetics in the Jewish Diaspora', in *Jews in the Hellenistic and Roman Cities*, ed. John R. Bartlett (London: Routledge, 2002), 134–5.

[27] Cf. Philip Vielhauer, 'Johannes, der Täufer', in *RGG, Dritte Auflage* (Tübingen: J.C.B. Mohr (Paul Siebeck), 1959), 3.805.

cleansed by repentance, if they had not believed that John's baptism would confer on them some sort of spiritual boon. And they probably would not have thought so unless John himself encouraged the belief. That belief, moreover, reflects a default Jewish position, namely that expiation of sin is accomplished by sincere repentance *in combination with* rituals of atonement, not in isolation from them.[28]

Both *Ant.* 18.116–17 and 1QS 3.6–9, then, are polemical, and neither supports the conclusion that John artificially separated his baptism from forgiveness of sins and the impartation of the Spirit. Rather, both passages are directed at misunderstandings and abuses that arose out of precisely the reality we have been discussing: water rites were intimately connected with forgiveness and spiritual endowment, and therefore some people thought they would automatically obtain those blessings when they came to the water.

John as salvation-bringer

Assuming that my line of reasoning so far has carried conviction, I now make bold to reconstruct the original form of the saying about the 'Coming One' with which this essay began. Many exegetes have preferred the Q form of the saying, which contrasts John's water baptism with baptism in fire and the Spirit, to the Markan form, which contrasts water baptism with Spirit baptism alone.[29] Moreover, some interpreters, including Dibelius, have thought that the original contrast was simply 'I baptize you with water, but he will baptize you with fire.'[30] If that is right then, in line with the previous argument, baptism with the Spirit may have been implied in John's reference to his water baptism. But it is also possible, I think, that John *did* mention the Spirit explicitly, linking it with water rather than fire:

JOHN THE BAPTIST	'THE COMING ONE'
I baptize you	but he will baptize you
in water	in fire
and the Holy Spirit	

---

[28] See Klawans, *Impurity*, 139: Josephus is 'overemphasizing the prerequisite of repentance over the power of the ritual itself to effect atonement'. Klawans grants that John probably would not have baptized a person whom he did not feel to be repentant, but also thinks that 'one cannot deny that there was [in John's mind] some power to the ritual itself. ... Indeed, almost all Jews would have agreed that atonement was effected by sincere repentance *and* rituals of atonement of one sort or another. If John rejected this consensus and believed that personal repentance alone was effective, then his baptism would not have been necessary'.

[29] See e.g. Dunn, *Baptism*, 8–14, and the authorities he cites. The eschatological connotations of fire cohere well with the atmosphere of John's ministry in general and the associated Q passage (Mt. 3.7–10//Lk. 3.7–9) in particular. Mark, moreover, does not seem to like the idea of eschatological punishment, which is vanishingly rare in his Gospel, and it is plausible that he removed the reference to fire from the form of John's saying that came down to him.

[30] Dibelius, *Überlieferung*, 56–8. For some of the scholars who have concurred with Dibelius's reconstruction of the saying, see Dunn, *Baptism*, 8 n. 1. Dibelius was partially anticipated by Charles Augustus Briggs, *The Messiah of the Gospels* (New York: C. Scribner's, 1894), 67 n. 4, though his reasoning was different from Dibelius's. More recently, Mason, 'Fire', 170, has arrived at the same conclusion.

It is easy to see how this saying could have morphed into the Markan and Q forms under pressure from the early Christian conviction that only Jesus imparts the Spirit. Mark takes the reference to the Spirit from the left-hand, John-the-Baptist column and *substitutes it* for the reference to fire in the right-hand, 'Coming-One' column; the Q form, on the other hand, takes the reference to the Spirit out of the left-hand column and *adds* it to the reference to fire on the right.

If this reconstruction and the arguments that have supported it are right, some common approaches to John stand in need of correction. First, it cannot be claimed, as is frequently done, that John saw his ministry solely as one of anticipation. In a classic statement of this position, Joachim Jeremias contrasted John's ministry with that of Jesus: 'John the Baptist remains within the framework of *expectation*; Jesus claims to bring *fulfilment*. John still belongs in the realm of the *law*, with Jesus, the *gospel* begins ... Here is the gulf which separates the two men, despite all the affinities between them' (emphasis in original).[31] James Dunn, similarly, characterizes John's ministry as an essentially preparatory one, in which the 'not yet' element prevails: 'It does *not* mark the beginning of the eschatological event; it does *not* initiate into the new age' (emphasis in original).[32] Against such reconstructions, I have argued that John saw his baptism as an eschatological sacrament – not only because it anticipated the eschaton but also because it already imparted, through the Spirit, the forgiveness that was part and parcel of the new age. As Otto Böcher already argued, then, John probably regarded himself, not merely as a precursor, but as a *Heilsmittler*, a bringer of salvation.[33]

Correlated with this, it will not do to characterize John's ministry as one of judgement, as opposed to Jesus's ministry of grace.[34] In John's eyes, rather, *he* was the preacher of the good news that God's eschatological victory was already manifesting itself in the earthly sphere. As a sign of that spreading victory, and as its vanguard, his baptism was conveying the joyful realities of the new age: forgiveness of sins and the Spirit that made it possible.[35] For John, *now* is the day of salvation, though the window of opportunity is closing; John urges his hearers to avail themselves of this last opportunity before it is too late. Soon there will be time only for the visitation of fire, the mopping-up operation executed by the warlike Davidic Messiah. John,

---

[31] Joachim Jeremias, *New Testament Theology. Part One: The Proclamation of Jesus* (New York: Scribner, 1971), 49.
[32] Dunn, *Baptism*, 14. I note with interest the use of italics in both quotations to underline what, in the authors' view, John was obviously not trying to do.
[33] Böcher, 'Wasser', 203, cites Vielhauer, 'Johannes', 3.805, as a precursor. Vielhauer notes the close connection between John's baptism and his person (John immerses the baptizand, the baptizand does not immerse him- or herself). He concludes 'dass J. sich nicht nur als Vorläufer des Richters, sondern in eins damit als Mittler des Heils verstanden hat'.
[34] For citations from scholars such as Renan, Strauss, Harnack and Dibeliuis, down to the Jesus Seminar in our own day, see Marcus, *John the Baptist*, 203 n. 68. See also Eugen Drewermann, *Das Markusevangelium* (Olten: Walter Verlag, 1987–8), 129 n. 2, who claims that Jesus's proclamation of God's forgiveness 'presupposes the *failure* of the Baptist's preaching of judgment' (emphasis in original: setzt ... das Scheitern *an der Gerichtspredigt des Täufers voraus*).
[35] I therefore disagree with Josef Ernst, *Johannes der Täufer: Interpretation – Geschichte – Wirkungsgeschichte*, BZNW 53 (Berlin: De Gruyter, 1989), 355–6, who asserts that the association of John with joy in Lk. 1.14 conflicts with the tenor of his ministry.

then, does indeed announce judgement. But it is explicitly not his task, but that of the coming Messiah.

The Christian appropriation of John

Leo Tolstoy's *Anna Karenina* contains this remarkable passage:

> Levin had often noticed in arguments between the most intelligent people that after enormous efforts, an enormous expenditure of logical subtleties and words, the arguers finally became aware that what they had so long been struggling to prove to one another had long ago, from the beginning of the argument, been known to both, but that they loved different things, and would not specify what they loved for fear of being attacked. He had often had the experience that suddenly in an argument you grasp what it is your opponent loves and at once you love it too, and immediately you find yourself agreeing, and then all the arguments fall away as useless. Sometimes, too, he had experienced the opposite: expressing at last what you yourself love, what you have been devising your arguments to defend, you happen to express it well and genuinely, and you find your opponent at once agreeing and calling a halt to the argument.[36]

Let me try out Levin's theory by telling you what I love, what lurks behind the enormous expenditure of logical subtleties and words in this essay, so that my potential opponents may suddenly agree and stop arguing. I love the idea of reclaiming as a *Heilsmittler* a figure who has sometimes been disparaged as the epitome of Jewish judgmentalism. I love the idea of showing that realized eschatology, which has often been portrayed as a Christian invention, was already a reality for John the Baptist and his predecessors at Qumran.

But I am also a Christian, and I recognize that demoting John as a *Heilsmittler* may have been an inevitable by-product of developing a distinctive Christian identity. As adherents of a crucified Messiah, the Christians needed to advance a convincing rationale for choosing to follow him – something that counterbalanced the disgrace and ostracism associated with Jesus's crucifixion and other norm-busting features of the movement.[37] The Christians themselves associated this turnaround with powerful experiences of the Spirit that followed Jesus's resurrection (Jn 20.22; Acts 2, etc.), experiences that confirmed for them that Jesus rather than anyone else, including John, was the decisive salvation-bringer of the new aeon.

It would have been theoretically possible for the Christians to place John and Jesus on a continuum of Spirit-reception; their message could have been, 'You can also have through Jesus what was already available through John', just as Matthew portrays John and Jesus proclaiming the same message about the kingdom of God (Mt. 3.2; 4.17).

---

[36] Translation altered from Leo Tolstoy, *Anna Karenina* (trans. Constance Garnett), Project Gutenberg EBook, https://www.gutenberg.org/files/1399/1399-h/1399-h.htm, accessed 1 April 2021.
[37] Cf. Wayne A. Meeks, 'The Man from Heaven in Johannine Sectarianism', *JBL* 91 (1972), 44–72.

That this proved impossible is probably due in part to the developing competition between the Christian movement and that of the Baptist, which is evident not only in Acts 19 but also in other passages throughout the New Testament. These, in a heavy-handed way, emphasize John's inferiority to Jesus and thus inadvertently reveal the threat he and his followers were perceived to pose to the Christian mission so long as they resisted absorption into it. In Mt. 3.14–15, for example, the First Evangelist inserts an invented dialogue between John and Jesus in which John at first refuses to baptize Jesus because '*I* have need to be baptized by *you*'. Even more significant are the frequent expressions of the inferiority theme in the Fourth Gospel, where the narrator emphatically asserts that John was *not* the light but only a witness to it (Jn 1.7–8), and where John himself 'confessed, and did not deny, but confessed' that he was not the Christ, but only his forerunner (1.20–3) and that, in the end, 'he must increase, but I must decrease' (3.30). This competition did not die out with the end of the first century; the Pseudo-Clementine literature acknowledges and argues against followers of John who still revered him as the Messiah into the second, third and fourth centuries,[38] and the Mandean literature provides indirect evidence for the continuation of the cult into even later times.[39]

Nor is this competition solely an invention of the church. Rather, it probably goes back in essence to Jesus himself, who in one Q logion says that the lowliest person in the kingdom of God is greater than John and in another may relegate him to the bygone era of the Law and the prophets.[40] This sort of relativizing of a predecessor by a successor is a phenomenon often seen in new religious movements, as demonstrated, for example, by Malcolm X's changing relation to Elijah Muhammad and Bahā' Allāh's changing relation to the Bāb.[41] But it is also similar to the way in which, according to Harold Bloom, one 'strong poet' often relativizes and deliberately misreads another who has gone before him.[42] As Dennis Feeney put it in a BBC radio discussion of Roman satire, 'Poets always create their own predecessors.'[43]

Yet the competition between the Jesus and Baptist movements did not, in most Christian circles we know of, result in Baptists being treated in the hostile manner reserved for Pharisees and other outright opponents of Jesus and the church.[44] They were usually regarded, rather, as a receptive mission field, as people to whom the way

---

[38] See n. 44.
[39] On the Mandean evidence, see Marcus, *John the Baptist*, 19–22, and, on the competition hypothesis in general, see chapter 1 of that book.
[40] On Mt. 11.7–11//Lk. 7.24–8 and Mt. 11.13//Lk. 16.16, see Marcus, *John the Baptist*, 90–1.
[41] For the examples of the Nation of Islam and the Bahā'ī movement, see Marcus, *John the Baptist*, 91–6.
[42] Harold Bloom, *The Anxiety of Influence: A Theory of Poetry* (New York: Oxford University Press, 1973). One of Bloom's premiere examples is William Blake, who claimed to understand John Milton's poetry better than Milton himself did: 'Milton wrote in fetters when he wrote of Angels and God, and at liberty when of Devils and Hell, ... because he was a true Poet and of the Devils party without knowing it' ('The Marriage of Heaven and Hell', in D. V. Erdman, *The Complete Poetry and Prose of William Blake: Newly Revised Edition*, Anchor Books (New York: Doubleday, 1988), 35).
[43] *In Our Time*, 22 April 2010.
[44] For a comparison with the treatment of the Pharisees, see Joel Marcus, 'Johannine Christian and Baptist Sectarians', in *John and Judaism: A Contested Relationship in Context*, ed. R. Alan Culpepper and Paul A. Anderson, Resources for Biblical Study 87 (Atlanta, GA: SBL Press, 2017), 155–63. In a late redactional layer of the Pseudo-Clementines (*Hom.* 2.17, 23; *Hom.* 3.22–3//*Rec.* 2.8), John

of God must simply be explained more accurately (cf. Acts 18.26). This was partly because of the undeniable historical links between John and Jesus; everyone (except apparently Josephus) knew that Jesus had begun his ministry within the Baptist fold.[45] But it was probably also because the two leaders never came to open blows. John may have remained sceptical about Jesus's messiahship, and Jesus may have relegated John to a secondary status in the kingdom, but he was still *in* the kingdom, or close to it, and the ambiguity of the two men's relations left room for the dialogue between their followers to continue after their deaths.

The most important way in which Jesus's followers acknowledged their link with the Baptist movement was, of course, by turning John's central rite into the cornerstone of their own sacramental practice. How John's disciples felt about this is not explicitly recorded. Acts of cultural appropriation often provoke both pride and irritation: pride that features of our culture are being recognized as valuable, irritation that they are being exploited by powerful outsiders. If we possessed actual literature from the Baptists of the early Christian centuries, it would probably reveal ambivalence of this sort.[46]

To return, then, to the overarching theme of this volume: the appropriation, reuse and transformation of Old Testament water rites in the Qumran community, the John the Baptist movement and early Christianity is a premier example of the way in which practices shape religious identity and are in turn shaped by its permutations. In ancient Israel, recurrent water rites were believed by their practitioners to confer ritual purity, which was sometimes conflated with forgiveness of sins.[47] Ezekiel 36 projects such practices onto an eschatological backdrop, prophesying a definitive shower of forgiveness through the power of the Spirit. The water imagery here becomes metaphorical, but the hope is real. Centuries later, the Qumranians reconcretize the imagery; their repeated immersions impart forgiveness of sins, but now through a foretaste of Ezekiel's eschatological Spirit, which sets them apart not only from the surrounding gentile world but also from their fellow Jews. John the Baptist inherits these conceptions, but once again transforms them, turning baptism into a once-and-for-all rite that does not need to be repeated because it imparts not just a foretaste but the eschatological Spirit in its fullness. Finally, Jesus and the early Christians adopt John's rite but relegate John himself and his baptism to precursor status, because for them Jesus (and therefore not John) is the eschatological *Heilsmittler*, and therefore his baptism rather than John's imparts forgiveness through the power of the Spirit.

---

is treated in a hostile manner. This is mirrored by the way Jesus becomes a false prophet in some Mandean texts. But in earlier layers of the Pseudo-Clementines (*Rec.* 1.54.8; 1.60.1), it is John's disciples, who acclaim him as Messiah, who are opposed, not John himself; see Marcus, *John the Baptist*, 14–22.

[45] On the significance of Josephus's ignorance of the link between John and Jesus, see Marcus, *John the Baptist*, 84.

[46] On the day I finished the first draft of this essay, I came across an article in *The New York Times* entitled, 'Why Is Everybody Always Stealing Black Music?' (*The New York Times Magazine*, 18 August 2019, pp. 60–7). In the article the author, Wesley Morris, speaks about 'the conflation of pride and chagrin I've always felt anytime a white person inhabits blackness with gusto. It's: *You have to hand it to her.* It's: *Go, white boy. Go, white boy. Go.* But it's also: *Here we go again*' (p. 62).

[47] See e.g. Num. 8.6–7; Ps. 51.7; Ezek. 36.25–31; 1QS 3.8–9; cf. Marcus, *John the Baptist*, 69–70, 74–6.

In the transition from Qumran to John, as well as from John to Jesus and the early Christians, the need to distinguish oneself from one's predecessor plays a major role in redefining the appropriated tradition. We can imagine a lively debate between a Qumranian, an adherent of the Baptist, and a follower of Jesus about whose immersion really imparts the Spirit (cf. Jn 3.25). As in all such debates, the subtext is the identity of the elect community.

10

Tradition and authority in scribal culture: A comparison between the *Yaḥadic* Dead Sea Scroll texts and the Gospel of Matthew

Loren T. Stuckenbruck[1]

Introduction

One of the main emphases of the Gospel of Matthew is its portrayal of Jesus as one who gives instruction. In the text, while his teaching is often addressed to his disciples (Mt. 5.1), it is also directed at the disciples of John the Baptist (9.14), the crowds (cf. 7.28; 11.7; 12.46; 13.2, 34; 15.10; 22.33; 23.1) and leaders with whom he debates (12.38; 15.1; 16.1; 19.3; 22.41; cf. 16.12). Beyond the narrative itself, which looks back to the time of Jesus, scholars frequently recognize that the disciples of Jesus, whether in full or presented as a subgroup (e.g. Peter, James, John) or individual (i.e. Peter), function at least in part as a cipher for the 'community' within which the gospel has taken shape several generations after Jesus's time.[2] Thus, the function of Jesus's teaching, so clearly on display in the text, relates to two temporal frameworks, one having to do with what Jesus *said* during his activity in Galilee and Judea and one having to do with what Jesus *is saying* within the gospel's contemporary setting.

There is reasonable consensus that many of Jesus's sayings, in contrast to the gospels of Mark and Luke, are organized into larger, almost self-contained units of instruction, each of which carries a particular emphasis. While there is some discussion on the number of these units,[3] teachings of Jesus are blocked together around at least the following texts and themes: chapters 5–7 (the 'Sermon on the Mount', on ideal religiosity), 10 (on mission), 13 (parables, on the kingdom of heaven), 18 (life among Jesus's followers), 23 (woes against 'scribes and Pharisees') and 24–5 (discourse concerning eschatological events). These discourses are interspersed and framed by

---

[1] I am grateful to Joseph Verheyden for an insightful response to this essay and for comments by other participants in the Australian Catholic University conference.
[2] See Warren Carter, *Households and Discipleship: A Study of Matthew 19–20*, JSNTSS 105 (Sheffield: JSOT Press, 1994).
[3] See e.g. the discussion on whether there are five or six by Craig S. Keener, *The Gospel of Matthew: A Socio-Rhetorical Commentary* (Grand Rapids, MI: Eerdmans, 2009), 37–8.

narratives that focus more on Jesus's deeds, events and smaller units of teaching.[4] This alternating shift, which reflects the writer's editorial and compositional activity, reinforces at every turn different aspects of Jesus's authority, whether expressed through his deeds (Mt. 9.6, 8; 21.23-4, 27) or through his teaching (7.29; 28.18-20; cf. 11.27). Though claimed to be unprecedented, Jesus in the gospel is made to pass on some of his authority to his disciples (10.1; cf. 11.25-6; 28.19-20).

Whether and, if so, how the disciples of Jesus function as channels of an authority that extends to the time of the gospel's composition shall be considered in this essay by casting a glance at a pool of tradition among the Dead Sea Scrolls. Before this is done, it is appropriate to offer preliminary reflections that provide warrant for the discussion.

First, we note that Jesus's authority as a teacher is not novel to Matthew. Matthew's emphasis builds on tradition, whether by material found in Mark (esp. 1.22, 27; 4.1-34; 13.1-36)[5] or, more generally, by material shared with the Gospel of Luke ('Q'), a source primarily centred around Jesus's sayings.[6] To the extent that Matthew received not only instructions attributed to Jesus but also claims about the singular nature of his teaching, he has adapted these traditions, organizing and editing them to form further units of instruction that, in turn, enhanced the authority of his Jesus even more.

That Matthew's Gospel shaped Jesus tradition – here, we are concerned with his teaching – to reinforce that, for example, he is modelled on, yet superior to Moses, goes without saying.[7] Is it possible, though, to go further by proposing a series of (a) phenomenological and (b) tradition-historical questions. With reference to (a), we note that it is one thing to recognize the gospel's emphasis on Jesus as teacher, while it is another to inquire into what this emphasis meant for the author-editor, insofar as he too aimed to instruct. In what sense can claims about Jesus be understood as claims, however thinly veiled, about 'Matthew' himself?[8] This issue gains specificity when several points are acknowledged. First, there is the distinction, well-worn in form-critical scholarship during the twentieth century, between sayings tradition and narrative. The former involves the transmission of Jesus's instructions in content, whether in discrete units or as collections, while the latter contextualizes and links the sayings material in relation to a storyline, whether consisting of units with shorter *logia* or furnishing narrative that could have given rise to poignant pronouncements (as, e.g. *apothegmata* in disputes and 'controversy stories' [*Schul-* and *Streitgespräche*]). Studies by Rudolf Bultmann and others focused on the *logia* of Jesus in order to trace

---

[4] So Matthew chapters 4, 8-9, 11-12, 14-17, 19-22, and 26-8. See the treatment of the issue, with an overview of previous scholarship, by W. D. Davies and D. A. Allison, *Matthew*, 3 vols, ICC (Edinburgh: T&T Clark, 1988), 1:58-72.

[5] Thus, the focus here on Matthew should not detract from the importance of Jesus as teacher in the Gospel of Mark. Remarkably, use of the verb 'teach' (διδάσκω) for Jesus's activity in Mark (twelve times) exceeds the number of instances in Matthew (five: 5.2; 7.29; 11.1; 13.54; 22.16). In addition to the verb, Jesus is called or designated 'teacher' no less than thirteen times in Mark (4.38; 5.35; 9.17, 38; 10.17, 20, 35, 51; 12.14, 19, 32; 13.1; 14.14), compared to ten times in Matthew (8.19; 9.11; 10.24; 12.38; 17.24; 19.16; 22.16, 24, 36; 23.8; 26.18; also, twice indirectly in 10.24-5), i.e. more often than the very gospel in which Jesus's role as teacher is emphasized.

[6] In addition, see the special material preserved in Lk. 4.32, 36.

[7] E.g. Dale C. Allison, *The New Moses: A Matthean Typology* (Eugene: Wipf & Stock, 1993, repr. 2013).

[8] This essay assumes that the gospel, though attached in the second century to 'Matthew', was the product of a composer-editor who was initially formally anonymous.

their earliest form and the settings within which they arose. In this vein, the focus was thus on Jesus tradition *behind* the texts, and less on the activity that produced the texts that we have. Second, the emergence of redaction-critical study, more than form-critical approaches, drew attention to editorial processes and theological outlooks of the evangelists, with the implication that they understood themselves as entitled to shape traditions they inherited. Although 'redaction criticism' paved the way for a study of the text traditions as embedded within the larger strategy of a narrator, the results of analysis remained focused on the Synoptic gospels' claims about Jesus. The following discussion shifts focus onto the author behind Matthew's Gospel to consider the degree to which his presentation of Jesus *reflects a strategy of self-validation in which he may be thought to have engaged*. Third, while it may already seem obvious, the question explored here has little to do with a recovery of a 'historical Jesus' or of the Matthean portrait of Jesus in any specific sense and, instead, attempts to throw light on the function of *language about* Jesus for the evangelist. The question addressed in this essay can thus be more precisely formulated: How is the significance of Matthew's claim concerning the authoritative nature of Jesus's teaching related to his own activity as organizer and interpreter of that tradition? In other words, how does the authority claimed for Jesus reflect on the authority the gospel may be claiming for itself?

The tradition-historical problem (b) is more difficult to address: If we are to understand Matthew's use of Jesus tradition as a form of self-authorization, what might account for it? Although appealing to an ideal figure to enhance one's own message would not have been novel in antiquity, is there a particular tradition-historical context or stream of discourse that puts us in a better position to understand Matthew? I shall argue below that, for all the differences, selected portions of the Dead Sea Scrolls provide an illuminative context.

To be sure, Jesus was not the only teacher in the ancient world about whom much could be said on the basis of surviving sources. Philosophical traditions that arose in the Greek-speaking Mediterranean world come to mind, especially in relation to how individuals (e.g. Socrates, Epicurus) are portrayed by heirs to their thought and 'schools' bearing their name.[9] On the Jewish side, the most well-known named teachers during the late Second Temple period to whom instructions and debates are attributed in rabbinic literature are Hillel and Shammai.[10] Without either discounting their potential significance for contextualizing Jesus in Matthew's Gospel or the transmission processes associated with them, the present essay draws 'the Teacher of Righteousness' (or 'Teacher') among the Dead Sea Scrolls into the conversation.[11] This

---

[9] In this regard, possible parallels to Plato's handling of Socrates would provide a useful analogy: Socrates is not known to have written anything and, arguably, Socrates functioned as a cipher for promoting Plato's own philosophical ideas; cf. esp. Lloyd Gerson, 'The Myth of Plato's Socratic Period', *Archiv für Geschichte der Philosophie* 96 (2014), 403–30 (with bibliography from recent scholarship).

[10] More emphasis has been devoted, however, to treating them as historical figures than to how each functioned as models for those writing about them; see e.g. James H. Charlesworth and Loren L. Johns, *Hillel and Jesus: Comparisons of Two Major Religious Figures* (Philadelphia, PA: Fortress, 1997).

[11] Two important monograph-length studies have compared Jesus as teacher in Matthew's Gospel with the Teacher of Righteousness in the Dead Sea Scrolls: Samuel Byrskog, *Jesus the Only Teacher: Didactic Authority and Transmission in Ancient Israel, Ancient Judaism and the Matthean Community*, ConBNT 24 (Stockholm: Almqvist & Wiksell, 1994); and John Yueh-Han Yieh, *One*

vantage point holds promise for several reasons: (1) the relative contemporaneity of sources about the Teacher to Matthew (they date to the late second and first centuries BCE); (2) sources referring to the Teacher, as Matthew to Jesus, were composed one or more generations after he was alive; and (3) these sources, as Matthew, yield information about the past while ultimately attending to more immediate concerns. These points are elaborated below.

The Teacher of Righteousness in the Dead Sea Scrolls

Much has been written about the Teacher by Dead Sea Scrolls specialists. A majority of scholars agree that slightly varying references in the texts to '(the) Teacher of Righteousness' and related designations refer to one and the same individual. The scrolls mention him some seventeen times in the following texts:

- Habakkuk Pesher (1QpHab, copied early second half of first cent. BCE) – i 13; ii 2; v 10; vii 4; viii 3; ix 9–10; and xi 5;
- Micah Pesher (1QpMic = 1Q14, second half of first cent. BCE) – 10.6;
- 4QPsalms Pesher[a] (4QpPs[a] = 4Q171, late first cent. BCE to early first cent. CE) 1–10 iii 15, 19, iv 8, 27;
- 4QPsalms Pesher[b] (4QpPs[b] = 4Q173, late first cent. BCE to early first cent. CE) 1.4 and 2.2;
- unidentified *pesher* fragment (4Q172) 7.1; and
- Cairo Geniza (CD) recension to the Damascus Document which refers to 'one who teaches righteousness' (יורה הצדק; CD A I 11, vi 11).

A further six may refer to him with similar expressions:

- CD B xx 1 and 14: 'the unique teacher' (מורה היחיד);
- CD B xx 28 and 4QIsaiah Pesher[c] (4QpIsa[c] = 4Q163, mid-first cent. BCE) 21.6: simply '(the) teacher' (מורה); and
- 4QPsalms Pesher[a] (4Q171) 1–10 i 27: 'the interpreter of knowledge' (מליץ דעת).[12]

Until relatively recently, most Scrolls research has been concerned with the Teacher's historical identity.[13] However, inquiry into the socio-rhetorical function of the many

---

Teacher: Jesus' Teaching Role in Matthew's Gospel, BZNT 124 (Berlin: de Gruyter, 2004). While these publications ultimately centre on explaining claims being made *about* Jesus, I attempt to redirect attention to how they lend authority to the evangelist's project.

[12] For further references, see CD A vi 7 (4Q267 2.15), CD A vii 17 (4Q266 iii 19; 4Q269 5.2), 4QpIsa[c] 46.2 and 4QpHos[b] 5–6.2.

[13] For discussions regarding a historical identification of the Teacher and other sobriquets among the Dead Sea Scrolls, see Philip R. Callaway, *The History of the Qumran Community*, JSPSup 3 (Sheffield: JSOT Press, 1988); and James H. Charlesworth, *The Pesharim and Qumran History: Chaos or Consensus?* (Grand Rapids, MI: Eerdmans, 2002).

sobriquets among the Scrolls leads to a different focus.[14] In relation to the Teacher, we may ask why the anonymous writers of the texts listed above refer to the Teacher. To address this, we not only review *what* the sources say regarding the Teacher but also consider what this would have meant for the *Yaḥad* authors themselves. The presentation of the Teacher in the Scrolls can be summarized under the following points.[15]

Priest. The Teacher is expressly identified as 'the priest' (הכוהן). This is most clearly stated in two passages.[16] The first of these is 4QpPsalms[a] 1–10 iii 15–16 in the context of a commentary on Psalm 37. The commentary responds to lemma that cites Ps. 37.23–4, which states that one who, 'though he stumble, will not fall headlong, for Yahweh holds him by the hand'. In the comment, this figure is identified as 'the Priest, the Teacher of [Righteousness, whom] God [ch]ose to stand (לעמוד)'.[17] The text adds that God 'established him to build for him a congregation of [....]'. Thus, in his function as priest, the Teacher is understood as having founded and shaped the character of the writer's community.[18] The other passage is 1QpHab ii 8: here a figure, probably the Teacher, is given the title 'priest'. The reference occurs in an interpretation of Hab. 1.5. After those 'who have not believed' for associating with the 'Man of the Lie' and not aligning themselves with the Teacher (cf. 1QpHab ii 2 and 6), the interpretation mentions 'traitors' who in the latter days 'will not believe when they hear all that will ha[ppen t]o the last generation from the mouth of the Priest' (ii 6–8). If referring to the Teacher, the text takes his priestly identity for granted, emphasizing that in the final generation, his instruction has met with rejection.[19]

Authoritative Interpreter. The Teacher is portrayed as an unequalled interpreter of the prophets and the Torah. As such, the Teacher's importance is recounted in an interpretation of Hab. 2.2 in 1QpHab vii 4–5. The phrase 'that the one who reads it may run', reiterated from the fuller lemma (cited in 1QpHab vi 15–16) is related by the writer to 'the Teacher of Righteousness, to whom God made known all the mysteries of the words of his servants the prophets'. Significantly, the text distinguishes between the Teacher and the prophet Habakkuk. Habakkuk was simply a recorder of knowledge about the future age; the Teacher, however, has actually understood God's plan for

---

[14] See esp. Matthew A. Collins, *The Use of Sobriquets in the Dead Sea Scrolls*, LSTS 67 (London: Bloomsbury, 2009), 16–37.

[15] For fuller discussion, see Loren T. Stuckenbruck, 'The Legacy of the Teacher of Righteousness in the Dead Sea Scrolls', in *New Perspectives on Old Texts*, ed. Esther G. Chazon, Betsy Halpern-Amaru and Ruth A. Clements, STDJ 88 (Leiden: Brill, 2010), 23–49, 29–44.

[16] Less certain is a reference to the attempted seizing of 'the priest and the men of his council' by 'Ephraim and Manasseh' in 4QpPs[a] 1–2 ii 18–20 (interpretation of Ps. 37.14–15).

[17] The Hebrew לעמוד can also be translated 'as a pillar'.

[18] The priestly character could be maintained, without immediate association with the Jerusalem Temple. Rulings in the Damascus Document requiring the involvement of priests reflect a self-understanding of the community along cultic lines; cf. e.g. CD A ix 13–14 (par. 4Q267 9 i 8); CD A xiii 5–6 (par. 4Q271 5 ii 20; see also the skin disease passages in 4Q266 6 i; 4Q267 iv; 4Q269 7; 4Q272 1 i; 4Q273 4 ii).

[19] For purposes of this discussion, it is important that the Teacher is remembered this way and matters less what historical reality lies behind it, i.e. whether the Teacher was a 'high priest', as many scholars have maintained; cf. the extensive bibliography in Stuckenbruck, 'The Legacy of the Teacher of Righteousness', 30–1 n. 18.

'the consummation of the age'. The interpreter construes the Hebrew imperfect 'may run' (ירוץ, *yaruṣ*) in Hab. 2.2 as a recent event of full disclosure. The author suggests that with the Teacher a 'final age' has dawned, one that God 'will prolong ... and will surpass everything the prophets have said' (vii 7–8).

As already implied in 1QpHab ii, the Teacher's authority is indisputable and determinative for all else. Reading 1QpHab ii and vii together yields a clear portrait of the Teacher's instruction as *the* criterion for what it means to be faithful to God. His revelation is complete; it pertains to '*all* the words of his servants the prophets' in ii 8–9 and to '*all* the mysteries of the words of his servants the prophets' in vii 4–5. The writer leaves the impression that the Teacher offered a running interpretation of the prophets, perhaps even of Habakkuk itself. The Habakkuk Pesher, however, does *not* so much cite the Teacher's interpretations, as it does those of the unidentified writer. Following the extraordinary claim about the Teacher, the text applies the words of Habakkuk to the community of the author's own time. What the Teacher began has been 'prolonged' (יארוך) to a time, when 'the men of truth who do the Torah' (vii 10–11) are exhorted to be patient. Thus, though the Teacher and the writer both live in 'the last generation' (ii 7) and 'final age' (vii 7), the writer's time is distinguishable from that of the Teacher. The Teacher's unique authority to interpret prophetic tradition is foundational for the later community of interpreters that included the author. In this sense, the Teacher's authority is not functionally unique. His activity is not simply marked out in order to reinforce that he has inaugurated a new era; rather, his authority is paradigmatic for the writer, who in turn can determine what the sacred text means for his own circumstances. Significantly, the writer assumes for himself a mantel of authority he attributes to the Teacher and, in this respect, bridges and blends the increasing gap between his and the Teacher's time (vii 9–14). It is *his and not, in the immediate sense, the Teacher's* message, which exhorts the community not to relax their 'service of the truth' (vii 11–12). The Teacher signifies a new era in which the writer finds a warrant for his own appropriation of Habakkuk.

The Teacher is also linked in several passages to Torah interpretation. In this respect, the claims made about him as a unique interpreter thereof are implicit. Several examples point in this direction. An interpretation of Hab. 1.13b in 1QpHab v 10–12 accuses 'the Man of the Lie', as one in conflict with the Teacher, of having rejected the Torah (cf. also the interpretation of Hab. 1.4a in 1QpHab i 10). Even more clearly, in an interpretation of Hab. 2.4b, 1QpHab viii 1–3 links fidelity to the Teacher with faithful observance of the Torah. The outcome of such obedience is deliverance by God 'from the house of judgment'. In 1QpHab viii 2 loyalty to the Teacher is associated with the community's 'toil' (עמלם). It is possible that this term refers to a form of suffering that the writer assigns to the community. Thus, by referring to the Teacher's fidelity in the next phrase, it is possible that the Teacher serves as a model with whom they not only identify their faithfulness to Torah but also their own rejection and suffering (cf. e.g. 1QpHab v 10–11; ix 9–10; xi 4–6; 4QpPs[a] 3–10 iv 6).[20]

---

[20] Cf. also 4QpPs[a] at 1–10 iv 8–9, which makes Ps. 37.32-3 refer to the conflict between the Wicked Priest and the Teacher of Righteousness while claiming that 'the Torah was sent to him (i.e. the Teacher)'.

Further association of the Teacher with Torah interpretation occurs in the Damascus Document as at CD B xx 27–32. Here, listening to his instruction is tantamount, for example, to 'not abandoning the correct laws when they hear them', being atoned, experiencing deliverance and trusting in God's 'holy name'. This link of the Torah with the Teacher may also be apparent in a statement about 'the Interpreter of the Torah' (דורש התורה), whose statutes are to be followed by community members 'until there arises one who will teach righteousness in the end of days' (CD A vi 9–11; cf. vii 18–19).[21]

If the writers and their community regarded the Teacher as initiator of a 'fulfilment' hermeneutic (1QpHab vii 1–5), they would find themselves able to adopt the same sort of activity by reading sacred tradition as a repository for revelation about their contemporary circumstances. It would not simply have been a matter of *imitation*. Presentist concerns could also dictate the *way* they presented the Teacher; the assumption of continuity would have made it easy to project onto him at least some of their own activities and statements about him.

Founder of the Community. At least two texts regard the Teacher as having founded a community or shaped a movement of the faithful. The first is 4QpPsalms Pesher[a] 1–10 iii 15–16 mentioned above. The Teacher, called 'the Priest', is the one whom God established 'to build for him a congregation of …[.' The Damascus Document (cf. CD A i 1–17) offers a slightly different scenario: for an already existing movement[22] – a group which, though 'a root of planting … in the goodness of [God's] soil', were 'as those who grope for a way for twenty years' (i 7–10a) – God 'raised the Teacher of Righteousness to guide them in the way of his heart' (i 11). If there is anything to the account in the text of CD A, then the author of 4QPsalms Pesher[a], while emphasizing the Teacher as *the* movement's founder, glosses over his link to the community's earlier origins.

One in Conflict with Other Authorities. As mentioned above (p. 184), 'traitors', aligned with 'the Man of the Lie', are presented in the Habakkuk Pesher as having opposed the Teacher's instruction (1QpHab ii 1–5).[23] A further sobriquet used for the Teacher's opponents is 'the Men of Mockery' (CD B xx 1; 4QpIsa[b] = 4Q162 2.6, 10) who, in turn, may be associated with the figure designated 'the Man of Mockery' (CD A i 14 par. 4Q266 2 i 18). A related designation is 'Spouter of the Lie' (1QpHab x 9; 1QpMic = 1Q14 8–10.4; cf. CD A viii 13), which, though perhaps to be identified with the Man of the Lie, nowhere occurs in immediate conjunction with the Teacher. Among the *Yaḥad* texts, two figures stand out as having been in conflict with the Teacher: 'the Man of the Lie' and 'the Wicked Priest'. Rather than attempting to identify one or both of them, it is enough to recognize here that when referring to them, authors were, as

---

[21] In several texts, writers offer authoritative interpretations of texts, including Pentateuchal tradition, without mentioning the Teacher's activity; see esp. 'thematic' *pesharim* such as in 4QCommGen in 4Q252–254 and 4Q254a, 4Q174 (4QFlorilegium), 4Q175 (4QTestimonia), 4Q177 (4QCatena A), 4Q180–181 (4QAges of Creation), 4Q464 (4QExposition on the Patriarchs) and 11Q13 (11QMelchizedek).

[22] See Philip R. Davies, 'The Teacher of Righteousness and the "End of Days"', in Davies, *Sects and Scrolls: Essays on Qumran and Related Topics*, SFSHJ 134 (Atlanta, GA: Scholars Press, 1996), 89–94.

[23] It is unclear whether these are precisely the same group as the 'traitors' mentioned in 1QpHab v 8; 4QIsaiah Pesher[c] (4Q163) 4–7 ii 6; and 4QDamascus Document[a] (4Q266) 2 i 6 par. CD A i.

with the Teacher, appealing to the recent *past* while doing so with more *contemporary* concerns.

Several passages link 'the Man of the Lie' to a conflict that resulted in a split in the movement. As mentioned above, 1QpHab ii 1-4 associates him with the 'traitors' who did not show fidelity to the Teacher (ii 2-4). More about the conflict is reported in 1QpHab v 8-12: references to 'traitors' and 'a wicked one' in Hab. 1.13b are, respectively, interpreted as 'the House of Absalom and the men of their counsel', on the one hand, and to 'the Man of the Lie who rejected the Torah in the midst of their council', on the other, with the former having been 'quiet at the rebuke of the Teacher of Righteousness'. The text does not indicate whether this event involved an open debate with (an) opponent(s) or involved an altercation within the earlier movement that split as a result (as in CD A i par. 4Q266 2 i). The former would suggest that the 'traitors' and 'the Man of the Lie' belonged to an outside group from which the Teacher may have anticipated support, while the latter would conceive of the opponents as having been part of the community itself. The second, especially given its correspondence to CD A i, seems the more plausible of the alternatives. In the text (CD A i 10-ii 1) terms applied to the Teacher's opponent are reminiscent of the Man of the Lie and Spouter of the Lie. The Teacher is said to have 'made known to the latter generations what he (God) did in the last generation in the congregation of *traitors* – they are those that depart from the way ... when there arose the Man of Mockery who spouted on Israel waters of *the lie* and led them into a chaos without the way'. The Teacher is presented as having criticized the Man of Mockery's leadership (cf. 1QpHab x 5-13 and 4QpPs^a 1-10 iv 14).

If the Man of Mockery, the Man of the Lie and the Spouter of the Lie are sobriquets for the same individual, then the Man of the Lie in the Habakkuk Pesher is associated with a group which in the Damascus Document is also described as 'those who sought smooth things' (cf. CD A i 18-20 par. 4Q266 2 i 21-23), to whom the more fixed sobriquet 'Seekers of Smooth Things' would subsequently be attached.[24] Whereas 'traitors' refers a group from the past, the Seekers of Smooth Things, who may already have existed during the Teacher's time, occur mostly in texts linked to events from a later period, that is, closer and perhaps even contemporary to the time of the authors. The latter, then, would have linked the Teacher's time to that of the authors, who construed the 'founding' events referred to in CD A i 18-20 as a pattern of conflict that persists into their present. It is possible, though uncertain, that the authors behind the Nahum Pesher and 4Q177 retrojected the Seekers of Smooth Things into the past so that language about the Teacher's conflict is accommodated to that existing one. In this case, depictions of the Teacher's experience would have functioned as the lens through which to understand the present.

The *Wicked Priest* is the other character, with whom the Teacher is presented as having been in conflict. Although often thought of as the Teacher's quintessential nemesis, the Wicked Priest is a more slippery figure. Whereas statements about the

---

[24] Cf. 1QHodayoth^a x 17 [reconstructed]; 4QIsaiah Pesher^c 23 ii 10; Nahum Pesher = 4Q169 3-4 i 2, 7; 3-4 ii 2, 4; iii 3, 6; 4Q177 7.2 and 9.4.

Teacher predominantly occur in the perfect (and therefore refer to past events),[25] the Wicked Priest is also a figure of the past[26] whose activity, however, extends beyond the Teacher's time so that he even turns up in the future.[27] Some therefore propose that the sobriquet was being applied to *any* high priest, whether he was in conflict with the Teacher or with the community at any point in its past or present.[28] Whether or not this holds, we note that the Wicked Priest frequently occurs in texts that do not mention the Teacher. Thus, his significance for writers of the *pesharim* was larger than his immediate relation to the Teacher.

According to two *pesharim*, the Wicked Priest persecuted or even attempted to kill the Teacher: 1QpHab xi 4–8 and 4QpPs^a 1–10 iv 7–8. These texts are as follows:

'Woe to anyone who causes his companion to be drunk, mixing in his anger, making drunk in order that he might gaze upon their feasts' (Hab. 2.15). Its interpretation concerns the Wicked Priest, who pursued the Teacher of Righteousness, to swallow *him* up with his poisonous fury to the House of Exile. And at the end of the feast, the repose of the Day of Atonement, he appeared to *them* to swallow *them* up and to make *them* stumble on the day of fasting, *their* restful Sabbath. (1QpHab xi 4–8)

'The wicked one lies in ambush for the righteous one and seeks [to put him to death. Yah]weh [will not abandon him into his hand,] n[or will he] allow him to be condemned as guilty when he comes to trial' (Ps. 37.32–3). Its interpretation concerns [the] Wicked [Pri]est, who w[aited in ambush for the Teach]er of Right[eousness and sought to] have him put to death. (4QpPs^a 1–10 iv 7–8)

The former passage implies that conflict arose based on different calendrical practices by the Teacher and his community, on the one hand, and the Jerusalem Temple under the aegis of the Wicked Priest, on the other.[29] In the text, the Wicked Priest attempted to subvert the Teacher: he is reported to have attempted to confound, perhaps even by force, the community's Yom Kippur observance. The latter passage may more generally

---

[25] This especially in the *pesharim*. Of course, the possibility remains that he may also be presented as an eschatological figure, as in CD A vi 11: 'the one who will teach righteousness in the end of days'.

[26] See esp. 1QpHab viii 9–13, 16; ix 10; xi 5–8, 12–14; and 4QpPs^a 1–10 iv 9 (though the subject of the verb is uncertain).

[27] As suggested by the imperfect verbs associated with his activity in 1QpHab at x 3–5, xi 14 and xii 5, while a partly restored participle (צ[ו]פ[ה]) has been proposed for 4QpPs^a 1–10 iv 9; cf. F. García Martínez and E. J. C. Tigchelaar, *The Dead Sea Scrolls Study Edition*, 2 vols (Leiden: Brill, 1997–8), 1:346.

[28] This 'Groningen hypothesis' was argued by A. S. van der Woude, 'Wicked Priest or Wicked Priests? Reflections on the Identification of the Wicked Priest in the Habakkuk Commentary', *JJS* 23 (1982), 349–59; and F. García Martínez, *inter alia*, in 'The Origins of the Essene Movement and of the Qumran Sect', in *The People of the Dead Sea Scrolls*, ed. F. García Martínez and J. Trebolle Barrera, trans. W. G. E. Watson (Leiden: Brill, 1995), 77–96. See the critical evaluation by Timothy H. Lim, 'The Wicked Priests of the Groningen Hypothesis', *JBL* 112 (1993), 415–25.

[29] See esp. S. Talmon, 'The Calendar Reckoning of the Sect from the Judean Desert', in *Aspects of the Dead Sea Scrolls*, ed. C. Rabin and Y. Yadin, ScrHier 4 (Jerusalem: Hebrew University Magnes Press, 1965), 162–99, *contra* Callaway, *History of the Qumran Community*, 160–1.

refer to the same event while, however, using stronger language, implying the Wicked Priest intended to kill the Teacher.[30]

The way the writer of the Habakkuk Pesher presents the conflict is significant. The event not only happened to the Teacher but also, as the *italicized* pronouns in the citation show, to his community. The writer understood himself (and the community of his own time) as heirs to and participants in the persecution of the Teacher. The writer interprets 'their feasts' in Hab. 2.15 as a reference to the more specific event, the Day of Atonement. The author thus not only reports an event of persecution, he also coordinates it with a festival that must also have been observed by his community. It is likely that his community could not observe Yom Kippur without, at the same time, recalling what had happened to the Teacher. The Teacher's location in 'the House of Exile', which was away from Jerusalem, would have reinforced or even justified the author and his community's Torah observance away from the Jerusalem cult (where the wrong calendar was in force). Appealing to this event and reporting it as having taken place on the Yom Kippur would have been a rallying point for the later community that observed it.[31]

Without referring to the Teacher, the Habakkuk Pesher initially mentions the Wicked Priest in terms of divine punishment in the past and condemnation in the future. His initial standing as one 'called by the name of truth' (1QpHab viii 9) is followed by a description of his decadence through haughtiness, amassing of wealth and religious impurity (viii 8–13). Then a twofold interpretation of Hab. 2.7–8a in 1QpHab viii 13–ix 7 ensues that centres on two phrases 'and you will become to them as booty' and 'all the rest of the peoples will plunder two'. Both these statements are applied to punishments meted out on the Wicked Priest for his wrongdoing, including 'evil diseases' and 'vengeful acts on the carcass of his flesh'. Significantly, both phrases in Hab. 2.8a are also interpreted in relation to a future punishment of 'the last priests of Jerusalem' who, like the Wicked Priest in the past, 'will amass wealth', make ill-gotten profit and be delivered into the army of the Kittim (ix 5–7). The analogy between the Wicked Priest and the last priests indicates how much the writer regards the latter as heirs of the former. The passage leads to the citation and interpretation of Hab. 2.8b that refers to the iniquity that the Wicked Priest committed against 'the Teacher of Righteousness and the men of his council', the latter of whom are called 'his (God's) chosen' (ix 9–12a). Not only here but also in the following passage that interprets Hab. 2.9–11, the text elaborates on the Wicked Priest's punishment, which is both past and future (ix 12b–x 5; cf. further xi 14 and xii 5). The text of Habakkuk is made to describe

---

[30] The text has to be restored: צ[פה למור]ה הצד]ק. The plausibility of the restoration is strengthened if the event corresponds to 1QpHab xi. See Maurya P. Horgan, 'Psalm *Pesher* 1 (4Q171 = 4QPs^a = 4QpPs37 and 45)', in *The Dead Sea Scrolls: Hebrew, Aramaic, and Greek Texts with English Translations. Volume B: Pesharim, Other Commentaries, and Related Documents*, ed. James H. Charlesworth and Henry W. Rietz, PTSDDS Project (Tübingen: Mohr Siebeck; Louisville, KY: Westminster John Knox Press, 2002), 6–23, 18–19.

[31] On Yom Kippur in the Scrolls, see other *Yaḥadic* texts: 1QS viii 6 (par. 4Q259 ii 15–16), 10; ix 4 (par. 4Q258 vii 4–5); and perhaps even 11QMelchizedek (= 11Q13) ii 7–8. See further 4Q156 (4QTgLev; 2 Aramaic fragments preserving parts of Lev 16); the Temple Scroll (= 11QTemple) xxv 10–xxvii 10, which amplifies the biblical account (xxvii 5 adds: 'may this day be to them a remembrance'); 4QAges of Creation A (= 4Q180 1.7–10); Book of Giants at 4Q203 7 i 6; and Jub. 5.17–19.

events from the remote and recent past as evidence of punishment that assures it will also take place in the future. Thus, the language about the Wicked Priest's fate blurs clear distinctions between the past, present and the future. By the same token, the iniquity he carried out against the Teacher is not simply a past event; the author reactivates it through scripture interpretation in order to address the present and to project a just outcome onto the future. If the Wicked Priest's persecution of the Teacher is the same as that which is coordinated with the Day of Atonement in 1QpHab xi, then this conflict is a pattern that transcends the past and defines the community's continuing story.

There is a sense in which it is not past events regarding the Wicked Priest, the Teacher and their respective communities that gave rise to the Habakkuk Pesher (or other similar writings). Instead, the work takes its chronological point of departure in more present circumstances that, inspired by the Teacher's activity, invited commentary of a prophetic tradition. The Teacher's claim to be *the* interpreter of sacred tradition and his conflicts with opponents function as a determinative frame of reference for the anonymous writer and his community's identity. The Teacher inaugurated a new period of faithfulness that reassures, exhorts and challenges 'the men of truth' and 'doers of the Torah' (vii 10–11), to be faithful in his wake.

Summary. Although the *Yaḥad* texts refer to the Teacher as an ideal figure of the recent past, the information that they convey is sketchy and fragmentary. Very little can be known about him as a historical figure. Less interest is shown in identifying him by name, locating his activity within a specific (e.g. Hasmonean) period, or in providing any kind of sustained account. The *pesharim* authors are concerned with his role in inaugurating a movement to which they belonged, with his authoritative interpretation of scripture, and with his conflicts with the Man of the Lie, the Wicked Priest and groups aligned to them. For all the Teacher's importance, no single saying or instruction is explicitly derived from him. In referring to the Teacher, writers were 'presentist' in orientation. At the same time, the activity they attributed to him marked the dawning of a new age that lent their interpretations an authority in their own right. There is therefore a real gap between historical information about what the Teacher taught and the abundance of interpretations offered by those who wrote about him. For those who wrote texts that refer to him, *that* the Teacher of Righteous taught with singular authority is *prime facie* as important as *what* he said.

From the Teacher to Jesus, and from *Pesher* authors to the Matthean evangelist

Before insights for Matthew's Gospel from the foregoing consideration of texts from the Dead Sea Scrolls can emerge, it is appropriate to indicate some obvious differences between the literatures and to identify more precisely where to place the contribution being offered. First, altogether unlike the texts referring to the Teacher, the Gospel of Matthew expressly attributes a large number of sayings to Jesus himself. Indeed, apart from the words attributed to John the Baptist, there is hardly an instruction in the gospel that is not attributed to Jesus as speaker. In other words, the transmission of words coming from Jesus himself or at least their attribution to Jesus was hugely significant for the writer. Second, and following from the point just made, the Gospel of Matthew – even beyond the accounts of Mark and Luke – explicitly has Jesus quoting and interpreting specific scriptures (see further below), whereas the Dead Sea texts reviewed only refer *in principle* to the Teacher's interpretation of (and presumably, appeal to) scripture without citing any specific or clear instance of such. Third, the presentation of Jesus in the gospel is a sustained one that follows a rough chronology; it shapes the work as a whole, while the fragmentary statements about the Teacher, among several *Yaḥadic* compositions, commensurate to an orientation around commentary, take a text or combination of texts as an organizing point of departure. References to the Teacher among the Scrolls, therefore, offer snapshots of different events and show little deliberate attempt to follow a running narrative sequence. Fourth, and finally, Matthew's Gospel speaks of 'fulfilment' of sacred texts (1.22; 2.15, 17, 23; 4.14; 8.17; 12.17; 13.14, 35; 21.24; 27.9; cf. 26.54, 56), while the Dead Sea documents do not formally refer to the fulfilment of prophecy (cf. most clearly only 11QTemple=11Q19 lxi 3) so that, in a strict sense, it is difficult to speak of the *pesher* texts as engaging in 'fulfilment hermeneutics'. In addition, the formal sequence in the Dead Sea texts of *lemma followed by interpretation* contrasts with Matthew,[32] in which an event or occurrence is *first told before appeal is made to this or that sacred tradition.* Despite these formal differences, however, it is the shared *presentist* orientation of interpretation relating to an ideal figure from the recent past that remains significant. Although Matthew and the *Yaḥad* orientated scrolls almost exclusively have this feature in common, it is difficult not to find a sociological – perhaps even a tradition-historical – connection between the scribal cultures of each. In any case, and in view of the last comment, these more conspicuous differences do not take away from allowing a reading of the Dead Sea texts to comprehend Matthew's presentation of Jesus in a new light.[33] Here we sketch several interrelated comparisons that provide cause for further research.

Formal anonymity in the shadow of an ideal figure. The first point of note is the *formal* anonymity of the authors writing about their respective ideal figures who wielded influence in relative recent times. While the second century CE would see the attachment of proper names to gospel narratives in the New Testament, there is no effort *within the gospels themselves* to identify the writers in this way, just as the writers of documents referring to the Teacher remain fully anonymous, that is, without proper

---

[32] That is, formal citations in Matthew are *introduced* by foregoing content, occurring in narrative events about Jesus (or John the Baptist) at the apex of a pericope rather than in the middle or at the beginning; cf. Mt. 1.22–3; 2.5–6, 15, 17–18; 3.3; 4.15–16; 8.17; 11.10; 12.17–21; 13.35; 21.4–5; and 27.9–10.

[33] Such comparisons do not relate as clearly to the main argument offered here. For example, there are hints that both the Jesus movement and that to which the Teacher was attached emerged from another. This is the case with Jesus in relation to John the Baptist (e.g. Mt. 3.1–17; Mk 1.1–11; Lk. 3.1–22), while a similar claim is made for the Teacher (cf. p. 185). Moreover, in both instances the sources about them overwhelmingly emphasize the singularity of their importance as agents of divine revelation (on the Teacher, cf. 1QpHab ii and vii and 4QpPs^a 1–10 iii, see pp. 183–4 above).

name.³⁴ Similarly, unlike Jewish, Jewish-Christian apocalyptic and related literature, as well as later apocryphal accounts, the narratives or fragments of information about Jesus and the Teacher, respectively, are not provided under a proper name of an ideal author or figure of the more distant past (often called 'pseudepigrapha').³⁵

Relation between the ideal figure as authoritative interpreter and the author's own interpretive activity. We have observed the abundance of material in the Dead Sea Scrolls, especially among *pesharim*, that offers *presentist* interpretations of a variety of 'scripture' traditions. In that context, finding ultimate meaning of a sacred text in the present could be authorized by drawing attention to the Teacher's foundational activity. In the case of Matthew's Gospel, analysis can be similarly focused. On the one hand, the narrator portrays a range of events relating to Jesus's life and activity as *the* fulfilment of words from scripture tradition. In contrast to Mark and Luke, the Matthean evangelist augments the narrative about Jesus with ten quotations that have been 'fulfilled' (1.22; 2.15, 17, 23; 4.14; 8.17; 12.17–21; 13.35; 21.4–5; 27.9; cf. also Mt. 26.54 par. Mk 14.49).³⁶ Given this acknowledged tendency, we may ask what may have provided a warrant for the gospel writer to do so with such confidence. Thus, on the other hand, and analogous to the Dead Sea *pesharim*, is the answer to be found in the text to present Jesus, not simply as teacher (cf. Mt. 7.29; cf. 28.18) but also and especially as one who interprets Jewish scripture as well? If we look beyond the narrator's use of quotations as commentary *about* Jesus, *sayings attributed to Jesus himself* may be queried to ascertain whether they reinforce the text's own interpretive emphasis. The question thus emerges: Does the presentation of Jesus map onto a strategy that authorizes the writer to do the same? To put the question another way, does the evidence for Jesus as interpreter in the gospel match the way the writer interprets Jewish scriptures?

Several observations indicate a special interest in Matthew to present Jesus as an interpreter of Jewish scriptures. First, near the beginning of the Sermon on the Mount the text has Jesus make a series of programmatic statements found in none of the other gospel traditions. According to Mt. 5.17, Jesus underscores that 'I have not come to abolish but to *fulfil* (viz. the law and the prophets)'. The following antitheses in 5.21–48 are each introduced by the phrase 'you have heard it said (ἠκούσατε ὅτι ἐρρέθη)',³⁷ while

---

[34] Notwithstanding the possibility that the actual author may have been known to some of his contemporaries; see Simon J. Gathercole, 'The Alleged Anonymity of the Canonical Gospels', *JTS* 69 (2018), 447–76.

[35] The term 'pseudepigraphon' should not detract from authorial claims on the part of the actual authors of such compositions. Instead, it reflects a different kind of strategy in which the authors themselves blend into (or wear the mask of) an ideal character to become the protagonist themselves; cf. Loren T. Stuckenbruck, '"Apocrypha" and "Pseudepigrapha"', in *Early Judaism: A Comprehensive Overview*, ed. John J. Collins and Daniel C. Harlow (Grand Rapids, MI: Eerdmans, 2012), 179–203.

[36] To be sure, Matthew may have been guided by received tradition; cf. e.g. the use of Mk. 14.49 in Mt. 26.54: Jesus explains that his arrest is taking place 'in order that the scriptures might be fulfilled' (without quotation). The use of fulfilment quotations by the Matthean narrator contrasts with Luke's Gospel, in which such claims are attributed to Jesus himself (so in Lk. 4.21; 22.37; 24.44; implicitly 21.24 and 22.16), with only the prologue containing general notice to that effect by the writer (1.1). Thus, for all the influence on Matthew that might be inferred through comparison within the Synoptic tradition, the correlation between both narrator and Jesus as interpreters of scripture in Matthew is strongest.

[37] Only Mt. 5.31, which, in referring to Deut. 24.1–3 does not actually cite the tradition *verbatim*, reduces the formula to 'it was said (ἐρρέθη)'.

the voice of Jesus pronounces an interpretation, each introduced by the declaration, 'but I say to you' (ἐγὼ δὲ λέγω ὑμῖν; vv. 21-2, 27-8, 31-2, 33-4, 38-9, 43-4). While the interpretation of sacred tradition here has received considerable attention, it is less often noticed that Jesus is made to assume vocabulary that the narrator has already used. The text has already claimed that events surrounding Jesus's birth, his sojourn to Egypt and his healing activity have occurred in order to *fulfil* scripture (ἵνα πληρωθῇ; 1.22; 2.15, 17, 23; 4.14). In these instances, each explicit citation expresses that the event fulfils *what was spoken* (τὸ ῥηθέν). Here, in the first discourse of the gospel, this twinned vocabulary is put on the lips of Jesus, who interprets tradition in a way that corresponds to what the narrator has done thus far. Although the kinds of interpretation in the antitheses and those in the narrative of Matthew 1-4 differ, the characterization of Jesus's advent in 5.17-18 in terms of fulfilment suggests a link between Jesus's self-presentation in the text and the implicit claim to authoritative interpretation by the narrator.

Second, in instances in which tradition is shared with Mark, Matthew's Gospel accentuates Jesus's role as interpreter. A clear instance can be observed in the parable chapter. Whereas the citation from Isa. 6.9-10 in Mk 4.12 (and Lk. 8.10) is merely introduced by 'so that' (ἵνα), the Matthean text has Jesus refer to the limited understanding of his teaching in parables as prophecy being fulfilled: 'with them indeed is fulfilled the prophecy of Isaiah that says' (ἀναπληροῦται ... ἡ προφητεία ... ἡ λέγουσα, 13.14). Significantly, whereas Mark concludes the parable discourse with Jesus's wide dissemination of parables in contrast to a more private disclosure of 'all things' to his disciples (Mk 4.34), Matthew stays with the theme of the parables' reception (13.33-5), thus offering an *inclusio* to the foregoing citation of Isaiah 6. As in 13.14, though more strictly following the narrator's introductory formula, Ps. 78.2 is introduced as follows: 'so that what was spoken through the prophet might be fulfilled, saying (ὅπως πληρωθῇ τὸ ῥηθὲν διὰ τοῦ προφήτου λέγοντος)'. The restricted perception of the parables is interpreted twice as the fulfilment of prophecy in the text, on the lips of Jesus at first, before being followed by the narrator's voice which quotes another tradition. Another instance illustrates the Matthean Jesus's augmented role as interpreter. A narrator's opening citation of Mal. 3.1 (an amalgam with Exod. 23.20) and Isa. 40.3 in reference to John the Baptist's activity in Mk 1.2-3 is retained in Mt. 3.3, which only quotes Isa. 40.3. As for Malachi 3, Matthew postpones its interpretation to a part of the narrative in which Jesus *himself* speaks about John the Baptist. In 11.10, Matthew has Jesus introduce the same combination of Malachi 3 and Exodus 23 in a formal way that, as in 13.14, is reminiscent of the gospel's style ('this is the one concerning whom it is written'; οὗτός ἐστιν περὶ οὗ γέγραπται). Whereas the Marcan citation in 1.2-3 is introduced by 'as it is written in the prophet Isaiah (καθὼς γέγραπται ἐν τῷ Ἡσαΐᾳ τῷ προφήτῃ)', the introduction formula attributed to Jesus in Mt. 11.10 is modelled on the Matthean formula in 3.3 ("*this is the one of whom* the prophet Isaiah *spoke* when he said"; οὗτος γάρ ἐστιν ὁ ῥηθείς).

Third, further instances of formal citation may be noted briefly, in which the portrayal of Jesus as interpreter has in Matthew been taken over from tradition found in Mark, on the one hand, as well as from material shared with Luke, on the other. On the basis of Mk 7.10, which refers to what 'Moses said', Mt. 15.4 has Jesus cite several commandments from the Decalogue, attributing them to 'God' (cf. Exod. 20.12; 21.17; Deut. 5.16; Lev. 20.9). A similar case occurs in Mt. 15.7-9 (cf. Mk 7.6-7), although Matthew does not include the formulaic 'it is written' (γέγραπται; though without a quotation, cf. also Mt. 17.12 par. Mk 9.12). Furthermore, Matthew expands the Marcan Jesus's interpretation of scripture in the form of a question. In Mark the formula, 'have you not read', initially attributed to Jesus without a quotation in 2.25, introduces a citation of Exod. 3.6 by Jesus in 12.26 (to Exod. 3.6) with the same formula. Matthew retains the formula from Mk 12.36 in 22.31-2, but also applies it in several other Jesus sayings, whether as an insertion into paralleled tradition (Mt. 19.4-5 par. Mk 10.5-8) or as a formula in a pericope altogether without Marcan parallel (Mt. 21.16 and 21.42 par. Lk. 20.17, which has a different formula: 'what is it that is written'). Finally, in the temptation narrative, Matthew has Jesus appeal to scripture all three times in response to the devil with the formulaic 'it is written' (Mt. 4.4, 6, 10), whereas in the final instance the Lukan version introduces Jesus's appeal with 'it has been said' (Lk. 4.12).

Although it cannot be argued that the Matthean gospel has done so at every turn, it remains clear that the narrator, whether through additional material or redactional activity, has shaped and significantly strengthened sayings by Jesus that interpret scripture. This additional emphasis on Jesus's activity as interpreter correlates with the license Matthew takes to present further events in the narrative as instances of scripture fulfilment. Thus, not only does the gospel draw on and re-present interpretations by Jesus in order to address and teach a contemporary community of faith, Jesus's mode and manner of interpretation takes on a paradigmatic function in the text. Jesus's authority becomes Matthew's authority; and, if Matthean departures from received tradition (Mark and material shared with Luke) are in view, the gospel's way of presenting Jesus provided a warrant for the writer to engage with tradition in an analogous way. Matthew's Gospel, then, joined the chorus of those in the Jesus movement who remembered Jesus as a teacher, and then augmented that portrait to reinforce his message to a community in conflict with contemporary groups which emphasized teaching emanating from scribal learning.[38] The similar relation between the *pesher* authors and the Teacher of Righteousness in the Scrolls makes this dynamic easier to recognize.

Shared scribal culture. The notion of backward projection from (a) later writer(s) to an ideal figure, as seen in the Scrolls, may throw further light on the role of the evangelist in Matthew's Gospel. In this connection, the significance of the term 'scribe' merits attention. It is, of course, impossible to know the degree to which Jesus himself engaged in writing and, if at all, whether this would have had anything to do with his teaching activity.[39] Similarly, in the Scrolls the Teacher, however learned or how much

---

[38] It is not a matter of determining whether or not Jesus himself was literate; however, the need to present him as learned or even as an authoritative interpreter thoroughly acquainted with the scriptures would have reflected Matthean interest; see the valuable study of Chris Keith, *Jesus against the Scribal Elite* (Grand Rapids, MI: Baker, 2014).

[39] In neither Matthew nor the Scrolls, respectively, is Jesus or the Teacher formally presented this way, though some scholars have argued that the Teacher composed some of the *Hodayoth*; cf. Gerd Jeremias, *Der Lehrer der Gerechtigkeit*, SUNT 2 (Göttingen: Vandenhoeck & Ruprecht, 1962), 168-77, who distinguishes between 'Teacher' and 'non-Teacher' hymns; and Hartmut Stegemann, 'The Number of Psalms in *1QHodayot*ᵃ and Some of Their Sections', in *Liturgical Perspectives: Prayer*

authority he enjoyed, is never formally linked to writing activity. Nevertheless, while Matthew nowhere remembers Jesus as one who wrote, he achieves a certain parity between Jesus and 'the scribes', with whom he is often seen to be in conflict, sometimes in tandem with other groups such as Pharisees, elders and chief priests (see esp. Mt. 5.20; *7.29* [par. Mk 1.22]; *9.3* [par. Mk 2.6]; 12.38; 15.1; 16.21; *17.10*; 20.18; 21.15; 23.2, 13, 15, 23, 25, 27, 29; 26.57; 27.41).[40] The following question emerges: if Jesus is not being expressly remembered as one who wrote, how does the evangelist establish continuity between Jesus and his own activity as writer? Matthew's use of tradition found in Mark makes clear that he knew and received tradition about Jesus's debates with scribes, who are frequently coupled with Pharisees.[41] However, the distinguishing emphasis in Matthew on the need of his followers to exceed the righteousness of the scribes and Pharisees (5.20) and the series of invectives against both groups throughout chapter 23 reflect circumstances with which the evangelist more immediately had to do. By analogy, writers of some of the Dead Sea texts may have retrojected their own contemporary conflicts with 'Seekers of Smooth Things' into the Teacher's past when the main opponents of the Teacher are branded as 'traitors' (see summary on p. 189 above). In Matthew, the scribes and Pharisees are given such a prominent role among Jesus's opponents, not only because some of this occurs in the received tradition (i.e. from Mark) but also because this reflects more contemporary debates between the gospel's community and other Jews who had contesting understandings of Jewish religious identity. In this context, Jesus is made in retrospect to offer authoritative guidance for the Matthean community. This is comparable to appeals by writers of *pesharim* to the Teacher of Righteousness's activities and selected events in his life to reaffirm and reinforce their identity as faithful Jews a generation or two later.

And yet, Jesus himself is never actually designated as a 'scribe' who, as such, debates with other scribes. If, however, we instead focus on the positive or ideal use of the term in special material in Matthew, more can be said. The woe pronouncements against 'scribes and Pharisees' in chapter 23 (vv. 13, 15, 23, 25, 27, 29) have Jesus refer to 'prophets, sages, and scribes' (23.34) whom he will send and who will be persecuted. These last mentioned 'scribes' are thus aligned with Jesus, who commissions them alongside the others. Moreover, the parables discourse in chapter 13 concludes with the remarkable saying attributed to Jesus: 'There every scribe who has been trained for the kingdom of heaven is like the master of a household who brings out of his treasure what is new and what is old' (13.52). On the basis of literary context of the gospel as a whole, Lamar A. Cope has argued the writer has inscribed a veiled reference to himself into a Jesus *logion*. Whether or not this thesis holds in a strict sense, the

---

and Poetry in Light of the Dead Sea Scrolls, ed. Esther G. Chazon with Ruth A. Clements and Avital Pinnick, STDJ 48 (Leiden: Brill, 2003), 191–234, who optimistically singled out fourteen 'psalms' composed by the Teacher.

[40] The scribes are treated alone in the italicized references. On the other hand, Jesus's interaction with 'a scribe' (in the singular), as in Mark's Gospel, is more sympathetic and far less polemical (Mt. 8.19 par. Mk 12.32); more, see the notion of 'scribes' alongside 'prophets' and 'wise men' being persecuted in Mt. 23.34.

[41] Mk 1.22; 2.6, 16 ['scribes of the Pharisees']; 3.22; 7.1, 5; 8.31; 9.11, 14; 10.33; 11.18, 27; 12.28, 35, 38; 14.1, 43, 53; 15.1, 31.

scribe trained for the kingdom of heaven represents the ideal; at the very least, the term aligns with the narrator's own interests, expressed by the protagonist Jesus himself.[42] The designation 'scribe', here as an idealized socio-religious category, suggests also how much Jesus's interactivity with the scribes was important for the evangelist. Without singling out Jesus as a scribe, his use of the category in the singular projects onto Jesus the commendation of a scribal paragon that stands in contrast with the scribes whom Jesus, as cipher for the writer, vehemently criticizes. What Matthew's Gospel claims for Jesus as teacher, both on the basis of traditions received and added emphases, holds true for the evangelist who writes in his wake.

Conclusion

In some sense, the foregoing discussion, with its focus on Matthean communicative strategy, might not initially seem methodologically novel. However, none of the established critical approaches – whether redaction, social-scientific criticism or narrative literary analysis – sufficiently addresses the implications of the evangelist's relation to and use of Jesus tradition as a way to understand how this evangelist *authorized his presentation of Jesus as fulfilment of divine purpose*. It is hoped that through a renewed appreciation of how the Yaḥad writers blended their time with that of the Teacher, whose activity they redeployed, we are in a better position to explain how Matthew's Gospel could model its authority on that attributed to Jesus.

---

[42] Lamar A. Cope, *Matthew: A Scribe Trained for the Kingdom of Heaven*, CBQMS 15 (Washington, DC: Catholic Biblical Association, 1976), 13–30. See already Ernst von Dobschütz, 'Matthew as Rabbi and Catechist', in *The Interpretation of Matthew*, 2nd edn, ed. Graham Stanton (Edinburgh: T&T Clark, 1995), 27–38 (translated by Robert Morgan from the original publication of 1928).

11

Remember the poor: Early Christian reception of a Jewish communal responsibility

John M. G. Barclay

It is universally recognized that the early Christian movement inherited the multistranded tradition of Jewish discourse concerning the poor. Whether or in what ways that tradition was distinctive in the ancient world is a separate question, but no one can doubt that Jewish social sensibilities concerning poverty and wealth, and Jewish texts on this topic (sometimes cited, often not), were influential on a wide range of Christian texts and practices. This is a paradigm case of 'reception' in the sense that a textual and cultural tradition, which was internally diverse and itself in constant motion, was not just passively 'received' but actively refocused, adapted and reapplied. What is more, this is a tradition strongly correlated with social practice and communal identity such that this topic speaks directly to our enquiry into the role of reception in the social imagination of early Christianity. To voice concern for the poor, and to put that concern into any sort of practice, was not an 'ethic' in the narrow sense of an individualized virtue; it was a matter of communal commitment.

In a modern, Western context, we are inclined to read the ancient traditions concerning care for 'the poor' as examples of 'charity' or 'almsgiving', whose paradigm is the practice of one-way, even anonymous gifts to the destitute. Such gifts were certainly practised in antiquity – for instance, the tossing of coins to desperate beggars – but the traditions we will explore here range across a much wider spectrum of practices, including mechanisms to support those who were in danger of destitution but not already in it.[1] The poor in antiquity lived highly precarious lives, in which any number of shocks (a failed harvest, a hike in food prices, illness, accident, unemployment or the death of a family income earner) could plunge them into debt and the threat of destitution. Their survival in such conditions depended on a network of reciprocated support to carry them through periods of crisis that were inevitable, but unpredictable. Normally the household and wider circles of kin would be the main support system,

---

[1] I label as 'destitute' those who lived below subsistence level, and thus in imminent danger of death unless they or others took emergency measures. The 'poor' (a loose and elastic category in our sources, as in modern discourse) I define as those living at or not more than two significant shocks above a 'bare bones' subsistence level. For economic levels in the Roman Empire, see W. Scheidel and S. J. Friesen, 'The Size of the Economy and the Distribution of Income in the Roman Empire', JRS 99 (2009), 61–91, who reckon that 82 per cent of the population lived in these two categories.

but kinship networks were sometimes broken, inaccessible or unable to assist to a sufficient degree. In these circumstances, one needed wider circles of friends, neighbours or patrons on whom one could depend. Destitution is the sign (then as now) that all networks of support have collapsed or proven inadequate.[2]

To what extent and in what ways did a community wider than immediate kin feel responsible to assist the poor? Given the standard expectations of reciprocity in the ancient world, any assistance that was significant and more than merely fleeting would reflect or create ties of social connection. Even loans implied a degree of trust, reflecting social ties between creditors and debtors and/or the persons who stood surety for them. Gifts or benefits, large or small, normally carried no legal duties, but they established or reinforced ties of social obligation. Those who felt responsible for the poor enacted a form of social solidarity: to assist the poor was to grant them social recognition, as members of one's community. Thus, an 'ethic' of concern for the poor concerned not just personal morality but also social identity. It identified the givers with those to whom they gave.[3]

In the ancient Jewish tradition, responsibility for its most vulnerable members was constitutive of the Jewish community. And since that community was also defined by its relationship to the divine – like most ancient communities, but in its own distinctive way – its social connections and responsibilities were permeated by sacred obligations and rites. As the social environment of the Jewish tradition changed, geographically and politically, so did the expressions of Jewish community and its social ties: concern for the poor meant different things in different contexts. But as this ever-shifting tradition was adopted by Christian communities, differently configured and with somewhat distinctive understandings of God, this 'same' tradition of social responsibility came to reflect and even constitute their social identity in subtly different ways.

In this essay, we will explore these social dynamics by noting select examples of reception and change. Starting from an influential text (Deuteronomy 15), we will discuss two very different instantiations of Jewish care for the poor, one from village life in the homeland (the family resource-pooling regulations of the Damascus Document) and one from an urban context in the Diaspora (the book of Tobit). We will then examine two examples of Christian reception of the Jewish tradition, Paul's collections for Jerusalem and a Roman Christian text from the early second century (the Shepherd of Hermas). What I hope to make evident is the malleability of this Jewish tradition and its relatively easy adaptation and reconfiguration in early Christian communities. But I will also highlight how concern for the poor operated as a kind of 'symbolic clamp', holding communities together and defining their limits.[4] From this perspective

---

[2] Among the best recent discussions of poverty in antiquity, see M. Atkins and R. Osborne (ed.), *Poverty in the Roman World* (Cambridge: Cambridge University Press, 2006); G. E. Gardner, *The Origins of Organized Charity in Rabbinic Judaism* (Cambridge: Cambridge University Press, 2015).

[3] On the complex social dynamics of gifts in the ancient world, see J. M. G. Barclay, *Paul and the Gift* (Grand Rapids, MI: Eerdmans, 2015); M. L. Satlow (ed.), *The Gift in Antiquity* (Chichester: Wiley-Blackwell, 2013).

[4] See P. Brown, *Poverty and Leadership in the Later Roman Empire* (Hanover: University Press of New England, 2002), 6, on the relation of the rich to the poor in the later Empire: 'Their relation to the poor acted, as it were, as a symbolic clamp. It bracketed and held in place an entire society.'

we may see how the application of this socio-economic tradition to newly constituted communities loyal to Christ both connected Christian communities to their Jewish heritage *and* sharpened their sense of difference.

The Jewish tradition and its adaptations

The scriptural traditions regarding concern for the poor are highly diverse, in genre, tone, address and content, ranging from legislation to prophetic critiques of injustice, together with accounts of exemplary patrons and miscellaneous wisdom sayings. The various terms for 'poor' range in meaning and reference, and particular classes of the vulnerable (widows, the fatherless, resident aliens) and the destitute (in debt bondage or hunger) come in and out of focus. Some of these traditions have their roots in a village- and kinship-based tradition, where the whole community is responsible to ensure that none of its members slide into hopeless debt, hunger, the forfeiture of land or the loss of children (to debt slavery). In many Ancient Near Eastern (ANE) traditions, this 'lower-class communitarianism'[5] is made the responsibility of the king, an application paralleled in some scriptural texts (e.g. Psalm 72) and deployed in the prophets' criticism of the urban elite (the product of monarchy).[6] In the Torah, and especially in Deuteronomy, this ethos is expected to permeate the whole nation, as a single community responsible for one another in covenant with God. The special attention given to the widow and the orphan (the fatherless) concerns the fact that they have lost both a vital source of income and the network connections that depend on the adult male; hence, they are easily exploited in loans and disputes. The resident alien and the Levite possess no land and therefore lack an economic base. Much of the Torah instruction is driven by a concern that the land given by God should be securely inhabited by the people to whom God gave it: if the poor slide into destitution through debt, they will be forced to sell their land or (the ultimate horror) their children.[7] Care for the marginal represents anxiety for the survival of the community who belong to the land.

This is the frame for the instructions on debt cancellation in Deut. 15.1–11. Even if debt carries no interest, it traps the poor into a downward spiral, as property put up in security is lost through failure to repay; in the ancient world, unrepayable debt often led to flight, the sale of land or self-sale into slavery. The instructions in Deuteronomy 15 are utopian, and self-consciously so,[8] but they attempt to deal with the problem of

---

[5] I derive the label from J. Scott, *The Moral Economy of the Peasant: Rebellion and Subsistence in Southeast Asia* (New Haven, CT: Yale University Press, 1990).
[6] For analysis of the ANE tradition, see H. Bolkestein, *Wohltätigkeit und Armenpflege in vorchristlichen Altertum* (Utrecht: A Oosthoek Verlag, 1939). For the Hebrew Bible materials, see W. J. Houston, *Contending for Justice: Ideologies and Theologies of Social Justice in the Old Testament* (London: T&T Clark, 2006).
[7] For the sale of children into slavery, see Joel 3.1–6 (Hebrew 4.1–6); Neh. 5.1–5.
[8] Note the contrast between 'there will be no-one in need among you' (15.4) and 'there will never cease to be some in need upon the land' (15.11).

debt by cancelling it on a periodic basis, resetting the status quo every seven years. Three features are notable for our purposes:

1. First, the person whose debt is to be cancelled is repeatedly and emphatically described as 'your brother': in fact, 'neighbour' is redefined in these terms (15.2) and the label 'brother' is used multiple times in what follows (15.3, 7, 9, 11, 12).[9] Help is to be supplied 'if there is among you anyone in need, a brother in any of your towns within the land that the LORD your God is giving you' (15.7). 'Brother' is not primarily a matter of emotion: it categorizes the recipient in terms that carry the strongest moral and social obligations. The nation (contrasted with foreigners, 15.3) is here imagined in kinship terms, as if the circle of kin extends all the way out to the extremities of the community and all the way down to the bottom of its economic scale. As Houston writes, 'The appeal to brotherhood is not the result of the natural relationship of all Israelites: the relation of all Israelites as brothers (and sisters) is the result of the law's appeal to treat each other as such.'[10] Such laws *construct* the community by its responsibilities to the poor, through the label it accords them and the duties that attend that label. 'Brothers' here means all those in the land, within the covenant with God. But it is a term that will be easily transferred to other communities, and other types of community, within or outside the land.
2. The law on debt release is specific and connected to occupation of the land. But there are plenty of commands in this passage that could be generalized: 'Since there will never cease to be some in need in the land (or: on the earth), I therefore command you, "Open your hand to your poor and needy brother in your land"' (Deut. 15.11). The geographical notice is ambiguous, making such exhortations applicable anywhere. The instruction that one should lend even when the seventh year is close (15.9) is given a moral tone ('give willingly', 'do not be malicious'), which locates the motivation for obedience internally, within the 'heart' (15.7, 9), not externally in the law. Thus, even those not directly beholden to this law may be addressed by its exhortations, attuned (on other grounds) to its moral requirements.
3. Thirdly, divine reciprocation is built into the rationale of these instructions. Loans expect repayment (just as gifts expect a return gift), but the instruction to give a loan even when the year of cancellation is near (15.9–10) requires creditors to lend at the evident risk of losing their loan/gift.[11] How do you motivate someone to give/lend, even where there is little to no chance of a return? This is where God takes on a special role: God will judge you if you do not follow this instruction (negative reciprocity) and reward you if you do (positive reciprocity). If you are mean, 'your neighbour might cry to the LORD against you, and you

---

[9] The NRSV's gender-neutral 'member of the community' loses the valence of the original 'his/your brother' (Hebrew: אחיך; Greek: ὁ ἀδελφός σου). The label is found elsewhere in Deuteronomy (e.g. Deut. 17.15; 23.20–1) and is prominent in the Jubilee legislation (Leviticus 25).
[10] Houston, *Contending for Justice*, 183.
[11] Although the context is the cancellation of *debts*, the language of *gift* here is intertwined with debt, and sometimes dominant (e.g. 15.10).

would incur guilt. Give liberally, and be ungrudging when you do so, for on this account the LORD your God will bless you in all your work and in all that you undertake' (15.9–10). An appeal to God against you and over your head will bring dire results; but a loan given even when it might not be repaid will bring divine blessing. Deuteronomic theodicy – the assurance that God will punish evil and reward the good – is here of special importance when there is little to no prospect of a human return. There is an ultimate, full and guaranteed return in the form of divine blessing – here expected in this life, but open to interpretation later in an eschatological frame.[12]

Space precludes examining other scriptural traditions, which proved equally adaptable to different circumstances: the influential book of Proverbs, for instance, was not only altered in translation but also supplemented and adapted for many different contexts. Here we can consider just two examples where these scriptural traditions were recycled, selected and enhanced within the Jewish tradition, one from the homeland and one from the Diaspora.

A particularly intriguing example of social practice is reflected in the Damascus Document, which contains regulations for the partial pooling of resources among poor families. There is much about this text and those who drew it up that we cannot know, but it seems to represent an effort to create secure networks of mutual support among families in Judean villages.[13] Unlike the Qumran Rule of the Community, which concerns unmarried males pooling all of their goods, those who wrote and lived by the Damascus Document continued in family life, and retained private possessions.[14] But they were obviously dissatisfied with the brutal realities of normal economic life, characterized by 'wicked wealth' (CD VI.15) and a grasping Temple elite (CD VI.16–17), and they formed a pact to enact biblical social ideals by adding to their normal family self-support an extra layer of community solidarity.[15] The most

---

[12] For the importance of divine return, see G. A. Anderson, *Charity: The Place of the Poor in the Biblical Tradition* (New Haven, CT: Yale University Press, 2013). For its significance in early Christian texts (which in this sense retain the structure of reciprocity), see e.g. N. Eubank, *Wages of Cross-Bearing and Debt of Sin: The Economy of Heaven in Matthew's Gospel* (Berlin: de Gruyter, 2013); D. J. Downs, *Alms: Charity, Reward, and Atonement in Early Christianity* (Waco, TX: Baylor University Press, 2016).

[13] For discussion, see C. M. Murphy, *Wealth in the Dead Sea Scrolls and in the Qumran Community* (Leiden: Brill, 2002), 25–102. Most of the key information is found in the CD texts, but some additional details are found in the related Qumran texts (4Q266–273). I cite from CD-A unless otherwise indicated.

[14] Josephus and Philo, in their depictions of the Essenes, idealize something analogous to the total pooling found in the *Community Rule*: the abjuration of family life, a period of probation and the complete renunciation of personal property (Josephus, *War* 2.119–61; *Ant.* 18.18–22; Philo, *Omn. Prob. Lib.* 75–91; *Hyp.* 11.1–18). This requires the renunciation of marriage because of the clash in economic commitments that would ensue between family and community (Philo, *Hyp.* 11.14–17; and Josephus, *Ant.* 18.21, moralizing this matter with gender stereotypes). Both also use the language of 'brotherhood' (Josephus, *War* 2.122; Philo, *Omn. Prob. Lib.* 79) associating it with shared property (Josephus) and equality (Philo). Josephus refers to another, less demanding group, who allowed marriage, but he seems to know almost nothing about it (*War* 2.160–1).

[15] Their continuation of private wealth in households is evident in references to slaves, fields, debts, property and marriage (e.g. CD XII.10; XVI.17; IX.10–12; VI.6–7; 4Q271 3.1–10). For the origin of

fascinating part of this, for our purposes, is that they set aside 'holy portions' (קדשׁים, CD VI.20; perhaps an echo of the third tithe, Deut. 26.13), and pooled them under the authority of a supervisor (מבקר, CD XIII.7–9). The rule was to set aside two days' wages each month (so about 8 per cent of income), and to put that in the control of the supervisor who took the role of the father in a community of 'brothers' (CD VI.20; VII.1; XIII.9; XIV.5). This money would be used to support 'the injured' and 'the poor and needy', specifically 'the elder who is bent', 'the afflicted' (perhaps the long-term sick), 'the prisoner of a foreign people' (someone kidnapped and enslaved?), 'the girl who has no redeemer' (i.e. male relative able to pay her dowry) and 'the youth who has no-one looking after him' (the orphan; CD XIV.13–17). These categories of need require either major expense beyond the everyday expenditure of a family (the dowry, the ransom) or long-term cost (the afflicted, the orphan) – costs beyond the capacity of a poor family and their immediate circle of kin. These communities of fellow Jews banded together to form a social security network, with tight rules on admission, on the declaration of wealth and on the responsible use of property. Lev. 19.17–18 is a key text in this regulation, but it is striking that 'You shall love your neighbour as yourself' (Lev. 19.18) is altered to read 'You shall love *your brother* as yourself' (CD VI.20-1). It is the kinship language that best expresses the depth of mutual commitment in these groups, since kin are the innermost circle in the concentric circles of social relations, and those with the strongest and most open-ended obligations. The groups regulated by this Document may have been an unusual phenomenon on the Judean landscape, but in their heightened expression of Jewish ideals they demonstrate the significance of reliable networks and the innovative ways in which the Jewish tradition was developed to meet economic and social needs.[16]

The novel-like story of Tobit, which circulated in many textual forms, parades the example of a Jewish communal patron in the Diaspora.[17] As is made clear from the start, this is the story of a man who 'walked in the ways of truth and righteousness all the days of my life, and performed many acts of compassion on my brothers and my nation who went with me in exile to Ninevah' (1.3; cf. 1.16; 14.2).[18] The content of these deeds is variously described: sharing the third tithe with orphans and widows (1.8); giving food and clothing to those who lacked it (1.17; 4.16); sharing the Passover meal with the poor (2.2-3); and burying the dead who had been left unburied (1.17–18; 2.3-8). The text presents an elaborate parallel between the God who has 'mercy' (ἔλεος) on

---

this material, and its later redaction, see C. Hempel, *The Laws of the Damascus Document: Sources, Tradition and Redaction* (Leiden: Brill, 1988), 138–40.

[16] B. J. Capper has claimed, from uncertain evidence, that the Essene communities (both celibate and married) operated an extensive system of poor care throughout Judaea. For bibliography, and cogent arguments against Capper's theses, see T. J. Murray, *Restricted Generosity in the New Testament* (Tübingen: Mohr Siebeck, 2018), 120–9. There is no evidence, for instance, that the money pooled from wages in CD XIV would be used for anyone beyond the families who were bound together by commitment to abide by these rules.

[17] For the main textual traditions, see S. Weeks, S. Gathercole and L. Stuckenbruck (eds), *The Book of Tobit: Texts from the Principal Ancient and Medieval Traditions* (Berlin: de Gruyter, 2004). Following their notation, G1 stands for Codex Vaticanus and G2 for Sinaiticus.

[18] The phrase ἐλεημοσύνας πόλλας ἐποίησα suggests acts (not attitudes), and I translate 'acts of compassion'; the usual translations, 'almsgiving' or 'charity/charitable acts' evoke modern notions of one-way beneficence that do not fit the ancient context.

the people of Israel in exile (at least, on those who remain true to him; e.g. 3.1; 8.15-17; 13.1-17) and the righteous people who are themselves compassionate on their fellow Jews. The vicissitudes in Tobit's own life (reduced to poverty when he becomes blind) are a parable of the fact that no one could count themselves economically secure.

The acts of compassion detailed here are directed to those in, or on the edge of destitution, but they are not given randomly: they are channelled specifically to those labelled 'brothers' (ἀδελφοί). The text plays repeatedly on the kinship relations that are operative among Jews in the Diaspora, aided by the cherished tradition of Jewish endogamy (4.12-13; 7.1-13). Carefully directed acts of compassion not only recognize these ties but to some extent construct them. Tobias is instructed to find for the Passover meal 'any of our brothers in need, who are mindful of the Lord' (2.2), that is, those in good standing within the social-religious community of Jews. Later, Tobit gives a set of instructions on the performance of acts of compassion on 'all those who practise righteousness' (4.6-7 G1; cf. 4.17 G1: 'and not to sinners'). These social acts of support ensure the survival of members of the Jewish community whose lives were dislocated in the Diaspora and provide a network of care that stretches right across this community as an extended kinship of 'brothers'.[19] 'Brotherly' commitment to the poorest Jews serves as a 'clamp' to hold this diverse Diaspora community together.

This commitment is expressed in reciprocal benefits circulating among people who were intermittently in surplus or in need, as conditions changed. Tobit, the benefactor, when he is sick and unable to work, is himself the recipient of benefaction from his relatives, his wife and his wife's employers (2.10-14). When he suggests laying up good treasure for the day of 'necessity' (ἀνάγκη, 4.9 G1), he is probably speaking of the accrual of social credit: by helping others in need, they will feel obliged to help in return when you are in crisis yourself. The fact that the instruction to give applies to those who may have little to share, but are still instructed to give it (4.8 G1), indicates that such ties of reciprocity extend right through the community, as peer-to-peer benefaction, and are not just confined to the relations between rich patrons and poor beneficiaries. But behind and beyond human reciprocity there is also the guarantee of a divine return: 'Compassion, for those who practise it, is a good gift in the sight of God' (4.11 G1) and 'if you serve God, you will be repaid' (4.14 G1).[20] This repayment seems to be envisaged primarily as survival, or prosperity, in this life (as for Tobit). It is in this sense that acts of compassion 'deliver from death and keep you from going into the darkness' (4.10; 12.9-10): they keep you alive, by ensuring future support from others (as granted and guaranteed by God).[21] But in an eschatological register deliverance from death could mean other things besides, especially when it is combined with

---

[19] The use of the label 'brother' and the repeated references to the commandments of God (4.5) and the law of Moses (1.8; G2) indicate the influence of the Torah on this text, and perhaps specifically Deut. 15.1-11; see e.g. the reference to the non-begrudging eye (Deut. 15.10) in Tob. 4.7, 16 G1, noted by J. A. Fitzmyer, *Tobit* (Commentaries on Early Jewish Literature; Berlin: de Gruyter, 2003), 176. Thus the land-oriented instructions of the Torah are here adapted and applied to life in the Diaspora.

[20] Cf. the negative equivalent: 'If you do not turn your face away from the poor, the face of God will not be turned away from you' (4.7 G1).

[21] As Moore notes, 'There is … no hint here of belief in an afterlife' (C. A. Moore, *Tobit*, AB (New York: Doubleday, 1996), 168). For discussion of this Tobit text, and its parallels in Sirach, see Downs, *Alms*, 57-81.

'purging every sin' (12.9). Indeed, when Tobit is read, as scripture, by early Christians, the reward of rescue from death will be open to interpretation as a reference to eternal salvation.[22]

These two illustrations of the adaptable Jewish tradition indicate that 'reception' of Jewish tradition on this topic had been going on for centuries before the birth of the Christian movement. The varied materials were fluid and could be selected, developed or reframed in many different ways. What seems clear, however, is that the reception of these traditions helped constitute the identity of Jewish communities. Concern for the poor articulated their solidarity across economic differences, and its practice clarified the ties of responsibility that bound those communities with each other and with God. Thus, their reception and adaptation in early Christian communities means more than the development of a 'moral' tradition or practice. We are alerted to the fact that the ways in which Christian communities felt economically responsible for one another will index the forms in which *their* networks were constituted and defined.

Early Christian reception and its social significance

One could draw up an extensive inventory of evidence for the utilization and development of Jewish traditions regarding concern for the poor within the early Christian movement.[23] Jesus was remembered for prophetic-style critiques of the rich and for his pronouncement of blessings or good news regarding 'the poor' (e.g., Lk. 4.18, citing Isa. 61.1–2). James describes piety in scriptural terms as 'visiting orphans and widows in their distress' (Jas 1.27) and lambasts manipulative employers for their treatment of workers in terms drawn straight from the prophets (Jas 5.1–6). 2 Clement weaves material from Proverbs ('love covers a multitude of sins', Prov. 10.12) with motifs probably derived from Tobit ('fasting is better than prayers, and compassionate action is better than both,' 2 Clem. 16.4; cf. Tob. 12.8–9). Deuteronomy 15 makes its mark on a variety of texts: Acts 4.34 portrays the fulfilment of Deut. 15.4 ('there was no-one in need among them'), while the Synoptics have Jesus echo the conviction from the same passage that 'you will always have the poor among you,' though with different implications (Mk 14.7 and parallels; Deut. 15.11); 1 John shares its horror at 'closing one's heart' against one's 'brother' (1 Jn 3.17; Deut. 15.7). The passage in Isaiah 58 about the true 'fast' (sharing bread with the hungry, giving them clothes and accommodation and not neglecting 'relatives of your own kin') is a particular favourite in early Christian texts, cited by, for instance, Barnabas, Justin, Theophilus and Tertullian.[24]

---

[22] One of the earliest Christian allusions to Tobit may be Polycarp, *Phil.* 10.2, where the connection between almsgiving and deliverance from death is significant: *cum potestis benefacere, nollite differre, quia eleemosyna de morte liberat* (see discussion in Downs, *Alms*, 230–1). For the heavy use of this motif in Cyprian, see Downs, *Alms*, 233–71. I am grateful to Simon Gathercole for impressing on me at our Colloquium the importance of Tobit for early Christian reception of the Jewish tradition of support for the poor.

[23] I define as 'Christian' those whose cultural traditions, Jewish or non-Jewish, were inflected by allegiance to Jesus; my time limits are the first two centuries CE.

[24] Barn. 3.1–5; Justin, *Dial.* 15; *1 Apol.* 37.8; Theophilus, *Autol.* 3.12; Tertullian, *Marc.* 4.16.16; 17.8; 31.3; etc.

Where human reciprocation is unlikely or inappropriate, God is again invoked as the one who will give a return: 'your Father who sees in secret will reward you' (Mt. 6.4) and 'you will be blessed ... for you will be repaid at the resurrection of the righteous' (Lk. 14.14). As we shall see, the promise of an eschatological reward can change the evaluation of wealth itself, but the notion that concern for the poor is bound up with the community's relationship to God is a familiar Jewish motif now capable of fresh expression in a Christian mode (cf. Mt. 25.31–46, with Jesus as the new point of focus).

We can discuss here just two examples of Christian reception and will highlight their significance in the formation of communal identity. The first comes from the very first generation, concerning financial support by gentile assemblies for 'the poor among the saints' in Jerusalem; the second from the second century, when the Shepherd of Hermas attempts to forge Christian solidarity by directing the responsibilities of the rich.

Paul's assemblies constituted new networks of social belonging, sometimes cutting across and sometimes supplementing the household networks of believers. When Paul calls for the exercise of love in these assemblies, and 'having the same care for one another' (1 Cor. 12.25), this has real material significance, though in an informal and open-ended way, without institutionalized 'pooling'.[25] This is not normally expressed as caring for 'the poor', because most of these believers were themselves poor. Paul is calling for them to support one another, in their fluctuating conditions of surplus or need; he is not looking for patrons or wealthy individuals to act as benefactors towards the rest.[26] Thus the Thessalonian believer-artisans, whose θλῖψις must have had negative economic consequences, are urged to show φιλαδελφία to one another (again, the 'brother' language carries high expectations), to work with their own hands, and to be dependent on one another, not on outsiders (1 Thess. 4.9–12).[27] The Corinthians are chided for securing their own financial needs (or those of their families) to the detriment of their 'brothers' (1 Cor. 6.1–8) and are expected to practise the Lord's Supper as a shared meal (κοινόν not ἴδιον), as a ritualized signal of their material obligations to one other (1 Cor. 11.17–34). The Galatians are to 'bear one another's burdens' (Gal. 6.2), fulfilling the command to 'love your neighbour as yourself' (Gal. 5.14; Lev. 19.18). However, as in the Damascus Document, the title 'brother' normally takes the place of 'neighbour', since it carries more far-reaching expectations of 'good works' directed to 'the household of faith' (Gal. 6.10). Such instructions articulate a vision of assemblies as networks of mutual support, bound together through gift in recognition of one another as brothers (and sisters) 'in Christ'.

---

[25] Virtual pooling (a sense of common belonging, with undefined but real responsibilities for material support, as in Gal. 6.6) may be distinguished from actual pooling, such as we have noted in the Damascus Document; and that may operate across a spectrum from partial to complete pooling of resources. Luke's depiction of the practice among Jerusalem believers is hazy and historically uncertain (Acts 2–5); the first clear evidence of a permanent common fund, with financial oversight in its collection and distribution, comes from 1 Tim. 5.3–16 and Ignatius, *Pol.* 4.3.

[26] See B. W. Longenecker, *Remember the Poor: Paul, Poverty, and the Greco-Roman World* (Grand Rapids, MI: Eerdmans, 2010).

[27] For this reading of the paragraph, see R. Schellenberg, 'Subsistence, Swapping, and Paul's Ethic of Generosity', *JBL* 137 (2018), 215–34.

This vision is spelled out most extensively in relation to a programme of long-distance benefaction, a project requiring fulsome theological underpinning (e.g. in 2 Corinthians 8–9). At the Jerusalem conference (Gal. 2.1–10) there is agreement that the Antioch-based mission of Barnabas and Paul need not require gentiles to be circumcised, so long as they recognize their connection to the assemblies of Jews 'in Christ' established by the 'pillar' apostles. This bond (reflected in 'the right hand of κοινωνία', Gal. 2.9) is to be expressed in material terms: they (the Antioch-based network of assemblies) are to 'remember the poor' (Gal. 2.10), which (as in Rom. 15.26) means 'the poor' among the believers in Jerusalem. This poverty may be related to famines in Judaea (Josephus, *Ant.* 20.50–1), or may derive from the 'persecution' of believers in Judaea (i.e. the fracturing of networks), of which Paul was highly conscious (1 Thess. 2.14) and in which he had played a part (Gal. 1.23). In either case, this project, reflected in Acts 11.27–30, was a crucial symbol of unity among those who expressed allegiance to Christ as Messiah or Lord.[28] It cemented the commitment of non-Jewish believers to a Jerusalem-sourced movement, distinguishing the givers from other gentiles (they were uncircumcised but had a special relationship with Jerusalem) and the recipients from other Jews (the gift was given not to all Jews, but only to these). Just as gentile 'sympathizers' expressed their ties to the Jewish people by giving benefactions to Judaea, to the Temple or to local synagogue communities, so the gentile believers created by the Antioch mission were to articulate their links to the Jewish Christ-movement in this material form – though to Christ-believers only, not to entire synagogue communities nor to the 'nation' as a whole.[29]

To 'remember' the poor is not simply to recall their existence. The verb is freighted with the sense of social commitment and means both to assert a social bond and to activate it. As Brown puts it, 'To "remember," to "hold in the mind," was not to store away a fact: It was to assert a bond; it was to be loyal and to pay attention to somebody.'[30] Just as God 'remembered' his covenant (Exod. 6.15) or his covenant partners (Noah, Abraham, David, Gen. 8.1; 19.29; Ps. 132.1), or as Israelites 'remembered' their God (Ps. 42.8) or their Spartan 'brothers' (1 Macc. 2.11), so 'remembering' the poor indicates the activation of a social tie, across a distance in

---

[28] I take Gal. 2.10 to reflect an initial project, securing the relationship between Antioch believers and the 'assemblies in Christ' in Judaea (c.48–49 CE). Later, after his split with Antioch, Paul revived the idea of a Jerusalem-gift, adapting it for a different group of assemblies in his better-known collection for the 'saints' in Jerusalem (c.52–55 CE). Gal. 2.10 does not refer to that later collection but to an earlier expression of the same idea, where monetary support creates social solidarity between gentile believers and the church in Jerusalem. See discussion in D. J. Downs, *The Offering of the Gentiles: Paul's Collection for Jerusalem, in its Chronological, Cultural, and Cultic Contexts* (Tübingen: Mohr Siebeck, 2008), 33–59; M. C. de Boer, *Galatians: A Commentary* (Louisville, KY: Westminster John Knox Press, 2011), 126–8.

[29] For gentile benefactions, see the famine-relief of Helena of Adiabene (Josephus, *Ant.* 20.49–50; *War* 4.567; 5.55), and gifts to the Temple (b Yoma 38a; Josephus, *Ant.* 18.82); for gentile gifts to local Jewish communities, see Lk. 7.4; Acts 10.2, 22; Julia Severa in Acmonia (*MAMA* 6.264, first century CE).

[30] P. Brown, *The Ransom of the Soul: Afterlife and Wealth in Early Western Christianity* (Cambridge, MA: Harvard University Press, 2015), 39.

time, in geographical location or in social status.³¹ What is envisaged here is the recognition of a 'symbolic clamp' between believers in Christ across ethnic difference and geographical distance.³²

When Paul later revived this idea, and gave it fresh expression in the assemblies founded independently of Antioch, it is again clear that the gift ('for the poor among the saints in Jerusalem', Rom. 15.26) serves a material need *within the frame* of a social commitment. Paul envisages the Christian movement as spreading the 'good news' from Jerusalem (Rom. 15.19) and takes all gentile believers as therefore beholden, by a debt of gratitude, to those who granted them a share in these 'spiritual' benefits (Rom. 15.27). This is the law of reciprocity, once again, now operative across a geographical, political and ethnic gap, and after a considerable passage of time. As Ogereau has argued, if the Macedonians and Achaeans have agreed κοινωνίαν τινὰ ποιήσασθαι (Rom. 15.26), this does not mean something vague like 'share fellowship' or something overspecific like 'make a contribution': it concerns the creation of 'some kind of partnership or association with socio-political ramifications, which Paul envisaged between the gentile churches and their Jerusalem counterparts, and which would ultimately manifest itself in the form of a concrete monetary gift'.³³ Indeed, one might say, the gift constitutes the partnership that would otherwise be harder to recognize by either side. The difficulty that Paul had in eliciting this gift from his assemblies, and his fear lest it might not be accepted (Rom. 15.31), suggests that the partnership would only be effectuated through the success of this project.

Thus, here again, concern for 'the poor' is an expression of social responsibility and mutual belonging, but this time at a distance and in the service on a *new* social configuration which is established precisely through this concern. The very distance across which the link was established made the tie all the more significant. As Malkin has argued in relation to the long-distance ties created through Greek colonization,

> Awareness of 'sameness' occurs not when people are close to each other (in fact, that is when they pay particular attention to their differences) but when they are far apart. It is distance that creates the virtual centre. The more the connecting links are stretched, the stronger they become. The farther the shores of these maritime

---

³¹ This is one reason why I do not agree with Longenecker's reading of 'remember the poor' (Gal. 2.10) as Jerusalem's concern that Paul's gentile churches continue the Jewish tradition of concern for the poor in their immediate localities (Longenecker, *Remember the Poor*, 157–206). Generosity to the poor is never articulated in such terms in the Jewish tradition (Eccl. 9.15 is only an apparent exception: 'remember' there means recall from the past), while 'remembering' suggests a distance of some sort, and makes excellent sense if this is required from gentile converts at a geographical distance from Jerusalem. One does not have to revive the old thesis that the Jerusalem believers were known collectively as 'the poor' (Ebionim) to have Jerusalem require that Jewish and gentile Christ-believers in Antioch express their solidarity through a material contribution towards their urgent needs.
³² See J. S. Kloppenborg, *Christ's Associations* (New Haven, CT: Yale University Press, 2019), 245–64: 'As a performance of citizenship in a fictive translocal polity, [Paul's] *epidosis* constructed a polity that bridged a conspicuous ethnic and political chasm' (263).
³³ J. Ogereau, 'The Jerusalem Collection as κοινωνία: Paul's Global Politics of Socio-Economic Equality and Solidarity', *NTS* 58 (2012), 360–78, 371.

settlements, the closer the Greeks felt to one another. In other words, colonization was to a significant degree responsible for the rise of Hellenism.[34]

Something similar may be traced in Paul's collection for Jerusalem. In the first place, the intense diplomacy required for this collection tied (some of) Paul's assemblies together, linking Macedonia with Achaea and (theoretically) Galatia, and requiring delegates to be appointed to travel and to work with each other in this common cause (2 Cor. 8.16–24). But the direction of all this effort towards 'the saints' in Jerusalem was intended to tie them all collectively to Jerusalem, in what Paul envisaged would be an ongoing reciprocal sharing of surplus, where the excess of each side would meet the need of the other (2 Cor. 8.13–14).[35] Because this financial transfer was voluntary, its eventual collection meant so much more than a tax or tribute: it indicated active, willed engagement with Jerusalem. Despite the cultural and geographical distance, it indicated the holding of something significant in common. But because nothing like this had ever happened before – a monetary gift from *these* particular gentiles to *those* particular Jews (not Jerusalem in general but Jews who were labelled 'the saints') – this gift helped to establish a new social phenomenon, whose basis was common dependence on Christ.[36] In other words, a Jewish cultural tradition is here received and reapplied to create a new social entity, in which identity is subtly redefined.

The complexity of this phenomenon is evident in the way Paul frames this gift in terms that are both traditionally Jewish and reconfigured 'in Christ'. In the extended exhortation of 2 Corinthians 8–9, the reciprocity between Corinth and Jerusalem is explained in terms drawn from the manna incident in Exodus 16 (2 Cor. 8.14–15). The distribution of God-supplied surplus is demonstrated from Greek Psalm 111 (2 Cor. 9.9). Paul's stress on the spirit in which the gift is given has links both to motifs from Deuteronomy 15 (καθὼς προῄρηται τῇ καρδίᾳ, μὴ ἐκ λύπης, 2 Cor. 9.7; cf. Deut. 15.10: καὶ οὐ λυπηθήσῃ τῇ καρδίᾳ) and to the Greek form of Prov. 22.8, readapted to read 'God loves a cheerful giver' (ἱλαρὸν γὰρ δότην ἀγαπᾷ ὁ θεός, 2 Cor. 8.7). As in the Jewish tradition, God's agency as rewarder of gift is here prominent, with reciprocity built into Paul's expectations at multiple levels. But all of this is also newly framed by reference to the Christ-gift, with the first and strongest warrant being 'the gift (χάρις) of our Lord Jesus Christ, who because [or although] he was rich for your sakes became poor, so that by his poverty you might become rich' (2 Cor. 8.9). The foundational divine gift in this new frame is not the land but the 'inexpressible gift' of God in Christ

---

[34] I. Malkin, 'Networks and the Emergence of Greek Identity', *Mediterranean Historical Review* 18 (2003), 56–74, 59. Cf. I. Malkin, *A Small Greek World: Networks in the Ancient Mediterranean* (Oxford: Oxford University Press, 2011).

[35] For the reciprocal expectations, see J. M. G. Barclay, 'Manna and the Circulation of Grace: A Study of 2 Corinthians 8:1–15', in *The Word Leaps the Gap: Essays on Scripture and Theology in Honor of Richard B. Hays*, ed. J. R. Wagner, C. K. Rowe and A. K. Grieb (Grand Rapids, MI: Eerdmans, 2008), 409–26.

[36] For the label, 'the saints', probably the self-designation of Jerusalem Christians (derived, perhaps, from Daniel 7), see P. Trebilco, *Self-Designations and Group Identity in the New Testament* (Cambridge: Cambridge University Press, 2011), 140–6. The label gives the gift an additional sacral layer of significance, like the labelling of contributions in CD VI.20 as 'sacred portions' (see above).

(2 Cor. 9.15). The new Christological focus matches the new configuration of the people, who are clamped together by this practical gift.

Paul's project may have failed, but his instinct was right, that nothing would serve better to bind together the disparate elements of the new Jesus movement than the practice of gift to those in need of material resources. Elsewhere, we could trace the importance of shared meals and of hospitality, both given and refused, in the creation and delimitation of new Christian networks (2–3 John; Didache 11–12). Once concern for the poor is merged with the Christian discourse of love, it can take on a new and powerful set of resonances closely connected to the Christ-event and to the love expressed therein (1 John 3–4). The welcoming of visiting 'brothers' who were part of an authorized network now testifies to 'your love before the assembly' (3 John 6) – the practice of hospitality *constituting* the network, and not just reflecting it. The same social practices that solidified Diaspora communities (as seen in Tobit) knitted together networks of 'brothers in Christ', the same 'ethic' serving to constitute different (even if overlapping) networks.

One of the clearest illustrations of this effect may be found in the Shepherd of Hermas, which is throughout concerned with the reluctance of wealthier Christians to share their resources with poorer members of the church. The relentless emphasis of this document on repentance reflects the concern of the author(s) concerning 'half-hearted' commitment (διψυχία), a problem especially connected with 'the rich'. The second Parable (Similitude) is especially revealing in this regard and will form the focus of our discussion.

Similitude 2, on the symbiosis of the vine and the elm, articulates Hermas's vision for a community held together across socio-economic difference by the practice of care for the poor. Unlike the peer-to-peer support operative in the Pauline churches, here the structure is closer to informal patronage, as the rich seem to be securely better off than those they are instructed to aid. Although scholars dispute which is the vine and which the elm in this Similitude, I consider the vine, whose rotten fruit lies on the ground, to be the rich, whose spiritual fruitfulness is compromised by their wealth.[37] The essential point for our purposes is that the two constituents of the church are said to flourish only when they are bound together in reciprocal benefit. When the vine trails along the ground it bears only a little, rotten fruit: in the same way, 'the rich person has money, but is poor towards the Lord, since he is distracted by his wealth', his prayers being 'weak, small, and of no real effect' (Sim. 2.5 (51.5)). But just as the vine, when draped over the elm, produces good fruit, so the rich 'depend on' (ἐπαναπαύομαι) the poor, whose thanks and prayers to God are far more powerful (2.5 (51.5)). This latter notion draws on the biblical motif of God's attention to the prayers of the poor (Exod. 22.23; Deut. 15.9; 24.13, 15, etc.; cf. Hermas, Vis. 3.9.6 (17.6)), and the confidence that they are powerful may reflect the fact that those on the economic

---

[37] For discussion of the Parable, and its interpretation, see C. Osiek, *Rich and Poor in the* Shepherd of Hermas: *An Exegetical-Social Investigation* (Washington, DC: CBA, 1983), 78–90; C. Osiek, *The Shepherd of Hermas*, Hermeneia (Minneapolis, MN: Fortress, 1999), 161–4; M. Leutzsch, *Die Wahrnehmung sozialer Wirklichkeit im 'Hirten des Hermas'* (Göttingen: Vandenhoeck & Ruprecht, 1989), 113–37.

edge are liable to pray with particular intensity, and if they survive that itself shows that their prayers were effective. But if the rich depend on the poor in this regard, the poor depend on the rich for their material support. So 'those who are poor who pray to the Lord on behalf of the rich bring completion to their wealth (πληροφοροῦσι τὸ πλοῦτος αὐτῶν), while those who are rich and supply the poor with what they need bring completion to their lives' (πληροφοροῦσι τὰς ψυχὰς αὐτῶν, Sim. 2.8 (51.8)).

This formula encapsulates the reciprocity at the heart of this relationship. The wealthy are here presented as *needing* the prayers of the poor, because their own prayers are insufficient. Throughout the Shepherd of Hermas the wealthy are regarded as spiritually disabled, distracted from their service to God by their wealth and by the business that creates it: 'Those involved in numerous business dealings are also involved in numerous sins, since they are distracted by their affairs and do not serve as the Lord's slaves' (Sim. 4.5 (53.5)). When the poor pray for them they are also invoking God's involvement in this reciprocal relationship such that the generosity of the rich will be returned by God: 'He (the rich) believes that if he helps the poor he will be able to receive his reward from God' (Sim. 2.5 (51.5); 'he will not be abandoned by God, but will be recorded in the books of the living' (2.9 (51.9)).

But if the poor thus help the rich to make their wealth spiritually valuable, the rich serve the poor by keeping them alive. The Shepherd of Hermas is unusually blunt about the realities of poverty in the ancient world: it notes how malnutrition harms the body and causes it to waste away (Vis. 3.9.3 (17.3); cf. 3.13.2 (21.2)), while those who are destitute suffer such physical misery and psychological torment that they are inclined to commit suicide (Sim. 10.4.2–3 (114.2–3)). Elsewhere, clear instructions are given (echoing the biblical tradition) regarding generosity to the poor, giving to *everyone* who asks (Hermas, Man. 2.4–7 (27.4–7)), supporting widows and orphans (Man. 8.10 (38.10)), being a lenient creditor (Man. 8.10 (38.10)) and practising 'social fasting' (giving away the money one saves by going without food oneself, Sim. 5.3.7–8 (56.7–8)). Thus the wealth of the rich serves not a private (and therefore contestable) function, funding luxury, greed and immoderate desires. It serves a communal and sacred function, by keeping poor believers alive. And although the poor can provide, of course, no material return, and although there is no reference here to the honour that is the usual recompense of wealthy benefactors, the rich are assured that their generosity will be noticed by God.

Thus, once again, care for the poor serves to 'clamp' a society together, though now the social entity thus held in place is the church community in Rome. Where the Hebrew scriptures were concerned about the loss of the poor (to starvation, landlessness, slavery or flight), in the Shepherd of Hermas this tradition of concern for the poor preserves both the poor and the rich. The text frequently expresses anxiety lest wealthier Christians drift away from the church: their business dealings are liable to compromise their faith, both morally and religiously, causing them to 'deny their Lord' (Vis. 3.6.5 (14.5); Sim. 6.2.4 (62.4); 8.6.4 (72.4)). Socially, their wealth necessitates the cultivation of networks outside the church and ties them to 'the world', not least as patrons of non-believers. 'Entangled in their business dealings, they do not join themselves to the saints' (Sim. 8.8.1 (74.1)); gaining honour among 'gentiles' (γενόμενοι ἐνδοξότεροι παρὰ τοῖς ἔθνεσιν), 'they have abandoned the truth and have not joined themselves to the righteous, but lived with gentiles' (μετὰ τῶν ἐθνῶν συνέζησαν, Sim. 8.9.1 (75.1)). How does one tie such wealthy and well-connected people into the church? By persuading them to deploy their wealth *within the church* through supporting its poorer members. Wealthy Christians in the Roman churches (which were voluntary associations) had somewhere else to go. The Shepherd of Hermas uses the Jewish tradition of care for the poor to bind them into the Christian community by persuading them to make a deep financial commitment to its poorer members.

This was, one might think, a high-risk policy: if the church makes demands on the rich, they might have further reason to walk away. But the Shepherd of Hermas raises the stakes high. To hold onto one's wealth, or to invest it in homes, luxuries and the creation of more wealth, is not only to be greedy and selfish: it is also to invest in 'this age' and to put in jeopardy one's eternal salvation. This warning against those who are 'invested in this age, who rejoice in their wealth and do not cling to the good things yet to come' (Vis. 1.1.8 (1.8)), is elaborated in the first Parable (Similitude 1) which invokes the insecurity of foreigners who invest insecurely in their cities where they reside, while properly having greater loyalty to the laws and customs of their homeland. Building on Jewish eschatology, radicalized in relation to wealth, this Parable requires the rich to alienate themselves from their comfortable social conditions and to invest in the 'city' to which they will return:

> Instead of fields, then, purchase souls/lives (ψυχαί) that have been afflicted, insofar as you can, and take care of widows and orphans and do not neglect them; spend your wealth and all your furnishings for such fields and houses as you have received from God. For this is why your Master made you rich, that you may carry out these ministries for him. It is much better to purchase the fields, goods, and houses you find in your own city when you return to it. (Sim. 1.8–9 (50.8–9), with echoes of Mk 10.29–30 and parallels, and Lk. 16.9)

Care for the poor thus becomes an eschatological investment, which simultaneously secures the future of the rich, maintains the poor and strengthens the Christian community in Rome.

The examples chosen here can only be suggestive, but we may summarize our conclusions as follows:

1. The biblical traditions about care for the poor were sufficiently varied and adaptable to be received in multiple contexts and put to diverse uses. Their vocabulary and motifs received various modulations and developments in Jewish communities long before (and long after) they were received and deployed by the first Christians. Among Christians potent terms (e.g. 'brothers') could take on new meanings, and old motifs (reciprocity) acquire different, eschatological resonances. But that is no more 'novel' than the kinds of adaptation we find already in our Jewish sources.
2. In both Jewish and Christian traditions, the social uses of money are explicitly part of a sacred economy. Thus the theological warrants for generosity in

the Jewish tradition are taken over in early Christianity, but also adapted and developed in new ways. We have noted the specifically Christological connotations of gift in 2 Corinthians 8–9, and the newly inflected eschatology of the Shepherd of Hermas; other early Christian texts would offer further examples of a reshaped theology of money and gift. Such reframing of a long tradition is a classic feature of reception and is part and parcel of the new social configurations that developed in early Christianity.

3. We have emphasized that care for the poor is a *community-constituting* ethic, not primarily a matter of personal morality. Thus, the reception and reapplication of this tradition inevitably forged new communal identities. Financial practices of this sort created bonds of accountability and responsibility, and indexed the social allegiances of the rich. As the Christian movement self-consciously crossed ethnic boundaries and identified its internal commonality as shared allegiance to Christ, this Jewish tradition became constitutive of a movement that overlapped with, but did not wholly match, the Jewish communities who were its bearers. It tied gentile converts to some (but not all) Jews, and held together communities which had become largely or even purely gentile. In this new context, it served, as before, to support the poor in their struggle for survival, but it also clarified the social loyalties of the rich. In fact, in tracing the *social* meaning of this ethic, we have become conscious of how *different* communities, and different kinds of community, may be constituted by the creative reception of the very *same* tradition.[38]

---

[38] For its later, post-Constantinian, significance, see P. Brown, *Through the Eye of a Needle: Wealth, the Fall of Rome, and the Making of Christianity in the West, 350–550 AD* (Princeton, NJ: Princeton University Press, 2012).

Bibliography

Ackerman, Susan, 'The Blind, the Lame, and the Barren Shall Not Come into the House', in *Disability Studies and Biblical Literature*, ed. Candida R. Moss and Jeremy Schipper. New York: Palgrave Macmillan, 2011, 29–46.

Ahmed, Luise, *Bilder von den Anderen*, JAC Ergänzungsband Kleine Reihe 14. Münster: Aschendorff Verlag, 2016.

Aliau-Milhaud, Agnès, 'Progrès du texte, progrès de l'individu dans le Commentaire de Jean d'Origène: les techniques d'exégèse appliquées au thème du progrès', in *Origeniana Nona: Origen and the Religious Practice of His Time*, ed. Gyorgy Heidl and Robert Somos, BETL 228. Leuven: Peeters, 2009, 13–23.

Aliau-Milhaud, Agnès, 'La composition du prologue du Commentaire sur Jean d'Origène', *Adamantius* 22 (2016), 6–24.

Allert, Craig D., *Revelation, Truth, Canon and Interpretation: Studies in Justin Martyr's Dialogue with Trypho*, VC Sup. Leiden: Brill, 2002.

Allison, Dale C., 'A Plea for Thoroughgoing Eschatology', *JBL* 113 (1994), 651–68.

Allison, Dale C., *Constructing Jesus: Memory, Imagination, and History*. Grand Rapids, MI: Baker Academic Press, 2010.

Allison, Dale C., *The New Moses: A Matthean Typology*. Eugene: Wipf & Stock, 1993, repr. 2013.

Anderson, Gary A., *Sin: A History*. New Haven, CT: Yale University Press, 2009.

Anderson, Gary A., *Charity: The Place of the Poor in the Biblical Tradition*. New Haven, CT: Yale University Press, 2013.

Assmann, Jan, *Religion and Cultural Memory: Ten Studies*, trans. Rodney Livingstone. Stanford, CA: Stanford University Press, 2006.

Atkins, M., and R. Osborne (eds), *Poverty in the Roman World*. Cambridge: Cambridge University Press, 2006.

Attridge, H. W., *The Epistle to the Hebrews: A Commentary on the Epistle to the Hebrews*, Hermeneia. Philadelphia, PA: Fortress, 1989.

Aune, David E., *The Cultic Setting of Realized Eschatology in Early Christianity*, NovTSup 28. Leiden: Brill, 1972.

Aune, David E., *Revelation 17–22*, Word Biblical Commentary, vol. 52C. Nashville, TN: Thomas Nelson, 1998.

Bailey, J. W., 'The Temporary Messianic Reign in the Literature of Early Judaism', *JBL* 53 (1934), 170–87.

Baltzly, Dirk, 'Plato's Authority and the Formation of Textual Communities', *CQ* 64 (2014), 793–807.

Barclay, John M. G., 'Mirror-Reading a Polemical Letter: Galatians as a Test Case', *JSNT* 31 (1987), 73–97.

Barclay, John M. G., *Jews in the Mediterranean Diaspora from Alexander to Trajan (323 BCE–117 CE)*. Edinburgh: T&T Clark, 1996, repr. HCS 33, Berkeley: University of California Press, 2010.

Barclay, John M. G., 'Apologetics in the Jewish Diaspora', in *Jews in the Hellenistic and Roman Cities*, ed. John R. Bartlett. London: Routledge, 2002, 141–60.

Barclay, John M. G., *Against Apion*, Flavius Josephus, Translation and Commentary 10. Leiden: Brill, 2007.

Barclay, John M. G., 'Manna and the Circulation of Grace: A Study of 2 Corinthians 8:1–15', in *The Word Leaps the Gap: Essays on Scripture and Theology in Honor of Richard B. Hays*, ed. J. R. Wagner, C. K. Rowe and A. K. Grieb. Grand Rapids, MI: Eerdmans, 2008, 409–26.

Barclay, John M. G., 'Hostility to Jews as Cultural Construct: Egyptian, Hellenistic and Early Christian Paradigms', in *Josephus und das Neue Testament: Wechselseitige Wahrnehmungen. II. Internationales Symposium zum Corpus Judaeo-Hellenisticum. 25.–28. Mai 2006, Greifswald*, ed. Christfried Böttrich and Jens Herzer, WUNT 1/209. Tübingen: Mohr Siebeck, 2012, 365–85.

Barclay, John M. G., *Paul and the Gift*. Grand Rapids, MI: Eerdmans, 2015.

Bardy, G., and M. Lefèvre, *Hippolyte. Commentaire sur Daniel*, Sources Chrétiennes. Paris: Éditions du Cerf, 1947.

Barkman, Heather, 'Virgins, Monsters, Martyrs, and Prophets: Tertullian's Species of Women', *Ottawa Journal of Religion* 4 (2012), 41–57.

Barth, Fredrik, *Ethnic Groups and Boundaries: The Social Organization of Culture Difference*, Reissued. Long Grove, IL: Waveland Press, 1969, repr. 1998.

Bauer, Walter, 'Chiliasmus', in *RAC*, vol. 2, ed. Theodor Klauser. Stuttgart: Hiersemann, 1954, 1073–8.

BeDuhn, Jason David, '"Because of the Angels": Unveiling Paul's Anthropology in 1 Corinthians 11', *JBL* 118 (1999), 295–320.

Berchman, Robert M., *From Philo to Origen: Middle Platonism in Transition*, BJS 69. Chico, CA: Scholars, 1984.

Bertrand, D., 'Typologie des références à la Bible dans le Discours sur la prière', in *Origeniana Sexta: Origène et la Bible/Origen and the Bible*, ed. G. Dorrival and A. le Boulluec, BETL 118. Leuven: Peeters, 1995, 229–41.

Best, Ernest, *A Critical and Exegetical Commentary on Ephesians*, ICC 39.1. Edinburgh: Clark, 1998.

Betcher, Sharon V., 'Disability and the Terror of the Miracle Tradition', in *Miracles Revisited: New Testament Miracle Stories and Their Concepts of Reality*, ed. Stefan Alkier and Annette Weissenrieder. Berlin: de Gruyter, 2013, 161–81.

Bietenhard, Hans, *Caesarea, Origenes und die Juden*. Stuttgart: Kohlhammer, 1974.

Black, Matthew, 'The Patristic Accounts of Jewish Sectarianism', *BJRL* 41 (1959), 285–303.

Blischke, Folker, 'Die *Sapientia Salomonis* und Paulus', in *Sapientia Salomonis (Weisheit Salomos)*, ed. Karl-Wilhelm Niebuhr. Tübingen: Mohr Siebeck, 2015, 273–91.

Bloom, Harold, *The Anxiety of Influence: A Theory of Poetry*. New York: Oxford University Press, 1973.

Bobichon, Philippe, 'Autorités religieuses juives et «sectes» juives dans l'œuvre de Justin Martyr', *Revue des Études Augustiniennes* 48 (2002), 3–22.

Bobichon, Philippe, *Justin Martyr, Dialogue avec Tryphon: Édition critique, traduction, commentaire*, 2 vols, Paradosis. Fribourg: Éditions universitaires de Fribourg, 2003.

Bobichon, Philippe, 'Composite Features and Citations in Justin Martyr's Textual Composition', in *Composite Citations in Antiquity Volume 1: Jewish, Graeco-Roman, and Early Christian Uses*, ed. Sean A. Adams and Seth M. Ehorn, LNTS. London: Bloomsbury, 2016, 158–81.

Böcher, Otto, 'Wasser und Geist', in *Verborum Veritas: Festschrift für Gustav Stählin zum 70. Geburtstag*, ed. Otto Böcher and Klaus Haacker. Wuppertal: Theologischer Verlag Rolf Brockhaus, 1970, 197–209.
Bodsch, I., 'Sacrarium Agrippinae', in *Ornamenta Ecclesiae. Kunst und Künstler der Romanik in Köln*, vol. 2, ed. A. Legner. Köln: Schnütgen-Museum, 1985, 157–78.
den Boeft, J., and J. N. Bremmer, 'Notiunculae Martyrologicae IV', *VigChr* 45 (1991), 105–22.
de Boer, Martinus C., *Johannine Perspectives on the Death of Jesus*, Contributions to Biblical Exegesis and Theology 17. Kampen: Kok Pharos, 1996.
de Boer, Martinus C., *Galatians: A Commentary*. Louisville, KY: Westminster John Knox Press, 2011.
Böhlemann, Peter, *Jesus und der Täufer. Schlüssel zur Theologie und Ethik des Lukas*, SNTSMS 99. Cambridge: Cambridge University Press, 1997.
Bolkestein, H., *Wohltätigkeit und Armenpflege in vorchristlichen Altertum*. Utrecht: A Oosthoek Verlag, 1939.
Bovon, François, *A Commentary on the Gospel of Luke*, 3 vols, trans. Christine M. Thomas, Donald S. Deer and James Crouch, Hermeneia. Minneapolis, MN: Fortress, 2002–13.
Boyarin, Daniel, *A Radical Jew: Paul and the Politics of Identity*. Berkeley: University of California Press, 1994.
Boyarin, Daniel, 'Justin Martyr Invents Judaism', *Church History* 70.3 (2001), 427–61.
Boyarin, Daniel, *Border Lines: The Partition of Judaeo-Christianity*. Philadelphia: University of Pennsylvania Press, 2004.
Boyd-Taylor, Cameron, 'Afterlives of the Septuagint: A Christian Witness to the Greek Bible in Byzantine Judaism', in *The Jewish-Greek Tradition in Antiquity and the Byzantine Empire*, ed. James Aitken and James Carleton Paget. Cambridge: Cambridge University Press, 2014, 135–51.
Brawley, R., 'Discourse Structure and the Unseen in Hebrews 2:8 and 11:1. A Neglected Aspect of the Context', *CBQ* 55 (1993), 81–98.
Briggs, Charles Augustus, *The Messiah of the Gospels*. New York: C. Scribner's, 1894.
Bright, P., 'Origenian Understanding of Martyrdom and its Biblical Framework', in *Origen of Alexandria: His Work and His Legacy*, ed. C. Kannengiesser and W. Petersen. Notre Dame, IN: University of Notre Dame Press, 1988, 180–99.
Brouwer, Jacob, 'Gott, Christus, Engel, Männer und Frauen: Chronologisch-thematische Bibliographie zu 1Kor 11,2–16', in *Frauen, Männer, Engel: Perspektiven zu 1Kor 11,2–16*, ed. Torsten Jantsch, BTS 152. Neukirchen-Vluyn: Neukirchener Theologie, 2015, 187–235.
Brown, Peter, *The Body and Society: Men, Women, and Sexual Renunciation in Early Christianity*. London: Faber and Faber, 1988.
Brown, Peter, *Poverty and Leadership in the Later Roman Empire*. Hanover: University Press of New England, 2002.
Brown, Peter, *Through the Eye of a Needle: Wealth, the Fall of Rome, and the Making of Christianity in the West, 350–550 A.D.* Princeton, NJ: Princeton University Press, 2012.
Brown, Peter, *The Ransom of the Soul: Afterlife and Wealth in Early Western Christianity*. Cambridge, MA: Harvard University Press, 2015.
Brown, Raymond E., *The Gospel According to John*, AB 29 & 29A. Garden City, NY: Doubleday, 1966–70.
Brown-Tkacz, C., 'The Seven Maccabees, Three Hebrews and a Newly Discovered Sermon of St. Augustine (Mayence 50)', *REA* 41 (1995), 59–78.

Byrskog, Samuel, *Jesus the Only Teacher: Didactic Authority and Transmission in Ancient Israel, Ancient Judaism and the Matthean Community*, ConBNT 24. Stockholm: Almqvist & Wiksell, 1994.
Callaway, Philip R., *The History of the Qumran Community*, JSPSup 3. Sheffield: JSOT Press, 1988.
Carter, Warren, *Households and Discipleship: A Study of Matthew 19–20*, JSNTSS 105. Sheffield: JSOT Press, 1994.
Castro Varela, María do Mar, and Nikita Dhawan, *Postkoloniale Theorie: Eine kritische Einführung*, BibS(N) 12. Bielefeld: Transcript, 2005.
Cataldo, Jeremiah W., 'The Other: Sociological Perspectives in a Post-Colonial Age: Imagining and Remembering the Other and Constructing Israelite Identities in the Early Second Temple Period', in *Imagining the Other and Constructing Israelite Identity in the Early Second Temple Period*, ed. Ehud Ben Zvi, LHBOTS 591. London: Bloomsbury, 2014, 1–9.
Charlesworth, James H., *The Pesharim and Qumran History: Chaos or Consensus?* Grand Rapids, MI: Eerdmans, 2002.
Charlesworth, James H., and Loren L. Johns, *Hillel and Jesus: Comparisons of Two Major Religious Figures*. Philadelphia, PA: Fortress, 1997.
Clements, Ruth, 'Peri Pascha: Passover and the Displacement of Jewish Interpretation within Origen's Exegesis', PhD diss., Harvard Divinity School, 1997.
Clements, Ruth, 'Origen's Hexapla and Christian-Jewish Encounter in the Second and Third Centuries', in *Religious Rivalries and the Struggle for Success in Caesarea Maritima*, ed. Terence L. Donaldson. Waterloo: Wilfrid Laurier Press, 2000, 303–29.
Cocchini, Franchesca, *Il Paolo di Origene: Contributo alla storia della ricezione delle epistole paoline nel III secolo*, Verba Seniorum 11. Rome: Edizioni Studium, 1992.
Cohen, Shaye J. D., 'Yavneh Revisited: Pharisees, Rabbis and the End of Jewish Sectarianism', in *Society of Biblical Literature 1982 Seminar Papers*, ed. Keith Harold Richards, SBL Seminar Papers. Chico, CA: Scholars Press, 1983, 45–61.
Cohen, Shaye J. D., 'Were Pharisees and Rabbis the Leaders of Communal Prayer and Torah Study in Antiquity? The Evidence of the New Testament, Josephus, and the Early Church Fathers', in *Evolution of the Synagogue: Problems and Progress*, ed. Howard Clark Kee and Lynn H. Cohick. Harrisburg: Trinity Press International, 1999, 89–105.
Cohick, Lynn, 'Virginity Unveiled: Tertullian's Veiling of Virgins and the Historical Women in the First Three Centuries A.D.', *AUSS* 45 (2007), 19–34.
Collins, D. J., 'The Renaissance of the Maccabees: Old Testament Jews, German Humanists, and the Cult of the Saints in Early Modern Cologne', in *Dying for the Faith, Killing for the Faith*, ed. G. Signori. Leiden: Brill, 2012, 209–45.
Collins, John J., *Jewish Wisdom in the Hellenistic Age*. Edinburgh: T&T Clark, 1997.
Collins, John J., *Between Athens and Jerusalem: Jewish Identity in the Hellenistic Diaspora*, 2nd edn, The Biblical Resource Series. Grand Rapids, MI: Eerdmans, 2000.
Collins, Matthew A., *The Use of Sobriquets in the Dead Sea Scrolls*, LSTS 67. London: Bloomsbury, 2009.
Cooper, Kate, *The Virgin and the Bride: Idealized Womanhood in Late Antiquity*. Cambridge, MA: Harvard University Press, 1996.
Cope, Lamar A., *Matthew: A Scribe Trained for the Kingdom of Heaven*, CBQMS 15. Washington, DC: Catholic Biblical Association, 1976.
D'Angelo, Mary Rose, 'Veils, Virgins, and the Tongues of Men and Angels: Women's Heads in Early Christianity', in *Off with Her Head! The Denial of Women's Identity*

in *Myth, Religion, and Culture*, ed. Howard Eilberg-Schwartz and Wendy Doniger. Berkeley: University of California Press, 1995, 131–64.
Daniel-Hughes, Carly, '"Wear the Armor of Your Shame!": Debating Veiling and the Salvation of the Flesh in Tertullian of Carthage', *SR* 39 (2010), 179–201.
Daniel-Hughes, Carly, *The Salvation of the Flesh in Tertullian of Carthage: Dressing for the Resurrection*. New York: Palgrave Macmillan, 2011.
Daniel-Hughes, Carly, 'We Are Called to Monogamy: Marriage, Virginity, and the Resurrection of the Fleshly Body in Tertullian of Carthage', in *Coming Back to Life: The Permeability of Past and Present, Mortality and Immortality, Death and Life in the Ancient Mediterranean*, ed. Fred Tappenden and Carly Daniel-Hughes. Montreal: McGill University Library, 2017, 239–65.
Danielou, Jean, *The Theology of Jewish Christianity*. London: Darton, Longman and Todd, 1964.
Davies, Philip R., 'The Teacher of Righteousness and the "End of Days"', in *Sects and Scrolls: Essays on Qumran and Related Topics*, SFSHJ 134. Atlanta, GA: Scholars Press, 1996, 89–94.
Davies, W. D., and D. A. Allison, *Matthew*, 3 vols, ICC. Edinburgh: T&T Clark, 1988.
Dawson, John David, *Christian Figural Reading and the Fashioning of Identity*. Berkeley: University of California Press, 2001.
DeSilva, D., 'An Example of How to Die Nobly for Religion: The Influence of 4 Maccabees on Origen's Exhortatio ad Martyrium', *JECL* 17 (2009), 337–55.
Dibelius, Martin, *Die urchristliche Überlieferung von Johannes der Täufer*, FRLANT 15. Göttingen: Vandenhoeck & Ruprecht, 1911.
von Dobschütz, Ernst, 'Matthew as Rabbi and Catechist', trans. Robert Morgan, in *The Interpretation of Matthew*, 2nd edn, ed. Graham Stanton. Edinburgh: T&T Clark, 1995, 27–38.
Dorman, Anke, 'The Other Others: A Qumran Perspective on Disability', in *Imagining the Other and Constructing Israelite Identity in the Early Second Temple Period*, ed. Ehud Ben Zvi and Diana Vikander Edelman. London: T&T Clark, 2014, 297–316.
Downs, D. J., *The Offering of the Gentiles: Paul's Collection for Jerusalem, in Its Chronological, Cultural, and Cultic Contexts*. Tübingen: Mohr Siebeck, 2008.
Downs, D. J., *Alms: Charity, Reward, and Atonement in Early Christianity*. Waco, TX: Baylor University Press, 2016.
Drake, Susanna, *Slandering the Jew: Sexuality and Difference in Early Christian Texts*. Philadelphia: University of Pennsylvania Press, 2013.
Drewermann, Eugen, *Das Markusevangelium*. 2 vols. Olten: Walter Verlag, 1987–8.
den Dulk, Matthijs, *Between Jews and Heretics: Refiguring Justin Martyr's Dialogue with Trypho*. London: Routledge, 2018.
den Dulk, Matthijs, 'Justin Martyr and the Authorship of the Earliest Anti-Heretical Treatise', *VC* 72.4 (2018), 471–83.
Dunderberg, Ismo, 'Moral Progress in Early Christian Stories of the Soul', *NTS* 59.2 (2013), 247–67.
Dunn, Geoffrey D., 'Rhetoric and Tertullian's *de Virginibus Velandis*', *VC* 59 (2005), 1–30.
Dunn, James D. G., *Baptism in the Holy Spirit*. London: SCM, 1970.
Dunn, James D. G., *The Partings of the Ways between Christianity and Judaism and their Significance for the Character of Christianity*, 2nd edn. London: SCM, 2006.
Eastman, David L., *Paul the Martyr: The Cult of the Apostle in the Latin West*. Atlanta, GA: Society of Biblical Literature, 2011.

Edsall, Benjamin A., 'Greco-Roman Costume and Paul's Fraught Argument in 1 Corinthians 11.2–16', *JGRChJ* 9 (2013), 132–46.
Edsall, Benjamin A., *Paul's Witness to Formative Christian Instruction*, WUNT 2/365. Tübingen: Mohr Siebeck, 2014.
Edwards, Catharine, *The Politics of Immorality in Ancient Rome*. Cambridge: Cambridge University Press, 1993.
Edwards, Mark J., 'Origen on Christ, Tropology, and Exegesis', in *Metaphor, Allegory, and the Classical Tradition: Ancient Thought and Modern Revisions*, ed. G. R. Boys-Stones. Oxford: Oxford University Press, 2003, 235–56.
Eisenbaum, P. M., *The Jewish Heroes of Christian History: Hebrews 11 in Literary Context*, SBLDS 156. Atlanta, GA: Scholars Press, 1997.
El Mansy, Aliyah, *Exogame Ehen: Die traditionsgeschichtlichen Kontexte von 1 Kor 7,12–16*, BWANT 206. Stuttgart: W. Kohlhammer, 2015.
Erdman, D. V., *The Complete Poetry and Prose of William Blake: Newly Revised Edition*, Anchor Books. New York: Doubleday, 1988.
Ernst, Josef, *Johannes der Täufer: Interpretation – Geschichte – Wirkungsgeschichte*, BZNW 53. Berlin: de Gruyter, 1989.
Eubank, N., *Wages of Cross-Bearing and Debt of Sin: The Economy of Heaven in Matthew's Gospel*. Berlin: de Gruyter, 2013.
von Euw, A., 'Die Makkabäerbrüder. Spätjüdische Märtyrer der christlichen Märtyrerverehrung', in *Monumenta Judaica. 2000 Jahre Geschichte und Kultur der Juden am Rhein, Handbuch*, vol. 1, ed. K. Schilling. Cologne: Kölnisches Stadtmuseum, 1963, 782–6.
Evans, Robert, *Reception History, Tradition and Biblical Interpretation: Gadamer and Jauss in Current Practice*. Scriptural Traces: Critical Perspectives on the Reception and Influence of the Bible 4. London: Bloomsbury T&T Clark, 2014.
Eyl, Jennifer, 'The Apocryphal Acts of the Apostles', in *The Oxford Handbook of New Testament, Gender and Sexuality*, ed. Benjamin Dunning. Oxford: Oxford University Press, 2019, 387–406.
Fabian, Johannes, *Time and the Other: How Anthropology Makes Its Object*, repr. New York: Columbia University Press, 2014.
Falls, Thomas B., and Thomas P. Halton (trans.), *St. Justin Martyr: Dialogue with Trypho*, Selections from the Fathers of the Church 3. Washington, DC: Catholic University of America Press, 2003.
Farmer, William, and Denis Farkasfalvy. *The Formation of the New Testament Canon*. New York: Paulist, 1983.
Fee, Gordon D., *The First Epistle to the Corinthians*, NICNT. Grand Rapids, MI: Eerdmans, 1987.
Felski, Rita, *The Limits of Critique*. Chicago: University of Chicago Press, 2015.
Ferguson, Everett, *The Early Church at Work and Worship: Volume 2. Catechesis, Baptism, Eschatology, and Martyrdom*. Cambridge: James Clarke & Co, 2014.
Finney, Mark, 'Honour, Head-Coverings and Headship: 1 Corinthians 11.2–16 in Its Social Context', *JSNT* 22 (2010), 31–58.
Fitzmyer, J. A., *Tobit*, Commentaries on Early Jewish Literature. Berlin: de Gruyter, 2003.
Foucault, Michel, *The Archaeology of Knowledge*. New York: Pantheon Books, 1969, repr. 1972.
Fredriksen, Paula, 'Origen and Augustine on Paul and the Law', in *Law and Lawlessness in Early Judaism and Early Christianity*, ed. David Lincicum et al., WUNT 1/420. Tübingen: Mohr Siebeck, 2019, 67–88.

Frend, W. H. C., *Martyrdom and Persecution in the Early Church: A Study of a Conflict from the Maccabees to Donatus*. Oxford: Blackwell, 1965.
Friedrich, G., *Die Verkündigung des Todes Jesu im Neuen Testament*, Biblisch-Theologische Studien 6. Neukirchen-Vluyn: Neukirchener Verlag, 1982.
Froehlich, Karlfried, 'Montanism und Gnosis', *Orientalia Christiana Analecta* 195 (1973), 91–111.
Gaca, Kathy L., *The Making of Fornication: Eros, Ethics and Political Reform in Greek Philosophy and Early Christianity*, HCS 39. Berkeley: University of California Press, 2003.
Gallagher, E. L., and J. Meade, *The Biblical Canon Lists from Early Christianity: Texts and Analysis*. Oxford: Oxford University Press, 2017.
Gamble, Harry Y., *Books and Readers in the Early Church: A History of Early Christian Texts*. New Haven, CT: Yale University Press, 1995.
Gamble, Harry Y., 'The Book Trade in the Roman Empire', in *The Early Text of the New Testament*, ed. Charles E. Hill and Michael J. Kruger. Oxford: Oxford University Press, 2012, 23–36.
García Martínez, Florentino, 'The Origins of the Essene Movement and of the Qumran Sect', in *The People of the Dead Sea Scrolls*, ed. F. García Martínez and J. Trebolle Barrera, trans. W. G. E. Watson. Leiden: Brill, 1995, 77–96.
García Martínez, Florentino, and Eibert J. C. Tigchelaar (ed.), *The Dead Sea Scrolls Study Edition*, 2 vols. Leiden: Brill, 1997–8.
Gardner, G. E., *The Origins of Organized Charity in Rabbinic Judaism*. Cambridge: Cambridge University Press, 2015.
Gardner, Jane F., *Frauen im antiken Rom: Familie, Alltag, Recht*. München: C. H. Beck, 1995.
Gathercole, Simon J., 'The Alleged Anonymity of the Canonical Gospels', *JTS* 69 (2018), 447–76.
Georges, Tobias, '"… herrlichste Früchte echtester Philosophie." – Schulen bei Justin und Origenes, im frühen Christentum sowie bei den zeitgenössischen Philosophen', *Millennium* 11.1 (2014), 23–38.
Gerber, Christine, 'Die alte Braut und Christi Leib: Zum ekklesiologischen Entwurf des Epheserbriefs', *NTS* 59.2 (2013), 192–221.
Gerber, Christine, 'Paulus als Ökumeniker: Die Interpretation der paulinischen Theologie durch den Epheserbrief', in *Reception of Paul in Early Christianity: The Person of Paul and His Writings through the Eyes of His Early Interpreters*, ed. Jens Schröter, BZNW 234. Berlin: de Gruyter, 2018, 317–54.
Gerson, Lloyd, 'The Myth of Plato's Socratic Period', *Archiv für Geschichte der Philosophie* 96 (2014), 403–30.
Gese, Michael, *Das Vermächtnis des Apostels: Die Rezeption der paulinischen Theologie im Epheserbrief*, WUNT 2/99. Tübingen: Mohr Siebeck, 1997.
Gögler, Rolf, *Zur Theologie des biblischen Wortes bei Origenes*. Düsseldorf: Patmos-Verlag, 1963.
Gonzalez, Eliezer, *The Fate of the Dead in Early Third Century North African Christianity*. Tübingen: Mohr Siebeck, 2014.
Goodenough, Erwin R., *An Introduction to Philo Judaeus*, 2nd edn. Lanham, MD: University Press of America, 1962, repr. 1986.
Goodman, Martin, 'Sacred Scripture and "Defiling the Hands"', *JTS* 41 (1990), 99–107.
Goodman, Martin, *Judaism in the Roman World: Collected Essays*. Leiden: Brill, 2007.

Gorman, Robert J., and Vanessa B. Gorman, *Corrupting Luxury in Ancient Greek Literature*. Ann Arbor: University of Michigan Press, 2014.

Gosbell, Louise A., *'The Poor, the Crippled, the Blind, and the Lame': Physical and Sensory Disability in the Gospels of the New Testament*, WUNT 2/469. Tübingen: Mohr Siebeck, 2018.

Greer, R. A. (ed. and trans.), *Origen: An Exhortation to Martyrdom, Prayer, First Principles. Book IV, Prologue to the Commentary on the Song of Songs, Homily XXVII on Numbers*, CWS. London: SPCK, 1979.

Gregerman, Adam, *Building on the Ruins of the Temple: Apologetics and Polemics in Early Christianity and Rabbinic Judaism*, TSAJ. Tübingen: Mohr Siebeck, 2016.

Greschat, Katharina, '"Worte Gottes, verkündigt von den Aposteln": Evangelienzitate bei Justin', in *Gospels and Gospel Traditions in the Second Century: Experiments in Reception*, ed. Jens Schröter, Tobias Nicklas and Joseph Verheyden, BZNW 235. Berlin: de Gruyter, 2019, 175–91.

Guéraud, Octave, and Nautin, Pierre (eds), *Origène: Sur la Pâque: Traité inédit publié d'après un papyrus de Toura*. Paris: Beauschesne, 1979.

Guillaumin, M.-L., 'Une jeune fille qui s'appelait Blandine', in *Epektasis: Mélanges patristiques offerts au Cardinal J. Daniélou*, ed. J. Fontaine and C. Kannengiesser. Paris: Beauchesne, 1972, 93–8.

Gundry-Volf, Judith M., 'Gender and Creation in 1 Corinthians 11:2–16: A Study in Paul's Theological Method', in *Evangelium-Schriftauslegung-Kirche: Festschrift für Peter Stuhlmacher zum 65. Geburtstag*, ed. Jostein Ådna et al. Göttingen: Vandenhoeck & Ruprecht, 1997, 151–71.

Guyot, P., and R. Klein, *Das frühe Christentum bis zum Ende der Verfolgungen: eine Dokumentation*, vol. 1, Texte zur Forschung 60. Darmstadt: Wissenschaftliche Buchgesellschaft, 1994.

Hagner, D. A., *Hebrews*, NIBC 14. Peabody, MA: Hendrickson, 1990.

Hall, Stuart, 'New Ethnicities', in *'Race', Culture and Difference*, ed. James Donald. London: Sage, 1992, 252–9.

Hamm, D., 'Faith in the Epistle to the Hebrews: The Jesus Factor', *CBQ* 52 (1990), 270–91.

von Harnack, Adolf, *The Expansion of Christianity in the First Three Centuries*, 2 vols, trans. James Moffatt. London: Williams & Norgate, 1904.

von Harnack, Adolf, *Ist die Rede des Paulus in Athens ein ursprünglicher Bestandteil der Apostelgeschichte? Judentum und Judenchristentum in Justins Dialogue mit Trypho, nebst einer Collation der Pariser Handschrift Nr. 450*, TU. Leipzig: Hinrichs, 1913.

Hartmann, P., 'Origène et la théologie du martyre d'après le PROTREPTIKOS de 235', *ETL* 34 (1958), 773–824.

Heath, Jane, '"Textual Communities": Brian Stock's Concept and Recent Scholarship on Antiquity', in *Scriptural Interpretation at the Interface between Education and Religion: In Memory of Hans Conzelmann*, ed. Florian Wilk. Leiden: Brill, 2019, 5–34.

Heine, Ronald E., *Origen: Scholarship in Service of the Church*. New York: Oxford University Press, 2010.

Heither, Theresia, *Translatio Religionis: Die Paulusdeutung des Origenes in seinem Kommentar zur Römerbrief*. Cologne: Bohlau, 1990.

Hellholm, David, 'Ailments of Immortality in the Afterlife: Apocalyptic and Eschatological Notions of Eternal Life', in *The Eucharist – Its Origins and Contexts. Sacred Meal, Communal Meal, Table Fellowship in Late Antiquity, Early Judaism, and Early Christianity*, ed. David Hellholm and Dieter Sanger. Tübingen: Mohr Siebeck, 2017, 1851–90.

Hempel, C., *The Laws of the Damascus Document: Sources, Tradition and Redaction*. Leiden: Brill, 1988.

Hengel, Martin, *The Zealots: Investigations into the Jewish Freedom Movement in the Period from Herod I until 70 A.D*. Edinburgh: T&T Clark, 1961, repr. 1989.

van Henten, J. W., 'The Tradition-Historical Background of Rom. 3.25: A Search for Pagan and Jewish Parallels', in *From Jesus to John: Essays on Jesus and New Testament Christology in Honour of Marinus de Jonge*, ed. M. C. de Boer, JSNTSup 84. Sheffield: JSOT Press, 1993, 101–28.

van Henten, J. W., 'Zum Einfluß jüdischer Martyrien auf die Literatur des frühen Christentums (2: Die Apostolischen Väter)', in *Aufstieg und Niedergang der römischen Welt II.27/1*, ed. W. Haase and H. Temporini. Berlin: de Gruyter, 1993, 700–23.

van Henten, J. W., *The Maccabean Martyrs as Saviours of the Jewish People: A Study of 2 and 4 Maccabees*, JSJSup 57. Leiden: Brill, 1997.

van Henten, J. W., 'The Christianization of the Maccabean Martyrs: The Case of Origen', in *Martyrdom and Persecution in Late Ancient Christianity: Festschrift Boudewijn Dehandschutter*, ed. J. Leemans, BETL 241. Leuven: Peeters, 2010, 333–52.

van Henten, J. W., 'The Reception of Daniel 3 and 6 and the Maccabean Martyrdoms in Hebrews 11:33–38', in *Myths, Martyrs, and Modernity: Studies in the History of Religions in Honour of Jan N. Bremmer*, ed. J. Dijkstra et al. Leiden: Brill, 2010, 359–77.

van Henten, J. W., 'The Passio Perpetuae and Jewish Martyrdom: The Motif of Motherly Love', in *Perpetua's Passions: Multidisciplinary Approaches to the Passio Perpetuae et Felicitatis*, ed. J. Bremmer and M. Formisano. Oxford: Oxford University Press, 2012, 118–33.

van Henten, J. W., and H. Walvoort, 'The Re-Interpretation of the Maccabean Mother and Her Sons by Frater Magdalius Iacobus Gaudensis in the Framework of the Cult of the Maccabees in Cologne', *LIAS* 46 (2019), 1–28.

Hermans, Theo, *Origène: Théologie des sacrificielle du sacerdoce des Chrétiennes*, TH 102. Paris: Beauchesne, 1996.

Hill, Charles E., 'The "Epistula Apostolorum": An Asian Tract from the Time of Polycarp', *JECS* 7.1 (1999), 1–53.

Hill, Charles E., 'Cerinthus, Gnostic or Chiliast? A New Solution to an Old Problem', *JECS* 8.2 (2000), 135–72.

Hill, Charles E., *Regnum Caelorum: Patterns of Millennial Thought in Early Christianity*, 2nd edn. Grand Rapids, MI: Eerdmans, 2001.

Himmelfarb, M., 'The Ordeals of Abraham: Circumcision and the "Aqedah" in Origen, the "Mekhilta", and "Genesis Rabbah"', *Henoch* 30 (2008), 289–310.

Hirner, R., 'Die Makkabäerschrein in St. Andreas zu Köln', PhD diss., Rheinische Friedrich-Wilhelms-Universität Bonn, 1970.

Hirshman, Marc G., *A Rivalry of Genius: Jewish and Christian Biblical Interpretation in Late Antiquity*. Albany: State University of New York Press, 1996.

Holladay, William L., *A Commentary on the Book of the Prophet Jeremiah*, 2 vols, Hermenia. Minneapolis, MN: Fortress, 1986–9.

Horbury, William, 'Messianism among Jews and Christians in the Second Century', *Augustinianum* 28 (1988), 71–88.

Horgan, Maurya P., 'Psalm *Pesher* 1 (4Q171 = 4QPs^a = 4QpPs37 and 45)', in *The Dead Sea Scrolls: Hebrew, Aramaic, and Greek Texts with English Translations. Volume B: Pesharim, Other Commentaries, and Related Documents*, ed. James H. Charlesworth and Henry W. Rietz, PTSDDS Project. Tübingen: Mohr Siebeck; Louisville, KY: Westminster John Knox Press, 2002, 6–23.

Horrell, David G., and Katherine M. Hockey (eds), *Ethnicity, Race, Religion: Identities and Ideologies in Early Jewish and Christian Texts, and in Modern Biblical Interpretation*. London: Bloomsbury, 2018.
Houston, W. J., *Contending for Justice: Ideologies and Theologies of Social Justice in the Old Testament*. London: T&T Clark, 2006.
Hummel, E. L., *The Concept of Martyrdom according to St. Cyprian*, Studies in Christian Antiquity 9. Washington, DC: Catholic University of America, 1946.
Israel, Hephzibah, 'Translation and Religion: Crafting Regimes of Identity', *Religion* 49.3 (2019), 323–42.
Jacobs, A., *The Remains of the Jews: The Holy Land and Christian Empire in Late Antiquity*. Stanford, CA: Stanford University Press, 2004.
Jacobsen, Anders-Christian, *Christ the Teacher of Salvation: A Study on Origen's Christology and Soteriology*, Adamantiana 6. Münster: Aschendorff, 2015.
Jantsch, Torsten, 'Einführung in die Probleme von 1Kor 11,2–16 und die Geschichte seiner Auslegung', in *Frauen, Männer, Engel: Perspektiven zu 1Kor 11,2–16*, ed. Torsten Jantsch, BTS 152. Neukirchen-Vluyn: Neukirchener Theologie, 2015, 1–60.
Jensen, Sune Q., 'Othering, Identity Formation and Agency', *Qualitative Studies* 2.2 (2011), 63–78.
Jeremias, Gerd, *Der Lehrer der Gerechtigkeit*, SUNT 2. Göttingen: Vandenhoeck & Ruprecht, 1962.
Jeremias, Joachim, *New Testament Theology. Part One: The Proclamation of Jesus*. New York: Scribner, 1971.
Johnson, Luke Timothy, *The Gospel of Luke*, SP 3. Collegeville, PA: Liturgical Press, 1991.
Joslyn-Siemiatkoski, D., *Christian Memories of the Maccabean Martyrs*. New York: Palgrave Macmillan, 2009.
Kamesar, Adam, 'The Virgin of Isaiah 7:14: The Philological Argument from the Second to the Fifth Century', *JTS* 41 (1990), 51–75.
Käsemann, Ernst, 'The Disciples of John the Baptist in Ephesus', in *Essays on New Testament Themes*, NTL. Philadelphia, PA: Fortress, 1952, repr. 1964, 136–48.
Käsemann, Ernst, 'The Pauline Doctrine of the Lord's Supper', in *Essays on New Testament Themes*. Philadelphia, PA: Fortress, 1947–8, repr. 1964, 108–35.
Keener, Craig S., *The Gospel of Matthew: A Socio-Rhetorical Commentary*. Grand Rapids, MI: Eerdmans, 2009.
Keith, Chris, *Jesus against the Scribal Elite*. Grand Rapids, MI: Baker, 2014.
Kirchhoff, Renate, *Die Sünde gegen den eigenen Leib: Studien zu pornē und porneia in 1 Kor 6,12–20 und dem sozio-kulturellen Kontext der paulinischen Adressaten*, SUNT 18. Göttingen: Vandenhoeck & Ruprecht, 1994.
Kister, M., 'Allegorical Interpretations of Biblical Narratives in Rabbinic Literature, Philo and Origen: Some Case Studies', in *New Approaches to the Study of Biblical Interpretation in Judaism of the Second Temple Period and Early Christianity. Proceedings of the Eleventh International Symposium of the Orion Center for the Study of the Dead Sea Scrolls and Associated Literature, Jointly Sponsored by the Hebrew University Center for the Study of Christianity, 9–11 January, 2007*, ed. G. A. Anderson, R. A. Clements and D. Satran. Leiden: Brill, 2013, 133–83.
Klawans, Jonathan, *Impurity and Sin in Ancient Judaism*. Oxford: Oxford University Press, 2000.
Kloppenborg, J. S., *Christ's Associations*. New Haven, CT: Yale University Press, 2019.
Knust, Jennifer Wright, *Abandoned to Lust: Sexual Slander and Ancient Christianity, Gender, Theory, and Religion*. New York: Columbia University Press, 2006.

Knust, Jennifer Wright, *Unprotected Texts: The Bible's Surprising Contradictions about Sex and Desire*. New York: HarperOne, 2011.

Knust, Jennifer Wright, '"Who Were the Maccabees?": The Maccabean Martyrs and Performances on Christian Difference', in *Martyrdom: Canonisation, Contestation and Afterlives*, ed. I. Saloul and J. W. van Henten. Amsterdam: Amsterdam University Press, 2020, 79–103.

Koch, Dietrich-Alex, *Die Schrift als Zeuge des Evangeliums: Untersuchungen zur Verwendung und zum Verständnis der Schrift bei Paulus*, BHT 69. Tübingen: Mohr Siebeck, 1986.

Koetschau, P., *Origenes Werke 1, Die Schrift vom Martyrium. Buch 1–4 gegen Celsus*, GCS. Leipzig: J. C. Hinrich, 1899.

Konradt, Matthias, *Gericht und Gemeinde: Eine Studie zur Bedeutung und Funktion von Gerichtsaussagen im Rahmen der paulinischen Ekklesiologie und Ethik im 1 Thess und 1 Kor*, BZNW 117. Berlin: de Gruyter, 2003.

Konradt, Matthias, 'Die Gefäßmetapher in 1 Thess 4,4: Ein neuer Versuch zur Deutung von 1 Thess 4,4f.,' *BZ* 62.2 (2018), 245–69.

Kornhardt, H., 'Exemplum: Eine bedeutungsgeschichtliche Studie', PhD diss., Georg-August-Universität Göttingen, 1936.

Kraft, Robert, 'Files and Information on Early Jewish and Early Christian Copies of Greek Jewish Scriptures'. Available online: http://ccat.sas.upenn.edu/rak//earlylxx/jewishpap.html (accessed 26 March 2020).

Kuhn, Heinz-Wolfgang, *Enderwartung und gegenwärtiges Heil. Untersuchungen zu den Gemeindeliedern von Qumran mit einem Anhang über Eschatologie und Gegenwart in der Verkündigung Jesu*, SUNT 4. Göttingen: Vandenhoeck & Ruprecht, 1966.

Laato, Antti, 'Justin Martyr Encounters Judaism', in *Encounters of the Children of Abraham from Ancient to Modern Times*, ed. Antti Laato and Pekka Lindqvist. Leiden: Brill, 2010, 97–123.

Lamberton, Robert, *Homer the Theologian: Neoplatonist Allegorical Reading and the Growth of the Epic Tradition*. Berkeley: University of California Press, 1986.

de Lange, Nicholas R. M., *Origen and the Jews: Studies in Jewish–Christian Relations in Third Century Palestine*. Cambridge: Cambridge University Press, 1976.

de Lange, Nicholas R. M., 'Jewish Transmission of Greek Bible Versions', in *XIII Congress of the International Organization for Septuagint and Cognate Studies*, ed. Melvin K. H. Peters. Atlanta, GA: SBL Press, 2008, 109–17.

Latour, Bruno, *Reassembling the Social: An Introduction to Actor-Network-Theory*. Clarendon Lectures in Management Studies. Oxford: Oxford University Press, 2005.

Lauro, Elizabeth Ann Dively, *The Soul and Spirit of Scripture in Origen's Exegesis*. Leiden: Brill, 2005.

Lawrence, Louise J., *Sense and Stigma in the Gospels: Depictions of Sensory–Disabled Characters*. Oxford: Oxford University Press, 2013.

Le Boulluec, Alain, *La notion d'hérésie dans la littérature grecque, IIe-IIIe siècles*, 2 vols. Paris: Etudes augustiniennes, 1985.

Lebreton, J., 'La source et la caractère de la mystique d'Origène', *Analecta Bollandiana* 67 (1949), 55–62.

Lehtipuu, Outi, *Debates over the Resurrection of the Dead: Constructing Early Christian Identity*. Oxford: Oxford University Press, 2015.

Leutzsch, M., *Die Wahrnehmung sozialer Wirklichkeit im 'Hirten des Hermas'*. Göttingen: Vandenhoeck & Ruprecht, 1989.

Lietaert Peerbolte, L. J., 'Man, Woman, and the Angels in 1 Cor 11:2–16', in *The Creation of Man and Woman: Interpretations of the Biblical Narratives in Jewish and Christian Traditions*, ed. Gerard P. Luttikhuizen, TBN 3. Leiden: Brill, 2000, 76–92.
Lieu, Judith, *Image and Reality: The Jews in the World of the Christians in the Second Century*. London: T&T Clark, 1996.
Lieu, Judith, 'Accusations of Jewish Persecution in Early Christian Sources, with Particular Reference to Justin Martyr and the Martyrdom of Polycarp', in *Tolerance and Intolerance in Early Judaism and Christianity*, ed. Graham N. Stanton and Guy G. Stroumsa. Cambridge: Cambridge University Press, 1998, 279–95.
Lieu, Judith, *Christian Identity in the Jewish and Graeco-Roman World*. Oxford: Oxford University Press, 2004 (2nd edn 2011).
Lieu, Judith, *Neither Jew nor Greek? Constructing Early Christianity*. London: T&T Clark, 2005.
Lim, Timothy H., 'The Wicked Priests of the Groningen Hypothesis', *JBL* 112 (1993), 415–25.
Lim, Timothy H., 'The Defilement of the Hands as a Principle Determining the Holiness of Scriptures', *JTS* 61 (2010), 501–15.
Linebaugh, Jonathan A., 'Announcing the Human: Rethinking the Relationship between Wisdom of Solomon 13–15 and Romans 1.18–2.11', *NTS* 57.2 (2011), 214–37.
Litchfield, H. W., 'National *Exempla Virtutis* in Roman Literature', *HSCP* 25 (1914), 1–71.
Loader, William R. G., *Philo, Josephus, and the Testaments on Sexuality: Attitudes Towards Sexuality in the Writings of Philo and Josephus and in the Testaments of the Twelve Patriarchs*, Attitudes towards Sexuality in Judaism and Christianity in the Hellenistic Greco-Roman Era. Grand Rapids, MI: Eerdmans, 2011.
Loader, William R. G., *The Pseudepigrapha on Sexuality: Attitudes towards Sexuality in Apocalypses, Testaments, Legends, Wisdom, and Related Literature*, Attitudes towards Sexuality in Judaism and Christianity in the Hellenistic Greco-Roman Era. Grand Rapids, MI: Eerdmans, 2011.
Loader, William R. G., *The New Testament on Sexuality*, Attitudes towards Sexuality in Judaism and Christianity in the Hellenistic Greco-Roman Era. Grand Rapids, MI: Eerdmans, 2012.
Loader, William R. G., *Making Sense of Sex: Attitudes towards Sexuality in Early Jewish and Christian Literature*. Grand Rapids, MI: Eerdmans, 2013.
Long, Lynne, 'Introduction: Translating Holy Texts', in *Translation and Religion: Holy Untranslatable?*, ed. Lynne Long. Bristol: Multilingual Matters, 2005, 1–15.
Longenecker, B. W., *Remember the Poor: Paul, Poverty, and the Greco-Roman World*. Grand Rapids, MI: Eerdmans, 2010.
de Lubac, Henri, *History and Spirit: The Understanding of Scripture according to Origen*, trans. Anne Englund Nash. San Francisco, CA: Ignatius, 2007.
Lumpe, A., 'Exemplum', in *RAC*, vol. 6, ed. Theodor Klauser. Stuttgart: Hiersemann, 1966, 1229–57.
Luz, Ulrich, *A Commentary on Matthew*, 3 vols, trans. James E. Crouch, Hermeneia. Minneapolis: Fortress, 2001–7.
MacKinnon, Catharine A., *Women Human? And Other International Dialogues*. Cambridge, MA: Belknap, 2006.
MacIntyre, Alasdair C., *After Virtue: A Study in Moral Theory*. 3rd edn. Bloomsbury Revelations. London: Bloomsbury Academic, 2014.
Magness, Jodi, *The Archaeology of Qumran and the Dead Sea Scrolls*, Studies in the Dead Sea Scrolls and Related Literature. Grand Rapids, MI: Eerdmans, 2002.

Malherbe, Abraham J., *The Letters to the Thessalonians: A New Translation with Introduction and Commentary*, AB 32B. New Haven, CT: Yale University Press, 2004.

Malkin, I., 'Networks and the Emergence of Greek Identity', *Mediterranean Historical Review* 18 (2003), 56-74.

Malkin, I., *A Small Greek World: Networks in the Ancient Mediterranean*. Oxford: Oxford University Press, 2011.

Manor, T. Scott, *Epiphanius' Alogi and the Johannine Controversy: A Reassessment of Early Ecclesial Opposition to the Johannine Corpus*, Leiden: Brill, 2016.

Marcus, Joel, *Mark: A New Translation with Introduction and Commentary*, AYB 27/27A. New Haven, CT: Yale University Press, 2000-9.

Marcus, Joel, 'Johannine Christian and Baptist Sectarians', in *John and Judaism: A Contested Relationship in Context*, ed. R. Alan Culpepper and Paul A. Anderson, Resources for Biblical Study 87. Atlanta, GA: SBL Press, 2017, 155-63.

Marcus, Joel, *John the Baptist in History and Theology*, Studies on Personalities of the New Testament. Columbia: University of South Carolina Press, 2018.

Martens, Peter W., *Origen and Scripture: The Contours of the Exegetical Life*, OECS. Oxford: Oxford University Press, 2011.

Mason, Steve, 'Fire Water and Spirit: John the Baptist and the Tyranny of Canon', *SR* 21 (1992): 163-80.

Massaux, Édouard, *The Influence of the Gospel of Saint Matthew on Christian Literature before Saint Irenaeus: Book 3, the Apologists and the Didache*, trans. Norman J. Belval and Suzanne Hecht, New Gospel Studies. Leuven: Peeters; Macon: Mercer, 1990.

Matthews, Shelly, 'Thinking of Thecla: Issues in Feminist Historiography', *JFSR* 17 (2001), 39-55.

Mazzinghi, Luca, *Weisheit*, IECOT 21. Stuttgart: W. Kohlhammer, 2018.

McDonald, Lee Martin, *The Formation of the Christian Biblical Canon*. Peabody, MA: Hendrikson, 1995.

McDonald, Lee Martin, *The Formation of the Bible, Vol. 1, The Old Testament: Its Authority and Canonicity*. London: Bloomsbury T&T Clark, 2017.

McGuckin, John A., 'Origen's Doctrine of the Priesthood, I & II', *Clergy Review* 70 (1985), 277-86, 318-25.

Meeks, Wayne A., 'The Man from Heaven in Johannine Sectarianism', *JBL* 91 (1972), 44-72.

Meier, John P., *A Marginal Jew: Rethinking the Historical Jesus*, 5 vols, ABRL. New Haven, CT: Yale University Press, 1991-2016.

Meyers, Eric M., 'Khirbet Qumran and Its Environs', in *The Oxford Handbook of the Dead Sea Scrolls*, ed. Timothy H. Lim and John J. Collins, Oxford Handbooks in Religion and Theology. Oxford: Oxford University Press, 2010, 21-43.

Mitchell, David T., and Sharon L. Snyder, *Narrative Prosthesis: Disability and the Dependencies of Discourse*. Ann Arbor: University of Michigan Press, 2000.

Moessner, David P., *Lord of the Banquet: The Literary and Theological Significance of the Lukan Travel Narrative*. Harrisburg, PA: Trinity Press International, 1989.

Molitor, H., 'Helias Marcaeus', in *Contemporaries of Erasmus: A Biographical Register of the Renaissance and the Reformation*, vol. 2, ed. P. G. Bietenholz and T. B. Deutscher. Toronto: University of Toronto Press, 1986, 381-2.

Moore, C. A., *Tobit*, AB. New York: Doubleday, 1996.

Morgan, Teresa, 'Society, Identity and Ethnicity in the Hellenic World', in *Ethnicity, Race, Religion: Identities and Ideologies in Early Jewish and Christian Texts, and in*

Modern Biblical Interpretation, ed. David G. Horrell and Katherine M. Hockey. London: Bloomsbury, 2018, 23–45.

Morris, Wesley, 'Why Is Everybody Always Stealing Black Music?', *New York Times Magazine*, 18 August 2019, 60–7.

Moss, Candida R., 'Christian Funerary Banquets and Martyr Cults', in *The Eucharist – Its Origins and Contexts: Sacred Meal, Communal Meal, Table Fellowship in Late Antiquity, Early Judaism, and Early Christianity*, ed. David Hellholm and Dieter Sanger. Tübingen: Mohr Siebeck, 2017, 819–28.

Moss, Candida R., *Divine Bodies: Resurrecting Perfection in the New Testament and Early Christianity*. New Haven, CT: Yale University Press, 2019.

Moss, Candida R., and Joel S. Baden, '1 Thessalonians 4.13–18 in Rabbinic Perspective', *NTS* 58.2 (2012), 199–212.

Moss, Candida R., and Liane M. Feldman, 'The New Jerusalem: Wealth, Ancient Building Projects and Revelation 21–2', *NTS*, forthcoming.

Müller, P. G., *ΧΡΙΣΤΟΣ ΑΡΧΗΓΟΣ, Der religionsgeschichtliche und theologische Hintergrund einer neutestamentlichen Christusprädikation*, Europäische Hochschulschriften Series 23, 28. Frankfurt: Peter Lang, 1973.

Murphy, C. M., *Wealth in the Dead Sea Scrolls and in the Qumran Community*. Leiden: Brill, 2002.

Murphy-O'Connor, Jerome, 'Sex and Logic in 1 Corinthians 11:2–16', *CBQ* 42 (1980), 482–500.

Murray, T. J., *Restricted Generosity in the New Testament*. Tübingen: Mohr Siebeck, 2018.

Musurillo, H. A., *The Acts of the Christian Martyrs*. Oxford: Clarendon Press, 1972.

Nautin, Pierre, *Origène: Sa vie et son oeuvre*. Paris: Beauchensne, 1977.

Neuschäfer, Bernhard, *Origenes als Philologe*, 2 vols, Schweizerische Beiträge zur Altertumswissenschaft 18.1–2. Basel: Friedrich Reinhardt, 1987.

Newsom, Carol A., *The Self as Symbolic Space: Constructing Identity and Community at Qumran*, STDJ 52. Atlanta, GA: SBL Press, 2004.

Newsom, Carol A., 'Constructing "We, You, and the Others" through Non-Polemical Discourse', in *Defining Identities: We, You, and the Other in the Dead Sea Scrolls*, ed. Florentino García Martínez and Mladen Popović, STDJ 70. Leiden: Brill, 2008, 13–21.

Nickelsburg, George W. E., and Michael E. Stone, *Early Judaism: Texts and Documents on Faith and Piety*, rev. edn. Minneapolis, MN: Fortress Press, 2009.

Niebuhr, Karl-Wilhelm, 'Ethik und Tora: Zum Toraverständnis in *Joseph und Aseneth*', in *Joseph und Aseneth*, ed. Eckart Reinmuth, SAPERE 15. Tübingen: Mohr Siebeck, 2009, 187–202.

Niebuhr, Karl-Wilhelm, 'Die *Sapientia Salomonis* im Kontext hellenistisch-römischer Philosophie', in *Sapientia Salomonis (Weisheit Salomos)*, ed. Karl-Wilhelm Niebuhr. Tübingen: Mohr Siebeck, 2015, 219–56.

Niebuhr, Karl-Wilhelm, 'Einführung in die Schrift', in *Sapientia Salomonis (Weisheit Salomos)*, ed. Karl-Wilhelm Niebuhr. Tübingen: Mohr Siebeck, 2015, 30–3.

Niehoff, Maren R., 'Circumcision as a Marker of Identity: Philo, Origen and the Rabbis on Gen. 17:1–14', *JSQ* 10 (2003), 89–123.

Niehoff, Maren R., 'A Jewish Critique of Christianity from Second-Century Alexandria: Revisiting the Jew Mentioned in Contra Celsum', *JECS* 21 (2013), 151–7.

Niehoff, Maren R., 'Origen's Commentary on Genesis as a Key to Genesis Rabbah', in *Genesis Rabbah in Text and Context*, ed. Sarit Kattan Gribetz et al., TSAJ 166. Tübingen: Mohr Siebeck, 2016, 129–53.

Ogereau, J., 'The Jerusalem Collection as κοινωνία: Paul's Global Politics of Socio-Economic Equality and Solidarity', *NTS* 58 (2012), 360–78.
Olyan, Saul M., '"Anyone Blind or Lame Shall Not Enter the House": On the Interpretation of Second Samuel 5:8b', *CBQ* 60.2 (1998), 218–27.
Olyan, Saul M., *Rites and Rank: Hierarchy in Biblical Representations of Cult*. Princeton, NJ: Princeton University Press, 2000.
Olyan, Saul M., *Disability in the Hebrew Bible: Interpreting Mental and Physical Differences*. New York: Cambridge University Press, 2008.
O'Meara, J. J., *Origen, Prayer, Exhortation to Martyrdom: Translated and Annotated*, Ancient Christian Writers 19. Westminster: Newman Press, 1954.
Osiek, C., *Rich and Poor in the* Shepherd of Hermas: *An Exegetical-Social Investigation*, Washington, DC: CBA, 1983.
Osiek, C., *The Shepherd of Hermas*, Hermeneia. Minneapolis, MN: Fortress, 1999.
Otto, Jennifer, *Philo of Alexandria and the Construction of Jewishness in Early Christian Writings*, OECS. Oxford: Oxford University Press, 2018.
Oulton, J. E. L., and H. Chadwick, *Alexandrian Christianity*, The Library of Christian Classics. Philadelphia, PA: Westminster Press, 1954.
Padgett, Alan G., *As Christ Submits to the Church: A Biblical Understanding of Leadership and Mutual Submission*. Grand Rapids, MI: Baker Academic, 2011.
Paschke, Boris, 'Ambiguity in Paul's References to Greco-Roman Sexual Ethics', *ETL* 83.1 (2007), 169–92.
Payne, Philip B., *Man and Woman, One in Christ: An Exegetical and Theological Study of Paul's Letters*. Grand Rapids, MI: Zondervan, 2009.
Perkins, Judith, *The Suffering Self: Pain and Narrative Representation in the Early Christian Era*. London: Routledge, 1995.
Perler, O., 'Das vierte Makkabäerbuch, Ignatius von Antiochien und die ältesten Martyrerberichte', *Rivista di archeologia cristiana* 25 (1949), 47–72.
Perrin, Nicholas, 'What Justin's Gospel Can Tell Us about Tatian's: Tracing the Trajectory of the Gospel Harmony in the Second Century and Beyond', in *The Gospel of Tatian: Exploring the Nature and Text of the Diatessaron*, ed. Matthew R. Crawford and Nicholas J. Zola, The Reception of Jesus in the First Three Centuries. London: Bloomsbury, 2019, 93–109.
Perrone, Lorenzo (ed.), *Die neuen Psalmenhomilien: Eine kritische Edition des Codex Monacensis Graecus 314*, GCS N.F. 19/Origenes Werke 13. Berlin: de Gruyter, 2016.
Peters, W., 'Der Anspruch des Kölner Makkabäer-Klosters auf einen Platz in der Ursulalegende', *Annalen des Historischen Vereins für den Niederrhein insbesondere das alte Erzbistum Köln* 211 (2008), 5–31.
Petrey, Taylor, *Resurrecting Parts: Early Christians on Desire, Reproduction, and Sexual Difference*, Routledge Studies in the Early Christian World. London: Routledge, 2015.
Porton, Gary G., 'Diversity in Postbiblical Judaism', in *Early Judaism and Its Modern Interpreters*, ed. Robert A. Kraft and George W. E. Nickelsburg. Atlanta, GA: Scholars Press, 1986, 57–80.
Rabens, Volker, *The Holy Spirit and Ethics in Paul: Transformation and Empowering for Religious-Ethical Life*, WUNT 2/283. Tübingen: Mohr Siebeck, 2010.
Rajak, Tessa, *The Jewish Dialogue with Greece and Rome: Studies in Cultural and Social Interaction*. Leiden: Brill, 2001.
Rajak, Tessa, *Translation and Survival: The Greek Bible of the Ancient Jewish Diaspora*. Oxford: Oxford University Press, 2009.

Rajak, Tessa, 'Theological Polemic and Textual Revision in Justin Martyr's Dialogue with Trypho the Jew', in *Greek Scripture and the Rabbis*, ed. T. M. Law and Alison Salvesen. Leuven: Peeters, 2012, 127–40.

Raphael, Rebecca, *Biblical Corpora: Representations of Disability in Hebrew Biblical Literature*, LHBOTS 445. New York: T&T Clark, 2008.

Raphael, Rebecca, 'Whoring after Cripples: On the Intersection of Gender and Disability Imagery in Jeremiah', in *Disability Studies and Biblical Literature*, ed. Candida R. Moss and Jeremy Schipper. New York: Palgrave Macmillan, 2011, 103–16.

Raphael, Rebecca, 'Disability, Identity, and Otherness in Persian-Period Israelite Thought', in *Imagining the Other and Constructing Israelite Identity in the Early Second Temple Period*, ed. Ehud Ben Zvi and Diana Vikander Edelman. London: T&T Clark, 2014, 277–96.

Rautenberg, U., *Überlieferung und Druck: Heiligenlegenden aus frühen Kölner Offizinen*, Frühe Neuzeit, vol. 30. Tübingen: Max Niemeyer Verlag, 1996.

Rebillard, É., *Greek and Latin Narratives about the Ancient Martyrs*, Oxford Early Christian Texts. Oxford: Oxford University Press, 2017.

Reed, Annette Yoshiko, *Fallen Angels and the History of Judaism and Christianity: The Reception of Enochic Literature*. Cambridge: Cambridge University Press, 2005.

Reinmuth, Eckart (ed.), *Joseph und Aseneth*, SAPERE 15. Tübingen: Mohr Siebeck, 2009.

Reinmuth, Eckart, 'Joseph und Aseneth: Beobachtungen zur erzählerischen Gestaltung', in *Joseph und Aseneth*, ed. Eckart Reinmuth, SAPERE 15. Tübingen: Mohr Siebeck, 2009, 141–58.

Ricoeur, Paul, *Time and Narrative*, 3 vols, trans. Kathleen McLaughlin and David Pellauer. Chicago: University of Chicago Press, 1984.

Ricoeur, Paul, *Memory, History, Forgetting*. Chicago: University of Chicago Press, 2004.

Riggins, Stephen H., 'The Rhetoric of Othering', in *The Language of Politics of Exclusion: Other in Discourse*, ed. S. H. Riggins. Thousand Oaks, CA: Sage, 1997, 1–30.

Rogers, Trent A., *God and the Idols: Representations of God in 1 Corinthians 8–10*, WUNT 2/427. Tübingen: Mohr Siebeck, 2016.

Rohrbaugh, Richard L., 'The Pre-Industrial City in Luke-Acts: Urban Social Relations', in *The Social World of Luke-Acts: Models for Interpretation*, ed. Jerome H. Neyrey. Peabody, MA: Hendrickson, 1991, 125–49.

Rokeah, David, *Justin Martyr and the Jews*, Jewish and Christian Perspectives. Leiden: Brill, 2002.

Roller, M. B., 'Exemplarity in Roman Culture: The Cases of Horatius Cocles and Cloelia', *CP* 99 (2004), 1–56.

Roloff, Jürgen, *Die Offenbarung des Johannes*. Zürich: Theologischer, 1984.

Rose, C., *Die Wolke der Zeugen: Eine exegetisch-traditionsgeschichtliche Untersuchung zu Hebräer 10,32–12,3*, WUNT 2/60. Tübingen: Mohr Siebeck, 1994.

Roth, S. John, *The Blind, the Lame, and the Poor: Character Types in Luke-Acts*, JSNTSS 144. Sheffield: Sheffield Academic Press, 1997.

Rudolf, David J., *A Jew to the Jews: Jewish Contours of Pauline Flexibility in 1 Corinthians 9:19–23*, 2nd edn. Eugene: Pickwick, 2016.

Runia, David T., *Philo in Early Christian Literature: A Survey*, CRINT 3. Minneapolis, MN: Fortress, 1993.

Sage, M. M., *Cyprian*, Patristic Monograph Series 1. Philadelphia, PA: Philadelphia Patristic Foundation, 1975.

Saieg, Paul, 'Reading the Phenomenology of Origen's Gospel: Toward a Philology of Givenness', *MT* 31 (2015), 235–56.

Salvesen, Alison, 'Aquila, Symmachus and the Translation of Proof-Texts', in *Die Septuaginta: Texte, Wirkung, Rezeption*, ed. Wolfgang Kraus and Siegfried Kreuzer (in Verbindung mit Martin Meiser und Marcus Sigismund), WUNT 1/325. Tübingen: Mohr Siebeck, 2014, 154–68.

Sanchez, S. J. G., 'Justin Martyr: un homme de son temps', *Sacris Erudiri* 41 (2002), 5–29.

Sanders, E. P., *Paul and Palestinian Judaism: A Comparison of Patterns of Religion*, Philadelphia, PA: Fortress, 1977.

Sandt, H. W. M., and David Flusser, *The Didache: Its Jewish Sources and Its Place in Judaism and Christianity*, Compendia Rerum Iudaucarum Ad Novum Testamentum. Assen: Royal Van Gorcum; Minneapolis, MN: Fortress, 2002.

Satlow, M. L. (ed.), *The Gift in Antiquity*. Chichester: Wiley-Blackwell, 2013.

Saxer, V., *Morts. Martyrs. Reliques. En Afrique chrétienne aux premiers siècles. Les témoignages de Tertullien, Cyprien, et Augustin à la lumière de l'archéologie africaine*. Paris: Beauchesne, 1980.

Schäfer, Theo, *Das Priesterbild im Leben und Werk des Origenes*. Frankfurt am Main: Lang, 1977.

Scheidel, W., and S. J. Friesen, 'The Size of the Economy and the Distribution of Income in the Roman Empire', *JRS* 99 (2009), 61–91.

Schellenberg, R., 'Subsistence, Swapping, and Paul's Ethic of Generosity', *JBL* 137 (2018), 215–34.

Schiffman, Lawrence H., *The Eschatological Community of the Dead Sea Scrolls: A Study of the Rule of the Congregation*. Atlanta, GA: Scholars Press, 1989.

Schipper, Jeremy, 'Reconsidering the Imagery of Disability in 2 Samuel 5:8b', *CBQ* 67.3 (2005), 422–34.

Schironi, Francesca, *The Best of the Grammarians: Aristarchus of Samothrace on the Iliad*. Ann Arbor: University of Michigan Press, 2018.

Schmid, W., *Stifter und Auftraggeber im spätmittelalterlichen Köln*, Veröffentlichungen des Kölnischen Stadtmuseums 11. Cologne: Kölnisches Stadtmuseum, 1994.

Schreiber, Stefan, *Der erste Brief an die Thessalonicher*, ÖTK 13.1. Gütersloh: Gütersloher Verlagshaus, 2014.

Schürer, Emil, *The History of the Jewish People in the Age of Jesus Christ (175 B.C.–A.D. 135)*. Edinburgh: T&T Clark, 1973–87.

Scott, J., *The Moral Economy of the Peasant: Rebellion and Subsistence in Southeast Asia*. New Haven, CT: Yale University Press, 1990.

Sedgwick, Eve Kosofsky, *Between Men: English Literature and Male Homosocial Desire*. New York: Columbia University Press, 1985.

Seidman, Naomi, *Faithful Renderings: Jewish-Christian Difference and the Politics of Translation*. Chicago: University of Chicago Press, 2006.

Shuve, Karl, '"Put On the Dress of a Wife, So That You Might Preserve Your Virginity": Virgins as Brides of Christ in the Writings of Tertullian', in *The Symbolism of Marriage in Early Christianity and the Latin Middle Ages: Images, Impact, Cognition*, ed. Line Cecile Engh. Amsterdam: Amsterdam University Press, 2019, 131–54.

Simon, Marcel, *Verus Israel: A Study of the Relations between Christians and Jews in the Roman Empire (AD 135–425)*, trans. H. McKeating. Oxford: Oxford University Press, 1986.

Skarsaune, Oskar, *The Proof from Prophecy: A Study in Justin Martyr's Proof-Text Tradition: Text-Type, Provenance, Theological Profile*, NovT Sup. Leiden: Brill, 1987.

Skarsaune, Oskar, 'Justin and His Bible', in *Justin Martyr and his Worlds*, ed. Sara Parvis and Paul Foster. Minneapolis, MN: Fortress, 2007, 53–76.

Slusser, Michael, 'Justin Scholarship: Trends and Trajectories', in *Justin Martyr and his Worlds*, ed. Sara Parvis and Paul Foster. Minneapolis, MN: Fortress, 2007, 13–21.
Smith, Christopher R., 'Chiliasm and Recapitulation in the Theology of Irenaeus', *Vigiliae Christianae* 48.4 (1994), 313–31.
Smith, Geoffrey S., *Guilt by Association: Heresy Catalogues in Early Christianity*. Oxford: Oxford University Press, 2014.
Solevåg, Anna Rebecca, *Negotiating the Disabled Body: Representations of Disability in Early Christian Texts*. Atlanta, GA: SBL Press, 2018.
Spivak, Gayatri C., 'The Rani of Sirmur: An Essay in Reading the Archives', *HistTh* 24 (1985), 247–72.
Stegemann, Hartmut, 'The Number of Psalms in *1QHodayot*^{a} and Some of Their Sections', in *Liturgical Perspectives: Prayer and Poetry in Light of the Dead Sea Scrolls*, ed. Esther G. Chazon, Ruth A. Clements and Avital Pinnick, STDJ 48. Leiden: Brill, 2003, 191–234.
Stein, R. H., *An Introduction to the Parables of Jesus*. Philadelphia, PA: Westminster, 1981.
Stemberger, Günter, 'The Sadducees – Their History and Doctrines', in *The Cambridge History of Judaism*, ed. William Horbury, W. D. Davies and John Sturdy. Cambridge: Cambridge University Press, 1999, 428–43.
Stock, Brian, *The Implications of Literacy: Written Language and Models of Interpretation in the Eleventh and Twelfth Centuries*. Princeton, NJ: Princeton University Press, 1983.
Stoler, Ann Laura, *Carnal Knowledge and Imperial Power: Race and the Intimate in Colonial Rule*, repr. Berkeley: University of California Press, 2010.
Strecker, Christian, 'Identität im frühen Christentum? Der Identitätsdiskurs und die neutestamentliche Forschung', in *Religionsgemeinschaft und Identität: Prozesse jüdischer und christlicher Identitätsbildung im Rahmen der Antike*, ed. Markus Öhler, BibS(N) 142. Neukirchen-Vluyn: Neukirchener Theologie, 2013.
Stuckenbruck, Loren T., 'The Legacy of the Teacher of Righteousness in the Dead Sea Scrolls', in *New Perspectives on Old Texts*, ed. Esther G. Chazon, Betsy Halpern-Amaru and Ruth A. Clements, STDJ 88. Leiden: Brill, 2010, 23–49.
Stuckenbruck, Loren T., '"Apocrypha" and "Pseudepigrapha"', in *Early Judaism: A Comprehensive Overview*, ed. John J. Collins and Daniel C. Harlow. Grand Rapids, MI: Eerdmans, 2012, 179–203.
Tabernee, William, *Fake Prophecy and Polluted Sacraments*. Leiden: Brill, 2007.
Talmon, S., 'The Calendar Reckoning of the Sect from the Judean Desert', in *Aspects of the Dead Sea Scrolls*, ed. C. Rabin and Y. Yadin, ScrHier 4. Jerusalem: Hebrew University Magnes Press, 1965, 162–99.
Tannehill, Robert C., *The Narrative Unity of Luke-Acts: A Literary Interpretation*, 2 vols, FF. Minneapolis, MN: Fortress, 1986–90.
Taylor, Miriam S., *Anti-Judaism and Early Christian Identity: A Critique of the Scholarly Consensus*. Leiden: Brill, 1995.
Thomas-Olalde, Oscar, and Astride Velho, 'Othering and Its Effects – Exploring the Concept', in *Writing Postcolonial Histories of Intercultural Education*, ed. Heike Niedrig and Christian Ydesen, Interkulturelle Pädagogik und postkoloniale Theorie 2. Frankfurt am Main: Peter Lang, 2011, 28–34.
Thümmel, Hans G., *Origenes' Johanneskommentar Buch I–V*, STAC 63. Tübingen: Mohr Siebeck, 2011.
Tiedemann, Holger, *Die Erfahrung des Fleisches: Paulus und die Last der Lust*. Stuttgart: Radius, 1998.

Tilley, M. A., 'North Africa', in *The Cambridge History of Christianity*, vol. 1, ed. M. M. Mitchell and F. Young. Cambridge: Cambridge University Press, 2006, 381–96.
Tolstoy, Leo, *Anna Karenina*, trans. Constance Garnett. Project Gutenberg EBook, https://www.gutenberg.org/files/1399/1399-h/1399-h.htm, accessed 1 April 2021.
Torjesen, Karen Jo, *Hermeneutical Procedure and Theological Method in Origen's Exegesis*, PTS 28. Berlin: de Gruyter, 1985.
Tov, Emmanuel, 'The Septuagint between Judaism and Christianity', in *Textual Criticism of the Hebrew Bible, Qumran, Septuagint: Collected Essays III*, V.T.S 167. Leiden: Brill, 2015, 446–69.
Traeger, Jens-W., *Johannesapokalypse und johanneischer Kreis*. Berlin: de Gruyter, 1988.
Trebilco, P., *Self-Designations and Group Identity in the New Testament*. Cambridge: Cambridge University Press, 2011.
Trevett, Christine, *Montanism: Gender, Authority, and the New Prophecy*. Cambridge: Cambridge University Press, 1996.
Trible, Phyllis, *Texts of Terror*. Philadelphia, PA: Fortress, 1984.
Tsvetkova-Glaser, Anna, *Pentateuchauslegung bei Origenes und den frühen Rabbinen*. Frankfurt am Main: Peter Lang, 2010.
Ulrich, Jörg, 'What Do We Know about Justin's "School" in Rome?', *ZAC* 16.1 (2012), 62–74.
Upson-Saia, Kristi, *Early Christian Dress: Gender, Virtue, and Authority*, Routledge Studies in Ancient History 3. New York: Routledge, 2011.
Veltri, Guiseppe, *Ein Tora für den König Talmai: Untersuchungen zum Übersetzungsverständnis in der jüdisch-hellenistischen und rabbinischen Literatur*, TSAJ 41. Tübingen: Mohr Siebeck, 1994.
Verheyden, Joseph, 'Justin's Text of the Gospels: Another Look at the Citations in 1Apol. 15. 1–8', in *The Early Text of the New Testament*, ed. Charles E. Hill and Michael J. Kruger. Oxford: Oxford University Press, 2012, 313–35.
Vielhauer, Philipp, 'Johannes, der Täufer', in *RGG, Dritte Auflage*. Tübingen: J. C. B. Mohr (Paul Siebeck), 1959, 3:805.
Vogel, Manuel, 'Einführung', in *Joseph und Aseneth*, ed. Eckart Reinmuth, SAPERE 15. Tübingen: Mohr Siebeck, 2009, 3–31.
Völker, W., *Das Volkommenheitsideal des Origenes*, Beiträge zur historischen Theologie 7. Tübingen: Mohr, 1931.
Von Stritzki, M.-B. (trans.), *Aufforderung zum Martyrium*, Origenes: Werke mit Deutscher Übersetzung. Berlin: de Gruyter; Freiburg: Herder, 2010.
Wacholder, Ben Zion, '[Review of] *The Eschatological Community of the Dead Sea Scrolls: A Study of the Rule of the Congregation* by Lawrence H. Schiffman', *JBL* 110 (1991), 147–8.
Wallis, I. G., *The Faith of Jesus Christ in Early Christian Traditions*, SNTSMS 84. Cambridge: Cambridge University Press, 2005.
Warren, Meredith J. C., *Food and Transformation in Ancient Mediterranean Literature*, ed. Clare K. Rothschild, Writings from the Greco-Roman World Supplement Series 14. Atlanta, GA: SBL Press, 2019.
Wasserstein, Abraham, and Wasserstein, David J., *The Legend of the Septuagint: From Classical Antiquity to Today*. Cambridge: Cambridge University Press, 2006.
Watson, Francis, *Paul and the Hermeneutics of Faith*, 2nd edn. London: T&T Clark, 2004.
Watson, Francis, *Gospel Writing: A Canonical Perspective*. Grand Rapids, MI: Eerdmans, 2013.

Watson, Francis, 'The Epistula Apostolorum: English Translation from Coptic and Geʽez', in *An Apostolic Gospel: The 'Epistula Apostolorum' in Literary Context*. Cambridge: Cambridge University Press, 2020, 42–77.

Watson, Francis, and Sarah Parkhouse (eds), *Telling the Christian Story Differently: Counter-Narratives from Nag Hammadi and Beyond*, The Reception of Jesus in the First Three Centuries 5, LBS. London: T&T Clark, 2020.

Webb, Robert L., *John the Baptizer and Prophet: A Socio-Historical Study*, JSNTSup 62. Sheffield: JSOT Press, 1991.

Weeks, S., S. Gathercole, and L. Stuckenbruck (eds), *The Book of Tobit: Texts from the Principal Ancient and Medieval Traditions*. Berlin: de Gruyter, 2004.

White, Benjamin L., 'Justin between Paul and the Heretics: The Salvation of Christian Judaizers in the Dialogue with Trypho', *JECS* 26.2 (2018), 163–89.

White, L. Michael, and G. Anthony Keddie (eds), *Jewish Fictional Letters from Hellenistic Egypt: The Epistle of Aristeas and Related Literature*. Atlanta, GA: SBL Press, 2018.

Wilcke, H.-A., *Das Problem eines messianischen Zwischenreichs bei Paulus*, ATANT 51. Zürich: Zwingli, 1967.

Wilken, Robert L., 'The Restoration of Israel in Biblical Prophecy: Christian and Jewish Responses in the Early Byzantine Period', in *To See Ourseles as Others See Us: Christians, Jews, and Others in Late Antiquity*, ed. Jacob Neusner and Ernest D. Frerichs. Chico, CA: Scholars Press, 1985, 443–71.

Wilken, Robert L., 'Early Christian Chiliasm, Jewish Messianism, and the Idea of the Holy Land', *HTR* 79.11 (1986), 298–307.

Wolter, Michael, 'Identität und Ethos bei Paulus', in *Theologie und Ethos im frühen Christentum: Studien zu Jesus, Paulus und Lukas*, ed. Michael Wolter, WUNT 1/236. Tübingen: Mohr Siebeck, 2009, 121–69.

Wolter, Michael, *Der Brief an Römer: Röm 1–8*, EKKNT VI/1. Neukirchen-Vluyn: Neukirchener Theologie, 2014.

van der Woude, A. S., 'Wicked Priest or Wicked Priests? Reflections on the Identification of the Wicked Priest in the Habakkuk Commentary', *JJS* 23 (1982), 349–59.

Wright, Benjamin G., 'The Letter of Aristeas and the Reception History of the Septuagint', *BIOSCS* 39 (2006), 47–68.

Wright, Benjamin G., 'The Letter of Aristeas and the Question of Septuagint Origins Redux', *Journal of Ancient Judaism* 2 (2011), 304–26.

Yarbrough, O. Larry, *Not Like the Gentiles: Marriage Rules in the Letters of Paul*, SBLDS 80. Atlanta, GA: Scholars Press, 1985.

Yee, Tet-Lim N., *Jews, Gentiles and Ethnic Reconciliation: Paul's Jewish Identity and Ephesians*, SNTSMS 130. Cambridge: Cambridge University Press, 2005.

Yieh, John Yueh-Han, *One Teacher: Jesus' Teaching Role in Matthew's Gospel*, BZNW 124. Berlin: de Gruyter, 2004.

Young, F., *Biblical Exegesis and the Formation of Christian Culture*. Cambridge: Cambridge University Press, 1997.

Zanda, Emanuela, *Fighting Hydra-Like Luxury: Sumptuary Regulation in the Roman Republic*. London: Bloomsbury, 2011.

Zangenberg, Jürgen K., 'Joseph und Aseneths Ägypten: Oder: Von der Domestikation einer "gefährlichen" Kultur', in *Joseph und Aseneth*, ed. Eckart Reinmuth, SAPERE 15. Tübingen: Mohr Siebeck, 2009, 183–5.

Ziadé, R., *Les martyrs Maccabées: de l'histoire juive au culte chrétien: Les homélies de Grégoire de Nazianze et de Jean Chrysostome*, VCS 80. Leiden: Brill, 2007.

Index of Ancient Sources

Old Testament/Hebrew Bible

Genesis
1–2	38
2.23 LXX	133
2.23–4	26 n.41
2.24 LXX	133
6	51
6.1–2	51 n.22
6.1–4	6, 51
8.1	206
12.3	64 n.4
13.13	141 n.56
13.14	141 n.56
13.17	141 n.56
17.5	21 n.23
17.15	21 n.23
19.29	206
20.1–18	35
24.64–5	53, 54
24.65	52
38.2	71 n.36
41.45	74
43.32	74 n.54
49.10–1	26

Exodus
2.21	71 n.36
3.6	193
4.11	112 n.23, 114
6.15	206
16	208
20.12	193
20.17	80
21.17	193
22.23	209
23	192
23.20	192
34.14–6	70

Leviticus
5.2–3	36
7.15	33
10.10 LXX	80 n.80
12.3	96
16	188 n.31
17.7	70 n.34
18	70
18.22	70 n.31
19.14	113, 118, 121, 127
19.17–8	202
19.18	202, 205
20.5–6	70 n.34
20.9	193
20.13	70 n.31
20.24	80 n.81
20.26	80 n.81
21	110–11, 119–20, 122 n.60
21.16–23	109, 113 n.28, 118–19
21.17–8	109
21.18–20	109
21.20	109 n.13
21.21	109
21.22	109
21.23	110
22.17–33	110
25	200 n.9

Numbers
5.3	121 n.55
8.5–12	167
8.6–7	177 n.47
13.16	21 n.23
14.33	70 n.34
15.39	70 n.34
25.1	70 n.34

Deuteronomy		11.4 LXX	80 n.80
5.16	193		
5.21	80	*1 Kings*	
7.1–5	70	11.1–13	71
15	10, 198–9, 204	16.31–3	71
15.1–11	199, 203 n.19		
15.2	200	*2 Kings*	
15.3	200	13.21	36
15.4	199 n.8, 204		
15.7	200, 204	*1 Chronicles*	
15.9	200, 209	5.25	70 n.34
15.9–10	200, 201		
15.10	200 n.11, 203 n.19, 208	*2 Chronicles*	
15.11	199 n.8, 200, 204	21.11	70 n.34
15.12	200	21.13	70 n.34
17.15	200 n.9	24.20–2	92
23.1	111–12, 112 n.26, 113 n.28, 128	*Ezra*	
23.2–9	112 n.26	9–10	71
23.20–1	200 n.9		
24.1–3	191 n.37	*Nehemiah*	
24.13	209	5.1–5	199 n.7
24.15	209		
26.13	202	*Psalms*	
27.18	113, 118, 121, 127	22	150
31.16	70 n.34	22.10–6	151
32.7–9	151 n.23	22.15–8	150
32.36	99	24	21
		35.9 LXX	133 n.13
Judges		36	41 n.64
1–2	133	36.4 LXX	133
2.17	70 n.34	36.11 LXX	133 n.13
8.27	70 n.34	37	183
8.33	70 n.34	37.14–5	183 n.16
		37.23–4	183
1 Samuel		37.32–3	184 n.20, 187
2.33	112, 114	42.8	206
3.1 LXX	112	51	167
3.2 LXX	112, 118	51.1–2	169
4.13	112 n.25	51.7	177 n.47
4.15	112, 112 n.25, 118	51.10–2	169
		72	21, 199
2 Samuel		72.1	21
5.6	110, 110 n.16	73.27	70 n.34
5.6–8	110, 118	78.2	192
5.8	110–1, 111, 111 n.18, 113 n.28, 119, 119 n.48, 121, 121 n.55, 123–4	78.6 LXX	80
		99	21
		105.20 LXX	83
		106.39	70 n.34

Index of Ancient Sources

109.4	151	35	114–15
110	21	35.1–4	114
110.1–4	22 n.27	35.5–6	8, 114, 117, 119, 125
111 LXX	208	40.3	169 n.22, 192
117.14 LXX	105	42.7	114, 117, 119, 125
131 LXX	29 n.53	43.8–10	115 n.38
132.1	206	52.5	155 n.39
132.11	29, 29 n.53	52.10–54.6	21 n.24
138.11 LXX	133 n.13	53	21 n.24, 108 n.3
		53.7	42 n.73
Proverbs		53.8	21, 21 n.24, 22 n.29
4.9 LXX	133 n.13	54.11–4	141 n.56
10.12	204	55.2 LXX	133 n.13
19.17	132 n.8	56	112 n.26, 113
22.8 LXX	208	56.3–7	112, 118
		56.3	112
Ecclesiastes		56.4–5	112, 127–8
4.2	94, 105	56.6–7	112
9.15	207 n.31	56.7	113
		57 LXX	134
Song of Songs		57.4 LXX	134
2.8–9	114	58	204
		58.13 LXX	133 n.13
Isaiah		61.1	125
1.16–8	167	61.1–2	204
3.9–15	151 n.23	65.17–50	141 n.56
3.10 LXX	23	65.18	141 n.56
4.4	167	66.11 LXX	133 n.13
6	192		
6.9–10	192	*Jeremiah*	
7	21	2.20 LXX	70 n.34
7.10–6	21	3.1–10	70 n.34
7.10–7	29	10.25 LXX	80
7.13–4	5, 27	11.19	22 n.30
7.14	21–3, 21 n.27, 26–7, 29 n.53	31	115, 118
		31.1	115
11.1–5	164 n.4	31.7	115
26.19	125	31.8–9	8, 115, 118
29	114	31.8	117–18, 121, 124, 127
29.9 LXX	114 n.34	31.12	116
29.9–10	114	31.31–4	169
29.10	114		
29.18	8, 114, 117, 119–20, 124	*Ezekiel*	
		11.18–20	169
29.18–9	125	16.20–43	70 n.34
29.19–20	115	18.30–1	169
31.9	141 n.56	34 LXX	133
32.1	141 n.56	34.15 LXX	134
33.23	110	36	170–1, 177

36–9	141 n.56	**New Testament**	
36.24–8	169		
36.25–7	169	*Matthew*	
36.25–31	169, 177	1–4	192
36.25–33	167	1.22	190–2
36.35 LXX	133 n.13	1.22–3	190 n.32
37	141 n.56	1.23	26 n.43, 29, 29 n.53
		2.4	152
Daniel		2.5–6	190 n.32
3	91–2, 100	2.15	190–2, 190 n.32
3.16–8	98	2.17	190–2
6	92, 100	2.17–18	190 n.32
7	208 n.36	2.23	190–2
		3.1	167
Hosea		3.1–17	190 n.33
4.12 LXX	70 n.34	3.2	175
		3.3	190 n.32, 192
Joel		3.7–8	172
3.1–6	199 n.7	3.7–10	173 n.29
		3.11	163, 163 n.2, 167
Micah		3.14–5	176
2.9 LXX	134	3.16	166
4.6	117–18	3.16–7	164 n.3
4.6–7	8, 116–17, 119, 124, 128	4	180 n.4
		4.4	193
4.7	117	4.6	193
		4.10	193
Habakkuk		4.14	190–2
1.4	184	4.15–6	190 n.32
1.5	183	4.17	175
1.13	184, 186	5–7	179
2.2	183–4	5.1	179
2.4	184	5.2	180 n.5
2.7–8	188	5.17	191
2.8	188	5.17–8	192
2.9–11	188	5.20	194
2.15	187–8	5.21–2	192
		5.21–48	191
Zephaniah		5.27–8	192
3.19	117, 119	5.31	191 n.37
3.19–20	8, 117–18, 124, 128	5.31–2	192
		5.33–4	192
Zechariah		5.38–9	192
3.1–7	155	5.43–4	192
13.1	167	6.4	205
		7.28	179
Malachi		7.29	180, 180 n.5, 191, 194
1.6–14	121 n.55	8–9	180 n.4
3	192	8.1–4	125 n.71
3.1	192	8.17	190–1, 190 n.32

8.19	180 n.5, 194 n.40	17.24	180 n.5
9.1–26	125 n.71	18	179
9.2–8	125 n.71	19–22	180 n.4
9.3	194	19.3	179
9.6	180	19.4–5	193
9.8	180	19.16	180 n.5
9.11	180 n.5	20.18	194
9.14	179	21.1–17	107
9.27–31	125 n.71	21.4–5	190 n.32, 191
9.32–4	125 n.71	21.9	123
10	179	21.14	8, 123, 127–8
10.1	180	21.15	123, 194
10.24	180 n.5	21.16	193, 123
10.24–5	180 n.5	21.23–4	180
10.38	92	21.24	190
11–12	180 n.4	21.27	180
11.1	180 n.5	21.42	193
11.2–6	164	21.43	36
11.5	8, 125	22.1–14	126 n.77, 135 n.20
11.7	179	22.10	126 n.77
11.7–11	176 n.40	22.16	180 n.5
11.10	190 n.32, 192	22.23	153
11.13	176 n.40	22.24	180 n.5
11.25–6	180	22.31–2	193
11.27	180	22.33	179
12.17	190	22.36	180 n.5
12.17–21	190 n.32, 191	22.41	179
12.38	179, 180 n.5, 194	23	179, 194
12.46	179	23.1	179
13	179, 194	23.2	194
13.2	179	23.8	41, 180 n.5
13.14	190, 192	23.13	149, 149 n.17, 194
13.33–5	192	23.15	144
13.34	179	23.16	149
13.35	190–1, 190 n.32	23.16–7	120 n.52
13.52	194	23.23	149
13.54	180 n.5	23.24	149
14–17	180 n.4	23.25	194
15.1	179, 194	23.27	149, 194
15.4	192	23.29	194
15.7–9	193	23.34	194, 194 n.40
15.10	179	24–25	179
15.30–1	125	25.1–13	135 n.20
16.1	179	25.31–46	205
16.12	179	26–28	180 n.4
16.21	150, 150 nn.20,21, 194	26.3–4	150
16.24	92	26.18	180 n.5
17.10	194	26.28	167
17.12	193	26.47	150, 152

26.54	190–1, 191 n.36	11.18	194 n.41
26.56	190	11.27	194 n.41
26.57	194	12.14	180 n.5
27.9	190–1	12.18	153
27.9–10	190 n.32	12.19	180 n.5
27.41	194	12.26	193
28.18	191	12.28	194 n.41
28.18–20	180	12.32	180 n.5, 194, n40
28.19–20	180	12.35	194 n.41
		12.36	193
Mark		12.38	194 n.41
1.1–11	190 n.33	13.1	180 n.5
1.2–3	192	13.1–36	180
1.4	167–9	14.1	194 n.41
1.5	167	14.7	204
1.7–8	163 n.2	14.14	180 n.5
1.8	163, 168	14.24	167
1.10	166	14.43	194 n.41
1.10–1	164 n.3	14.49	191, 191 n.36
1.22	180, 194, 194 n.41	14.53	194 n.41
1.27	180	15.1	194 n.41
2.6	194, 194 n.41	15.31	194 n.41
2.16	194 n.41		
2.25	193	Luke	
3.22	194 n.41	1	166 n.16
4.1–34	180	1.1	191 n.36
4.12	192	1.14	174 n.35
4.34	192	1.15	166 n.16
4.38	180 n.5	1.35	29
5.35	180 n.5	1.41	166 n.16
7.1	194 n.41	1.42	29, 29 n.53
7.5	194 n.41	1.59	96
7.6–7	193	1.67	166 n.16
7.10	192	1.80	166 n.16
8.31	150 n.20, 150 n.21,	2.21	96
	194 n.41	3.1–22	166, 190 n.33
9.11	194 n.41	3.3	167
9.12	193	3.7–8	172
9.14	194 n.41	3.7–9	173 n.29
9.17	180 n.5	3.16	163, 163 n.2
9.38	180 n.5	3.20	164 n.5
9.43–8	114 n.35	3.21–2	164 n.3
10.5–8	193	4.12	193
10.17	180 n.5	4.18	204
10.20	180 n.5	4.18–9	125
10.29–30	211	4.21	191 n.36
10.33	194 n.41	4.32	180 n.6
10.35	180 n.5	4.36	180 n.6
10.51	180 n.5	7.4	206 n.29

Index of Ancient Sources 239

7.18–23	164	8.12	41
7.21	125	10.7	41
7.21–2	126	10.11	41
7.22	8, 125, 126 n.73	11.25	41
7.22–3	125	14.6	41
7.24–8	176 n.40	19.26	42
7.36–50	140 n.50	19.34	165 n.10
8.10	192	20.22	175
9.7–9	164 n.5		
9.22	150 nn.20–1	*Acts*	
11.42	149 n.16	2	175
11.52	149, 149 n.17	2–5	205 n.25
13.29	135 n.20, 138 n.43	2.38	165 n.11
14	126–7	4.34	204
14.7–11	126	8.30–5	42 n.73
14.12–4	126	10.2	206 n.29
14.13	126–7, 126 n.75	10.22	206 n.29
14.14	205	11.27–30	206
14.15	135 n.20	15.20	78
14.15–24	126	15.29	78
14.21	126–7, 126 n.73	16.1–5	34
14.21–4	8, 128	18.26	177
14.24	127	19	166, 168, 176
14.33	92	19.1–7	165
16.9	211	19.4	165, 167
16.16	176 n.40	23.6	153 n.30
20.17	193		
20.27	153	*Romans*	
21.24	191 n.36	1	80, 83
22.16	138 n.43, 191 n.36	1.5	64 n.4
22.37	191 n.36	1.13	64 n.4
23.20	135 n.20	1.16	83
24.44	191 n.36	1.18	48, 83
		1.18–32	82–3, 82 n.97, 83 n.100, 85
John		1.20	82
1.7–8	176	1.21	82 n.96
1.20–3	176	1.21–4	64 n.5, 82
1.29	41	1.23	83
1.33	163, 165 n.10	1.24	82 n.96
1.35–42	165 n.13	1.24–7	82–3
3.5	165 n.10	2.1–2	82
3.22–6	165 n.10	2.4–5	82 n.97
3.25	178	2.14–5	64
3.30	176	2.24	64 n.4, 155 n.39
4.4–15	165 n.10	2.28–9	96
5.3	122 n.61	2.29	35, 40, 45
6.63	43 n.80	3.2	37
7.38	165 n.10	3.22	83
7.38–9	165, 165 n.10		

3.29	64 n.4	7.17–24	48
4.14–5	64 n.4	7.25–6	48 n.3
5.5	164	7.31	48
5.12–21	83 n.98	7.32–5	48
6.3–4	164 n.8	7.39	78, 78 n.73
6.19	80 n.80	8	78
7.6	164, 164 n.8	8–10	48
7.7	80 n.87	9.20	34, 34 n.19
7.7–13	83 n.98	10	78
7.14	33	10.4	165 n.10
8.2–4	164	10.11	4, 42
8.9–11	164	11	50
8.10–1	164, 164 n.8	11.2–6	54
8.23	164	11.2–16	6, 47–8, 51, 54–6
9.24	64 n.4	11.3	53, 93
9.30–1	64 n.4	11.10	6, 48–51, 53, 57–60, 58 n.61
11.11–2	64 n.4		
11.13	64 n.4	11.13	50
11.25	64 n.4	11.16	50 n.51
14.17	164	11.17–34	205
15.4	4	12–14	48
15.16	64 n.4	12.2	64 n.4
15.18	64 n.4	12.13	164
15.19	207	12.25	205
15.26	206–7	15.23–8	129 n.1
15.27	207		
15.31	207	*2 Corinthians*	
		1.22	164
1 Corinthians		3.6	35 n.26, 38
1.23	64 n.4	3.14–8	42, 44
2.14–3.1	38, 41	4.4	64 n.4
2.16	6, 42	6.14	78 n.73
5	48, 70	6.14–5	64 n.4
5–7	78	8–9	206, 208, 212
5.1	64 n.4, 78, 81 n.90	8.7	208
6	48	8.9	208
6.1–8	205	8.13–4	208
6.6	64 n.4	8.14–5	208
6.11	79, 79 n.77, 164	8.16–24	208
6.12–20	80 n.83	9.7	208
7	50, 57	9.9	208
7.2	80 n.83	9.15	209
7.2–6	80		
7.8–9	48, 48 n.2	*Galatians*	
7.12–5	64 n.4	1.16–7	64 n.4
7.12–6	78	1.23	206
7.12–7	78 n.73, 84	2.1–10	206
7.14	80 n.80	2.2	64 n.4

2.8–9	64 n.4	*Philippians*	
2.9	206	3.20	130
2.10	206, 206 n.28, 207 n.31	4.13	105
2.11–5	64 n.4		
2.11–6	78	*Colossians*	
2.20	42	1.27	64 n.4
3.8	64 n.4	3.1–7	79 n.77
4.24	33	3.5–11	78 n.72
5.14	205	3.7	79
6.2	205		
6.6	205 n.25	*1 Thessalonians*	
6.10	205	1.4	78
		1.6	78
Ephesians		1.9	78–9
1.13	165 n.9	2.1	78
2.2–3	84	2.13	78
2.11	64 n.4	2.14	78, 206
2.11–2	83	2.14–6	78
2.11–3	64	2.15	78–9
2.12	83	2.16	78–9
2.14–5	78	3.4	78
3.1	6, 64, 64 n.4	3.7	78
3.6	64, 64 n.4	3.13	80
3.8	64, 64 n.4	4	79 n.76, 83, 129 n.1
4	83	4.1	79
4.1–16	84	4.3	79, 80
4.4–5	165 n.9	4.3–4	80
4.11	41	4.3–6	80, 85
4.17	64, 64 n.4, 83	4.3–8	79, 81
4.17–9	67 n.22, 82–5, 82 n.96	4.4	79–80, 80 n.84, 82
4.17–20	6, 63–5, 63 n.2, 79 n.77	4.5	6, 64 n.4, 79–81, 84
4.17–24	79, 83	4.6	79
4.18–9	64	4.7	80
4.20–1	84	4.7–8	79
4.22–4	83, 165 n.9	4.8	80–1
4.24–32	84	4.9–12	205
5.3	80 n.80, 83	4.12	79 n.78, 81, 81 n.94
5.3–5	65, 83, 85	4.13	81 n.94
5.3–7	63 n.2	5.6	81 n.94
5.3–14	83	5.15	79 n.78
5.5	84 n.102	5.23	80
5.5–6	84		
5.7	84	*2 Thessalonians*	
5.8–14	83	2.13	165 n.9
5.11	84		
5.22–33	84	*1 Timothy*	
5.22–6.9	84	1.12	105
		2.7	33, 64 n.4
		2.9	50

3.16	64 n.4	*1 John*	
5.3–16	205 n.25	3–4	209
		3.17	204
2 Timothy		5.6–8	165 n.9
4.17	64 n.4	*2 John*	29
		3 John	209
Titus		6	209
3.5	164		
		Revelation	
Hebrews		2	58
4.1–6	199 n.7	2.14	78 n.72
5.8–9	102	2.20–3	78 n.72
5.10	151	7.2–8	40
6.1–6	165 n.9	7.9–15	104
6.20	151	10.10	135 n.23
8.5	42	19.1–6	135 n.20
10.19–39	102	20	130, 130 n.4, 140
10.19–12.15	98, 103	20.1–6	129 n.1
10.32–4	102	20.4	139
10.36–9	102	21	139
11	98–9, 102, 105	21–2	130, 140
11.2	102	21.18–21	139
11.2–31	98, 102		
11.30–40	40	**Ancient Jewish Texts**	
11.32	98, 102		
11.33–8	90, 98, 102	Apocrypha and Pseudepigrapha	
11.34	90		
11.35	90, 95 n.36, 97, 103	*Tobit*	
11.35–6	88, 97, 102	1.3	202
11.36	90	1.8	202, 203 n.19
11.39	102	1.16	202
11.39–40	103	1.17	202
11.40	97, 102	1.17–8	202
12.1	102	2.2	203
12.1–3	102–3	2.2–3	202
12.2	90, 102	2.3–8	202
12.4–15	102	2.10–4	203
13.4	78	3.1	203
		4.5	203 n.19
James		4.6–7	203
1.27	204	4.7	203 nn.19–20
5.1–6	204	4.8	203
		4.9	203
1 Peter		4.10	203
3.1–3	78	4.11	203
3.3	50	4.12–3	203
3.4	40	4.13	71
4.1–6	78 n.72	4.14	203
		4.16	202, 203 n.19

4.17	203	6.20–2	95
7.1–13	203	6.21	92
8.15–7	203	6.23–8	95
12.8–9	204	6.24–5	100 n.59
12.9	204	6.24–8	95 n.37
12.9–10	203	6.26	99
13.1–17	203	6.28	95 n.40
14.2	202	6.30	95, 95 n.37, 104
		7	91–3, 95–6, 100–1
Wisdom of Solomon		7.1–6	92, 98
11.15	76	7.2	92–3, 95 n.37, 95 n.40
12.27	76	7.4	93, 96
13–14	64 n.5, 82	7.5–6	91
13–15	76 n.59, 78	7.6	92, 98–9, 103
13.1–9	76	7.9	95 nn.37, 40, 99
13.1–15.19	76	7.10	101
13.10–19	76	7.10–2	101
13.10–15.13	76	7.11	95 n.40, 101
14	80, 82–3	7.12	95 n.37, 101
14.1–10	76	7.14	95 n.37, 99
14.11–31	76–7	7.18	95 nn.35, 37, 100
14.12	76–7	7.19	93
14.15–21	76	7.20	90 n.17
14.21	76	7.20–3	90
14.23	76	7.25–6	100 n.60
14.23–4	77	7.29	100
14.23–9	77	7.30	95 nn.37, 40, 100
14.24	76	7.30–8	100
14.25	76	10.2	91
14.26	70 n.31, 83	10.5	91
14.27	76–7	15.4	91
15.1–4	82 n.97		
15.1–6	76	*4 Maccabees*	
15.7–13	76	1.3	80 n.87
15.14–9	76	2.6	80 n.87
16.1	76	7.21	98 n.55
19.11	133 n.13	9.6	95 n.39
		13.9	105 n.77
1 Maccabees		14.13	100 n.62
2.11	206	14.13–15.32	100 n.62
		15.23	100 n.62
2 Maccabees		15.29	100 n.62
4.47	96 n.41	16.1	95 n.39
6.18	92	16.3–4	100 n.62
6.18–21	93	17.2	98 n.55
6.18–31	93	17.7	95 n.39
6.18–7.42	98, 104	17.10	95 n.39
6.19	94–5	17.23	95 n.39

Index of Ancient Sources

Apocalypse of Moses
19.3	80 n.87

2 Baruch
29.3–30.1	141 n.55
40.1–4	141 n.55
72.2–74.3	141 n.55

1 Enoch
6	51
6.1–2	51 n.22
6.1–4	51
6.3–6	51
8.1–2	53, 53 n.30
45.3	164 n.4
45.6	164 n.4
48.10	164 n.4
55.3–4	164 n.4
60.7–8	135
62.3–5	164 n.4
62.14	135
93.3–10	141 n.55
93.11–7	141 n.55

2 Enoch
8.1–5	135 n.23

2 Esdras
2.38	135
19.25	133 n.13

4 Ezra
7.26–44	141 n.55
11.37–12.3	164 n.4
12.31–4	141 n.55
13.8–11	164 n.4

Joseph and Aseneth
1–21	74 n.51
2.1	74
2.3	74
3.3–4	75
3.6	74
4.7	75
4.9–10	74
5.7	75
6.4	74
7.1	74
7.5	75
8.5	74
8.5–6	75
8.5–7	75
9.5	74
10–17	75
11.7	75, 75 n.57
11.7–8	74
12.5	74
15.7	75
21.2–9	75

Jubilees
5.17–9	188 n.31

Letter of Aristeas
11–5	73
16	73
121–2	73
130–71	72
134	72
134–8	72
135	72
136–9	73
139	72–3, 78
142	72, 78
151	72–3
152	70 n.31, 72–3
235	73
306	18
321–2	73

Psalms of Solomon
17	164 n.4
17.21–46	163 n.2
17.22	163 n.2
17.36	163 n.2
17.37	163 n.2
17.38	163 n.2
17.40	163 n.2

Sibylline Oracles
3.185–6	70 n.31
3.573–600	70 n.33
3.594–600	70 n.31
3.651–64	164 n.4
8.145–9	141 n.60

Testament of Dan		De vita contemplativa	
5.5	70	48	134 n.18

Testament of Reuben		De decalogo	
4.6–7	70	173	80 n.87

Testament of Simeon		Quod Deus sit immutabilis	
5.3–4	80 n.82	7	167 n.20

Josephus

In Flaccum
184   134 n.15

Antiquitates Judaicae

		Hypothetica	
1.9–13	19	11.1–18	201 n.14
1.207	35 n.26	11.14–7	201 n.14
5.132	133 n.11		
6.34	133 n.11	De Iosepho	
8.93	155 n.42	44	134 n.18
12.11–118	19, 26		
13.78	155 n.42	Legatio ad Gaium	
18	171–2	168	134 n.18
18.18–22	201 n.14		
18.21	201 n.14	De migratione Abrahami	
18.82	206 n.29	204	134 n.15
18.116–7	171, 173		
20.49–50	206 n.29	De posteritate Caini	
20.50–1	206	32	134 n.15

Bellum Judaicum

		De vita Mosis	
2.119–61	201 n.14	2.12–3	134 n.18
2.122	201 n.14	2.25–44	19
2.160–1	201 n.14		
2.164–5	153 n.30	De specialibus legibus	
4.567	206 n.29	1.134	134 n.15
5.55	206 n.29	1.257–60	167 n.20

Contra Apionem

		1.303–4	134 n.15
2.148	74 n.53	2.99	134 n.18
2.190–220	70	2.240	134 n.18
2.199–201	70	4.84	80 n.87

Philo

Quod omnis probus liber sit

		75–91	201 n.14
De Abrahamo		79	201 n.14
133–6	134 n.18, 140 n.50		

De somniis

De cherubim		1.121	134
12	134, 134 n.14	1.123–4	134 n.17

De virtutibus
161–3   134 n.18

Pseudo-Philo,
De Jona
27.105–6   80 n.79

Dead Sea Scrolls

1QH^a (1QHoyadoth^a)
xvii [ix] 32–4   169
x 17   186 n.24
frag 2 1.13   169

1QM
vii 4–5   121 n.56

1QpHab
i 10   184
i 13   182
ii   184, 190 n.33
ii 1–4   186
ii 1–5   185
ii 2   182–3
ii 2–4   186
ii 6   183
ii 6–8   183
ii 7   183
ii 8   183
ii 8–9   184
v 8   185 n.23
v 8–12   186
v 10   182
v 10–1   184
v 10–2   184
vi 15–16   183
vii   184
vii 1–5   185
vii 4   182
vii 4–5   183–4
vii 7   184
vii 7–8   184
vii 9–14   184
vii 10–1   184, 189
vii 11–2   184
viii 1–3   184
viii 2   184
viii 3   182
viii 8–13   188

viii 9   188
viii 9–13   187 n.26
viii 13–ix 7   188
viii 16   187 n.26
ix 5–7   188
ix 10   187 n.26
ix 9–10   182, 184
ix 9–12a   188
ix 12b–x 5   188
x 3–5   187 n.27
x 5–13   186
x 9   185
xi   188 n.30, 189
xi 4–6   184
xi 4–8   187
xi 5   182
xi 5–8   187 n.26
xi 12–14   187 n.26
xi 14   187 n.27, 188
xii 5   187 n.27, 188

1QpMic (1Q14)
8–10.4   185
10.6   182

1QS   9
ii 25–iii 1   172
iii   171
iii 1–9   167
iii 2–3   172
iii 4–5   172
iii 6–7   169
iii 6–9   171–3
iii 8–9   177 n.47
iii 9   172
iv   170
iv 11–2   120 n.52
iv 20–2   167, 170–2
iv 20–3   169
viii 6   188 n.31
viii 10   188 n.31
ix 3–5   169
ix 4   188 n.31
xi 2–6   136 n.30

1QSa
ii 3–9   120, 127
ii 9–10   121
ii 11–23   135
ii 11–22   136 n.30

4Q72	118	4Q175 (4QTestimonia)	
			185 n.21
4Q156 (4QTgLev)	188 n.31		
		4Q177 (4QCatena A)	
4Q162 (4QpIsa^b)			185 n21, 186
2.6	185	7.2	186 n.24
2.10	185	9.4	186 n.24
4Q163 (4QpIsa^c)	182	4Q180-1 (4QAges of Creation)	
4-7 ii 6	185 n.23		185 n.21
21.6	182		
23 ii 10	186 n.24	4Q180 (4QAges of Creation A)	
46.2	182 n.12	1.7-10	188 n.31
4Q167 (4QpHos^b)		4Q203	
5-6.2	182 n.12	7 i 6	188 n.31
4Q169 (4QpNah)		4Q252-254 (4QComm Gen A-C)	
3-4 i 2	186 n.24		185 n.21
3-4 i 7	186 n.24		
3-4 ii 2	186 n.24	4Q254a (4QComm Gen D)	
3-4 ii 4	186 n.24		185 n.21
3-4 iii 3	186 n.24		
3-4 iii 6	186 n.24	4Q258	
		vii 4-5	188 n.31
4Q171 (4QpPs^a)			
	185	4Q259	
1-2 ii 18-20	183 n.16	ii 15-6	188 n.31
1-10 i 27	182		
1-10 iii	190 n.33	4Q266 (4QDamascus Documents^a)	
1-10 iii 15	182	2 i	186
1-10 iii 15-6	183, 185	2 i 6	185 n.23
1-10 iii 19	182	2 i 18	185
1-10 iv 7-8	187	2 i 21-3	186
1-10 iv 8	182	6 i	183 n.18
1-10 iv 8-9	184 n.20	8 i 6-9 (=cd xv 15-7)	
1-10 iv 9	187 nn.26-7		119
1-10 iv 14	186	iii 19	182 n.12
1-10 iv 27	182		
3-10 iv 6	184	4Q266-73	201 n.13
4Q172		4Q267	
7.1	182	2.15	182 n.12
		iv	183 n.18
4Q173 (4QpPs^b)		9 i 8	183 n.18
1.4	182		
2.2	182	4Q269	
		5.2	182 n.12
4Q174 (4QFlorilegium)		7	183 n.18
	185 n.21		

4Q271		A vi 15	201
3 1–10	201 n.15	A vi 16–7	201
5 ii 20	183 n.18	A vi 20	202, 208 n.36
		A vi 20–1	202
4Q272		A vii 1	202
1 i	183 n.18	A vii 17	182 n.12
		A vii 18–9	185
4Q273		A viii 13	185
4 ii	183 n.18	A ix 10–2	201 n.15
		A ix 13–4	183 n.18
4Q285	164 n.4	A xii 10	201 n.15
		A xiii 5–6	183 n.18
4Q396		A xiii 6	119 n.51
ii 1–3	120	A xiii 7–9	202
ii 3–4	120	A xiii 9	202
ii 5	120	A xiv	202 n.16
		A xiv 5	202
4Q464 (4QExposition on the Patriarchs)		A xiv 12–7	121, 127
	185 n.21	A xiv 13–7	202
		A xiv 14–6	119–20, n.51
4Q506		A xiv 14–7	121
frags 131–2 11–14	169	A xvi 17	201 n.15
		B xx 1	182, 185
4QMMT	110 n.14, 120	B xx 14	182
		B xx 27–32	185
11Q13 (11QMelchizedek)		B xx 28	182
	185 n.21		
ii 7–8	188 n.31	**Rabbinic Texts**	
11QT^a (11Q19) (11QTemple)		*b. Megillah*	
xxv	10–xxvii 10	8b–9b	19
	188 n.31		
xxvii 5	188 n.31	*b. Sanhedrin*	
xlv 12–4	121	153a	135
lxi 3	190		
		b. Sotah	
CD		49b	16
A	185, 201 n.13		
A i	185–6	*b. Yoma*	
A i 1–17	185	38a	206 n.29
A i 7–10a	185		
A i 10–ii 1	186	*m. Sotah*	
A i 11	182, 185	9.14	16
A i 14	185		
A i 18–20	186	*m. Yadayim*	
A vi 6–7	201 n.15	3.5	36 n.34
A vi 7	182 n.12		
A vi 9–11	185	*t. Yadayim*	
A vi 11	182, 187 n.25	2.14	36 n.34

Midrash Genesis
62.2   135

Apostolic Fathers

Barnabas
3.1–5   204 n.24

1 Clement
5.7   103 n.74

2 Clement
16.4   204

Didache
8.1   137 n.33
11–12   209

Shepherd of Hermas
Mandates
2.4–7 (27.4–7)   210
8.10 (38.10)   210

Similitudes
1   211
1.8–9 (50.8–9)   211
2   209
2.5 (51.5)   209–10
2.8 (51.8)   210
2.9 (51.9)   210
4.5 (53.5)   210
5.3.7–8 (56.7–8)   210
6.2.4 (62.4)   210
8.6.4 (72.4)   210
8.8.1 (74.1)   210
8.9.1 (75.1)   210–11
10.4.2–3 (114.2–3)   210

Visions
1.1.8 (1.8)   211
3.6.5 (14.5)   210
3.9.3 (17.3)   210
3.9.6. (17.6)   209
3.13.2 (21.2)   210

Ignatius

To Polycarp
4.3   205 n.25

Martyrdom of Polycarp
18.3   137 n.35

Polycarp

To the Philippians
10.2   204 n.22

Other Early Christian Literature

Epistula Apostolorum
19   139
19.14–5   139
21   139

Gospel of Thomas
64   126 n.77

Revelation of Peter
2   141 n.55

Pseudo-Clementines
Homilies
2.17   176 n.44
2.23   176 n.44
3.22–3   176 n.44

Recognitions
1.54.8   177 n.44
1.60.1   177 n.44
2.8   176 n.44

Augustine
Breviculus collationis cum Donatistis
3   88 n.9

Sermones
300   88 n.8, 89, 89 n.15
301   88 n.8, 89 n.15

Basil of Caesarea
De virginitate 59 n.63

Epistulae
6.2   88 n.9

Clement of Alexandria
Excerpta ex Theodoto
44.2   58 n.57

Hypotyposes
Fragment 1   49 n.11, 58 n.58

Paedagogus
2.1.4.3–4   137 n.32
2.1.5.3   137 n.32
2.1.7.3   138 n.41
2.12.119   139 n.46
3.2.12–3   139 n.46

Stromateis
1.22.148   28 n.48
1.22.149   28 n.49
2.1.14.4   137 n.32
3.6   132 n.8

Cyprian
Acta proconsularia
3–4   92 n.21

Epistulae
21.1–3   93 n.25
55.13–4   93 n.25

Ad Fortunatum
11   92, 99, 103

De lapsis
35   93 n.25

Ad Quirinum testimonia adversus Judaeos
3.16–7   89, 93, 100, 100 n.60

Epiphanius
Panarion (Adversus haereses)
30.13.6   28 n.46
14.3   28 n.46
48.14   140 n.53
51.3.1   140 n.52

Eusebius
Demonstratio evangelica
8.2.93   88 n.6

Historia ecclesiastica
3.28.2   139, 139 n.48, 140 n.51
3.39.1   136 n.25
4.22.7   157 n.55
5.1.22–4   105 n.78
5.1.27–8   105 n.78
5.1.56   105 n.78
5.8.10   27 n.44, 28
5.8.10–2   28 n.49
5.13   36 n.33
5.18.2   140 n.53
6.1   91 n.19
6.2   102 n.68
6.2.2–4   91 n.19
6.23.2   94 n.28
6.24–5   139
6.24.1   139
6.24.3   139
6.24.4   139
6.28   93 n.26

Gregory of Nazianzus
Discourse 15   88 n.7

Funerary oration 74   88 n.7

Hippolytus of Rome
Commentarium in Danielem
1.15–7   91
1.20–1   91
2.14–38   91
2.19.8   103
2.20   89, 98, 103
2.20.2   92
2.20.3   92
2.20.4   92
2.21   99, 103
2.21.1   92, 103
2.21.1–2   103
2.21.3   92, 103
2.35   89, 91–2, 98, 103
2.35.1   103
2.35.8   91, 103
4.3   91 n.20
20.3   98
20.4   98

Irenaeus
Epideixis tou apostolikou kērygmatos
18   51 n.23

Adversus Haereses
1.8.3   58 n.57
1.10.1   51 n.23

Index of Ancient Sources

1.26	28 n.46	35	25
3.1–5	27	36.3	26
3.3.4	141 n.57	37.8	204 n.24
3.9	27	40.6	26
3.19.1	27	46.1	19 n.20
3.19.3	27	47	25
3.20.2	27 n.44	48	25
3.21.1	27 nn.44, 45, 28–9	49.5	26
3.21.2	28	53.6	26
3.21.4	29 n.53	63.11	26
3.21.5	27 n.45	66	148 n.11
3.21.5–9	29	66–7	145 n.1
4.16.2	51 n.23	67	132 n.8
4.18	132 n.8		
5.33.2	130 n.4, 136 n.27	*Apologia II*	
5.33.3–4	136 n.25	5.3	51 n.23
5.35	141 n.56		

Jerome
Altercatio Luciferiani
7   168

Commentariorum in Jeremiam libri
66.20   138 n.41

De viris illustribus
18   141 n.58

John Chrysostom
De Eleazaro et septem pueris 88 n.9

Homilia in martyres 88 n.9, 100 n.62

De sanctis martyribus
50.647   88 n.9

Justin
Apologia I

26	25
31	25, 141 n.55
31.1	25
31.1–5	26
31.5	20 n.22, 25
31.5–6	26
31.7	25
31.8	25
32.1	26
33.1	26
34	25

Dialogus cum Tryphone

1.3	19 n.20
7.1–2	20
10	148 n.13
13.2–9	21 n.24
15	204 n.24
17	155, 155 n.39
17.3–4	149 n.15
17.15	23
18.1	149
27.5	151 n.25
29.3	151 n.25
32.2	21 n.24
32.6	22 n.27
33.1	21
33.1–2	151 n.26
34	21
34.1	21
36.2	21
37.4	151 n.25
40.4	152
42.4–5	141 n.55
43.3	21, 21 n.24
43.5–6	21, 21 n.26
43.8	21
51.2	150 n.19
52.3	152 n.27
63.3	22 n.27
64.5	21
66	21
66.2–3	21 n.25
67.1	21

67.1–2	22	*Martyrdom of Fructuosus*	
68.6	22, 24	3.3	137 n.37
68.7	22, 151 n.24		
71	24	Maximus the Confessor	
71.1	22 n.29	*On the Ecclesiastical Hierarchy*	
71.1–2	151 n.24	7	136 n.26
71.2	22		
71.3	21 n.27	Methodius of Olympus	
72–3	22	*Symposium*	
73.5	22	9.1–5	141 n.60
76.7	22 n.27, 150 nn.19–21		
78.1	152	Origen	
80	141 n.56	*Commentarius in Canticum*	
80.1	136 n.28, 140 n.54	Prologue 1	37 n.37
80.4	136 n.28, 152, 152 n.29, 155, 156 n.44	Prologue 3	37 n.38
		35.13	58 n.61
83	21		
83.2	22 n.27	*Commentarii in Evangelium Joannis*	
83.4	22 n.27	1.1	35 n.21, 40 n.54, 45 n.86
84	21 n.27		
84.3	151 n.24	1.1–89	42
84.3–4	22	1.17	97 n.47
86.3	151 n.26	1.2–8	40 n.55
98–106	150	1.9	40 n.57, 41 n.61
100	148 n.13	1.10	40 n.56
100–07	145 n.1	1.12–13	40 n.58
100.3	150 nn.19–20	1.14	41 n.62
102.5	151, 154	1.17	41 n.63
103.1	150	1.19–20	41 n.65
113.1–2	21	1.21–2	41 n.66
115	155	1.23	42 n.67
116.2	151 n.26	1.24	42 n.69
117.2	155	1.27	42 n.71
117.3	155	1.28–31	42 n.72
119.17	23	1.32	42 n.73
120.4–5	23	1.33	42 n.74
120.6	19 n.20	1.34	42 n.75
124.2–3	23	1.35	42 n.76
131.1	23, 151 n.23	1.36	43 n.77
133.2–3	151 n.23	1.41–2	34 n.19
133.7	23	1.44	43 n.78
136.2	23	1.47–74	43 n.79
137.2	154 n.35, 157 n.54	1.85	42 n.73
137.3	23	1.215	38 n.44
141	146 n.2	5	94 n.31
		10.172–3	42 n.69
Martyrologium Romanum		13.58	97 n.47
August 1	88 n.9		

Index of Ancient Sources

Commentarius in Evangelium Matthaei
1	94 n.31
11.12	34 n.16, 96 n.43
27	43 n80

Commentarii in Romanos
1.10.3	44 n.83
2.14.6	37 n.39
2.14.7	37 n.40
2.14.8	38 n.41
2.14.9	38 n.42
2.14.14	42 n.70
10–11	96 n.43
10.39.2	34 n.18
19	96 n.43

Fragmenta in Exodum
12.268	97 n.47

Fragmenta in Psalmos 1–150
43.1	97 n.47

Contra Celsum
1–2	159 n.61
1.43	36 n.31
2.1	34 n.16, 34 n.19
2.28	33 n.11
4.1	33 n.12
5.31	36 n.32
5.60	35 n.22
5.61–5	34 n.16
7.29	141 n.59
7.34	96 n.45
8.6	96
8.46	97 n.47

Homiliae in Canticum
3.3	43 n.82

Homiliae in Exodum
7.3	36 n.29
12.1	35 n.25

Homiliae in Genesim
2.2	36 n.33
3.4–5	96 n.43
3.5	34 n.16
5.1	34 n.15
6.1	33 n.13
6.3	35 n.26
7.6	35 n.25
13.3	35 n.24

Homiliae in Jeremiam
7.1	97 n.47
9.1	43 n.81
12.13.1–2	33 n.14
14.12.3	36 n.29

Homiliae in Jesu Nave
6.1	35 n.25
7.1	94 n.31
9.4	35 n.25
26.3	36 n.29

Homiliae in Judices
2.5	35 n.25
8.4	36 n.29

Homiliae in Leviticum
3.3.1	36 n.27
4.1.1	43 n.80
5.7.5	35 n.24
5.8.3	33 n.14
16.1–2	35 n.25

Homiliae in Lucam
23	58 n.60
23.8	49 n.9

Homiliae in Numeros
7.2.4	35 n.25
9.2.4	31
17.3.2	37 n.40

Exhortatio ad martyrium
2	95 n.39
2–3	101
3	101
4	101 n.67, 105 n.78
5	94, 95 n.38
6	94, 101 n.67
6–21	94
7	101 n.66
10–11	101 n.66
13	101
15	95 n.39
22	95, 95 n.40, 101, 104

22–7	94–5	Pamphilus	
23	94–7, 95 nn.39–40, 101 n.64, 105–6	*Apology for Origen*	
		113	140 n.50
24	95 n.40		
25	95 n.35, 95 nn.38,40, 101, 101 n.64	*Passion of Marian and James*	
		5.2	89 n.11
26	95, 95 nn.39–40, 100	6.10	89 n.11
27	94–5, 97, 100, 100 n.62, 101 n.64, 104, 106	11.3	137 n.36
		11.6	137 n.36
29	95 n.38	13	88
33	94, 100	13.1	90, 102
34	95 n.39	13.1–3	98 n.56
35	105 n.77		
37	95 n.39	*Passion of Montanus and Lucius*	
37–8	101 n.66	11.2	89 n.11
38	102	16	88, 102
39	95 n.39	16.3	90
41–4	95 n.39	16.3–4	98
42	95 n.38, 101	16.4	88, 90
47	95 n.38, 101 n.63	16.5	91, 91 n.18
49	95 n.39	21.3	89 n.11

De oratione

		Passion of Perpetua and Felicitas	
11.1	97 n.47		91 n.19
		4.6	105 n.78

De pascha

		4.10	135 n.23
6	42 n.67		
26	43 n.81	Pseudo-Justin	
38	44 n.84	*Cohortatio*	
		13	26 n.42

Philocalia

		Tertullian	
15.19	43 n.81	*De baptismo*	
27	97 n.47	10.5–6	168 n.21

De principiis

		De corona militis	
1.3.4	38 n.44	2.4	53 n.33
1.6.2	58 n.61	3.1	53 n.33
2.11.1	141 n.59	4.1	53 n.33
4.2.1	34 n.15	4.2	53 n.34
4.2.3	42 n.68	12.3	53 n.33
4.2.4	34 n.17	14.1	53, 53 nn.33,35, 54 n.36
4.2.5	35 n.21		
4.3.1–3	36 n.27		
4.3.3	44 n.84	*De cultu feminarum*	
4.3.8	34 n.16	1.1.2	52 n.28
4.3.14	38 n.44	1.2.1	52 n.29
		1.3.1	53 n.31

Selecta in Psalmos

		1.3.2–3	53
12.1084	97 n.47		

De jejunio adversus psychicos
17.7   138 n.39

Adversus Marcionem
3.24   138 n.39
4.16.16   204 n.24
17.8   204 n.24
31.3   204 n.24

De oratione
20   50
21.1   51 n.19, 56 n.50
21.2   51
22   54
22.1   56 n.50
22.5   51 n.21, 52 nn.25–7
22.5–6   49 n.8
22.10   52 n.20

De resurrectione carnis
61.5–7   138 n.40

Ad Scapulam
3.1   91 n.19
5   91 n.19

De virginibus velandis
1.1   54 nn.37, 39
1.2   56 n.47
1.3   56 n.48
1.4   55 n.45, 56 n.49
4   49 n.13
4.1   56, 56 n.50
7   54
7.2   49 n.8, 57 n.51
7.3–4   55 n.40
16.4   55, 55 n.43
16.5   56 n.45
16.6   56 n.45
17.9   55 n.44

Theophilus
Ad Autolycum
2.28   26 n.41
3.12   204 n.24

Tyconius of Carthage
Exposition of the Apocalypse
7.21   139 n.47

Victorianus
Commentary on the Apocalypse
215–16   136 n.24

Classical Literature

Acta Iustini
3.3   147 n.5

Aulus Gellius
2.24.12   137 n.32

Cicero
Pro Sexto Roscio Amerino
39   140 n.50

Galen
De propriorum animi cuiuslibet affectuum dignotione et curatione

1.9, K45   137 n.32

Herodotus
4.46   96 n.41
4.62   96 n.41
4.64–5   96 n.41

Historia Augusta
17.1   91 n.19
Livy
39.6   135 n.19

Malalas
Chronographia
206–7   88 n.9

Macrobius
Saturnalia
3.17.13   137 n.32

Musonius Rufus
Dissertationes
18b.55–65   137 n.32

Pliny the Elder
Naturalis historia
8.82　　　　　　　137 n.32

Rufus of Ephesus
On Satyriasis and Gonorrhea
19–20　　　　　　139 n.48

Suetonius
Gaius Caligula
24.1　　　　　　　140 n.50

Tacitus
Historiae

5.5　　　　　　　74 n.53

Inscriptions

MAMA
6.264　　　　　　206 n.29

Index of Authors

Ackerman, S. 112
Ahmed, L. 67
Aliau-Milhaud, A. 40
Allert, Craig D. 148
Allison, Dale C. 170, 171, 180
Anderson, G. A. 131, 132, 136, 137, 142, 201
Assmann, J. 31
Atkins, M. 198
Attridge, H. W. 98, 102
Aune, David E. 141, 170

Baden, Joel S. 129
Bailey, J. W. 29, 141
Baltzly, Dirk 36
Barclay, John M. G. 56, 71–4, 76–7, 172, 198, 208
Bardy, G. 91
Barkman, Heather 57
Barth, Fredrik 66
Bauer, Walter 136
BeDuhn, Jason David 49
Berchman, Robert M. 44
Bertrand, D. 95
Best, Ernest 64
Betcher, Sharon V. 125
Bietenhard, Hans 32
Black, Matthew 156–7
Blischke, Folker 82
Bloom, Harold 176
Bobichon, Philippe 148–51, 153–7
Böcher, Otto 165–6, 174
Bodsch, I. 87
den Boeft, J. 101
de Boer, Martinus C. 165, 206
Böhlemann, Peter 166
Bolkestein, H. 199
Bovon, François 125
Boyarin, Daniel 39, 146–7, 154–7
Boyd-Taylor, Cameron 17

Brawley, R. 98
Bremmer, J. N. 101
Briggs, Charles Augustus 173
Bright, P. 94
Brouwer, Jacob 48
Brown, Peter 47–8, 50, 131, 137, 198, 206, 212
Brown, Raymond E. 165
Brown-Tkacz, C. 89
Bultmann, Rudolf 180
Byrskog, Samuel 181

Callaway, Philip R. 182, 187
Capper, B. J. 202
Carter, Warren 179
Castro Varela, María do Mar 66, 69
Cataldo, Jeremiah W. 67
Chadwick, H. 35, 94, 96, 102
Charlesworth, James H. 181–2
Clements, Ruth 32, 38
Cocchini, Franchesca 33–4, 44
Cohen, Shaye J. D. 95, 154
Cohick, Lynn 55
Collins, D. J. 87–8
Collins, John J. 77
Collins, Matthew A. 183
Cooper, Kate 55
Cope, Lamar A. 194–5

D'Angelo, Mary Rose 55
Daniel-Hughes, Carly 57
Danielou, Jean 141–2
Davies, Philip R. 185
Davies, W. D. 180
Dawson, John David 39
DeSilva, D. 89, 94, 100
Dhawan, Nikita 66, 69
Dibelius, Martin 165, 173
von Dobschütz, Ernst 195
Dorman, Anke 119–22

Downs, D. J. 201, 203–4, 206
Drake, Susanna 38–9
Drewermann, Eugen 174
den Dulk, Matthijs 146–7, 152–3, 155–7
Dunderberg, Ismo 139–40
Dunn, Geoffrey D. 54
Dunn, James D. G. 16, 168, 173–4

Eastman, David L. 137
Edsall, Benjamin A. 48–9
Edwards, Catharine 142
Edwards, Mark J. 37
Eisenbaum, P. M. 98, 102–3
El Mansy, Aliyah 70, 78
Erdman, D. V. 176
Ernst, Josef 174
Eubank, N. 201
von Euw, A. 87
Evans, Robert 3
Eyl, Jennifer 135

Fabian, Johannes 68
Falls, Thomas B. 149
Farkasfalvy, Denis 138
Farmer, William 138
Fee, Gordon D. 49
Feldman, Liane M. 138
Felski, Rita 159
Ferguson, Everett 138
Finney, Mark 49
Fitzmyer, J. A. 203
Flusser, David 137
Foucault, Michel 65
Fredriksen, Paula 34
Frend, W. H. C. 89, 91
Friedrich, G. 102
Friesen, S. J. 197
Froehlich, Karlfried 140

Gaca, Kathy L. 69, 70
Gallagher, E. L. 97
Gamble, Harry Y. 146
García Martínez, Florentino 119, 187
Gardner, G. E. 198
Gardner, Jane F. 69
Gathercole, Simon J. 191, 202
Georges, Tobias 147
Gerber, Christine 84
Gerson, Lloyd 181

Gese, Michael 64, 82
Gögler, Rolf 43
Gonzalez, Eliezer 137
Goodenough, Erwin R. 134
Goodman, Martin 36, 156
Gorman, Robert J. 133
Gorman, Vanessa B. 133
Gosbell, Louise A. 107–9, 112, 122, 126, 127
Greer, R. A. 94
Gregerman, Adam 146
Greschat, Katharina 148–9, 153
Guéraud, Octave 44
Guillaumin, M.-L. 89
Gundry-Volf, Judith M. 49
Guyot, P. 91

Hagner, D. A. 97
Hall, Stuart 68
Halton, Thomas P. 149
Hamm, D. 98
von Harnack, Adolf 16–17, 156
Hartmann, P. 94, 100–1
Heath, Jane 31
Heine, Ronald E. 33, 36, 38, 40
Heither, Theresia 34
Hellholm, David 135
Hempel, C. 202
Hengel, Martin 172
van Henten, J. W. 87–90, 94, 98, 100
Hermans, Theo 40
Hill, Charles E. 130, 139, 141
Himmelfarb, M. 96
Hirner, R. 88
Hirshman, Marc G. 146–7, 159
Hockey, Katherine M. 65
Holladay, William L. 115
Horbury, William 141
Horgan, Maurya P. 188
Horrell, David G. 65
Houston, W. J. 199, 200
Hummel, E. L. 92

Israel, Hephzibah 15

Jacobs, A. 97, 105
Jacobsen, Anders-Christian 36
Jantsch, Torsten 48
Jensen, Sune Q. 66

Jeremias, Gerd 193
Jeremias, Joachim 174
Johnson, Luke Timothy 126
Joslyn-Siemiatkoski, D. 87–8

Kamesar, Adam 24
Käsemann, Ernst 164, 166
Keddie, G. Anthony 28
Keener, Craig S. 179
Keith, Chris 193
Kirchhoff, Renate 69
Kister, M. 96
Klawans, Jonathan 167, 173
Klein, R. 91
Kloppenborg, J. S. 207
Knust, Jennifer Wright 47, 49, 69, 88, 97, 105
Koch, Dietrich-Alex 31
Koetschau, P. 94
Konradt, Matthias 70, 79, 80–2
Kornhardt, H. 104
Kraft, Robert 17
Kuhn, Heinz-Wolfgang 170

Laato, Antti 147
Lamberton, Robert 35
de Lange, Nicholas R. M. 17, 32
Latour, Bruno 146, 159
Lauro, Elizabeth Ann Dively 32, 36
Lawrence, Louise J. 108, 122, 125
Lawson, R. P. 37
Le Boulluec, Alain 152–3, 155, 157
Lebreton, J. 101
Lefèvre, M. 91
Lehtipuu, Outi 140
Leutzsch, M. 209
Lietaert Peerbolte, L. J. 49
Lieu, Judith 31, 65–6, 130, 147, 154, 156–7
Lim, Timothy H. 36, 187
Linebaugh, Jonathan A. 82–3
Litchfield, H. W. 104
Loader, William R. G. 65, 69, 70–2, 77–8, 80–1
Long, Lynne 18–19
Longenecker, B. W. 205, 207
de Lubac, Henri 32, 34
Lumpe, A. 104
Luz, Ulrich 107, 123–5

MacIntyre, Alasdair C. 2–4
MacKinnon, Catharine A. 56
Magness, Jodi 170
Malherbe, Abraham J. 79. 80–1
Malkin, I. 207–8
Manor, T. Scott 140
Marcus, Joel 163, 166, 168–9, 174, 176–7
Martens, Peter W. 32, 34, 39
Mason, Steve 172–3
Massaux, Édouard 148, 150
Matthews, Shelly 55
Mazzinghi, Luca 76–7
McDonald, Lee Martin 97, 138
McGuckin, John A. 40
Meade, J. 97
Meeks, Wayne A. 175
Meier, John P. 166
Meyers, Eric M. 170
Mitchell, David T. 113, 124
Moessner, David P. 126
Molitor, H. 87
Moore, C. A. 203
Morgan, Theresa 66
Morris, Wesley 177
Moss, Candida R. 114–15, 125, 129, 136, 138
Müller, P. G. 102
Murphy, C. M. 201
Murphy-O'Connor, Jerome 49
Murray, T. J. 202
Musurillo, H. A. 88

Nautin, Pierre 34, 44
Neuschäfer, Bernhard 42, 95
Newsom, Carol A. 119, 121
Nickelsburg, George W. E. 72
Niebuhr, Karl-Wilhelm 74, 76
Niehoff, Maren R. 32–3, 96

Ogereau, J. 207
Olyan, Saul M. 108, 110–14, 116 17, 120–1
O'Meara, J. J. 94
Osborne, R. 198
Osiek, C. 209
Otto, Jennifer 38
Oulton, J. E. L. 94, 96, 102

Padgett, Alan G. 49
Parkhouse, Sarah 1

Paschke, Boris 91
Payne, Philip B. 49
Perkins, Judith 128
Perler, O. 89
Perrin, Nicholas 153
Peters, W. 87
Petrey, Taylor 138
Porton, Gary G. 156

Rabens, Volker 164
Rajak, Tessa 17–18, 23–4, 147
Raphael, Rebecca 108–9, 111, 113, 116–18, 122
Rautenberg, U. 88
Rebillard, É. 88, 90–1
Reed, Annette Yoshiko 51, 53, 59
Reinmuth, Eckart 74, 75
Ricoeur, Paul 146–7, 158–9
Riggins, Stephen H. 67
Rogers, Trent A. 77
Rohrbaugh, Richard L. 126
Rokeah, David 146–7, 154
Roller, M. B. 104
Roloff, Jürgen 135
Rose, C. 97–8, 102
Roth, S. John 108, 122, 125
Rudolf, David J. 34
Runia, David T. 32, 38

Sage, M. M. 89, 92
Said, E. 66, 68
Saieg, Paul 41
Salvesen, Alison 17, 23
Sanchez, S. J. G. 147
Sanders, E. P. 170
Sandt, H. W. M. 137
Satlow, M. L. 198
Saxer, V. 89
Schäfer, Theo 40
Scheck, Thomas P. 37
Scheidel, W. 197
Schellenberg, R. 205
Schiffman, Lawrence H. 136
Schipper, Jeremy 111
Schironi, Francesca 35
Schmid, W. 87
Schreiber, Stefan 78, 80–1
Schürer, Emil 133
Scott, J. 199

Sedgwick, Eve Kosofsky 55
Seidman, Naomi 18, 24
Shuve, Karl 55
Simon, Marcel 16–17
Skarsaune, Oskar 20, 23, 148
Slusser, Michael 146
Smith, Christopher R. 130, 136
Smith, Geoffrey S. 152, 155, 157
Smith, John Clark 36
Snyder, Sharon L. 113, 124
Solevåg, Anna Rebecca 108, 113, 122–3, 125
Spivak, Gayatri C. 66, 68
Stegemann, Hartmut 193
Stein, R. H. 135
Stemberger, Günter 156
Stock, Brian 31
Stoler, Ann Laura 69
Stone, Michael E. 72
Strecker, Christian 65
Stuckenbruck, Loren T. 183, 191, 202
Stuhlmacher, Peter 164

Tabernee, William 140
Talmon, S. 187
Tannehill, Robert C. 126–7
Taylor, Miriam S. 146–7, 154, 158
Thomas-Olalde, Oscar 66–7
Thümmel, Hans G. 41
Tiedemann, Holger 68, 70
Tigchelaar, Eibert J. C. 119, 187
Tilley, M. A. 93
Tolstoy, Leo 175
Torjesen, Karen Jo 32, 38, 43
Tov, Emmanuel 16, 118
Traeger, Jens-W. 135
Trebilco, P. 208
Trevett, Christine 140
Trible, Phyllis 125
Tsvetkova-Glaser, Anna 33

Ulrich, Jörg 147
Upson-Saia, Kristi 50, 57, 139

Veltri, Guiseppe 19
Velho, Astride 66–7
Verheyden, Joseph 148
Vielhauer, Philipp 172, 174
Vogel, Manuel 74

Völker, W. 101
Von Stritzki, M.-B. 96

Wacholder, Ben Zion 136
Wallis, I. G. 102
Walvoort, H. 87
Warren, Meredith J. C. 135
Wasserstein, Abraham 15, 18–19
Wasserstein, David J. 15, 18–19
Watson, Francis 1, 31, 41, 139
Webb, Robert L. 167
Weeks, S. 202
White, Benjamin L. 147
White, L. Michael 28

Wilcke, H.-A. 141
Wilken, Robert L. 141
Wolter, Michael 66, 81, 83
van der Woude, A. S. 187
Wright, Benjamin G. 18

Yarbrough, O. Larry 81
Yee, Tet-Lim N. 64
Yieh, John Yueh-Han 181
Young, F. 95

Zanda, Emanuela 137
Zangenberg, Jürgen K. 75
Ziadé, R. 101

Index of Subjects

allegory 33, 35, 39 n.52, 58, 96, 126
almsgiving. *See* gift
anti-gentile rhetoric 63–86
anti-Judaism 9, 64, 78 n.75, 129 n.1, 141
appropriation 2
   of Jewish traditions 4–8, 18, 30, 88, 145
   of John the Baptist 175–8
   of the Septuagint 16–17, 24, 30, 31
asceticism 8, 129–30, 132

baptism 9–10, 96, 163–78
boundaries 4, 7, 44, 66, 69, 212
   between Christians and others 78, 82, 85, 107
   between Jews and non-Jews 71–3, 78
   between Jews and Christians 32, 145

celibacy 48–60, 202 n.16
charity. *See* gift
chiliasm 129–30, 133, 136, 138–9, 141
circumcision 20, 34, 83, 96, 206
community
   construction of 1, 3, 30, 81, 83, 107–8, 147, 153, 200
   formation 9, 11, 15, 47, 50, 55, 65, 84, 200, 205, 207–8
   self-definition 47, 72, 132, 166, 169
   self-understanding 107, 111, 118, 127–8
competition
   between communities 5, 6, 9, 176
   in interpretation 3, 21

demarcation
   against others 64, 71, 81, 85–6
   of communities 39
differentiation 30, 32, 40–5, 66, 78, 137, 141, 178, 199
disability 7–8, 107–28

diversity
   in early Christianity 7, 8, 127
   in Second Temple Judaism 2, 7–8, 123, 127, 146, 154, 211

endogamy 70–1, 74, 84, 85, 203
ethnicity 3, 4, 5, 65

faith (*pistis*) 98–9, 103–4, 106
fasting 8, 130, 131, 137–8, 204, 210
feasting 8, 117–18, 130–9, 187–8
food
   and Jewish laws 69, 74, 92–5
   and survival 197, 202, 210
   See also fasting, feasting

gift 131–2, 137, 142, 197–212

heresy 27–30, 130, 140, 146, 150, 152, 155–8

identity 1, 5, 7–9, 15, 31–3, 64–5, 81–2, 110, 115–28
   Christian 39, 88, 106, 107, 130, 132, 143, 145, 159, 175
   Jewish 7, 88–96, 124, 145, 158–9
idolatry 6–7, 48, 65, 70, 72–7
impurity 36, 74
intertextuality 47, 49, 51–2

judaizing 4, 5, 89–97

Letter and Spirit 17, 32–9, 41
luxury 129–43, 210

Maccabean martyrs 5, 7, 87–106
martyrdom 87–106, 130, 132, 137
millenarianism. *See* chiliasm

Index of Subjects

Othering 6–7, 63–86, 111, 122. *See also* demarcation

parting of the ways 9, 15–17, 19, 65, 105
piety (*eusebeia*) 94, 98, 100–2, 106
postcolonial theory 15, 65–8
poverty 10–11, 131–2, 138 n.41, 197–212
purity 37, 109–13, 121, 167, 170–2, 177, 188

Rabbinic Judaism 16–17, 32–3, 135, 147, 154, 156
reception 1–11, 59, 160
  of Christian tradition 82–4, 129, 145–7
  as creative process 2–4, 5, 9, 10, 59–60
  of Jewish tradition 18, 50, 65, 84–5, 169, 197–8, 204, 208, 211–12
resurrection 130, 137–8, 140, 142, 152–3
reward 129–32, 142, 200–4, 205, 210

Septuagint 18
  as Christian source 133–5, 148
  legend of 5, 15–30, 151
sexual immorality 6–7, 68–75, 77, 80–3, 85
social imagination 1–6, 9, 47, 106, 113, 120, 145, 197
  defined 1
  Paul's 48, 60
  Tertullian's 55
spirit 9–10, 38, 163–78
supersession 5, 38, 39 n.52

translation of scripture 2, 5, 8. *See also* Septuagint

virginity 21–2, 27, 48–60. *See also* Celibacy

wealth 8–9, 131–43, 201, 209–11
women
  dress of 47, 50, 52–8
  voices of 56–7

www.ingramcontent.com/pod-product-compliance
Lightning Source LLC
Chambersburg PA
CBHW062127300426
44115CB00012BA/1841